ARABIC GRAMMAR

ARABIC GRAMMAR

Of the Written Language

with Arabic-English and English-Arabic Vocabulary

By

REV. G. W. THATCHER, M.A., A.D.

Formerly, Senior Tutor, Mansfield College, Oxford

KITAB BHAVAN

New Delhi-110002 (India)

KITAB BHAVAN
Publishers, Distributors, Exporters & Importers
1784, Kalan Mahal, Darya Ganj,
New Delhi - 1100 02 (India)

Phones : (91-11) 23277392/93, 23274686, 32906494
Fax : (91-11) 23263383

Website: www.nusratalinasri.com

Email : nasri@vsnl.com
: nusrat@bol.net.in

Reprinted : 2013

ISBN : 81-7151-230-5
Book Code No. : A00300

Printed & Published in India by :
Nusrat Ali Nasri for KITAB BHAVAN
1784, Kalan Mahal, Darya Ganj,
New Delhi - 1100 02 [India]

Preface

During the last ten years of my teaching of Arabic I have often found that my pupils had received much help from Harder's Arabic Grammar[1], and have been asked whether there was a similar work in English. When I was asked by the firm of Julius Groos to write such a work using Harder to any extent, I gladly consented, and trust this Grammar may be useful to many students of Arabic, who cannot read German.

The present work is a grammar of Arabic as in has been and is written. The spoken language varies in Arabia, Egypt, Syria, Morocco etc. But the written language is the same for all; the chief difference between the modern and ancient literature consisting in the introduction of new words to meet the requirements of advanced knowledge.

Each lesson should be thoroughly mastered before the next is studied. Each exercise should be carefully worked and compared with the key.

In the supplement only a few extracts from older books are given, as the Koran and other works of this class can easily be obtained. Special attention is given on the other hand to selection from modern novels, journals and correspondence.

To those who wish to study the grammar of the classical Arabic further I would recommend the last

---

1 Arabische Konversations-Grammatik mit besonderer Berucksichtigung der Schriftsprache von Ernst Haarder. Heidelberg. Julius Groos, 1898.

edition of Wright's Arabic Grammar published by the Cambridge University Press.

The various styles of Arabic handwriting may be studied in the Specimens d'ecritures Arabes (with key) published at the Imprimerie Catholique in Beyrouth.

A handy guide to Arabic literature is M. C. Stuart's "Arabic Literature" London 1903.

Sydney (New South Wales), September 1910

G. W. Thatcher.

Table of Contents.

First Part.

Second Part.

Introduction

§ 1.

Arabic characters are written from right to left. The alphabet (هِجَاءٌ hijā) consists of 28 characters (حَرْفٌ ḥarf, plur. حُرُوفٌ ḥurūf), which all represent consonants. Most of these letters are written in slightly different forms according to whether they 1. stand alone or 2. are joined to a preceding letter or 3. are joined to a preceding and a following letter or 4. are joined to a following letter only.

Names of the letters.	Standing alone.	Joined to preceding letter.	Joined to preceding and following letters.	Joined to following letter only.	Transcription.
أَلِفٌ alif[1]	ا	ـا	—	—	â
بَاءٌ bâ	ب	ـب	ـبـ	بـ	b
تَاءٌ tâ	ت	ـت	ـتـ	تـ	t
ثَاءٌ thâ	ث	ـث	ـثـ	ثـ	th
جِيمٌ jîm	ج	ـج	ـجـ	جـ	j
حَاءٌ ḥâ	ح	ـح	ـحـ	حـ	ḥ
خَاءٌ khâ	خ	ـخ	ـخـ	خـ	kh
دَالٌ dâl	د	ـد	—	—	d
ذَالٌ dhâl	ذ	ـذ	—	—	dh
رَاءٌ râ	ر	ـر	—	—	r

Names of the letters.	Standing alone.	Joined to preceding letter.	Joined to preceding and following letters.	Joined to following letter only.	Transcription.
زَاىْ zâi	ز	ـز	—	—	z
سِينْ sîn	س	ـس	ـسـ	سـ	s
شِينْ shîn	ش	ـش	ـشـ	شـ	sh
صَادْ ṣâd	ص	ـص	ـصـ	صـ	ṣ
ضَادْ ḍâd	ض	ـض	ـضـ	ضـ	ḍ
طَاءْ ṭâ	ط	ـط	ـطـ	طـ	ṭ
ظَاءْ ẓâ	ظ	ـظ	ـظـ	ظـ	ẓ
عَيْنْ ʿain	ع	ـع	ـعـ	عـ	ʿ
غَيْنْ ghain	غ	ـغ	ـغـ	غـ	gh
فَاءْ fâ	ف	ـف	ـفـ	فـ	f
قَافْ qâf	ق	ـق	ـقـ	قـ	q
كَافْ kâf	ك	ـك	ـكـ ـكـ	كـ كـ	k
لَامْ lâm	ل	ـل	ـلـ	لـ	l
مِيمْ mîm	م	ـم	ـمـ	مـ	m
نُونْ nûn	ن	ـن	ـنـ	نـ	n
هَاءْ hâ	ه	ـه	ـهـ	هـ	h
وَاوْ wâw	و	ـو	—	—	w
يَاءْ yâ	ى	ـى	ـيـ	يـ	y

Note 1. The letter ا (alif) has no sound of its own but is used merely a) as a support for hamza under certain conditions (see § 10), or b) to lengthen a preceding a vowel (see § 6)

or c) at the end of 3rd plur. of verbs (see § 6, Note 4). The first real consonant of the Arabic alphabet is ء (see §§ 3 and 10).

Note 2. When the letter tâ is used as the feminine ending of nouns or adjectives it is written as hâ (ه) with two dots (ة) and is called تَاء مَرْبُوطَة tâ marbūta, the ordinary tâ being called تَاء طَوِيلَة tâ ṭawîla. This tâ of the feminine ending is not pronounced in modern Arabic except when followed by a word beginning with a vowel sound. The modern usage is observed in the technical terms of this book e.g. hamza for هَمْزَة; hamzat al-waṣl for هَمْزَة الْوَصْلِ.

Note 3. In NW. Africa f is written ڢ and q ڧ.

Note 4. The following letters are sometimes used in foreign words: پ = p; چ = ch (as in *church*), ڤ = v.

§ 2.

The six letters و ز ر ذ د ا can only be joined to preceding not to following letters. These are called حُرُوف مُنْفَصِلَة, ḥurūf munfaṣila i.e. separate letters; the others are called حُرُوف مُتَّصِلَة ḥurūf muttaṣila i.e. united letters.

Among ordinary combinations of letters in writing are the following:

بح bâ-ḥâ	حجج ḥâ-jîm-jîm	لا or ﻼ (joined to preceding letter ـلا) lâm-alif
بى bâ-yâ	سح sîn-ḥâ	لح lâm-ḥâ
تح tâ-ḥâ	صح ṣâd-ḥâ	لم lâm-mîm
تى tâ-yâ	عج ʿain-jîm	مح mîm-ḥâ
جح jîm-ḥâ	فح fâ-ḥâ	مم mîm-mîm
حج ḥâ-jîm	فى fâ-yâ	نح nûn-ḥâ
	نى nûn-yâ	يح yâ-ḥâ
	هم hâ-mîm	يم yâ-mîm.

§ 3.

Pronunciation of the Consonants.

The following letters are pronounced like their English equivalents:

ب bā = b. ت tā = t. ث thā = th as in *think*. ج jīm = j. د dāl = d. ذ dhāl = dh = th as in *this*. ر rā = r. ز zai = z. س sīn = s as in *so*. ش shīn = sh as in *shot*. ف fā = f. ك kaf = k. ل lām = l. م mīm = m. ن nūn = n. ه hā = h. و wāw = w. ى yā = y. (و and ى are also used to lengthen a preceding u or i vowel see § 6).

The following represent sounds foreign to English:

ء hamza is a click produced by a quick compression of the upper part of the throat.

ح ḥā is an h pronounced with a strong expulsion of air from the chest.

خ khā is a guttural ch as in the Scotch "loch" but more from the throat.

ص ṣād, ض ḍād, ط ṭā and ظ ẓā form a group of emphatic sounds corresponding with س s, د d, ت t and ز z distinguished from them by the tongue being placed against the palate instead of against the teeth.

ع 'ain is a very strong guttural produced by compression of the throat and expulsion of the breath.

غ ghain has a hard sound between a snarling pronunciation of gh and r.

ق qāf is a k sound produced in the throat, (like the cawing of a crow).

§ 4.

Classification of the Letters.

1. Arabian grammarians divide the letters of the alphabet (حُرُوفُ ٱلْهِجَاء ḥurūf alhijā') into a) those

which are dotted (حُرُوف مُعْجَمَة ḥurūf muʿjama) and b) those which are not dotted (حُرُوف مُهْمَلَة hurūf muhmala).

2. More practical is the division into a) Sun letters (اَلْحُرُوفُ الشَّمْسِيَّة alhurūf ashshamsīya) namely ت, ث, د, ذ, ر, ز, س, ش, ص, ض, ط, ظ, ل, ن which assimilate the l of the Article, and b) Moon letters (اَلْحُرُوفُ الْقَمَرِيَّة alhurūf alqamarīya), comprising the other letters of the alphabet, which do not assimilate the l (see Lesson 1).

3. The letters ا alif, و wāw and ى yā are called Weak letters (حُرُوف الْعِلَّة hurūf alʿilla) because they are often interchanged or dropped under the influence of other letters. Contrasted with these, the other letters of the alphabet are called Sound letters (اَلْحُرُوفُ الصَّحِيحَة alhurūf aṣṣaḥīḥa).

§ 5.

Vowels.

Every consonant in a vocalised Arabic text is provided with a vowel sign or with a sign indicating the absence of a vowel.

The vowel signs (شَكْل shakl, Plur. أَشْكَال ashkāl or شُكُول shukūl) are three in number:

1. فَتْحَة fatḥa, a small diagonal stroke over a consonant = ă as in دَ da.

2. كَسْرَة kasra a small diagonal stroke under a consonant = ĭ as in دِ di.

2. ضَمَّة ḍamma, a small و above a consonant =

The sign indicating the absence of a vowel is ـْـ written above a consonant. It is called سُكُونٌ sukun or جَزْمَةٌ jazma e.g. كُنْ kun.

Note 1. The three vowel signs above do not actually represent all the vowel sounds used in pronunciation for while fatḥa preserves the ă sound after ح, خ, ع, غ it inclines to the sound of au in "taught" after the Emphatic letters ص, ض, ط, ق, and is usually thinned down to the sound of ĕ after the other letters as in كَلْبٌ kelbun.

Note 2. In Arabic a vowel is called a "movement" (حَرَكَةٌ ḥaraka) and so a consonant is either "moved" (مُتَحَرِّكٌ mutaḥarrik) i.e. provided with a vowel, or "resting" (سَاكِنٌ sākin) i.e. without vowel.

§ 6.

Long Vowels and Diphthongs.

The long vowels ā, ī, ū are expressed in Arabic by the signs ـَـ ـِـ ـُـ followed by ا, ى, و (written without sukūn), thus مَالٌ mālun "wealth", كِيسٌ kīsun "a purse", طُولٌ ṭūlun "length".

The diphthongs ai and au (now generally pronounced as English a and o) are written ـَيْ and ـَوْ as بَيْتٌ baitun "a house", خَوْفٌ khaufun "fear".

Note 1. In a few words ā is expressed by a short vertical stroke over a consonant as in هٰذَا hadhā "this", ذٰلِكَ dhālika "that", لٰكِنْ lākin "but", اللّٰهُ allāhu "God" etc.

Note 2. At the end of a word ā is often expressed by ـَـ followed by ى (without dots or sukūn), thus رَمَى ramā "he threw", إِلَى ila "unto". As soon as this ـى ceases to be final it returns to the form ـا e.g. رَمَاهُ ramāhu "he threw him". The Arabian grammarians call this ى the أَلِفٌ بِصُورَةِ ٱلْيَاءِ alif biṣurat alyā' "alif in the form of ya". The sign for ā at the end of a word (whether ا or ى) is called أَلِفٌ مَقْصُورَةٌ alif maqsūra "alif that can be shortened" because it is shortened when followed by a word beginning with hamzat alwaṣl (see § 11).

Note 3. In a few words ending in āt an older form of writing them with ـٰوةٌ or ـٰيةٌ occurs. These are حَيٰوةٌ or حَيَاةٌ ḥayātun "life", صَلٰوةٌ or صَلَاةٌ ṣalātun "prayer", زَكٰوةٌ or زَكَاةٌ zakātun "alms", تَوْرِيَةٌ or تَوْرَاةٌ taurātun "Torah" (the Mosaic Law).

Note 4. An ا is written but not pronounced after the و with which some verbal forms end e.g. كَتَبُوا katabū "they wrote" رَمَوْا ramau "they threw". The ا is also not pronounced in the word مِائَةٌ mi'atun "hundred".

§ 7.

Nunation.

At the end of nouns and adjectives, when indefinite, the three vowel signs are sometimes written double, thus ـٌ, ـٍ, ـً and are then pronounced *un*, *in*, *an*.

This is the so-called Nunation (تَنْوِينٌ tanwīn). The sign for *an* has ا as well, except after ة e.g. بَابًا bāban, خَلِيفَةً khalīfatan.

When however *an* is a contraction for *ayun* we find it written ـًى as هُدًى hudan (for hudayun); as a contraction for *awun* it is written ـًى or ـًا as عَصًى or عَصًا ʿaṣan (for ʿaṣawun).

§ 8.
Sukūn or Jazma.

The absence of a vowel after a consonant is indicated by the sign ـْ called سُكُونٌ sukūn or جَزْمَةٌ jazma e.g. قَتْلٌ qatlun "a killing", كَتَبَتْ katabat "she wrote".

The letters و and ى take sukūn when they form diphthongs, but not when they only lengthen vowels (see § 6).

For the omission of sukūn with the lām of the article see § 9.

A vowelless consonant is said to be سَاكِنٌ sākin "resting" (§ 5, note 2).

§ 9.
Tashdīd.

When a consonant occurs twice without a vowel sound between; it is written once only and the sign ـّ (called تَشْدِيدٌ tashdīd) is placed over it e.g. مَرَّ marra "he passed by", مَارٌّ mārrun "passing by". The consonantal sound however must be distinctly pronounced twice.

Tashdīd often indicates assimilation. Thus the ل of the Article أَلْ al is assimilated when the word to which it is prefixed begins with a Sun letter (see § 4). The ل is retained in writing but without sukūn; and tashdīd is written over the following letter e.g. شَمْسٌ shamsun "sun" becomes with the Article اَلشَّمْسُ ash-shamsu "the sun"; رَجُلٌ rajulun "a man" becomes اَلرَّجُلُ arrajulu "the man".

Again the ن of the words أَنْ 'an "that", مِنْ min and عَنْ 'an "from" is assimilated to the ل and م of لَا lā "not", مَا mā "what" and مَنْ man "who, whom" in أَلَّا allā = an-lā, "that not", مِمَّا mimmā and عَمَّا 'ammā "from what", مِمَّنْ mimman and عَمَّنْ 'amman "from him who": so also إِلَّا 'illa = 'in-lā "if not".

Sometimes the letters ت, ث, د, ذ, ض, ط, ظ are assimilated to a following ت.

Here also the letter assimilated is left in the writing but without sukūn, while a tashdīd is written over the ت e.g. أَرَدتَّ aratta = arad-ta, لَبِثتُّ labittu = labith-tu.

§ 10.

Hamza.

Hamza ـٔ (هَمْزَةٌ cf. § 1, Note 1 and § 3) is of two kinds 1. هَمْزَةُ ٱلْقَطْعِ hamzat alqaṭ', which cannot be dropped and 2. هَمْزَةُ ٱلْوَصْلِ hamzat alwaṣl, which is omitted under some circumstances (see § 11).

It is generally written above (with ـَ and ـُ) or under (with ـِ) one of the letters ا, و, ى but sometimes independently. The following are the rules for writing it:

I. At the beginning of a word it is always written with ا e.g. أَمْرٌ 'amrun, إِبْرَةٌ 'ibratun, أُذْنٌ 'udhnun.

II. In the middle of a word:

a) Preceded by ـَ a and 1. followed by ـَ a or sukūn it is written above ا e.g. سَأَلَ sa'ala, رَأْسٌ ra'sun; 2. followed by ـِ it is written above ى e.g. يَئِسَ ya'isa; 3. followed by ـُ u it is written above و e.g. بَؤُسَ ba'usa.

b) Preceded by ـِ i it is written above ى e.g. بِئْرٌ bi'run.

c) Preceded by ـُ u it is written above و when followed by a or u, above ى when followed by i, e.g. يُؤَلِّفُ yu'allifu, سُئِلَ su'ila.

d) Preceded by sukūn it is written above ا when followed by ـَ, over و when followed by u, over ى when followed by ـِ e.g., يَسْأَلُ yas'alu, يَبْؤُسُ yab'usu.

e) If hamza is preceded by ا or و of the long vowel, it is written a little above the line without any bearer e.g. تَسَاءَلَ tasā'ala, مَقْرُوءَةٌ maqrū'atun; if preceded by the ى of long ī, it is written above the stroke that joins the ى to the following letter e.g. خَطِيئَةٌ khaṭī'atun.

III. At the end of a word:

a) It is not affected by the vowel that follows it, but is written over ا after ـَ over و after ـُ, over ى after ـِ e.g. قَرَأَ qara'a, يَقْرَأُ yaqra'u, دَنُؤَ danu'a, خَطِئَ khaṭi'a.

b) After sukūn it has no bearer e.g. ضَوْءٌ ḍau'un, شَيْءٌ shai'un. With the ending *an* the hamza is written over the stroke connecting the previous letter with the ا e.g. شَيْئًا shai'an; if however the preceding letter cannot be connected the ا is omitted and the hamza written without bearer e.g. جُزْءًا juz'an.

§ 11.

Hamzat alwaṣl.

1. In some cases the hamza at the beginning of a word is no essential part of its form, but seems to

be written only to prevent a syllable from beginning with a vowel. In such cases, when it follows another word, the hamza is dropped with its vowel, a sign called waṣla ـٱـ (وَصْلَةٌ) is put in place of the hamza and the two words are read as one. If the preceding word does not end in a vowel, then one is given to it in accordance with the rules below (4). The Hamza in these cases is called هَمْزَةُ ٱلْوَصْلِ hamzat alwaṣl. The ا, though preserved in the writing, is not pronounced, neither has the waṣla any effect on the pronunciation.

Examples: عَبْدُ ٱلْقَادِرِ ʻabdu ʼlqādiri; وَٱنْصَرَفَ wa'nṣarafa (from وَإِنْصَرَفَ), رَأَيْتُ ٱبْنَ ٱلأَمِيرِ ra'aitu ʼbna ʼlamīri.

2. The hamza is hamzat alwaṣl:

a) In the Article أَلْ al e.g. عَبْدُ ٱلْقَادِرِ ʻabdu ʼlqādiri.

b) In the Imperative of the I form of the Verb (Lesson 16) e.g. قُلْتُ ٱكْتُبْ qultu ʼktub "I said: write".

c) In the Perfect, Imperative and Verbal noun of the VII, VIII IX and X forms of the verb (Less. 18) e.g. فَٱنْهَزَمَ fa'nhazama.

d) In the following eight words:

إِبْنٌ ibnun "son".	إِمْرُؤٌ imra'un or إِمْرُؤٌ imru'un "man".
إِبْنَةٌ ibnatun "daughter".	إِمْرَأَةٌ imra'atun "woman".
إِثْنَانِ ithnāni "two (Masc.).	إِسْمٌ ismun "name".
إِثْنَتَانِ ithanatāni "two (Fem.).	إِسْتٌ istun "buttock".

3. If the word preceding a hamzat alwaṣl does not end in a vowel, then the final consonant generally

receives a kasra —, e.g. قَدِ ٱنْصَرَفَ qadi 'nsarafa "he has already gone away". The nunation also takes — after it.

Exceptions. The Preposition مِنْ min "from" takes — before the Article as مِنَ ٱلْوَلَدِ mina 'lwaladi "from the boy"; in other cases it takes the usual — e.g. مِنِ ٱبْنِهِ mini 'bnihi "from his son".

The Personal pronouns هُمْ hum, كُمْ kum and أَنْتُمْ antum, the ending تُمْ tum of the 2nd Pers. Plur. Perf. of the verb and the Preposition مُذْ mudh (= مُنْذُ mundhu) "since" take ـُ u before the hamzat alwaṣl e.g. لَعَنَهُمُ ٱللهُ la'anahumu 'llāhu "May God curse them"; رَأَيْتُمُ ٱلْوَلَدَ ra'aitumu 'lwalada "You have seen the boy".

If the word preceding the hamza ends with ا, و or ى which lengthen the vowels before them, then although the writing is not altered, the vowel must be pronounced short (see § 13, 3) e.g. أَبُو ٱلْوَلَدِ abŭ'lwaladi, فِي ٱلدَّارِ fī 'ddāri.

If however the word ends in ـَىْ or ـَوْ, then the ى takes — and the و takes ـُ in place of the sukūn e.g. فِي عَيْنَيِ ٱلْمَلِكِ fī ainayi 'lmaliki "in the eyes of the king" مُصْطَفَوُ ٱللهِ mustafawu 'llāhi "the chosen ones of God".

The conjunctions لَوْ lau "if" and أَوْ au "or" follow the general rule and take — after the وِ.

4. The hamzat alwaṣl falls out of the writing as well as the pronunciation:

a) In the expression بِسْمِ ٱللّٰهِ bismi'llāhi (for بِٱسْمِ) "In the name of God".

b) In the word إِبْنٌ ibnun "son" when it comes between the name of the son and that of the father (and not at the beginning of a line) e.g. عُمَرُ بْنُ ٱلْخَطَّابِ 'umaru 'bnu 'lkhaṭṭāb "Omar the son of Alkhattab". If the إِبْنٌ is predicative the ا is preserved e.g. زَيْدٌ ٱبْنُ عَمْرٍو zaiduni'bnu 'amrin "Zaid is the son of Amr".

c) In the Article أَلْ al, if preceded by the Preposition لِ li "to, for" or the strengthening Particle لَ la "verily" e.g. لِلرَّجُلِ lirrajuli "to the man", لِلْوَلَدِ lilwaladi "to the boy", لَلْحَقُّ lalḥaqqu "verily the truth".

If the noun begins with ل, then the لْ of the Article falls out also e.g. لِلَّيْلَةِ (for لِلْلَيْلَةِ) lillailati "for the night". Similarly from أَللّٰهُ allāh "God" is formed لِلّٰهِ lillāhi "to God".

d) The ا of the hamzat alwaṣl may drop out, when preceded by the Interrogative particle أَ e.g. أَبْنُكَ abnuka (for أَٱبْنُكَ) "thy son"?

§ 12.
Madda.

If a hamza with fatḥa (a) is followed by a vowelless alif, then the hamza and vowel are dropped and one alif only is written, while above this is written a sign ~ called مَدَّةٌ madda (really the second alif written horizontally above) which is pronounced ā, e.g. آمِنْ

āminun (for أَأْمِنٌ), رَآهُ (for رَأَاهُ) ra'āhu, قُرْآنٌ qur'ānun (for قُرْأَانٌ).

Note. In many books the usual ا which lengthens the ـَ vowel, is provided with this sign, when it precedes hamza e.g. صَحْرَآءُ ṣaḥrā'u "desert".

§ 13.

The Syllable.

1. There are two kinds of syllable:

a) Open, consisting of a consonant and a short vowel e.g. كَتَبَ ka-ta-ba.

b) Closed, consisting of a consonant, short vowel and vowelless consonant e.g. the 2nd and 3rd syllables in كَتَبْتُمْ ka-tab-tum.

Syllables consisting of a consonant and a long vowel are considered closed since the letters ا و ي are considered vowelless consonants e.g. دَارِي dā-rī.

A consonant followed by the nunation is also considered as closed (as if the n were written) e.g. دَارٌ dā-rı

2. No syllable can begin with a vowelless consonant. If such a case arises from inflection in Arabic words, a hamzat alwaṣl with ا is prefixed e.g. اُكْتُبْ 'uktub "write" (for كْتُبْ ktub). In writing foreign words an unchangeable hamza (هَمْزَةُ القَطْعِ) is prefixed e.g. أَفْلَاطُونُ aflāṭūnu "Plato", or the first consonant is provided with a vowel e.g. فَرَنْسَا faransā (for fransā) "France".

3. No syllable can close with two vowelless consonants. If such a case arises from inflection, then one letter falls out e.g. قُولْ qūl becomes قُلْ qŭl "say", (cf. also § 6, Note 2 and § 11, 3).

The only exception to this rule is in the case of words in which these letters ا, و, ى lengthening a vowel are followed by a doubled consonant e.g. فَارٌّ fārrun, for فَارْرٌ from فَارِرٌ fārirun.

§ 14.
Accent.

1. In words of more than one syllable the accent is never on the last.

2. If the last syllable but one is closed, it receives the accent e.g. قَالَ qála, يَقُولُ yaqúlu, خَيَّاطُونَ khayyāṭúna, إِجْتَمَعْنَا ijtamáʿnā, أَخْبَرْنَاكُمْ akhbarnákum.

3. In words of three syllables, if the last but one is open, the accent falls on the last but two e.g. كَتَبَ kátaba. In words of four or more syllable. the accent is carried back until it meets with a closed syllable e.g. مَشْوَرَةٌ máshwaratun, تَجَنَّبَتَا tajánnabatā, مُكَاتَبَةٌ mukátabatun

§ 15.
Numerals.

1. In former times (and occasionally still in some artificial forms of literature) the letters of the alphabet are used to indicate numerals. In this case the order of the letters is that of the old Semitic alphabet, followed by the letters peculiar to the Arabic alphabet. This alphabet is called حُرُوفُ الأَبْجَدِ ḥurūf al'abjad.

1.	ا	20.	ك	200.	ر
2.	ب	30.	ل	300.	ش
3.	ج	40.	م	400.	ت
4.	د	50.	ن	500.	ث
5.	ه	60.	س	600.	خ
6.	و	70.	ع	700.	ذ
7.	ز	80.	ف	800.	ض
8.	ح	90.	ص	900.	ظ
9.	ط	100.	ق	1000.	غ
10.	ى				

This order is given in the following line:

أَبْجَدْ هَوَزْ حُطِّي كَلَمَنْ سَعْفَصْ قُرِشَتْ ثَخِذْ ضَظِغْ

but that used in NW. Africa differs slightly from this.

2. The numerals in general use now are:

١ ٢ ٣ ٤ ٥ ٦ ٧ ٨ ٩ ٠

1 2 3 4 5 6 7 8 9 0

These are read from left to right e.g. ١٨٩٧ 1897.

§ 16.

Abbreviations.

A stroke resembling a madda is generally (though not always) put above abbreviations e g. آلخ for إِلَى آخِرِهِ ilā ākhirihi "and so forth" (literally "to its end").

The following abbreviations are in common use after the names of certain persons: صعم = صَلَّى ٱللّٰهُ عَلَيْهِ وَسَلَّمَ salla 'llāhu ʿalaihi wasallama "God bless him and give him peace" used after the name of Mohammed.

عم = عَلَيْهِ ٱلسَّلَامُ ʿalaihi 'ssalāmu "Upon him be peace" used after the names of other prophets.

رضه = رَضِىَ ٱللّٰهُ عَنْهُ raḍiya 'llāhu ʿanhu "May God be pleased with him" used after the names of the Companions of Moḥammed.

رح = رَحِمَهُ ٱللّٰهُ raḥimahu 'llāhu "May God have compassion on him" used after the names of the dead.

Exercises in reading.

I.

بِ تَ لِ وَ أَبٌ بَلْ قُلْ حَمٌ قُمْ كُلْ طِبْ

ṭib kul qum ḥamun qul bal abun wa lī ta bi

سِرْ لَا مَا لَمْ عَنْ خُذْ ذُو نَمْ فِى دُمْ كَىْ يَدٌ

yadun kai dum fī nam dhū khudh ʿan lam mā lā sir

وَىْ لُبٌّ مَدَّ طِبٌّ دَلَّ كُلٌّ

kullun dalla ṭibbun madda lubbun wai

II.

كَتَبَ قَتَلَ فَرِحَ حَسُنَ شَرِبَ قَتْلٌ فَرَحٌ

faraḥun qatlun shariba ḥasuna fariḥa qatala kataba

حَسَنٌ حُسْنٌ طَالَ خَافَ ضَرْبٌ حَبْلٌ إِبِلٌ

ibilun ḥablun ḍarbun khāfa ṭāla ḥusnun ḥasanun

نُورٌ فِيلٌ بَيْتٌ جَارٌ مَوْتٌ قُمْتَ خِفْتِ رَأْسٌ

ra'sun khiftī qumta mautun jārun baitun fīlun nūrun

ظَهْرٍ بُخْلٌ بَحْرٍ نَهْرٍ بِكْرٍ أَكَلَ جَرَى

jarā akala bikrin nahrin baḥrin bukhlun ẓahrin

III.

كتبت كتبت كتاب . كاتب قلنا نفسا هارب

hāribun nafsan qulnâ kātibun kitābun katabtu katabat

يكتب تضرب أقتل فتش فتش أساس كتبتم

katabtum asāsun fattish fattasha aqtulu taḍribu jaktubu

فرحنا بعثوا تخرج كتابه شغلكم مكتوب

maktūbun shughlukum kitābuhu takhruju baʿathū fariḥnā

مفتاح جالسا سرطان تعبان طريقكم تختلفوا

takhtalifū ṭarīqukum taʿbānu saraṭānun jālisan miftāḥun

إختلاف إجتمعنا إتخذتم إحمرت تدارك

tadāraka iḥmarrat ittakhadhtum ijtamaʿnā ikhtilāfun

إضطربت تتذكر مومن آكل آخذ إلى على

ʿalā ilā ākhiḏun ākilun mu'minun tatadhakkaru iḍṭarabat

موسى إستئناس إستحلفيني مواخذة مولفون

mu'allifūna mu'ākhaḏatun istaḥlifīnī isti'nāsun mūsā

تأليفا

ta'lîfan

IV.

القطر المصرى يكون الزاوية الشمالية الشرقية من

أفريقية ويقال له ايضا وادى النيل لان قسمه الجنوبى واقع بين

سلسلتى جبال ويخترقه نهر النيل العظيم امساحته جغرافيا

اربعمائة الف ميل مربع واما مساحته المقاسة فهى ٦٥ الف

ميل مربع منه ...٥٧٣٦ فدان ارض زراعية ☆

وَيَحُدُّ هٰذَا ٱلْقُطْرَ مِنَ ٱلشَّمَالِ ٱلْبَحْرُ ٱلْمُتَوَسِّطُ وَمِنَ ٱلشَّرْقِ خَطٌّ يَمْتَدُّ مِنْ خَانِ يُونُسَ عَلَى ٱلْبَحْرِ ٱلْمُتَوَسِّطِ إِلَى ٱلسُّوَيْسِ عَلَى ٱلْبَحْرِ ٱلْأَحْمَرِ وَٱلْبَحْرُ ٱلْأَحْمَرُ وَمِنَ ٱلْجَنُوبِ بِلَادُ ٱلنُّوبَةِ وَمِنَ ٱلْغَرْبِ بِلَادُ بَرْقَةَ ۞

وَٱلنِّيلُ نَهْرٌ يَخْتَرِقُ ٱلْقُطْرَ ٱلْمِصْرِيَّ مِنَ ٱلْجَنُوبِ إِلَى ٱلشَّمَالِ فَإِذَا وَصَلَ إِلَى قُرْبِ ٱلْقَاهِرَةِ انْقَسَمَ إِلَى فَرْعَيْنِ يَسِيرُ أَحَدُهُمَا مَائِلًا إِلَى ٱلشَّرْقِ حَتَّى يَصُبَّ إِلَى ٱلْبَحْرِ ٱلْمُتَوَسِّطِ عِنْدَ مَدِينَةِ دِمْيَاطَ وَٱلْآخَرُ يَسِيرُ مَائِلًا إِلَى ٱلْغَرْبِ حَتَّى يَصُبَّ إِلَى ذٰلِكَ ٱلْبَحْرِ عِنْدَ ثَغْرِ رَشِيدَ ۞

وَيَنْقَسِمُ ٱلْقُطْرُ ٱلْمِصْرِيُّ بِهٰذَا ٱلْاعْتِبَارِ إِلَى قِسْمَيْنِ جَنُوبِيٍّ وَشَمَالِيٍّ أَوْ قِبْلِيٍّ وَبَحْرِيٍّ فَٱلْقِسْمُ ٱلْقِبْلِيُّ يُقَالُ لَهُ ٱلصَّعِيدُ أَوْ مِصْرُ ٱلْعُلْيَا يَمْتَدُّ مِنْ آخِرِ حُدُودِ مِصْرَ جَنُوبًا إِلَى نُقْطَةِ تَفَرُّعِ ٱلنِّيلِ وَٱلْبَحْرِيُّ يُقَالُ لَهُ مِصْرُ ٱلسُّفْلَى يَمْتَدُّ مِنْ نُقْطَةِ تَفَرُّعِ ٱلنِّيلِ إِلَى ٱلْبَحْرِ ٱلْمُتَوَسِّطِ ۞

وَيَنْقَسِمُ ٱلْوَجْهُ ٱلْبَحْرِيُّ إِلَى ثَلَاثَةِ أَقْسَامٍ مُتَوَسِّطٍ وَهُوَ ٱلْوَاقِعُ بَيْنَ فَرْعَيِ ٱلنِّيلِ وَقَدْ يُسَمَّى لِذٰلِكَ رَوْضَةَ ٱلْبَحْرَيْنِ وَيُقَالُ لَهُ أَيْضًا ٱلدِّلْتَا لِمُشَابَهَتِهِ بِحَرْفِ ٱلدَّالِ عِنْدَ ٱلْيُونَانِيِّينَ

وَشَرْقِيّ وَهُوَ ٱلْوَاقِعُ إِلَى شَرْقِيِّ ٱلدِّلْتَا وَيُقَالُ لَهُ ٱلْحُوفُ ٱلشَّرْقِيُّ

وَغَرْبِيّ وَهُوَ ٱلْوَاقِعُ إِلَى غَرْبِيِّهَا وَيُقَالُ لَهُ ٱلْحُوفُ ٱلْغَرْبِيُّ هٰذِهِ هِيَ

أَقْسَامُ ٱلْقُطْرِ ٱلْمِصْرِيِّ ٱلطَّبِيعِيَّةُ أَمَّا أَقْسَامُهُ ٱلْإِدَارِيَّةُ فَتَخْتَلِفُ

بِٱخْتِلَافِ ٱلْأَزْمَانِ ۞

Transcription and Translation.

alquṭru 'lmiṣrīyu yukauwinu 'zzāwiyata
The land the Egyptian forms the angle
'shshamālīyata 'shsharqīyata min afrīqiyatin wayuqālu
the northern the eastern of Africa and it is
lahu aiḍan wādi'nnīli li'anna qismahu
called also the valley of the Nile because its part
'ljanūbīya wāqiʿun baina silsilatai jibālin
the southern lies between two chains of mountains,
wayakhtariquhu nahru'nnīli 'l'aẓīmu
and cuts through it the river of Nile the mighty.
masāhatuhu jighrāfīyan arbaʿumi'ati alfi mīlin
Its area (is) geographically 400 000 square
murabbaʿin wa ammā masāḥatuhu 'lmuqāsatu
miles and as for its area the measured,
fahiya 65 alfa mīlin murabbaʿin minhā 5 736 000
it (is) 65 000 square miles, of which 5 736 000
faddānin arḍan zarāʿīyatan.
faddāns (are) seed ground

wayaḥuddu hādha 'lquṭra mina 'shshamāli 'lbaḥru
And bounds this land on the North the sea
'lmutawassiṭu wamina 'shsharqi khaṭṭun yamtaddu
the Mediterranean and on the East a line which extends
min khāni yūnusa ʿala 'lbaḥri 'lmutawassiṭi ila
from Khān Yunus on the sea the Mediterranean to
'ssuwaisi ʿala 'lbaḥri 'l'aḥmari wa 'lbaḥru 'l'aḥmaru
Suez on the sea the Red, and the sea the Red;
wamina 'ljanūbi bilādu 'nnūbati wamina
and on the South the district of Nubia; and on
'lgharbi bilādu barqata.
the West the district of Barqa.

wa 'nnīlu nahrun yakhtariqu
And the Nile (is) a river (which) cuts through
'lquṭra 'lmiṣrīya mina 'ljanūbi ila 'shshamāli
the land the Egyptian from the South to the North
fa 'idhā waṣala ilā qurbi 'lqāhirati
and when it comes to the neighbourhood of Cairo,
'nqasama ilā farʿaini yasīru aḥaduhumā mā'ilan
it divides into two branches, goes one of them tending
ila 'shsharqi ḥattā yaṣubba ila 'lbaḥri 'lmutawassiṭi
to the East until it flows into the sea the Mediterranean
ʿinda madīnati dimyāṭa wa 'l'ākharu yasīru mā'ilan
at the city of Damietta and the other goes tending
ila 'lgharbi ḥattā yaṣubba ilā dhālika 'lbaḥri ʿinda
to the West until it flows into that sea at
thaghri rashīda.
the frontier of Rosetta.

wayanqasimu 'lquṭru 'lmiṣrīyu bihādha
And is divided the land the Egyptian in this
'liʿtibāri ilā qismaini janūbīyin washamālīyin au
way into two parts, a southern and a northern, or
qiblīyin. wabaḥrīyin fa'lqismu 'lqiblīyu
a southern and a sea-coast, and the part the southern,
wayuqālu lahu .'ṣṣaʿīdu au miṣru 'lʿulyā yamtaddu
and it is called the Ṣaʿīd or Egypt the upper, extends
min ākhiri ḥudūdi miṣra janūban ilā
from the end of the limits of Egypt (on the) South to
nuqṭati tafarruʿi 'nnīli wa'lbaḥrīyu
the point of the branching of the Nile; and the sea-coast,
wayuqālu lahu miṣru 'ssuflā yamtaddu min nuqṭati
and it is called Egypt the lower, extends from the point
tafarruʿi 'nnīli ila 'lbaḥri 'lmutawassiṭi.
of the branching of the Nile to the sea the Mediterranean.

wayuqsamu 'lwajhu 'lbaḥrīyu ilā
And is divided the portion the sea-coast into
thalāthati aqsāmin mutawassiṭin wahuwa 'lwāqiʿu baina
three divisions, a middle, and it lies between
farʿayi 'nnīli waqad summiya
the two branches of the Nile, and it has been named
lidhālika rauḍatu 'lbaḥraini
on account of that the garden of the two rivers
wayuqālu lahu aiḍani 'dhdhaltā limushābahatihi
and it is called also the Delta on account of its

biharfi 'dhdhāli ʿinda 'lyūnānīyīna
resemblance to the letter dhal among the Greeks,
washarqīyin wahuwa 'lwāqiʿu ilā sharqīyi 'dhdhaltā
and an eastern, and it lies to the East of the Delta
wayuqālu lahu 'lḥaufu 'shsharqīyu wagharbīyin
and is called the border the Eastern, and a western
wahuwa 'lwāqiʿu ilā gharbīyiha wayuqālu lahu
and it lies to the West of it, and is called
'lḥaufu 'lgharbīyu hādhihi hiya 'aqsāmu
the border the Western. These are the divisions
'lquṭri 'lmiṣrīyi 'ṭṭabiʿīyatu 'ammā 'aqsāmuhu
of the land the Egyptian the natural. As for its divisions
'l'idārīyatu fatakhtalifu bi'khtilāfi
the administrative, they differ with the differing
'l'azmāni.
of the times.

First Part.

First Lesson.

(أَلدَّرْسُ ٱلأَوَّلُ 'addarsa l'awwalu.)

1. There is no indefinite article in Arabic.

2. The definite article for all genders and numbers is أَلْ 'al, which is prefixed to the noun which it defines, at the same time depriving it of the nunation (Intro. § 7), e.g. بَيْتٌ baitun "a house"; أَلْبَيْتُ 'albaitu "the house".

The hamza of the article is hamzat alwaṣl (Intro. § 11) and so when it follows another word is dropped with its vowel and in pronunciation the ل follows immediately the vowel of the preceding word e.g. بَابُ ٱلْبَيْتِ bābulbaiti "the door of the house"; بَابِ ٱلْبَيْتِ bābilbaiti "of the door of the house"; بَابَ ٱلْبَيْتِ bāb-albaiti "the door (accus.) of the house".

3. In pronunciation the ل of the article is assimilated to the Sun-letters (Intro. § 4, 2) ت ث د ذ ر ز س ش ص ض ط ظ ل ن when the word to which it is attached begins with one of these e.g. أَلرَّجُلُ 'arrajulu the man" أَلشَّمْسُ ashshamsu "the sun". In such words the ل is written without vowel-sign and tashdīd is placed over the Sun-letter.

4. Adjectives as attributes are placed after the nouns they qualify. If the noun has the article the adjective must have it also e.g. نَهْرٌ عَرِيضٌ nahrun ʿarīḍun "a wide river"; أَلنَّهْرُ ٱلْعَرِيضُ 'annahrulʿarīḍu "the wide river".

5. The copula "is" or "are" is not expressed in Arabic, e.g. اَلنَّهْرُ عَرِيضٌ 'annahru 'arīḍun "the river is wide".

6. The personal pronouns of the singular are:

أَنَا 'anā I.

أَنْتَ 'anta Thou (masc.).

أَنْتِ 'anti Thou (fem.).

هُوَ **huwa He.**

هِيَ **hiya She.**

Vocabulary.

بُسْتَانٌ bustānun a garden.

كَبِيرٌ kabīrun great, large.

بَيْتٌ baitun a house.

صَغِيرٌ ṣaghīrun small.

مَحَلٌّ maḥallun a place.

حَسَنٌ ḥasanun, كُوَيِّسٌ kuwaiyisun beautiful.

اَلنِّيلُ annīlu the Nile.

نَهْرٌ nahrun a river.

مَلِكٌ malikun a king.

عَادِلٌ 'ādilun just.

إِنْسَانٌ insānun a man.

بَحْرٌ baḥrun a sea.

قَصْرٌ qaṣrun a castle.

خُبْزٌ khubzun bread.

طَيِّبٌ ṭaiyibun good.

رَجُلٌ rajulun a man.

اَلْقَاضِي alqāḍī the judge (see Lesson 6, 2 Note 2).

تَعْبَانُ ta'bānu tired. (without nunation, see Lesson 41).

حَبِيبٌ ḥabībun a friend.

صَادِقٌ ṣādiqun upright.

شَارِعٌ shāri'un a street.

عَرِيضٌ 'arīḍun wide.

قَبِيحٌ qabīḥun bad, disgraceful.

Exercise 1.

ٱلْبُسْتَانُ كَبِيرٌ — ٱلْبُسْتَانُ ٱلْكَبِيرُ — ٱلْبَيْتُ ٱلصَّغِيرُ —
مَحَلٌّ حَسَنٌ — ٱلرَّجُلُ حَسَنٌ — إِنْسَانٌ قَبِيحٌ — ٱلنِّيلُ
نَهْرٌ — مَلِكٌ عَادِلٌ — ٱلْبَحْرُ كَبِيرٌ — قَصْرٌ كُوَيِّسٌ — خُبْزٌ
طَيِّبٌ — ٱلْخُبْزُ طَيِّبٌ — أَنَا رَجُلٌ — ٱلْقَاضِي رَجُلٌ طَيِّبٌ —
أَنْتَ تَعْبَانُ — هُوَ حَبِيبٌ طَيِّبٌ — ٱلرَّجُلُ هُوَ ٱلْحَبِيبُ
ٱلصَّادِقُ — ٱلشَّارِعُ عَرِيضٌ —

Transcription.

albustānu kabīrun. — albustānu ’lkabīru, — albaitu ’ṣṣaghīru. — maḥallun ḥasanun. — arrajulu ḥasanun. — insānun qabīḥun. — annīlu nahrun. — malikun ʿādilun. — albaḥru kabīrun. — qaṣrun kuwaiyisun. — khubzun ṭaiyibun. — alkhubzu ṭaiyibun. — anā rajulun. — alqāḍī rajulun ṭaiyibun. — anta taʿbānu. — huwa ḥabībun ṭaiyibun. — arrajulu huwa ’lḥabību ’ṣṣādiqu. — shshāriʿu ʿarīḍun.

Exercise 2.

The house is large. — The garden is a beautiful place. — Thou art a good man. — I am tired. — The beautiful castle and (وَ wa) the wide river. — The judge is upright. — I am an upright friend. — Thou art a bad man. — The wide street.

Second Lesson.

(ٱلدَّرْسُ ٱلثَّانِي)

The Feminine.

1. Most feminine words take the ending ـَةٌ atun (for this form of t see Intro. § 1, Note 2), e.g. إِبْنٌ

'ibnun "a son", إِبْنَةٌ 'ibnatun "a daughter"; كَبِيرٌ kabīrun "great", feminine كَبِيرَةٌ kabīratun.

2. The adjective agrees with the noun which it qualifies or is predicate to, e.g. اَلْاِبْنَةُ الْكَبِيرَةُ 'alibnatu 'lkabīratu "the big girl", اَلْاِبْنَةُ كَبِيرَةٌ 'alibnatu kabīratun "the girl is big (or old)".

3. Some words are feminine without having a feminine ending:

a) Nouns denoting females e.g. أُمٌّ 'ummun "a mother", عَرُوسٌ 'arūsun "a bride", هِنْدٌ Hindun (name of a woman).

b) Proper names of lands and cities e.g. مِصْرُ miṣru (without nunation) "Egypt, Cairo", اَلشَّامُ 'ashshāmu (always with article), "Syria, Damascus".

c) Names of those parts of the body which occur in pairs e.g. يَدٌ yadun "hand", رِجْلٌ rijlun "foot", عَيْنٌ 'ainun "eye" etc.

d) Many single words, among the commonest being:

أَرْضٌ 'arḍun, earth.	شَمْسٌ shamsun, sun.
خَمْرٌ khamrun, wine.	نَارٌ nārun, fire.
دَارٌ dārun, house.	نَفْسٌ nafsun, self, soul.
رِيحٌ rīḥun, wind.	سُوقٌ sūqun, market.

Note 1. Some words are used both as masculine and feminine, (see Less. 38).

Note 2. Other feminine endings are ـَى ā and ـَاءُ ā'u (see Less. 38).

Note 3. Nouns ending in ةٌ denoting males are masculine e.g. خَلِيفَةٌ khalīfatun "a caliph", طَرَفَةُ Ṭarafatu (the name of a poet).

Collectives.

4. Many words singular in form have a collective meaning e.g. حَجَرٌ ḥajarun "rock", زَيْتُونٌ zaitūnun "olives". To indicate a single object the feminine ending ةٌ atun is appended to such words e.g. حَجَرَةٌ ḥajaratun "a piece of rock, a stone", زَيْتُونَةٌ zaitūnatun "a (single) olive".

5. Interrogative sentences are introduced by the particles هَلْ or أَ. The latter is prefixed to the first word of the sentence.

Vocabulary.

جَدٌّ	jaddun a grandfather.	حَاضِرٌ	ḥāḍirun present, ready.
جَدَّةٌ	jaddatun a grandmother.	شَدِيدٌ	shadīdun strong, violent.
صَالِحٌ	ṣāliḥun honest.	حَكِيمٌ	ḥakīmun a wise man, physician.
جُنَيْنَةٌ	junainatun a garden.	طَيْرٌ	ṭairun a bird.
نَعَمْ	na'am yes.	طَالِعٌ	ṭāli'un rising (of the sun).
لَا	lā no.	مُظِلٌّ	muẓillun shady.
سَاعَةٌ	sā'atun an hour.	خَادِمٌ	khādimun a man-servant.
قَدِيمٌ	qadīmun old, ancient (of things).	خَادِمَةٌ	khādimatun a maid-servant.
جَدِيدٌ	jadīdun new.		
وَلَدٌ	waladun a boy		

مُطِيعٌ muṭîʿun obedient.
قَاهِرٌ qâhirun conquering.
نَظِيفٌ naẓîfun clean.
إِوَزٌّ {iwazzun goose (collective).
مَيِّتٌ maiyitun dead.
مَلِكَةٌ malikatun a queen.
غَارِبٌ {ghâribun setting (of the sun).
تُفَّاحٌ {tuffâḥun apple (collective).
شَجَرٌ {shajarun tree (collective).

Exercise 3.

ٱلْجَدُّ كَبِيرٌ — ٱلْجَدَّةُ كَبِيرَةٌ — ٱلاِبْنَةُ ٱلصَّغِيرَةُ — إِبْنٌ
صَالِحٌ — هَلِ ٱلْجُنَيْنَةُ كُوَيِّسَةٌ — نَعَمِ ٱلْجُنَيْنَةُ كُوَيِّسَةٌ — سَاعَةٌ
حَسَنَةٌ — ٱلْبَيْتُ قَدِيمٌ — ٱلدَّارُ جَدِيدَةٌ — ٱلْأُمُّ حَسَنَةٌ —
أَلْوَلَدُ حَاضِرٌ — رِيحٌ شَدِيدَةٌ — ٱلرِّيحُ شَدِيدَةٌ — أَأَنْتَ
تَعْبَانُ — نَعَمْ أَنَا تَعْبَانُ — هَلْ أَنْتَ ٱلْقَاضِي — لَا أَنَا ٱلْحَكِيمُ —
هَلْ هِيَ صَالِحَةٌ — لَا هِيَ قَبِيحَةٌ — ٱلشَّمْسُ طَالِعَةٌ — ٱلشَّجَرَةُ
ٱلْمِظَلَّةُ — ٱلْخَادِمَةُ مُطِيعَةٌ — مِصْرُ ٱلْقَاهِرَةُ (a name of Cairo)
— ٱلْيَدُ نَظِيفَةٌ — ٱلْإِوَزُّ طَيْرٌ — ٱلْإِوَزَّةُ ٱلْمَيِّتَةُ —

Transcription.

aljaddu kabîrun. — aljaddatu kabîratun. — alibnatu 'ṣṣaghîratu. — ibnun ṣâliḥun. — hali 'ljunainatu kuwaiyisatun. — naʿami 'ljunainatu kuwaiyisatun. — sâʿatun ḥasanatun. — albaitu qadîmun. — addâru jadîdatun. — al'ummu ḥasanatun. — alwaladu ḥâḍirun. — rîḥun shadîdatun. — arrîḥu shadîdatun. — a'anta taʿbânu. — naʿam anâ taʿbânu. — hal anta 'lqâḍi. —

lā ana 'lḥakīmu. — hal hiya ṣāliḥatun. — lā hiya qabīḥatun. — ashshamsu ṭāliʿatun. — ashshajaratu 'lmuzillatu. — alkhādimatu muṭīʿatun. — miṣru 'lqāhiratu. — alyadu naẓīfatun. — al'iwazzu ṭairun. — al'iwazzatu 'lmaiyitatu.

Exercise 4.

The mother is present. — A great fire. — Is the garden large? — No, the garden is small. — The new house is small. — The wind is violent. — Art thou (fem.) the grandmother? — Yes, I am the grandmother. — Tho beautiful daughter. — The king is just and the queen is beautiful. — The setting sun.

Third Lesson.

(أَلدَّرْسُ ٱلثَّالِثُ)

Number.

1. There are three numbers in Arabic: Singular (مُفْرَدٌ mufrad), Dual (مُثَنًّى muthanna or تَثْنِيَةٌ tathniya) and Plural (جَمْعٌ jamʿ).

2. The Dual is formed by adding to the word (either masc. or fem.) the termination ـَانِ āni for the nominative, ـَيْنِ aini for the other cases, e.g.

مَلِكٌ malikun a king; مَلِكَانِ malikāni two kings (nom.); مَلِكَيْنِ malikaini two kings (other cases).

مَلِكَةٌ malikatun a queen مَلِكَتَانِ malikatāni two queens (nom.) مَلِكَتَيْنِ malikataini two queens (other cases).

Note. In the fem. the ة is changed to ت wherever a suffix is added.

3. The Plural is of two kinds:

a) The Sound plural (أَلْجَمْعُ ٱلسَّالِمُ 'aljam' assālim) formed by the addition of endings to the singular.

b) The Broken plural (أَلْجَمْعُ ٱلْمُكَسَّرُ 'aljam' almukassar) formed by a change of vowels within the word and in some cases with an ending as well, (sed Lessons 4 and 5).

4. The Sound plural masc. of nouns and adjectives is formed by adding ـُونَ ūna for the nominative and ـِينَ īna for the other cases after the case-ending of the nominative singular has been dropped, e.g.

Singular.	Plural Nom.	Plural, other cases.
مَلِكٌ malikun.	مَلِكُونَ malikūna.	مَلِكِينَ malikīna.
كَثِيرٌ kathīrun.	كَثِيرُونَ kathīrūna.	كَثِيرِينَ kathīrīna.

The Sound plural of feminines is formed by changing ـَةٌ atun into ـَاتٌ ātun for the nominative and ـَاتٍ ātin for the other cases, e.g.

Singular.	Plural Nom.
خَادِمَةٌ khādimatun a maid-servant.	خَادِمَاتٌ khādimātun.

Plural, other cases
خَادِمَاتٍ khādimātin.

Note. Some feminine nouns take a masculine sound plural, e.g. سَنَةٌ sanatun a year Plur. سِنُونَ sinuna; some masculine nouns also take a feminine sound plural, e.g حَيَوَانٌ ḥayawānun animal, Plur. حَيَوَانَاتٌ ḥayawānātun.

5. Adjectives agree with their nouns not only in gender (see Less. 2, 2) but also in number except

that: a) when the noun is in the Sound fem. plur. the adjective is usually in the fem. singular, though it is occasionally in the fem. plur. when persons are indicated. b) Broken plurals being originally Collectives, take the adjective in the fem. sing. (see Lessons 4 and 5).

Examples of the regular agreement:

خَادِمٌ حَسَنٌ	khādimun ḥasanun a good (beautiful) servant.
خَادِمَةٌ حَسَنَةٌ	khādimatun ḥasanatun a good maid-servant.
خَادِمَانِ حَسَنَانِ	khādimāni ḥasanāni two good servants.
خَادِمَتَانِ حَسَنَتَانِ	khādimatāni ḥasanatāni two good maid-servants.
خَادِمُونَ حَسَنُونَ	khādimūna ḥasanūna good servants.

Example of exception a):

خَادِمَاتٌ حَسَنَةٌ	khādimātun ḥasanatun good maid-servants.

or as the noun indicates persons

خَادِمَاتٌ حَسَنَاتٌ khādimātun ḥasanātun.

6. The personal pronouns are:

هُوَ huwa he.	هُمَا humā they two (masc. and fem.).	هُمْ hum they (masc.).
هِيَ hiya she.		هُنَّ hunna they (fem.).
أَنْتَ anta thou (masc.).	أَنْتُمَا antumā you two (masc. and fem.).	أَنْتُمْ antum you (masc.).
أَنْتِ anti thou (fem.).		أَنْتُنَّ antunna you (fem.).
أَنَا anā I (masc. and fem.		نَحْنُ naḥnu we (masc. and fem.).

Vocabulary.

مُعَلِّمٌ	muʿallimun a teacher.	مَبْسُوطٌ	mabsūṭun contented.
مُعَلِّمَةٌ	muʿallimatun a (female) teacher.	زَعْلَانُ	zaʿlānu vexed
لَامِعٌ	lāmiʿun flashing.	لَيْلٌ	lailun night (collective).
لَيْلَةٌ	lailatun a night.	خَيَّاطَةٌ	khaijāṭatun a (female) tailor.
نَهَارٌ	nahārun a day.	مُسْلِمٌ	muslimun a Moslem.
مَشْغُولٌ	mashghūlun busy.	لَاعِبٌ	lāʿibun playing.
خَبَّازٌ	khabbāzun a baker.	حَارَةٌ	ḥâratun a quarter (of a town).
مُجْتَهِدٌ	mujtahidun industrious.	مُظْلِمٌ	muẓlimun dark.
غَائِبٌ	ghā'ibun absent.	كَسْلَانُ	kaslānu idle.
خَيَّاطٌ	khaiyāṭun a tailor.	نَجَّارٌ	najjārun a carpenter.

Exercise 5.

اَلْمُعَلِّمُ ٱلصَّالِحُ — اَلْمُعَلِّمُونَ صَالِحُونَ — اَلْعَيْنَانِ ٱللَّامِعَتَانِ — اَلْمُعَلِّمَاتُ حَاضِرَةٌ — هَلْ أَنْتُمْ مَبْسُوطُونَ — لَا نَحْنُ زَعْلَانُونَ — لَيْلَتَانِ وَنَهَارَانِ — هَلِ ٱلْقَاضِي مَشْغُولٌ — نَعَمْ هُوَ مَشْغُولٌ — اَلْخَبَّازُونَ مُجْتَهِدُونَ — اَلِابْنَتَانِ غَائِبَتَانِ — اَلْخَيَّاطُ وَٱلْخَيَّاطَةُ مَشْغُولَانِ — اَلْخَيَّاطُونَ وَٱلْخَيَّاطَاتُ مُجْتَهِدُونَ — اَلْمُسْلِمُونَ ٱلصَّالِحُونَ — وَلَدَانِ لَاعِبَانِ — اَلْحَارَاتُ نَظِيفَةٌ —

Transcription.

almuʿallimu ʾṣṣāliḥu. — almuʿallimūna ṣāliḥūna. — alʿaināni ʾllāmiʿatāni. — almuʿallimetu ḥāḍiratun. — hal antum mabsūṭūna. — lā naḥnu zaʿlānūna. — lailatāni wanahārāni. — hali ʾlqāḍī mashghūlun. — naʿam huwa mashghūlun. — alkhabbāzūna mujtahidūna. — alibnatāni ghāʾibatāni. — alkhaiyāṭu waʾlkhaiyāṭatu mashghūlāni. — alkhaiyāṭūna waʾlkhaijāṭātu muytahidāna. — almuslimūna ʾṣṣāliḥūna. — waladāni lāʿibāni. — alḥāratu nazīfatun.

Exercise 6.

The quarter (of the town) is clean. — The teachers are present. — A flashing eye. — Are you (two) industrious? — Yes, we are busy. — Are you vexed? — No, I am contented. — The Moslem is pious. — They (masc.) are absent. — The beautiful tailoresses are present. — The boy is industrious. — The night is dark. — The servants and maid servants are tired. — The physician is busy. — Two busy physicians. — Two clean hands. — Are the bakers idle? — Yes, and the carpenters are idle, they are tired.

Fourth Lesson.

(اَلدَّرْسُ اَلرَّابِعُ)

The Broken Plural.

Explanation. Arabic words with few exceptions (see Note) consist of three consonants called Radicals together with certain vowels and sometimes prefixes or suffixes. To indicate patterns or type-forms of words Arabian grammarians use the three consonants فعل the ف representing the first radical, the ع the second and the ل the third e.g. كَلْبٌ kalbun "a dog" is said to be of the form فَعْلٌ; كَبِيرٌ of the form فَعِيلٌ; ظِلٌّ (for ظِلْلٌ) of the form فِعْلٌ; أَحْمَرُ ʾaḥmaru "red" of the form أَفْعَلُ; تَعْبَانُ of the form فَعْلَانُ; مَبْسُوطٌ of the form مَفْعُولٌ.

Note. A few Arabic words have four radicals. The pattern فعلل is used for them.

There are 31 patterns of the Broken Plural (Less. 3, § 3). A complete list of these is given in Lessons 39 and 40. Among the most frequently used are:

a) أَفْعَالٌ e.g. أَوْلَادٌ 'aulādun plur. of وَلَدٌ waladun "a boy"; أَفْرَاسٌ 'afrāsun plur. of فَرَسٌ farasun "a horse"; أَشْرَافٌ 'ashrāfun plur. of شَرِيفٌ sharīfun "noble". In the same way are formed the plurals of طِفْلٌ ṭiflun "a baby"; مَطَرٌ maṭarun "rain"; وَقْتٌ waqtun "time".

b) فُعُولٌ e.g. بُحُورٌ buḥūrun plur. of بَحْرٌ baḥrun "sea"; أُسُودٌ 'usūdun plur. of أَسَدٌ 'asadun "a lion"; شُهُودٌ shuhūdun plur. of شَاهِدٌ shāhidun "a witness"; حُقُوقٌ ḥuqūqun plur. of حَقٌّ ḥaqqun "a right". In the same way are formed the plurals of قَلْبٌ qalbun "a heart"; جُنْدٌ jundun "an army"; مَلِكٌ malikun "a king".

c) فِعَالٌ e.g. كِلَابٌ kilābun plur. of كَلْبٌ kalbun "a dog"; رِجَالٌ rijālun plur. of رَجُلٌ rajulun "a man"; so also are formed the plurals of جَبَلٌ jabalun "a mountain"; رُمْحٌ rumḥun "a spear"; كَبِيرٌ kabīrun "great".

d) فُعُلٌ e.g. كُتُبٌ kutubun plur. of كِتَابٌ kitābun "a book"; مُدُنٌ mudunun plur. of مَدِينَةٌ madīnatun "a city"; سُفُنٌ sufunun plur. of سَفِينَةٌ safīnatun "a ship".

e) أَفْعُلٌ e.g. أَنْهُرٌ 'anhurun plur. of نَهْرٌ nahrun "a river"; أَشْهُرٌ 'ashhurun plur. of شَهْرٌ shahrun "a month"; أَرْجُلٌ 'arjulun plur. of رِجْلٌ rijlun "a foot".

Vocabulary.

The small letters after a word indicate that the Plural is of the form given under that letter in this lesson.

وَسِخٌ	wasikhun dirty.	طَوِيلٌ	ṭawīlun long.
صَعْبٌ	ṣaʿbun hard, difficult.	اَلْفُرَاتُ	alfurātu the Euphrates.
طَرِيقٌ	(d) ṭarīqun a way.	مُخْلِصٌ	mukhliṣun honest.
سَهِلٌ	sahilun easy.	سَرِيعٌ	sarīʿun swift.
عِلْمٌ	(b) ʿilmun knowledge, science.	اَلْمَاضِى	almāḍī the past.
نَافِعٌ	nāfiʿun useful.	اَلْعَالِى	alʿâlī the high.
شَرْطٌ	(b) sharṭun a condition.	حَرْفٌ	(b) ḥarfun a letter (of the alphabet).
ثَابِتٌ	thābitun firm, permanent.	عَرَبِيٌّ	ʿarabīyun Arabic, Arabian.
صَالِحٌ	(c) ṣāliḥun pious, honest.	سَيْفٌ	(b) saifun a sword.
		قَاطِعٌ	qāṭiʿun cutting.
حَارِسٌ	ḥārisun watchful.	نَاسٌ	nāsun peopl

Exercise 7.

هُوَ كِتَابٌ صَعْبٌ — كُتُبٌ صَعْبَةٌ — مِصْرُ وَٱلشَّامُ مَدِينَتَانِ

حَسَنَتَانِ — ٱلْمُدُنُ كُوَيِّسَةٌ — طُرُقٌ سَهِلَةٌ — ٱلْعُلُومُ

نَافِعَةٌ — ٱلشُّرُوطُ صَعْبَةٌ — حُقُوقٌ ثَابِتَةٌ — هُوَ شَاهِدٌ

صَالِحٌ — شُهُودٌ صِلَاحٌ — ٱلْكَلْبُ حَارِسٌ — ٱلْكِلَابُ ٱلْحَارِسَةُ —

ٱلْقُلُوبُ ٱلْمُخْلِصَةُ — سُفُنٌ سَرِيعَةٌ — الافراس حَسَنَةٌ —

الأَوْلَادُ مُطِيعُونَ — الأَمْطَارُ ٱلشَّدِيدَةُ — الأَوْقَاتُ ٱلْمَاضِيَةُ —
ٱلْجِبَالُ عَالِيَةٌ — ٱلْحُرُوفُ ٱلْعَرَبِيَّةُ — ٱلسُّيُوفُ قَاطِعَةٌ — الأَنْهُرُ
ٱلْكَبِيرَةُ — هُمْ نَاسٌ كِبَارٌ —

Transcription.

huwa kitābun ṣaʿbun. — kutubun ṣaʿbatun. — miṣru wa'shshāmu madīnatāni ḥasanatāni. — almudunu kuwaiyisatun. — ṭuruqun sahilātun. — alʿulūmu nāfiʿatun. — ashshurūṭu ṣaʿbatun. — ḥuqūqun thābitatun. — huwa shāhidun ṣāliḥun. — shuhūdun ṣilāḥun. — alkalbu ḥārisun. — alkilābu 'lḥārisatu. — alqulūbu 'lmukhliṣatu. — sufunun sarīʿatun. — al'afrāsu ḥasanatun. — al'aulādu muṭīʿūna. — al'amṭāru 'shshadīdatu. — al'auqātu 'lmāḍiyatu. — aljibālu ʿāliyatun. — alḥurūfu 'lʿarabīyatu. — assuyūfu qāṭiʿatun. — al'anhuru 'lkabīratu. — hum nāsun kibārun.

Exercise 8.

The dogs are swift and watchful. — It is a difficult way. — Difficult ways. — The industrious boys. — The Arabic letters are difficult. — They are (هُمْ) permanent rights. — An honest heart. — The high mountains are beautiful. — Are you great people? — No, .we are honest people. — Useful books. — The Arabian cities are dirty. — The Arabian sciences are difficult. — The swords are long. — The Nile and Euphrates are two great rivers. — The past month. — The little babies.

Fifth Lesson.

(أَلدَّرْسُ ٱلْخَامِسُ)

1. Further forms of the Broken Plural are:

f) فُعَلَاءُ e.g. وُزَرَاءُ wuzarā'u plur. of وَزِيرٌ wazīrun "a Vezir, minister"; أُمَرَاءُ 'umarā'u plur. of أَمِيرٌ 'amīrun "a prince"; سُفَرَاءُ sufarā'u plur. of سَفِيرٌ safīrun "an ambassador"; أُسَرَاءُ 'usarā'u plur. of أَسِيرٌ 'asirun "a captive".

This is a very common plural for words of the form فَعِيلٌ when they denote persons.

g) أَفْعِلَاءُ e.g. أَصْدِقَاءُ 'aṣdiqā'u plur. of صَدِيقٌ ṣadīqun "a friend"; أَنْبِيَاءُ 'anbiyā'u plur. of نَبِيٌّ nabīyun "a prophet"; أَقْرِبَاءُ 'aqribā'u plur. of قَرِيبٌ qarībun "a relative"; أَغْنِيَاءُ 'aghniyā'u plur. of غَنِيٌّ ghanīyun "rich".

h) فُعْلَانٌ e.g. فُرْسَانٌ fursānun plur. of فَارِسٌ fārisun "a rider"; بُلْدَانٌ buldānun plur. of بَلَدٌ baladun "a district"; قُضْبَانٌ quḍbānun plur. of قَضِيبٌ qaḍībun "a rod, sceptre".

2. Nouns with four radicals (فعلل) have the following Broken Plurals:

i) فَعَالِلُ e.g. كَوَاكِبُ kawākibu plur. of كَوْكَبٌ kaukabun "a star"; تَجَارِبُ tajāribu plur. of تَجْرِبَةٌ tajribatun "an attempt". In the same way are formed the plurals of جَوْهَرٌ jauharun "a jewel"; مَكْتَبٌ maktabun "a school, office"; مَكْتَبَةٌ maktabatun "a library".

k) فَعَالِيلُ e.g.

فَنَاجِينُ fanājīnu from فِنْجَانٌ finjānun "a cup".

صَنَادِيقُ ṣanādīqu from صُنْدُوقٌ ṣundūqun "a coffer".

خَنَازِيرُ khanāzīru from خِنْزِيرٌ khinzīrun "a pig".

In the same way are formed the plurals from سُلْطَانٌ sulṭānun "a sultan"; مَكْتُوبٌ maktūbun "a letter": قِنْدِيلٌ qindīlun "a lamp"

This form is used for the plural of all words of four radicals which have a long vowel between the third and fourth radicals.

l) فَعَالِلَةٌ a rare form used specially for living beings e.g. تَلَامِذَةٌ talāmidhatun pl. of تِلْمِيذٌ tilmīdhun "a scholar"

3. The following words deserve special notice:

إِبْنٌ 'ibnun "a son" plur. بَنُونَ banūna or أَبْنَاءٌ 'abnā'un.

إِبْنَةٌ 'ibnatun or بِنْتٌ bintun "daughter, girl", plur. بَنَاتٌ banātun.

أَخٌ 'akhun "brother", plur. إِخْوَةٌ 'ikhwatun or إِخْوَانٌ 'ikhwānun.

أُخْتٌ 'ukhtun "sister", plur. أَخَوَاتٌ 'akhawātun.

Note 1. Some nouns have two or more forms of Broken Plural e.g. بَحْرٌ bahrun "sea" has بُحُورٌ buhūrun, بِحَارٌ biḥārun, أَبْحُرٌ abhurun and أَبْحَارٌ abḥārun.

Note 2. Some words have different forms of the Broken Plural with different meanings e.g. بَيْتٌ baitun means "a house" or "a verse of poetry". In the former sense the Plural is بُيُوتٌ buyūtun, in the latter أَبْيَاتٌ abyātun.

Vocabulary.

فَارِغٌ fārighun empty. نَفِيسٌ nafīsun precious.

كَرِيمٌ karīmun noble.

(Other words in the lesson.)

Exercise 9.

اَلسُّفَرَاءُ حَاضِرُونَ وَالْوُزَرَاءُ غَائِبُونَ — اَلْأَمِيرُ أَسِيرٌ —
أَصْدِقَاءُ مُخْلِصُونَ — اَلنَّاسُ أَغْنِيَاءُ — اَلْبُيُوتُ الْعَالِيَةُ كُوَيِّسَةٌ —
مَكَاتِبُ نَافِعَةٌ — اَلسَّلَاطِينُ كِبَارٌ — اَلرِّمَاحُ طَوِيلَةٌ —
بَسَاتِينُ حَسَنَةٌ — اَلْمُعَلِّمُونَ مَبْسُوطُونَ وَالتَّلَامِذَةُ مُجْتَهِدُونَ —
اَلصَّنْدُوقُ فَارِغٌ — بُلْدَانٌ غَنِيَّةٌ — اَلْبِحَارُ (اَلْبُحُورُ) اَلْكَبِيرَةُ
— اَلْأَقْرِبَاءُ هُمُ الْأَصْدِقَاءُ — اَلْجَوْهَرُ النَّفِيسُ — اَلنَّفْسُ الْكَرِيمَةُ
— اَلْبَنُونَ مُجْتَهِدُونَ وَالْبَنَاتُ مُطِيعَاتٌ

Transcription.

assufarā'u ḥāḍirūna walwuzarā'u 'ghā'ibūna. — al'amīru asīrun. — aṣdiqā'u mukhliṣūna. — annāsu aghniyā'u. — albuyūtu 'l'āliyatu kuwaiyisatun. — makātibu nāfiʿatun. — assalāṭīnu kibārun. — arrimāḥu ṭawīlatun. — basātīnu ḥasanatun. — almuʿallimūna mabsūṭūna wa'ttalāmidhatu mujtahidūna. — aṣṣundūqu fārighun. — buldānun ghanīyatun. — albiḥaru (albuḥūru) 'lkabīratu. — al'aqribā'u humu 'l'aṣdiqā'u. — aljauharu 'nnafīsu. — annafsu 'lkarīmatu. — albanūna mujtahidūna wa'lbanātu muṭīʿātun.

Exercise 10.

The cups are empty. — The pigs are animals. — The Sultan is just. — The princes and ministers are present. — The letter is long. — Long letters. — Noble souls. — The scholars are busy. — The boys are contented, they are playing. — The horsemen are tired. — Are the ambassadors present? — No, they are absent. — Are you relatives? — Yes, and we are friends. — The big coffers. — The jewels are precious. — Beautiful verses. — The brothers and sisters are present and the sons and daughters are absent.

Sixth Lesson.

(اَلدَّرْسُ اَلسَّادِسُ)

Declension.

1. There are three cases in Arabic: the Nominative (رَفْعٌ raf'), Genitive, oblique or prepositional (جَرٌّ jarr) and Accusative (نَصْبٌ naṣb).

2. These cases are expressed:

a) When the word originally has nunation — whether it be a masc. sing. or fem. sing. or broken plural — by the endings *un*, *in*, *an*, (written ـٌ ـٍ ـًا ـً).

b) When the word has originally no nunation by *u* for the nom., and *a* for the other cases.

c) When the word is defined by the article or a following word in the genitive — whether it has nunation or not originally — by *u*, *i*, *a*.

Examples.

a) Nom سَارِقٌ sāriqun "a thief". خَادِمَةٌ khādimatun "a maid-servant". أَوْلَادٌ aulādun "children".

Gen. سَارِقٍ sāriqin. خَادِمَةٍ khādimatin. أَوْلَادٍ aulādin.

Acc. سَارِقًا sāriqan. خَادِمَةً khādimatan. أَوْلَادًا aulādan.

b) Nom. مَكَّةُ makkatu "Mecca". صَنَادِيقُ ṣanādīqu "coffers".

Gen. and Acc. مَكَّةَ makkata. صَنَادِيقَ ṣanādīqa.

c) Nom. اَلسَّارِقُ assāriqu. صَاحِبُ ٱلْبَيْتِ ṣāḥibu-'lbaiti "the master of the house"

Gen. اَلسَّارِقِ assāriqi. صَاحِبِ ٱلْبَيْتِ ṣāḥibi-'lbaiti.

Acc. اَلسَّارِقَ assāriqa. صَاحِبَ ٱلْبَيْتِ ṣāḥiba-'lbaiti.

Note 1. A word without original tanwīn is called by the Arabian grammarians غَيْر مُنْصَرِف ghair munsarif i.e. not (perfectly) declined. (see Less. 41).

Note 2. Words which end in ى preceded by kasra contract ـِيٌ iyun and ـِيٍ iyin into ـٍ in: ـِيُ iyu and ـِيِ iyi into ـِ i. In the Sound plural they drop the ـِي altogether e.g. قَاضٍ qāḍin "a judge" for قَاضِيٌ qāḍiyun (nom.) or قَاضِيٍ qāḍiyin (gen.) اَلْقَاضِي alqāḍī; "the judge" for اَلْقَاضِيُ alqāḍiyu (nom.) or اَلْقَاضِيِ alqāḍiyi (gen.) Plural. nom. قَاضُونَ qāḍūna; gen. قَاضِينَ qāḍīna. Other forms are uncontracted e.g. قَاضِيًا qāḍiyan (acc.).

Note 3. The forms of the dual and plural have already been given in Lesson 3 so that the declension of the noun is now complete.

3. All prepositions govern the genitive, thus:

فِي fī "in" as فِي بُسْتَانٍ fī bustānin "in a garden"; فِي مَكَّةَ fī makkata "in Mecca".

عَلَى ʿalā "on" as عَلَى ٱلْجِبَالِ ʿalā ʾljibāli "on the mountains".

لِ li "to, for" as لِلْوَلَدِ lilwaladi "for the boy" (see Intro. § 11, 4 c).

مِنْ min "from" as مِنَ ٱلْبُيُوتِ mina ʾlbuyūti "from the houses".

4. The relation of a word and its following genitive is called إِضَافَة iḍāfa; the governing word is called مُضَاف muḍāf and the genitive مُضَاف إِلَيْهِ muḍāf ilaihi.

The word that governs a genitive is itself definite but never takes the article, thus بَيْتُ رَجُلٍ baitu rajulin means "*the* house of a man".

بَيْتُ ٱلرَّجُلِ baitu 'rrajuli means "*the* house of the man".

When the governing word is indefinite the preposition لِ must be put before the following genitive e g. بَيْتٌ لِلرَّجُلِ baitun lirrajuli "a house of the man"; or one may say بَيْتٌ مِنْ بُيُوتِ ٱلرَّجُلِ baitun min buyūti 'rrajuli (literally) "a house from the houses of the man".

Vocabulary.

أَللّٰهُ	allāhu God.	أَحْمَدُ	aḥmadu Ahmed (name of a man).
سُوقٌ	sūqun a market.	وَاسِعٌ	wāsiʿun wide, spacious.
جَارٌ	jārun a neighbour.	عُمَرُ	ʿumaru Omar (name of a man).
قَبْلَ	qabla before.	زَيْدٌ	zaidun Zaid (name of a man).
صَاحِبٌ	ṣāḥibun master, owner, friend.	مَشْهُورٌ	mashhūrun renowned.
أَلْيَوْمَ	alyauma the day = to-day.	مَجْلِسٌ	majlisun assembly, council.
ظَهْرٌ	zahrun a back.	زَوْجَةٌ	zaujatun a sponse, wife.
مِفْتَاحٌ	miftāḥun a key.	رَأْسٌ	raʾsun a head, beginning.
بَابٌ	bābun (pl. أَبْوَابٌ abwābun) a gate, door.	حِكْمَةٌ	ḥikmatun wisdom.
مَفْتُوحٌ	maftūḥun open.	مَخَافَةٌ	makhāfatun fear.
رَفِيقٌ	rafīqun a companion.		

Exercise 11.

صَاحِبُ ٱلْبَيْتِ غَائِبٌ ٱلْيَوْمَ — ٱلْفَارِسُ عَلَى ظَهْرِ ٱلْفَرَسِ — ٱلْأَمِيرُ غَائِبٌ خَادِمُ ٱلْأَمِيرِ فِي ٱلدَّارِ — مِفْتَاحُ بَابِ ٱلْبَيْتِ — أَبْوَابُ ٱلْمَدِينَةِ مَفْتُوحَةٌ — عُمَرُ صَاحِبٌ لِزَيْدٍ — بَسَاتِينُ ٱلشَّامِ مَشْهُورَةٌ — كَلْبُ ٱلْوَلَدِ حَارِسٌ — كُتُبُ ٱلتَّلَامِذَةِ نَظِيفَةٌ — نَحْنُ أَصْدِقَاءُ ٱلرَّجُلِ — قَصْرُ ٱلْأَمِيرِ فِي ٱلْمَدِينَةِ — بُيُوتُ ٱلْمَدِينَةِ عَالِيَةٌ — ٱلرِّجَالُ حَاضِرُونَ فِي ٱلْمَجْلِسِ — زَوْجَةُ ٱلْقَاضِي حَسَنَةٌ — رَأْسُ ٱلْحِكْمَةِ مَخَافَةُ ٱللّٰهِ — بَيْتٌ مِنْ بُيُوتِ ٱلْأَمِيرِ فِي ٱلسُّوقِ — أَنْتُمْ حَاضِرُونَ فِي بُسْتَانِ ٱلْجَارِ — ٱلْجَارُ قَبْلَ ٱلدَّارِ ٱلرَّفِيقُ قَبْلَ ٱلطَّرِيقِ —

Transcription.

ṣāḥibu 'lbaiti ghā'ibuni 'lyauma. — alfārisu 'alā ẓahri 'lfarasi. — al'amīru ghā'ibun khādimu 'l'amīri fī'ddāri. — miftāḥu bābi'lbaiti. — abwābu 'lmadīnati maftūḥatun. — 'umaru ṣāḥibun lizaidin. — basātīnu 'shshāmi mashhūratun. — kalbu 'lwaladi ḥārisun. — kutubu 'ttalāmidhati naẓīfatun. — naḥnu aṣdiqā'u 'rrajuli. — qaṣru 'l'amīri fi'lmadīnati. — buyūtu 'lmadīnati 'āliyatun. — arrijālu ḥāḍirūna fī'lmajlisi. — zaujatu 'lqāḍī ḥasanatun. — ra'su 'lḥikmati makhāfatu 'llāhi. — baitun min buyūti 'l'amīri fī'ssūqi. — antum ḥāḍirūna fī bustāni 'ljāri. — aljrāu qabla 'ddāri 'rrafīqu qabla 'ṭṭarīqi.

Exercise 12.

Is the master of the servant in the house? — No, he is in the garden of the neighbour. — You are the friends of the man. — The merchant is present in the market of the city. — The door of the house is open. — The man's dogs (dogs of the man) are watchful. — The king's ministers are present in the council. — Is the physician present? — The physician is absent and the wife of the physician is present to-day. — Ahmed is a friend of the judge. — The gardens of the city are spacious. — The relatives of the physician are rich.

Seventh Lesson.

(اَلدَّرْسُ ٱلسَّابِعُ)

The Genitive (continued).

1. The Dual and Sound plural masc. lose their final ن with its vowel when they are followed by a genitive; thus the ending ـَانِ āni becomes ـَا ā, ـَيْنِ aini becomes ـَيْ ai, ـَتَانِ atāni becomes ـَتَا atā, ـَتَيْنِ ataini becomes ـَتَيْ atai, ـُونَ ūna becomes ـُو ū, ـِينَ īna becomes ـِي ī, e g.

بَيْتَا ٱلرَّجُلِ	baitā 'rrajuli the two houses of the man.
بَابَا بَيْتَيِ ٱلرَّجُلِ	bābā baitayi 'rrajuli the two doors of the two houses of the man.
إِبْنَتَا ٱلْوَزِيرِ	ibnatā 'lwazīri the two daughters of the minister.
بَيْتُ ٱبْنَتَيِ ٱلْوَزِيرِ	baitu 'bnatayi 'lwazīri the house of the two daughters of the minister.
مُعَلِّمُو ٱلْوَلَدِ	muʿallimū 'lwaladi the teachers of the boy.
كُتُبُ مُعَلِّمِي ٱلْوَلَدِ	kutubu muʿallimī 'lwaladi the books of the teachers of the boy.

2. The words أَبٌ abun "father", أَخٌ akhun "brother", حَمٌ ḥamun "father-in-law", ذُو dhu "master,

possessor" (only used with a genitive), فَمٌ famun "mouth" take the following forms before a genitive:

Nom.	أَبُو	abū	Acc.	أَبَا	abā	Gen. أَبِي	abī
"	أَخُو	akhū	"	أَخَا	akhā	" أَخِي	akhī
"	حَمُو	ḥamū	"	حَمَا	ḥamā	" حَمِي	ḥamī
"	ذُو	dhū	"	ذَا	dhā	" ذِي	dhī
"	فُو	fū	"	فَا	fā	" فِي	fī.

Thus:

أَبُو مُحَمَّدٍ abū muḥammadin Mohammed's father.

ضَرَبْتُ أَبَا زَيْدٍ darabtu abā zaidin I struck Zaid's father.

وَجْهُ ذِي حُسْنٍ wajhu dhī husnin the face of the beautiful man (literally "of the possessor of beauty").

3. A word cannot be separated from a genitive belonging to it, therefore if it is qualified by an adjective, the adjective must be put after the gemtive (and have the article), e.g.

بَيْتُ ٱلْوَزِيرِ ٱلْوَاسِعُ baitu 'lwazīri 'lwāsi'u "the spacious house of the Vezir".

An alternative form would be:

ٱلْبَيْتُ ٱلْوَاسِعُ لِلْوَزِيرِ. albaitu 'lwāsi'u lilwazīri.

4. If the genitive refers to two nouns, it must follow the first while the second takes the suffix of the personal pronoun (see Lesson 8) e.g.

بَيْتُ ٱلْوَزِيرِ وَبُسْتَانُهُ baitu 'lwazīri wabustānuhu "the Vezir's house and garden".

يَدَا ٱلْبِنْتِ وَرِجْلَاهَا yadā 'lbinti warijlāhā "the girl's hands (dual) and feet (dual)".

5. The genitive is often used partitively and to denote material e.g. قِطْعَةُ لَحْمٍ qiṭʿatu laḥmin "a piece of flesh"; فِنْجَانُ قَهْوَةٍ finjānu qahwatin "a cup of coffee"; كُرْسِيُّ خَشَبٍ kursīyu khashabin "a seat of wood".

6. The genitive often occurs after an adjective to define or limit its application, e.g. قَلِيلُ ٱلْعَقْلِ qalīlu 'lʿaqli "little of understanding" (i.e. as regards understanding) i.e. "stupid"; كَثِيرُ ٱلْمَالِ kathīru 'lmāli "abundant of wealth" i.e, "rich"; حَسَنُ ٱلْوَجْهِ ḥasanu 'lwajhi "beautiful of face".

Note. This genitive is improper and stands in place of a defining accusative, hence the rule in Lesson 6, 4 does not apply to the word before it, which can take the article when it is definite e.g.

إِبْنَةُ ٱلْوَزِيرِ ٱلْحَسَنَةُ ٱلْوَجْهِ حَاضِرَةٌ 'ibnatu 'lwazīri 'lḥasanatu 'lwajhi ḥāḍiratun "the beautiful daughter (lit. "the daughter the beautiful of face") of the Vezir is present".

7. Some nouns are used in Arabic with a following genitive denoting a quality, where in English an adjective is used. These nouns are such as صَاحِبٌ ṣāḥibun, plur. أَصْحَابٌ aṣḥābun "master, possessor"; ذُو dhū, dual, ذَوَا dhawā (with omission of the final ن before the genitive), plur. ذَوُو dhawū and the feminine sing. ذَاتُ dhātu, dual ذَاتَا dhātā, plur. ذَوَاتُ dhawātu "possessor"; أَبُو abū "father"; أُمُّ ummu "mother"; إِبْنُ ibnu "son", e.g.

صَاحِبُ عِلْمٍ ṣāḥibu ʿilmin "master of learning i.e. learned".

ذَاتُ حُسْنٍ dhātu ḥusnin "possessor of beauty i.e. beautiful (fem.)".

أَبُو لِسَانَيْنِ abū lisānaini "father of two tongues i.e. dissembling".

إِبْنُ خَمْسِينَ سَنَةً ibnu khamsīna sanatan "son of 50 years i.e. 50 years old".

Vocabulary.

أَبُو بَكْرٍ abū bakrin Abu Bekr, (name of a man).

قَبِيلَةٌ qabīlatun a tribe.

بَنُو أَسَدٍ banū asadin (sons of a lion), name of an Arabian tribe.

جَمَالٌ jəmālun beauty.

بُخْلٌ bukhlun miserliness.

ظِلٌّ ẓillun shadow.

زُهْدٌ zuhdun abstinence.

لُقْمَةٌ luqmatun a bit (of bread, meat &c.).

خُبْزٌ khubzun bread.

حَدِيدٌ ḥadīdun iron.

شَيْخٌ shaikhun an old man, head of a tribe, Sheikh.

مَعْرِفَةٌ maʿrifatun knowledge.

كِذْبٌ kidhbun a lie.

حُجْرَةٌ ḥujratun a room.

مَطْبَخٌ maṭbakhun a kitchen.

نِسَاءٌ nisā'un women.

تَاجِرٌ tājirun a merchant.

Exercise 13.

مُعَلِّمُوا ٱلْوَلَدِ أَصْحَابُ عِلْمٍ — ٱلرَّجُلُ ٱلْقَبِيحُ هُوَ أَبُو لِسَانَيْنِ — إِبْنُ أَبِي بَكْرٍ كَثِيرُ ٱلْمَالِ — إِبْنَتَا ٱلْوَزِيرِ حَسَنَتَا ٱلْوَجْهِ — بَابُ ٱلْبَيْتِ ٱلْوَاسِعِ مَفْتُوحٌ — هَلْ هُوَ ذُو عِلْمٍ — لَا هُوَ قَلِيلُ ٱلْعَقْلِ — كُتُبُ ذَوِي عِلْمٍ نَافِعَةٌ — قَبِيلَةُ بَنِي أَسَدٍ هِيَ قَبِيلَةٌ مِنَ ٱلْعَرَبِ — زَوْجَةُ ٱلْحَكِيمِ هِيَ ذَاتُ حُسْنٍ وَجَمَالٍ

— هَلِ ٱلْأَمِيرُ كَرِيمُ ٱلنَّفْسِ — لَا هُوَ كَثِيرُ ٱلْبُخْلِ — أَلشَّجَرَةُ
ذَاتُ ظِلٍّ — زُهْدُ أَبِي بَكْرٍ مَشْهُورٌ — عَيْنَا ٱبْنَةِ ٱلْقَاضِي
لَامِعَتَانِ — قِطْعَةُ لَحْمٍ كَبِيرَةٌ — لُقْمَةُ خُبْزٍ صَغِيرَةٌ — فِنْجَانُ
ٱلْقَهْوَةِ حَاضِرٌ — كُرْسِيُّ حَدِيدٍ فِي ٱلْبُسْتَانِ — شَيْخُ ٱلْقَبِيلَةِ
ٱلْكَثِيرُ ٱلْمَالِ صَالِحٌ —

Transcription.

muʿallimū ʾlwaladi aṣḥābu ʿilmin. — arrajulu ʾlqabīḥu huwa abū lisānaini. — ibnu abī bakrin kathīru ʾlmāli. — ibnatā ʾlwazīri ḥasanatā ʾlwajhi. — bābu ʾlbaiti ʾlwāsiʿu maftūḥun. — hal huwa dhū ʿilmin? Lā, huwa qalīlu ʾlʿaqli. — kutubu dhawī ʿilmin nāfiʿatun. — qabīlatu banī asadin hiya qabīlatun mina ʾlʿarabi. — zaujatu ʾlḥakīmi hiya dhātu ḥusnin wa jamālin. — hali ʾlʾamīru karīmu ʾnnafsi. — lā huwa kathīru ʾlbukhli. — ashshajaratu dhātu ẓillin. — zuhdu abī bakrin mashhūrun. — ʿainā ʾbnati ʾlqāḍī lāmiʿatāni. — qiṭʿatu lahmin kabīratun. — luqmatu khubzin ṣaghīratun. — finjānu ʾlqahwati ḥāḍirun. — kursīyu ḥadīdin fī ʾlbustāni. — shaikhu ʾlqabīlati ʾlkathīru ʾlmāli ṣāliḥun.

Exercise 14.

The boys are stupid. — The stupid boys are present. — The physicians (Broken plur. f) are learned. — The girls (Less. 5, 3) are beautiful. — The men present are learned and the women present are beautiful. — The tailor is bad, he is a liar (father of lying). — Abu Bekr's servant is present and the two maid-servants of Abu Bekr's brother are absent. — The cups are in the room. — No, they are (فِي) in the kitchen. — One of the sons (a son of the sons) of the sheikh is 50 years old. — Is the merchant rich? — Yes, he is rich and miserly (much of miserliness). — The learned are the friends of kings (Plur. b).

Eighth Lesson.

(اَلدَّرْسُ ٱلثَّامِنُ)

Pronominal Suffixes.

1. The Personal Pronouns (ضَمِيرٌ ḍamīr) exist in two forms: a) Independent i.e. standing alone (ضَمِيرٌ مُنْفَصِلٌ ḍamīr munfaṣil) or b) attached as Suffixes to nouns, verbs or prepositions (ضَمِيرٌ مُتَّصِلٌ ḍamīr muttaṣil). The Independent forms have already been given in Less. 3, 6).

2. The forms used when attached to words are:

	Sing.	Dual	Plur.
3rd Masc.	هُ hu	هُمَا humā	هُمْ hum.
3rd Fem.	هَا hā		هُنَّ hunna.
2nd Masc.	كَ ka	كُمَا kumā	كُمْ kum.
2nd Fem.	كِ ki		كُنَّ kunna.
1st Masc. and Fem.	ـِي ī		نَا nā.
(with a verb نِي nī).			

3. These Suffixes attached to a noun correspond to our Possessive Pronoun e.g. كِتَابُهُ kitābuhu "his book": attached to a verb or preposition they answer to our Personal Pronoun in the objective case e.g. ضَرَبَهُ ḍarabahu "he struck him"; مِنْهُ minhu "from him".

Note 1. Nouns to which these suffixes are attached employ the forms which they have before a genitive i.e. they drop the nunation and in the dual and plur. the ن; while the words أَبٌ أَخٌ حَمٌ have the forms given in Lesson 7 (except that with the 1st pers. pron. sing. they become أَبِي abī, أَخِي akhī, حَمِي ḥamī).

Note 2. The suffixes ه hu, هُمَا humā and هُمْ hum are changed to ه hi, هِمَا himā and هِمْ him when attached to a word ending in ــِ i, ــِي ī or ــَيْ ai e.g. كِتَابِهِ kitābihi "of his book", كِتَابَيْهِم kitābaihim "of their two books".

Note 3. The suffixes كُمْ kum and هُمْ hum become كُمُ kumu and هُمُ humu when they are followed by a word beginning with hamzat alwaṣl.

Note 4. The pronominal suffix of the 1st person sing. is always ي ya after a vowelless ا و ي.

4. The prepositions عِنْدَ ʿinda "with, in, in the possession of", مِنْ min "from" عَلَى ʿalā "on", إِلَى ilā "to, unto" are attached to the pronominal suffixes without change (e.g. عِنْدَهُ ʿindahu "in his possession", عَلَيْهِ ʿalaihi "on him") except in the case of the 1st person which is as follows: عِنْدِي ʿindī "with me", مِنِّي minnī "from me", عَلَيَّ ʿalaiya "upon me", إِلَيَّ ilaiya "unto me". لِ li "to, for" assumes the form لَ la before the suffixes except with the 1st person which is لِي lī "to me".

5. The English verb "to have" is usually expressed in Arabic not by a verb but by the prepositions لِ, عِنْدَ or مَعَ maʿ "with"; thus "Zaid has a book" may be expressed by لِزَيْدٍ كِتَابٌ or عِنْدَ زَيْدٍ كِتَابٌ or مَعَ زَيْدٍ كِتَابٌ.

6. The particle O! or Oh! in forms of address may be expressed in Arabic by يَا yā with the following

word in the nominative without nunation e.g. يَا زَيْدُ yā zaidu "oh Zaid", but with the following word in the accusative if that is followed by a genitive e.g. يَا سَيِّدَ ٱلنَّاسِ yā saiyida 'nnāsi "oh Lord of (the) men".

For further details see Lesson 16.

Vocabulary.

بَيْنَ	baina between, among.	عَائِشَةُ	'āishatu Ayesha, (name of woman).
وَرَقٌ	waraqun paper (collective).	خَيْطٌ	khaiṭun thread.
قَلَمٌ	qalamun a reed, pen.	إِسْمٌ	ismun name.
حِبْرٌ	ḥibrun ink.	سَاعَةٌ	sā'atun hour, watch.
زَيْنَبُ	zainabu Zainab (name of woman).	ذَهَبٌ	dhahabun gold.
سَيِّدٌ	saiyidun master, lord.	عَبْدُ ٱلرَّحْمٰنِ	'abdu 'rraḥmāni Abdurrahman, (name of man, literally "the servant of the Merciful").
سَيِّدَةٌ	saiyidatun mistress, lady.		
مَحْمُودٌ	maḥmūdun Mahmud, (name of man).	حِمَارٌ (pl. حَمِيرٌ)	ḥimārun an ass.
حَسَنٌ	ḥasanun Hasan, (name of man).	عَبْدٌ	'abdun a slave, servant.
فِضَّةٌ	fiḍḍatun silver.	أَوْ	au or.
فَاطِمَةٌ	fāṭimatun Fatima, (name of woman).	هِنْدُ	hindun Hind, (name of woman).

Exercise 15.

يَدِي نَظِيفَةٌ — يَدَاكُمْ نَظِيفَتَانِ — نَحْنُ بَيْنَ يَدَيْهِ —

يَا تِلْمِيذُ هَلْ عِنْدَكَ كِتَابُكَ — نَعَمْ يَا مُعَلِّمِي عِنْدِي كِتَابِي —

يَا تَلَامِذَةُ هَلْ لَكُمْ وَرَقٌ — نَعَمْ يَا مُعَلِّمُ لَنَا وَرَقٌ وَقَلَمٌ وَحِبْرٌ —
لِأَبِي بَكْرٍ ٱبْنَتَانِ ٱسْمُ كَبِيرَتِهِمَا هِنْدٌ وَٱسْمُ صَغِيرَتِهِمَا زَيْنَبُ —
يَا سَيِّدَتِي هَلِ ٱسْمُكِ فَاطِمَةُ — لَا يَا سَيِّدِي ٱسْمِي عَائِشَةُ — عِنْدَ
ٱلْخَيَّاطِينَ خَيْطٌ وَعِنْدَ ٱلنَّجَّارِينَ خَشَبٌ — بَيْتُنَا كَبِيرٌ وَوَاسِعٌ —
بُسْتَانُكُمْ صَغِيرٌ — أَبُوكُمْ وَأَخُونَا فِي ٱلسُّوقِ — يَا خَادِمَةُ هَلْ
صَاحِبُكِ حَاضِرٌ فِي ٱلْبَيْتِ — لَا هُوَ فِي بُسْتَانِهِ — ٱلسَّيِّدَةُ
حَسَنَةٌ يَدَاهَا وَرِجْلَاهَا صَغِيرَتَانِ — هَلْ مَعَكَ سَاعَةٌ — نَعَمْ
مَعِي سَاعَةُ ذَهَبٍ — هَلْ أَخُوهَا أَوْ أُخْتُهَا فِي ٱلْبَيْتِ —
أُخْتُهَا حَاضِرَةٌ وَأَخُوهَا فِي ٱلسُّوقِ

Exercise 16.

Abdurrahman has two sons, the name of the older (great) is Mahmud, the (name) of the younger (small) is Hasan. — O servant, is the physician present? — No, (O) my master, the physician is absent; the wife and son of the physician (Less. 7, 4) are present. — Hast thou a gold watch (watch of gold) or a silver one (watch of silver)? — I have a silver watch, (O) my master! — Have you horses (plur. a)? — Yes, we have horses and asses. — Are my servants in the market? — No, your servants are in the garden. — My brother's wife is beautiful (beautiful of face). — O my mistress, art thou content with (مِنْ) thy slave? — Yes, I am content. — He is content with his servant.

Ninth Lesson.

(اَلدَّرْسُ ٱلتَّاسِع)

Demonstrative Pronouns.

1. The Demonstrative Pronoun (إِسْمُ ٱلْإِشَارَة ism al-'ishāra) in its simplest form is: Masculine Sing. ذَا dhā for all cases; Dual nom. ذَانِ dhāni, gen. and acc. ذَيْنِ dhaini; Feminine, Sing. ذِى dhī, ذِهِ dhihi, تِى tī, تِهِ tihi, تَا tā for all cases; Dual nom. تَانِ tāni, gen. and acc. تَيْنِ taini.

Plural for both genders and all cases أُولَى ūlā or أُولَاءِ ūlā'i.

These forms are however rarely used.

2. The words for "this, these" are formed by prefixing هَا (written هٰ see Intro. § 6, note 1), to some of the simple forms above. They are:

Sing. masc. هٰذَا hādhā for all cases. Fem. هٰذِهِ hādhihi (rarely هٰذِى) for all cases.

Dual masc. nom. هٰذَانِ hādhāni. Fem. هٰتَانِ hātāni.

Gen. and acc. هٰذَيْنِ hādhaini. Fem. هٰتَيْنِ hātaini.

Plural هٰؤُلَاءِ hā'ulā'i for both genders and all cases.

3. The words for "that, those" are formed by adding كَ ka (in some cases with interpolated لِ) to the simple forms. They are:

Sing. masc. ذَاكَ dhāka or ذٰلِكَ dhālika; fem. تَاكَ tāka or تِيكَ tīka or usually تِلْكَ tilka for all cases.

Dual masc. nom. ذَانِكَ dhānika or ذَانِّكَ dhānnika; gen. and acc. ذَيْنِكَ dhainika or ذَيْنِّكَ dhainnika.

Fem. nom. تَانِكَ tānika or تَانِّكَ tānnika; gen. and acc. تَيْنِكَ tainika or تَيْنِّكَ tainnika.

Plural أُولَائِكَ ūlā'ika (more rarely أُولَاكَ ūlāka or أُولَالِكَ ūlālika) for both genders and all cases.

4. If the demonstrative qualifies a simple noun, it precedes it and the noun takes the article e.g. هٰذَا ٱلْكِتَابُ hādhā 'lkitābu "this book".

But if the noun is defined by a following genitive or a pronominal suffix the demonstrative is placed after these e.g. إِبْنُ ٱلْمَلِكِ هٰذَا ibnu 'lmaliki hādhā "this son of the king" كِتَابُكُمْ هٰذَا kitābukum hādhā "this book of yours".

5. If the demonstrative is used pronominally and as subject of a nominal sentence, then:

a) If the predicate is an indefinite noun, no copula is necessary e.g. هٰذَا كِتَابٌ hādhā kitābun "this is a book".

b) If the predicate is defined by the article the 3rd pers. pron. is used as a copula to prevent the demonstrative from being taken adjectivally (as in 4) e.g. هٰذَا هُوَ ٱلْوَلَدُ hādhā huwa 'lwaladu "this is the boy"

c) If the predicate is defined by a following genitive or a pronominal suffix, the demonstrative is put first and no copula is needed e.g. هٰذَا كِتَابُكُمْ "this is your book"

6. The Interrogative pronouns (إِسْمُ ٱلِاسْتِفْهَامِ ism alistifhām) are مَنْ man "who", مَا mā "what" (sometimes

مَاذَا mādhā), أَىٌّ aiyun fem. أَيَّةٌ aiyatun "which", كَمْ kam "how much? how many?"

مَنْ is indeclinable (مَبْنِىٌّ mabnī). The genitive relation is expressed by placing it after a noun e.g. كِتَابُ مَنْ kitābu man "whose book?"

مَا is also indeclinable. After some prepositions it is written مَ as لِمَ lima "for what? why?"

أَىٌّ, fem. أَيَّةٌ is declinable and is treated as a noun, so takes a following noun in the genitive e.g. أَىُّ رَجُلٍ aiyu rajulin "which man?" أَيَّةُ بِنْتٍ aiyatu bintin "which girl?"

كَمْ takes the following noun in the accusative e.g. كَمْ وَلَدًا kam waladan "how many boys?"

Note. The interrogative particles (أَ, هَلْ) are not used before the interrogative pronouns.

Vocabulary.

قَاتِلٌ qātilun killing.	أَنِيسٌ anīsun amiable.
لَحْظٌ laḥẓun glance.	شَخْصٌ shakhṣun person.
قَامُوسٌ qamūsun dictionary.	سَبَبٌ sababun cause.
مَنْظَرٌ manẓarun look.	مُصِيبَةٌ muṣībatun misfortune.
غَفْلَةٌ ghaflatun carelessness.	مَطْلُوبٌ maṭlūbun desire.
امْرَأَةٌ imra'atun woman, (in distinction from man).	سَنَةٌ sanatun year.
	عُمْرٌ 'umrun life.

Exercise 17.

هٰذَا ٱلْكِتَابُ نَافِعٌ — هٰذَا كِتَابٌ صَعْبٌ — كِتَابُ ٱلتِّلْمِيذِ
هٰذَا وَسِخٌ — يَا تَلَامِذَتِي كُتُبُكُمْ هٰذِهِ وَسِخَةٌ — هَاتَانِ
ٱلْعَيْنَانِ قَاتِلَتَانِ — لَحْظُ عَيْنَيْكَ هَاتَيْنِ قَاتِلٌ — هٰذَا هُوَ
ٱلْقَامُوسُ — هٰذِهِ هِيَ ٱلْخَادِمَةُ — ذٰلِكَ ٱلْمَنْظَرُ حَسَنٌ — هٰؤُلَاءِ
ٱلْأَشْخَاصُ مِنَ ٱلْكِبَارِ — تِلْكَ ٱلشَّجَرَةُ ذَاتُ ظِلٍّ — أُولَائِكَ
ٱلرِّجَالُ ذَوُو عِلْمٍ — هٰذَا بَيْتٌ وَاسِعٌ — هٰذِهِ خَادِمَةُ هٰؤُلَاءِ
ٱلْأَشْخَاصِ — خَادِمَةُ أُولَائِكَ ٱلْأَشْخَاصِ هٰذِهِ وَسِخَةٌ — بُسْتَانِي
هٰذَا مَشْهُورٌ فِي مَدِينَتِنَا — مَنْ حَاضِرٌ عِنْدَكُمْ — عِنْدَنَا حَاضِرٌ
خَادِمُنَا — مَا سَبَبُ هٰذِهِ ٱلْمُصِيبَةِ — سَبَبُ مُصِيبَتِنَا هٰذِهِ
غَفْلَتُنَا — لِمَ أَنْتُمْ حَاضِرُونَ وَهُمْ غَائِبُونَ — كَمْ شَخْصًا حَاضِرٌ
ٱلْيَوْمَ — هٰذِهِ ٱمْرَأَةٌ حَسَنَةٌ —

Exercise 18.

This is a good man and that (fem.) is a bad woman. — This is the judge. — This judge is upright and that physician is learned. — These friends of thine are rich. — This son of the sheikh is amiable and that daughter of his is beautiful (of face). — O my master, what is thy desire? — What I want (my desire) is paper (and) pen and ink. — Who is the minister's son, this or that? — This is the minister's son. — Whose son is Hasan? — Hasan is the son of Abdurrahman. — How many sons has Abdurrahman? — He has five. — Hast thou this book? — No, I have that. — This dictionary is useful. — What is thy name? — My name is Hasan. — How old art thou (how many years is thy life)? — I am 50 years old (my life is 50 years, or I am a son of 50 years). — These two men are friends.

Tenth Lesson.

(اَلدَّرْسُ ٱلْعَاشِرُ)

Adjectives.

1. Some of the commonest forms of adjectives (إِسْمُ صِفَةٍ ism ṣifa) are:

a) فَاعِلٌ fā'ilun (properly the present participle) e.g. صَادِقٌ ṣādiqun "upright", عَادِلٌ 'ādilun "just", جَاهِلٌ jāhilun "ignorant".

b) فَعِيلٌ fa'īlun e.g. سَعِيدٌ sa'īdun "happy", كَبِيرٌ kabīrun "great", كَثِيرٌ kathīrun "much, many".

c) فَعُولٌ fa'ūlun denoting intensity e.g. جَهُولٌ jahūlun "very ignorant", كَسُولٌ kasūlun "very lazy".

d) فَعْلَانُ fa'lānu (without nunation) e.g. تَعْبَانُ ta'bānu "tired", غَضْبَانُ ghaḍbānu "angry".

2. Adjectives denoting colours or bodily defects have the following form:

Masc. sing. أَفْعَلُ af'alu. Fem. sing. فَعْلَاءُ fa'lā'u. Plural for both genders فُعْلٌ fu'lun.

E.g.

Sing. Masc.		Fem.		Plural.	
أَسْوَدُ	aswadu, black	سَوْدَاءُ	saudā'u	سُودٌ	sūdun
أَبْيَضُ	abyaḍu, white	بَيْضَاءُ	baiḍā'u	بِيضٌ	bīḍun
أَحْمَرُ	aḥmaru, red	حَمْرَاءُ	ḥamrā'u	حُمْرٌ	ḥumrun
أَزْرَقُ	azraqu, blue	زَرْقَاءُ	zarqā'u	زُرْقٌ	zurqun
أَخْضَرُ	akhḍaru, green	خَضْرَاءُ	khaḍrā'u	خُضْرٌ	khuḍrun
أَصْفَرُ	aṣfaru, yellow	صَفْرَاءُ	ṣafrā'u	صُفْرٌ	ṣufrun
أَطْرَشُ	aṭrashu, deaf	طَرْشَاءُ	ṭarshā'u	طُرْشٌ	ṭurshun
أَخْرَسُ	akhrasu, dumb	خَرْسَاءُ	kharsā'u	خُرْسٌ	khursun
أَعْمَى	aʿmā, blind	عَمْيَاءُ	ʿamyā'u	عُمْيٌ	ʿumyun
أَعْرَجُ	aʿraju, lame	عَرْجَاءُ	ʿarjā'u	عُرْجٌ	ʿurjun
أَحْدَبُ	aḥdabu, humpbacked.	حَدْبَاءُ	ḥadbā'u	حُدْبٌ	ḥudbun.

Notice the absence of nunation in the Sing. (cf. Lesson 6, 3).

Note. The fem. of the dual changes hamza into و e.g. سَوْدَاوَانِ saudāwāni.

3. For the comparative and superlative of adjectives the so-called Elative is used (the إِسْمُ ٱلتَّفْضِيلِ ism attafḍīl). It is always of the form أَفْعَلُ afʿalu, e.g. صَعْبٌ ṣaʿbun "hard" Elative أَصْعَبُ aṣʿabu "harder". كَبِيرٌ kabīrun "great" Elative أَكْبَرُ akbaru "greater".

4. If the second and third radicals of an adjective are the same, they are written as one with the tashdīd in this form (cf. Less. 23); e.g. شَدِيدٌ shadīdun "violent"

(radicals شدد) makes its Elative أَشَدُّ ashaddu; (for أَشْدَدُ); قَلِيلٌ qalīlun "few", Elative أَقَلُّ aqallu.

5. The Elative as comparative is the same for all genders and numbers. It is followed by مِنْ to express the English "than", e.g.

زَيْدٌ أَكْبَرُ مِنْ عُمَرَ zaidun akbaru min ʿumara "Zaid is older than Omar".

هِنْدٌ أَكْبَرُ مِنْ زَيْنَبَ hindun akbaru min zainaba "Hind is older than Zainab".

اَلْبَنُونَ أَكْبَرُ مِنَ ٱلْبَنَاتِ albanūna akbaru mina 'lbanāti "the sons are older than the daughters".

6. The Elative as superlative is always defined by the article or a following genitive or a pronominal suffix. Its feminine is فُعْلَى fuʿlā (see Less. 38, 5. c.), e.g. اَلأَكْبَرُ al'akbaru "the greatest" (masc.) اَلْكُبْرَى alkubrā "the greatest" (fem.).

7. The substantives خَيْرٌ khairun "good" and شَرٌّ sharrun "evil" are used as Elatives with the meanings "better" and "worse", e.g.

هُوَ خَيْرٌ مِنْكَ huwa khairun minka "he is better than thou".

Vocabulary.

لَطِيفٌ laṭīfun pleasant.	لَوْنٌ launun colour.
وَجْنَةٌ wajnatun cheek.	صَيْفٌ ṣaifun summer.
بَحْرٌ bahrun sea (used also for the Nile).	شَعْرٌ shaʿrun hair.
نِسَاءٌ nisāʾun women (used as plur. of إِمْرَأَةٌ).	ثَقِيلٌ thaqīlun heavy
	مَدْرَسَةٌ madrasatun school.

جَامِعٌ	jāmiʿun mosque.	أَصْلٌ	aṣlun origin.
اَلْجَامِعُ ٱلْأَزْهَرُ	aljāmiʿu ʾl'azharu the mosque el-Azhar (in Cairo).	حَدٌّ	ḥaddun boundary, limit.
		جَزِيرَةٌ	jazīratun island.
شَرِيفٌ	sharīfun noble.	سَائِلٌ	sāʾilun beggar.
اَلْبَارِحَ	albāriḥa yesterday (used in acc. as adverb.).	شَوْقٌ	shauqun yearning.
		غَرْبٌ	gharbun West.

Exercise 19.

صَاحِبُكُمْ رَجُلٌ لَطِيفٌ — اَلْعَبْدُ ٱلْأَسْوَدُ فِي ٱلْحُجْرَةِ ٱلْحَمْرَاءِ — اَلْوَرَقُ أَبْيَضُ — اَلْوَرَقُ ٱلْأَبْيَضُ وَٱلْحِبْرُ ٱلْأَسْوَدُ عِنْدَ ٱلتَّلَامِذَةِ — وَجْنَتَا ٱلْبِنْتِ ٱلْحَمْرَاوَانِ لَطِيفَتَا ٱلْمَنْظَرِ (Less. 7, 6) — اَلْبَحْرُ ٱلْأَزْرَقُ وَٱلْبَحْرُ ٱلْأَبْيَضُ أَصْلُ بَحْرِ ٱلنِّيلِ — اَلنِّسَاءُ طُرْشٌ وَٱلرِّجَالُ خُرْسٌ — هُوَ أَصْفَرُ ٱللَّوْنِ (Less. 7, 6) فِي وَجْهِهِ — هٰذِهِ ٱلشَّجَرَةُ خَضْرَاءُ فِي ٱلصَّيْفِ — عَيْنَاهَا زَرْقَاوَانِ وَشَعْرُهَا أَسْوَدُ — اَلرَّجُلُ ٱلْجَهُولُ وَٱلْكَسُولُ قَبِيحٌ — هٰذَا ٱلطَّرِيقُ أَصْعَبُ مِنْ ذٰلِكَ ٱلطَّرِيقِ هُوَ أَصْعَبُ طُرُقِ ٱلشَّامِ — اَلذَّهَبُ أَثْقَلُ مِنَ ٱلْفِضَّةِ — اَلْمَدْرَسَةُ ٱلْكُبْرَى عِنْدَ ٱلْمُسْلِمِينَ فِي ٱلْجَامِعِ ٱلْأَزْهَرِ — زَيْدٌ قَلِيلُ ٱلْعَقْلِ وَعَمْرٌو أَقَلُّ ٱلْعَقْلِ مِنْهُ — مُحَمَّدٌ صَدِيقٌ حَسَنٌ وَحَسَنٌ صَدِيقٌ أَحْسَنُ مِنْهُ هُوَ أَحْسَنُ أَصْدِقَائِي — اَلرِّيحُ ٱلْيَوْمَ أَشَدُّ مِنْهَا ٱلْبَارِحَ (Less. 36, 7)

Exercise 20.

The lame girl is in the yellow room. — The girl's eyes are blue. — The black eyes of the girl are killing. — The slave is black. — The Red Sea is the boundary of the peninsula (island) of Arabia in the West. — The beggar is deaf and dumb. — My house is more spacious than thine (thy house), it is the most spacious of the houses of the city. — The Nile is wider than the Euphrates. — This book is better (أَحْسَنُ) than that (book), it is the best of the books. — Most men (أَكْثَرُ ٱلنَّاسِ literally "the most of the men") are idle. — My yearning for (إِلَى cf. Less. 8, 4) thee is more violent than for thy brother.

Eleventh Lesson.

(أَلدَّرْسُ ٱلْحَادِى عَشَرَ)

The Verb.

1. The Verb (فِعْلٌ fi'l) has usually three radical letters as كَتَبَ kataba to write, but may have four or more as تَرْجَمَ tarjama to translate, (see Less. 30).

Note. In dictionaries the Arabic verb is found in the form of the 3rd sing. masc. perf. active, while the infin. is given as the translation of it. Thus we say kataba "to write" although it really means "he wrote".

2. The 3rd sg. masc. perf. is of the forms فَعَلَ, فَعِلَ or فَعُلَ i.e. the first and third radicals always have a, while the second may have any one of the three a, i, u, verbs having i or u are generally intransitive and denote a state or quality, those with i denoting a temporary state as حَزِنَ ḥazina, to be sad; while those with u denote a lasting or permanent state as حَسُنَ ḥasuna, to be beautiful.

3. The verb has two main tenses: the Perfect (اَلْمَاضِي al-māḍī) denoting a finished action, and the Imperfect (اَلْمُضَارِعُ al-muḍāriʿ) denoting unfinished action. To these the Arabs add as a third the Imperative (اَلْأَمْرُ al-'amr).

4. The Perfect Stem is obtained by cutting off the last vowel of the 3rd sing. masc. perf., and the perfect is declined by adding to this stem the following endings:

Sing.			Dual			Plur.		
3. masc.	ـَ	a	3. masc.	ـَا	ā	3. masc.	ـُوا	ū
3. fem.	ـَتْ	at	3. fem.	ـَتَا	atā	3. fem.	ـْنَ	na
2. masc.	ـْتَ	ta	1. m. a. f.	ـْتُمَا	tumā	2. masc.	ـْتُمْ	tum
2. fem.	ـْتِ	ti				2. fem.	ـْتُنَّ	tunna
1. m. a. f.	ـْتُ	tu				1. m. a. f.	ـْنَا	nā

E.g.

Sing.	3. masc.	كَتَبَ	kataba he has written, (or he wrote).
„	3. fem.	كَتَبَتْ	katabat she has written.
„	2. masc.	كَتَبْتَ	katabta thou (man) hast written.
„	2. fem.	كَتَبْتِ	katabti thou (woman) hast written
„	1. masc. a. fem.	كَتَبْتُ	katabtu I have written.
Dual	3. masc.	كَتَبَا	katabā they two (men) have written.
„	3. fem.	كَتَبَتَا	katabatā they two (women) have written.
„	2. masc. a. fem.	كَتَبْتُمَا	katabtumā you two have written.

Plural 3. masc.	كَتَبُوا	katabū they (men) have written.
„ 3. fem.	كَتَبْنَ	katabna they (women) have written.
„ 2. masc.	كَتَبْتُمْ	katabtum you (men) have written.
„ 2. fem.	كَتَبْتُنَّ	katabtunna you (women) have written.
„ 1. masc. a. fem.	كَتَبْنَا	katabnā we have written.

In the same way from verbs of the forms فَعِلَ faʿila and فَعُلَ faʿula we have: شَرِبَ shariba "he drank", شَرِبَتْ sharibat "she drank" etc.: from كَرُمَ karuma "he was noble", كَرُمْتُ karumtu "I was noble" etc.

Note. The endings in the forms above are simply shortened forms of the personal pronouns used as nominatives except in the 3rd sing. masc. where the *a* is unexplained, in the 3rd sing. fem. where the *at* is the fem. ending and in the 3rd masc. plur. where the *u* is simply the sign of the plural. (The ا in this last ending is not pronounced and is introduced only to prevent the form being read at the beginning of the next word as "and".)

The chief rules for the Concord of subject and predicate are:

a) When the verb (فِعْلٌ fiʿl) precedes the subject (اَلْفَاعِلُ al-fāʿil) then:

1. If the subject is a sing. masc. or usually if it is a dual masc. or a sound plur. masc. the verb is put in the 3rd sing. masc.

كَتَبَ ٱلْمُعَلِّمُ kataba 'lmuʿallimu the teacher wrote.

كَتَبَ ٱلْمُعَلِّمَانِ kataba 'lmuʿallimāni the two teachers wrote.

كَتَبَ ٱلْمُعَلِّمُونَ kataba 'lmuʿallimūna the teachers wrote.

2. If the subject is a fem. sing. followed imme diately by the verb, or a dual fem. or a sound fem plur., or a broken plur., the verb is put in the 3rd sing. fem.

كَتَبَتِ ٱلْمُعَلِّمَةُ { katabati 'lmuʿallimatu the teacher (fem.) wrote.

كَتَبَتِ ٱلْمُعَلِّمَتَانِ { katabati 'lmuʿallimatāni the two teachers (fem.) wrote.

كَتَبَتِ ٱلْمُعَلِّمَاتُ { katabati 'lmuʿallimātu the teachers (fem.) wrote.

كَتَبَتِ ٱلتَّلَامِذَةُ katabati 'ttalāmidhatu the pupils wrote.

3. If the subject is a sing. fem. not immediately following the verb, or a collective (see Less. 2, 4), the verb may be in the 3rd sing. masc. or fem.

كَتَبَ (كَتَبَتْ) لَهُ ٱلْمُعَلِّمَةُ kataba (or katabat) lahu 'lmuʿallimatu, the teacher (fem.) wrote to him.

أَكَلَ (أَكَلَتِ) ٱلطَّيْرُ مِنْهُ akala (or akalati) 'ṭṭairu minhu, the birds (coll.) ate of it.

b) If the subject comes first the verb must agree with it in gender and number.

حَضَرَ ٱلْمُعَلِّمُونَ وَذَهَبُوا ḥaḍara 'lmuʿallimūna wadhahabū, the teachers were present and went away.

6. Sentences according to Arabian grammarians are of two kinds:

a) The Verbal sentence (ٱلْجُمْلَةُ ٱلْفِعْلِيَّةُ al-jumla al-fiʿlīya) when the verb (ٱلْفِعْلُ) is followed by the subject (called in this case ٱلْفَاعِلُ al-fāʿil) e.g. كَتَبَ زَيْدٌ kataba zaidun "Zaid has written".

b) The Nominal sentence (ٱلْجُمْلَةُ ٱلاسْمِيَّةُ al-jumla al-ismīya), when the subject (here called ٱلْمُبْتَدَأُ almubtada' "that (with which) is begun" comes first, whether the predicate (أَلْخَبَرُ alkhabar) be a noun or its equivalent, an adverbial clause or a verb e.g. زَيْدٌ وَلَدٌ zaidun waladun "Zaid is a boy". زَيْدٌ كَتَبَ zaidun kataba "Zaid (he) has written".

Note. The particle قَدْ qad is often put before the perfect to strengthen it. It may sometimes be translated "already", sometimes it may be omitted in translation.

Vocabulary.

فَهِمَ	fahima to understand.	نَهَارٌ	nahārun day.
قَوْلٌ	qaulun speech.	صَيْدٌ	ṣaidun hunt.
طَلَعَ	ṭalaʿa to rise (of the sun).	قَبِلَ	qabila to receive.
غَرَبَ	gharaba to set (of the sun).	ضَيْفٌ	ḍaifun guest.
شَمْسٌ	shamsun sun.	كَسَرَ	kasara to break.
قَمَرٌ	qamarun moon.	كُبَّايَةٌ	kubbāyatun glass.
قَصَدَ	qaṣada to strive after, make for.	بَعَثَ	baʿatha to send.
سَائِحٌ	sā'iḥun traveller.	فَلَّاحٌ	fallāḥun peasant.
دَخَلَ	dakhala to enter, go into.	حَاكِمٌ	ḥākimun governor.
خَرَجَ	kharaja to go out.	رَجَعَ	rajaʿa to return.
نَزَلَ	nazala to alight.	بَعُدَ	baʿuda to be distant.
مَاءٌ	mā'un water.	نَحْوَ	naḥwa towards, about.
خَمْرٌ	khamrun wine.	نِصْفٌ	niṣfun half.
حَوْشٌ	ḥaushun courtyard.	سَاعَةٌ	sāʿatun hour.

وَجَدَ	wajada to find.	غُلَامٌ	ghulāmun youth.
غَنِيٌّ	ghanīyun (plur. g) rich.	طَلَبَ	ṭalaba to seek, require.
فَتَحَ	fataḥa to open.	طَعَامٌ	ṭaʿāmun food.
فَرِحَ	fariḥa to rejoice.	جَلَسَ	jalasa to sit.

Exercise 21.

أَكَتَبْتَ ٱلْمَكْتُوبَ — لَا مَا كَتَبْتُ ٱلْمَكْتُوبَ — هَلْ فَهِمْتُمْ
قَوْلَنَا — نَعَمْ فَهِمْنَا قَوْلَكُمْ — طَلَعَتِ ٱلشَّمْسُ — غَرَبَ ٱلْقَمَرُ —
قَصَدَ ٱلشَّامَ ٱلسَّائِحُ وَخَادِمُهُ وَدَخَلَا ٱلْمَدِينَةَ — خَرَجْنَا مِنْ
بَابِ ٱلْمَدِينَةِ — طَلَعَ ٱلرِّجَالُ ٱلْجَبَلَ وَنَزَلُوا — هَلْ شَرِبْتُمْ
ٱلْمَآءَ (Intro. § 11, 3) — لَا مَا شَرِبْنَا ٱلْمَآءَ شَرِبْنَا ٱلْخَمْرَ — أَكَسَرْتُمَا
كُبَّايَةَ ٱلْمَآءِ أَنْتِ وَأَخُوكِ — لَا مَا كَسَرْنَا كُبَّايَةَ ٱلْمَآءِ — بَعَثْتُ
هٰؤُلَاءِ ٱلْفَلَّاحِينَ إِلَى بَيْتِ ٱلْحَاكِمِ — رَجَعْتَ إِلَى بَيْتِ أَبِيكَ —
بَعُدَتِ ٱلدَّارُ نَحْوَ نِصْفِ سَاعَةٍ — قَصَدْتُ (Intro. § 9)
هٰذِهِ ٱلدَّارَ وَوَجَدْتُ أَصْحَابَهَا مِنَ ٱلْأَغْنِيَاءِ — فَتَحَ لَهُ صَاحِبُ
ٱلدَّارِ بَابَ ٱلْحَوْشِ — خَرَجْتُ فِي هٰذَا ٱلنَّهَارِ إِلَى ٱلصَّيْدِ —
قَبِلُوا ٱلضَّيْفَ عِنْدَهُمْ هٰذِهِ ٱللَّيْلَةَ — فَرِحَ ٱلْغُلَامُ وَطَلَبَ مِنَ
ٱلرَّجُلِ ٱلطَّعَامَ —

Exercise 22.

The verb is always to be put at the beginning of sentences.

Have you written your letters (plur. k)? Yes, we have written our letters. — The beggar sought food from me. — The maidservant opened the door of the house. — Hast thou gone out to the hunt to-day? No, I did not go out to the hunt, I went into the city. (accus.). — Has the sun set? Yes, the sun has set and the moon has risen. — Mohammed and his sons entered the city and went out (dual) of it. — The men sat. — We returned from the hunt and sat. — They drank (the) coffee. — I received the guest at my house (عِنْدِى) this night. — O maidservant, hast thou returned from the market? I alighted at the house of (عِنْدَ) the peasants. — O girl, hast thou understood what I say (my speech)?

Twelfth Lesson.

(أَلدَّرْسُ ٱلثَّانِى عَشَرَ)

The Verb with Suffixes.

1. When a personal pronoun is the direct object of a verb it is attached to it as a suffix in one of the forms given in Lesson 8 e.g. ضَرَبْتُكَ ḍarabtuka "I have struck thee", ضَرَبَنِى ḍarabani "he has struck me".

Note. The otiose ا in the 3rd plur. masc. is omitted before the suffixes e.g. ضَرَبُونِى ḍarabūni "they have struck me"; and ـُو ū is added to the 2nd plur. masc. before the suffixes e.g. ضَرَبْتُمُوهَا ḍarabtumūhā "you have struck her".

2. The verb كَانَ kāna "to be" is weak (مُعْتَلّ muʿtall. See Less. 23, 1) and its conjugation will be explained in Less. 27, but it is needed so often that the Perfect is given here.

Sing.	3. masc.	كَانَ	kāna he was.
„	3. fem.	كَانَتْ	kānat she was.
„	2. masc.	كُنْتَ	kunta thou (m.) wast.
„	2. fem.	كُنْتِ	kunti thou (f.) wast.
„	1. masc. a. fem.	كُنْتُ	kuntu I was.
Dual	3. masc.	كَانَا	kānā they two (m.) were.
„	3. fem.	كَانَتَا	kānatā they two (f.) were.
„	2. masc. a. fem.	كُنْتُمَا	kuntumā you two were.
Plur.	3. masc.	كَانُوا	kānū they (m.) were.
„	3. fem.	كُنَّ	kunna they (f.) were.
„	2 masc.	كُنْتُمْ	kuntum you (m.) were.
„	2. fem.	كُنْتُنَّ	kuntunna you (f.) were.
„	1. masc. a. fem.	كُنَّا	kunnā we were.

3. The Perfect of كَانَ is used with the Perf. of another verb to express the Pluperfect of the latter, the subject being often placed between the two verbs e.g.

كَانَ زَيْدٌ كَتَبَ { kāna zaidun kataba Zaid had written.

كَانَ ٱلرِّجَالُ شَرِبُوا { kāna ʾrrijālu sharibū the men had drunk, (cf. Less. 11, 3 b).

4. When كَانَ is used as a copula its predicate (خَبَرٌ khabar) is put in the accusative (نَصْبٌ naṣb (see Less. 30, § 12), e.g.

كَانَتْ فَاطِمَةُ ٱبْنَةَ ٱلْمَلِكِ { kānat fāṭimatu 'bnata 'lmaliki Fatima was the king's daughter.

كَانَ زَيْدٌ وَلَدًا { kāna zaidun waladan Zaid was a boy.

كَانَ ٱلْبُسْتَانُ كَبِيرًا { kāna 'lbustānu kabīran the garden was large.

5. Any verb in Arabic may govern its own Verbal Noun (مَصْدَرٌ masdar) in the accusative. When an adjective is attached to this, the two words together are translated in English by an adverb e.g. فَرِحَ فَرَحًا عَظِيمًا fariḥa faraḥan 'aẓīman, he rejoiced greatly (literally "he rejoiced a great rejoicing", cf. Less. 34).

Vocabulary.

بَلَغَ balagha to reach.

خَبَرٌ { khabarun (pl. أَخْبَارٌ akhbārun) news.

خَتَمَ khatama to seal.

أَخَذَ akhadha to take.

هَرَبَ haraba to flee.

سَلِمَ { salima to be sound, whole.

حَزِنَ ḥazina to be sad.

حُزْنٌ ḥuznun sadness.

تَرَكَ { taraka to leave, abandon.

تَاجِرٌ { tājirun (pl. تُجَّارٌ tujjārun) merchant.

ضَرْبٌ { darbun stroke, blow.

مُهِمٌّ { muhimmun important.

مَمْلُوكٌ { mamlūkun (plur. مَمَالِيكُ mamālīku) Mamluke.

حَاكِمٌ { ḥākimun (pl. حُكَّامٌ ḥukkāmun) ruler, governor.

عَلِيٌّ ʿalīyun Ali (name of man).

قَتَلَ qatala to kill.

قَلْعَةٌ qalʿatun fortress, citadel.

سَلِيمٌ salīmun Selim, (name of man).

بَلْ bal but.

بِضَاعَةٌ biḍāʿatun (pl. بَضَائِعُ baḍāʾiʿu), wares, goods.

سَمِعَ samiʿa to hear.

أَسَرَ asara to take prisoner.

عَدُوٌّ ʿadūwun (pl. أَعْدَاءٌ aʿdāʾun) enemy.

Exercise 23.

هَلْ ضَرَبَكَ زَيْدٌ — لَا مَا ضَرَبَنِى زَيْدٌ بَلْ ضَرَبَتْنَا هِنْدٌ — أَفَهِمْتُمُونَا — نَعَمْ فَهِمْنَاكُمْ — بَلَغَنَا هٰذَا ٱلْخَبَرُ — طَلَبْنَاهُ وَمَا وَجَدْنَاهُ — كَتَبَ لَهُ مَكْتُوبًا وَخَتَمَهُ — أَخَذَ ٱلرِّجَالُ ٱلْخَمْرَ وَشَرِبُوهَا — هَرَبَتِ ٱلْبَنَاتُ وَسَلِمْنَ — حَزِنَ ٱلْمَلِكُ حُزْنًا شَدِيدًا — هَلْ تَرَكَ ٱلتُّجَّارُ بَضَائِعَهُمْ — نَعَمْ تَرَكُوهَا فِى ٱلدَّارِ — كُنْتُ قَدْ سَمِعْتُ أَخْبَارًا مُهِمَّةً — أَكَلَا وَشَرِبَا قَلِيلًا مِنَ ٱلْخَمْرِ — ٱلْمَمَالِيكُ كَانُوا حُكَّامًا فِى مِصْرَ — مُحَمَّدُ عَلِي قَتَلَهُمْ فِى قَلْعَةِ ٱلْقَاهِرَةِ — كَانَ ٱسْمُهُ سَلِيمًا — كَانَ مَلِكًا عَظِيمًا ذَا مَالٍ كَثِيرٍ (Less. 7, 2) — كَانَ ٱلرِّجَالُ ضَرَبُوهُمْ ضَرْبًا شَدِيدًا — مَا كُنْتُ حَاضِرًا عِنْدَكُمْ —

Exercise 24.

Have you struck them (fem.)? No, we have not struck them, the men have struck them. — This news (plur.) has reached me. — The king was just. — This sheikh was learned. — Wast thou present yesterday in the assembly? — No, I was absent. — O children, were you diligent? — O girl, hast thou understood me? — I have understood thee. — The girls were present and rejoiced greatly. — Her name was Hind. — The king took the enemies prisoner and killed them. — O merchants, where are your wares, have you left them in the house? — Have you heard it? — We have heard it. — Hast thou (أَنْتَ) written it, or did thy sister write it? — They both wrote it.

Thirteenth Lesson.

(أَلدَّرْسُ ٱلثَّالِثَ عَشَرَ)

The Imperfect.

1. The Imperfect tense (أَلْمُضَارِعُ almuḍāriʿ) expresses an action still unfinished and is translated in English by the present, the future or when used without a conjunction after another verb by the present participle e.g. جَلَسَ ٱلنَّاسُ يَشْرَبُونَ ٱلْخَمْرَ jalasa ʼnnāsu yashrabūna ʼlkhamra "the men sat drinking (literally "they were drinking") wine".

2. The Imperfect Stem consists of the three radicals of the verb, the first having no vowel, the second having a, i, or u (the dictionary always tells which is used with each verb). The persons are expressed by prefixing ya, ta, ʼa and na to the stem with the addition in some cases of suffixes also. The Moods are indicated by adding the vowels u for the Indicative, a for the Subjunctive to the last radical, which is left without vowel for the Jussive.

Prefixes and suffixes added to imperfect stem in indicative mood:

3. masc.	يَـْـــُ	3. masc.	يَـْـــَانِ	3. masc.	يَـْـــُونَ
3. fem.	تَـْـــُ	3. fem.	تَـْـــَانِ	3. fem.	يَـْـــْنَ
2. masc.	تَـْـــُ	2. m. a. f.	تَـْـــَانِ	2. masc.	تَـْـــُونَ
2 fem.	تَـْـــِينَ			2. fem.	تَـْـــْنَ
1. m. a. f.	أَـْـــُ			1. m. a. f.	نَـْـــُ

Full form of Imperfect Indicative of كَتَبَ -u (*i.e. imperf. stem = ktub*):

Sing.	3. masc.	يَكْتُبُ	yaktubu he writes (or will write).
„	3. fem.	تَكْتُبُ	taktubu she writes.
„	2. masc.	تَكْتُبُ	taktubu thou (masc.) writest.
„	2. fem.	تَكْتُبِينَ	taktubīna thou (fem.) writest.
„	1. masc. a. fem.	أَكْتُبُ	aktubu I write.
Dual	3. masc.	يَكْتُبَانِ	yaktubāni they two (masc.) write.
„	3. fem.	تَكْتُبَانِ	taktubāni they two (fem.) write.
„	2. masc. a. fem.	تَكْتُبَانِ	taktubāni you two write.
Plur.	3. masc.	يَكْتُبُونَ	yaktubūna they (masc.) write.
„	3. fem.	يَكْتُبْنَ	yaktubna they (fem.) write.
„	2. masc.	تَكْتُبُونَ	taktubūna you (masc.) write.
„	2. fem.	تَكْتُبْنَ	taktubna you (fem.) write.
„	1. masc. a. fem.	نَكْتُبُ	naktubu we write.

3. The vowel of the second letter of the imperfect stem must be ascertained from the dictionary. The following points however may be noted:

a) Most verbs whose second or third radical is a guttural (i.e. ح خ ع غ ء ه) take a — e.g. فَتَحَ fataḥa, Imperf. يَفْتَحُ yaftaḥu; مَنَعَ mana'a "to hinder, Imperf. يَمْنَعُ yamna'u. There are however many exceptions as دَخَلَ dakhala "to enter", Imperf. يَدْخُلُ yadkhulu; بَلَغَ balagha "to reach", Imperf. يَبْلُغُ yablughu; رَجَعَ raja'a "to return", Imperf. يَرْجِعُ yarji'u.

b) Verbs of the form فَعِلَ fa'ila generally take — as شَرِبَ shariba "to drink", Imperf. يَشْرَبُ yashrabu; exceptions however occur as حَسِبَ ḥasiba "to esteem", Imperf. يَحْسِبُ yaḥsibu. (حَسَبَ ḥasaba "to reckon" makes يَحْسُبُ yaḥsubu).

c) Verbs of the form فَعُلَ fa'ula take ـُ as كَرُمَ karuma "to be noble", Imperf. يَكْرُمُ yakrumu.

4. The Imperfect in itself denotes only unfinished action, but it may be made to indicate the future by putting the independent word سَوْفَ saufa before it or prefixing the contraction سَ sa, e.g. سَوْفَ يَكْتُبُ saufa yaktubu or سَيَكْتُبُ sayaktubu "he will write".

5. The Imperfect of كَانَ (which generally has a future meaning) is:

Sing. 3. masc.	يَكُونُ yakūnu	he will be.
" 3. fem.	تَكُونُ takūnu	she will be.

Sing. 2. masc.		تَكُونُ	takūnu thou (m.) wilt be.
„ 2. fem.		تَكُونِينَ	takūnīna thou (f.) wilt be.
„ 1. masc. a. fem.		أَكُونُ	akūnu I shall be.
Dual 3. masc.		يَكُونَانِ	yakūnāni they two (m.) will be.
„ 3. fem.		تَكُونَانِ	takūnāni they two (f.) will be.
„ 2. masc. a. fem.		تَكُونَانِ	takūnāni you two will be.
Plur. 3. masc.		يَكُونُونَ	yakūnūna they (m.) will be.
„ 3. fem.		يَكُنَّ	yakunna they (f.) will be.
„ 2. masc.		تَكُونُونَ	takūnūna you (m.) will be.
„ 2. fem.		تَكُنَّ	takunna you (f.) will be.
„ 1. masc. a. fem.		نَكُونُ	nakūnu we shall be.

6. The Perf. of كَانَ used with the Imperf. of another verb gives to the second one the meaning of the Latin imperf. e.g. كَانَ زَيْدٌ يَلْعَبُ kāna zaidun yal'abu "Zaid was playing".

7. The Imperf. of كَانَ used with the Perf. of another verb gives to the latter the meaning of the Future-perfect e.g. يَكُونُ زَيْدٌ كَتَبَ yakūnu zaidun kataba "Zaid will have written".

Vocabulary.

شَارِعٌ shāri'un street.	تَوْفِيقٌ taufīqun success (of God).
لَعِبَ la'iba to play.	عَرَفَ 'arafa to know.
اَللّٰهُ allāhu God.	أَغْنِيَاءُ aghniyā'u (plur. of غَنِيٌّ ghanīyun) rich.

قَدْرٌ qadrun value.

ثَمَنٌ thamanun price.

حَمَلَ ḥamala to carry.

أَ . . . أَمْ a . . . am or (in a double question).

قَرْيَةٌ qaryatun village.

قَبْرٌ qabrun grave.

أَحَدٌ aḥadun one (with suffix أَحَدُهُمْ aḥaduhum one of them).

ذَهَبَ dhahaba to go away.

أَيْنَ aina where? whither?

دُخَانٌ dukhānun smoke, tobacco.

شَرِبَ دُخَانًا shariba dukhānan, to smoke (literally "to drink smoke").

بَعْدَ baʿda after (of time).

بَعْدَهُ baʿdahu afterwards.

غَدًا ghadan to-morrow.

حَقٌّ ḥaqqun right.

حَمَّالٌ ḥammālun porter.

حِمْلٌ ḥimlun load, burden.

ظُهْرٌ ẓuhrun midday.

بَعْدَ ٱلظُّهْرِ baʿda 'ẓẓuhri, in the afternoon.

Exercise 25.

خَرَجَ ٱلْغُلَامُ يَلْعَبُ فِي ٱلشَّارِعِ — تَرَكْتُهُ يَلْعَبُ — نَطْلُبُ كُلُّنَا مِنَ ٱللّٰهِ ٱلتَّوْفِيقَ — أَتَعْرِفُ ٱلرَّجُلَ — لَا لَا أَعْرِفُهُ — كَثِيرُونَ مِنَ ٱلْأَغْنِيَاءِ لَا يَعْرِفُونَ قَدْرَ ٱلْعِلْمِ — مَا تَطْلُبُونَ مِنِّي — نَطْلُبُ مِنْكَ ثَمَنَ بَضَائِعِنَا — أَتَحْمِلُنِي أَمْ أَحْمِلُكَ — كَانَ ٱلشَّيْخُ يَقْصِدُ ٱلْقَرْيَةَ — يَحْمِلُونَ ٱلْمَيِّتَ إِلَى ٱلْقَبْرِ — يَكُونُ أَحَدُنَا حَمَلَ صَاحِبَهُ — أَيْنَ تَذْهَبَانِ أَنْتَ وَأَخُوكَ — نَذْهَبُ إِلَى ٱلشَّامِ — جَلَسَ ٱلرِّجَالُ يَشْرَبُونَ

دُخَانًا — جَلَسَتِ ٱلنِّسَاءُ يَشْرَبْنَ ٱلْقَهْوَةَ — نَحْنُ كُنَّا حَاضِرِين

نَلْعَبُ — يَا بِنْتُ لِمَاذَا لَا تَكْتُبِين (accus. cf. Less. 12, 4)

مَكْتُوبَكِ — سَوْفَ أَكْتُبُهُ بَعْدَهُ — يَا أَصْحَابِي أَتَذْهَبُون

إِلَى ٱلصَّيْدِ مَعَنَا — نَعَمْ يَا سَيِّدِي سَنَكُونُ حَاضِرِين

عِنْدَكُمْ غَدًا —

Exercise 26.

Dost thou smoke? — I do not smoke. — Will you two be present to-morrow with us? — No, we shall be absent. — What does he desire from me? — He desires his right from me. — The girl sat playing with us. — Zaid knew (use كَانَ with imperf.) the sheikh of the tribe. — I did not know him. — The porter will carry the load to (إِلَى) thy house. — Dost thou understand what I say (my speech)? — No, I do not understand it. — The men were present going to the hunt. — When wilt thou return from the hunt? — I shall return to-morrow — Will this news (plur.) reach him? — It will reach him in the afternoon. — The king will be just. — The sheikh smoked (كَانَ with imperf.) much tobacco. — O merchant, wilt thou send the wares to my house? — The porter will bring them to thee.

Fourteenth Lesson.

(أَلدَّرْسُ ٱلرَّابِعُ عَشَرَ)

The Moods of the Imperfect.

1. The Imperfect (أَلْمُضَارِع almuḍāri') has three Moods which are distinguished by the vowel of the third

radical. In this it resembles the noun with its three case-endings. (Hence the term مُضَارِعٌ which means "resembling".)

Note. Arabian grammarians treat the imperfect as a noun, thus, where we should say that the conjunction أَنَّ anna "that" requires the Subjunctive Mood, the Arab says that the particle أَنَّ governs the imperf. in the accusative.

The three Moods are

1) The Indicative ending in ـُ corresponding to the nominative and hence called اَلْمُضَارِعُ الْمَرْفُوعُ almuḍāriʿ almarfūʿ, e.g. يَكْتُبُ yaktubu.

2) The Subjunctive ending in ـَ corresponding to the accusative and called اَلْمُضَارِعُ الْمَنْصُوبُ almuḍāriʿ almanṣūb e.g. يَكْتُبَ yaktuba.

3) The Jussive with a vowelless ending corresponding to the genitive and called اَلْمُضَارِعُ الْمَجْزُومُ almuḍariʿ almajzūm e.g. يَكْتُبْ yaktub.

Note. The Jussive originally ended in ـِ which is now dropped, but reappears before a word beginning with hamzat alwaṣl e.g. يَكْتُبِ الْكِتَابَ yaktubi-lkitāba.

2. The Imperfect Subjunctive is declined as follows:

Singular.			Dual.		
3. masc.	يَكْتُبَ	yaktuba.	3. masc.	يَكْتُبَا	yaktubā.
3. fem.	تَكْتُبَ	taktuba.	3. fem.	تَكْتُبَا	taktubā.
2. masc.	تَكْتُبَ	taktuba.	2. m. a. f.	تَكْتُبَا	taktubā.
2. fem.	تَكْتُبِي	taktubī.			
1. m. a. f.	أَكْتُبَ	aktuba.			

Plural.

3. masc.	يَكْتُبُوا	yaktubū.
3. fem.	يَكْتُبْنَ	yaktubna.
2. masc.	تَكْتُبُوا	taktubū.
2. fem.	تَكْتُبْنَ	taktubna.
1. m. a. f.	نَكْتُبَ	naktuba.

Note 1. In the 2nd sing. fem. and in the 2nd and 3rd dual and plur. mascl. the final ن of the Indicative is dropped. In the 2nd and 3rd plur. the otiose ا is added at the end except when a suffix is attached to the verb e.g. يَكْتُبُوهُ yaktuūbhu.

Note 2. The Imperf. Subjunctive of كَانَ is declined like the indic. subject to the same changes in the endings as in the verb above.

3. The Subjunctive is used after the conjunctions أَنْ an "that", أَلَّا allā (see Intro. § 9) "that not", حَتَّى ḥattā "until, so that", لِ li, كَيْ kai, لِكَيْ likai, لِأَنْ li'an "so that", لِئَلَّا li alla (لِأَنْ لَا li'an la) "so that not", فَ fa and وَ wa when they mean "so that", أَوْ au when it means "unless that, until that" and لَنْ lan "not" (used as negation of the future), e.g. طَلَبَ أَنْ يَحْضُرَ ṭalaba an yahḍura "he required that he should be present".

Note. لَنْ is a contraction for لَا يَكُونُ أَنْ la yakūnu an "it will not be that".

Vocabulary.

The vowel after a verb is that of the second radical in the imperfect.

كَشَفَ	kashafa (i) to uncover, examine.	أَمْرٌ	amrun command, affair.

أَمَرَ amara (u) to command (takes acc. of the person).

سَمَحَ samaha to allow (with لِ for the person and بِ for the thing).

غُرْفَةٌ ghurfatun room.

صَرَفَ ṣarafa to spend (time).

فِرَاشٌ firāshun bed.

رَقَدَ raqada (u) to sleep.

قَصَدَ qaṣada (i) to intend.

عَاقِلٌ ʿāqilun intelligent.

مَوْجُودٌ maujūdun existing.

مَفْقُودٌ mafqūdun wanting, not present.

نَظَرَ naẓara (u), to see.

عَمِلَ ʿamila (a), to do.

أَمَامَ amāma before (of place).

وَعَدَ waʿada to promise (with acc. of the person).

سِرٌّ sirrun a secret.

بَيْنَ baina between.

Exercise 27.

طَلَبَ ٱلْقَاضِى مِنْكُمْ أَنْ تَحْضُرُوا عِنْدَهُ — أَمَرْتُهُمَا أَنْ يَجْلِسَا
— حَضَرَ ٱلتَّاجِرُ عِنْدِى لِيَطْلُبَ ٱلْبَضَائِعَ — هَلْ فَتَحْتَ لَهُمُ
ٱلْبَابَ لِيَدْخُلُوا عِنْدَنَا — سَأَفْتَحُ ٱلْبَابَ لَهُمْ — حَضَرَ ٱلْقَاضِى
لِيَكْشِفَ ٱلْأَمْرَ — لَا يَتْرُكُ ٱلْعَاقِلُ ٱلْقَلِيلَ ٱلْمَوْجُودَ لِيَطْلُبَ
ٱلْكَثِيرَ ٱلْمَفْقُودَ — خَرَجَ ٱلرِّجَالُ لِيَذْهَبُوا إِلَى ٱلصَّيْدِ — طَلَبَ
ٱلْغُلَامُ مِنَ ٱلرَّجُلِ أَنْ يَسْمَحَ لَهُ بِغُرْفَةٍ نَظِيفَةٍ لِيَصْرِفَ لَيْلَتَهُ
فِيهَا — فَتَحْتُ ٱلْبَابَ حَتَّى أَدْخُلَ ٱلْغُرْفَةَ —

Exercise 28.

We require thee (from thee) (fem.) to be present **(see Less.** 16, 6) with us. — He entered the bed to **sleep (so** that he might sleep). — The women intended to go out of (from) the house. — I sent a boy with him to see what (مَا) he would do. — Mohammed and his servant intended to go to (إِلَى) the market. — I shall return to the house to see what thou art doing. — I have commanded the servant to appear (be present) before me. — They went away until they entered the city. — I have promised him that that shall be a secret between me and (between) him.

Fifteenth Lesson.

(اَلدَّرْسُ ٱلْخَامِسَ عَشَرَ)

The Jussive.

1. The Jussive Mood (اَلْمُضَارِعُ ٱلْمَجْزُومُ almuḍāriʿ almajzūm) has the same forms as the Subjunctive except that where the 3rd radical is the last letter, it takes jazma (sukūn) e.g.

Singular.			Dual.		
3. masc.	يَكْتُبْ	yaktub.	3. masc.	يَكْتُبَا	yaktubā.
3. fem.	تَكْتُبْ	taktub.	3. fem.	تَكْتُبَا	taktubā.
2. masc.	تَكْتُبْ	taktub.	2. masc.	تَكْتُبَا	taktubā
2. fem.	تَكْتُبِي	taktubī.			
1. m. a. f.	أَكْتُبْ	aktub.			

Plural.

3. masc.	يَكْتُبُوا	yaktubū.
3. fem.	يَكْتُبْنَ	yaktubna.
2. masc.	تَكْتُبُوا	taktubū.
2. fem.	تَكْتُبْنَ	taktubna.
1. m. a. f.	نَكْتُبْ	naktub.

2. The verb كَانَ in the Jussive loses its و (see Less. 27) when the last radical is vowelless (see Intro. § 13, 3) e.g.

Singular.			Dual.		
3. masc.	يَكُنْ	yakun	3. masc.	يَكُونَا	yakūnā
3. fem.	تَكُنْ	takun	3. fem.	تَكُونَا	takūnā
2. masc.	تَكُنْ	takun	2. m. a. f.	تَكُونَا	takūnā
2. fem.	تَكُونِي	takūnī			
1. m. a. f.	أَكُنْ	akun.			

Plural.

3. masc.	يَكُونُوا	yakūnū
3. fem.	يَكُنَّ	yakunna
2. masc.	تَكُونُوا	takūnū
2. fem.	تَكُنَّ	takunna
1. m. a. f.	نَكُنْ	nakun.

3. The Jussive is used:

a) Alone, especially in the 3rd pers. to express a command e.g. يَكْتُبْ yaktub "let him write". In this sense it is generally strengthened by a prefixed لِ e.g. لِيَكْتُبْ liyaktub "let him write". If فَ precedes this particle, the لِ loses its vowel e.g. فَلْيَكْتُبْ falyaktub "so let him write".

b) After لَا lā used for prohibitions (لَا ٱلنَّهْيِ lā annahyi) e.g. لَا تَكْتُبْ lā taktub "do not write". لَا تَكُنْ غَائِبًا lā takun ghā'iban "be not absent".

c) After لَمْ lam used to deny a statement. Here the Imperf. has the force of the Perf. e.g. لَمْ يَكْتُبْ lam yaktub "he has not written". It is also used after لَمَّا lammā in the sense "not yet".

d) In the protasis and apodosis of conditional sentences, (see Less. 57).

Note. The jussive may be rendered more emphatic by adding anna or an, thus forming the so-called modus energicus 1 and 2, e.g.

		Modus energicus I.		Modus energicus II.	
Sing.	3. masc.	يَكْتُبَنَّ	yaktubanna he shall write	يَكْتُبَنْ	yaktuban.
„	3. fem.	تَكْتُبَنَّ	taktubanna	تَكْتُبَنْ	taktuban.
„	2. masc.	تَكْتُبَنَّ	taktubanna	تَكْتُبَنْ	taktuban.
„	2. fem.	تَكْتُبِنَّ	taktubinna	تَكْتُبِنْ	taktubin.
„	1. m. a. f.	أَكْتُبَنَّ	aktubanna	أَكْتُبَنْ	aktuban.
Dual	3. masc.	يَكْتُبَانِّ	yaktubānni.		
„	3. fem.	تَكْتُبَانِّ	taktubānni.		
„	2. m. a. f.	تَكْتُبَانِّ	taktubānni.		
Plur.	3. masc.	يَكْتُبُنَّ	yaktubunna	يَكْتُبُنْ	yaktubun.
„	3. fem.	يَكْتُبْنَانِّ	yaktubnānni.		
„	2. masc.	تَكْتُبُنَّ	taktubunna	تَكْتُبُنْ	taktubun.
„	2. fem.	تَكْتُبْنَانِّ	taktubnānni.		
„	1. m. a. f.	نَكْتُبَنَّ	naktubanna	نَكْتُبَنْ	naktuban.

These forms (not much used) are employed for exhortation and are often strengthened by prefixing the particle لَ, e.g. لَيَكْتُبَنَّ layaktubanna "let him surely write". They are also used after the prohibitive لَا, e.g. لَا تَكْتُبَنَّ lā taktubanna "thou shalt not write".

Vocabulary.

جَانِبٌ	jānibun side.	غَضِبَ	ghaḍiba to be angry (followed by عَلَى).
ضِيقٌ	ḍīqun anxiety, need.	قَدَرَ	qadara(i) to be able.
مَنَعَ	manaʿa to prevent.	غَيْرٌ	ghairun another (noun).
دُخُولٌ	dukhūlun entrance.	غَيْرُهُ	another than he.
شَيْءٌ	shai'un thing.	كَذَبَ	kadhaba(i) to lie.
غَرِيبٌ	gharībun strange pl. غُرَبَاءُ ghurabā'u.	فَ	fa and.
دَقِيقَةٌ	daqīqatun minute.	قَالَ	qāla to say.
مَوْضِعٌ	mauḍiʿun } place.	نُورٌ	nūrun light.
مَكَانٌ	makānun } place.		

Exercise 29.

لَمْ يَكُنْ يَسْمَحُ ٱلْوَزِيرُ أَنْ يَجْلِسَ رَجُلٌ فِي جَانِبِهِ — لَا تَتْرُكْ صَدِيقَكَ فِي ٱلضِّيقِ. — عَرَفَهُ ٱلرِّجَالُ وَلَمْ يَمْنَعُوهُ مِنَ ٱلدُّخُولِ فَدَخَلَ — قَلْبُهَا لَمْ يَكُنْ يَفْرَحُ لِشَيْءٍ — يَا بِنْتُ لَا تَفْتَحِي ٱلْبَابَ لِلْغُرَبَاءِ — لَا تَحْزَنُوا يَا أَوْلَادُ (Less. 16, 4 a) — نَحْنُ تَعْبَانُونَ فَلْنَجْلِسْ دَقِيقَةً فِي هٰذَا ٱلْمَوْضِعِ — لَا تَغْضَبُوا

عَلَيْنَا — لَمْ يَقْدِرُوا أَنْ يَرْجِعُوا إِلَى ٱلْمَدِينَةِ — نَظَرَ ٱلْوَلَدُ
دَارًا وَلَمْ يَكُنْ غَيْرُهَا فِي تِلْكَ ٱلْمَكَانِ — دَخَلَ مَعَهُ ٱلْكَلْبُ
وَلَمْ يَتْرُكْهُ — قَالَ ٱللهُ لِيَكُنْ نُورٌ فَكَانَ نُورٌ —

Exercise 30.

I did not (مَا) know the affair and did not (لَمْ) understand it. — O boys, do not open the door. — O girl, do not lie. — The pupils were idle and did not (لَمْ) write the letter. — O boys, be not idle. — They heard your speech and did not understand it. — Do not leave your friends in (the) anxiety. — Do not prevent me from entrance to (عِنْدَ) you. — Be not angry with me, o girl. — Let us drink (the) coffee. — The father and his son were not able to return to their house (. . . that they should return).

Sixteenth Lesson.

(أَلدَّرْسُ ٱلسَّادِسُ عَشَرَ)

The Imperative.

1. The Imperative فِعْلُ ٱلْأَمْرِ fi'l al'amr is formed from the Jussive by omitting the pronominal prefix, but as a word in Arabic must not begin with a vowelless letter (see Intro. §. 2) a hamzat alwasl (Intro. § 11) supported by ا is prefixed. This hamza takes the vowel ـُ if the second radical has ـُ, but ـِ if the second radical has ـَ or ـِ e.g.

كَتَبَ kataba, Jussive يَكْتُبْ yaktub, Imperative أُكْتُبْ uktub.

ضَرَبَ ḍaraba, Jussive يَضْرِبْ yaḍrib, Imperative إِضْرِبْ iḍrib.

مَنَعَ mana'a, Jussive يَمْنَعْ yamna', Imperative إِمْنَعْ imna'.

إِذْهَبْ إِلَى ٱلْبَابِ وَٱفْتَحْهُ idhhab ilā 'lbābi waftaḥhu "go to the door and open it".

2. The Imperative is naturally found in the 2nd pers. only:

Sing.	2. masc.	أُكْتُبْ	uktub
„	2. fem.	أُكْتُبِي	uktubī
Dual	2. masc. and fem.	أُكْتُبَا	uktubā
Plur.	2. masc.	أُكْتُبُوا	uktubū
„	fem.	أُكْتُبْنَ	uktubna.

The Imper. of كَانَ is:

Sing.	2. masc.	كُنْ	kun
„	2. fem.	كُونِي	kūnī
Dual	2. masc. and fem.	كُونَا	kūnā
Plur.	2. masc.	كُونُوا	kūnū
„	2. fem.	كُنَّ	kunna.

3. The Imperative is negatived by لَا with the Jussive (see Less. 15, 3 b).

4. Direct address (the vocative) is introduced by:

a) The particle يَا yā followed by a noun, which, if it stands alone is put in the nom. without the article and without nunation in the sing.; but if it is followed by a genit. is put in the accus. e.g. يَا وَلَدُ yā waladu "O boy!"; يَا عَبْدَ ٱللّٰهِ yā ʿabda 'llahi "O Abdallah!" (literally "servant of God").

b) The particle أَيُّهَا aiyuhā; fem. أَيَّتُهَا aiyatuhā; strengthened form يَا أَيُّهَا yā aiyuhā followed by a noun in the nom. and always with the article e g. يَا أَيُّهَا ٱلتِّلْمِيذُ yā aiyuhā 'ttilmidhu "O scholar!"

For further details see Less. 48, 1.

Present Participle.

5. The Present Participle (إِسْمُ ٱلْفَاعِلِ ism alfāʿil, nomen agentis) is of the form فَاعِلٌ e.g. كَاتِبٌ kātibun "writing".

The Participle is declined like other nouns and generally has a sound plural e.g.

		Masc.			Fem.	
Sing.	nom.	كَاتِبٌ	kātibun	writing	كَاتِبَةٌ	kātibatun
,,	acc.	كَاتِبًا	kātiban	,,	كَاتِبَةً	kātibatan
,,	gen.	كَاتِبٍ	kātibin	,,	كَاتِبَةٍ	kātibatin
Dual	nom.	كَاتِبَانِ	kātibâni	,,	كَاتِبَتَانِ	kātibatāni
,,	acc. gen.	كَاتِبَيْنِ	kātibaini	,,	كَاتِبَتَيْنِ	kātibataini
Plur.	nom.	كَاتِبُونَ	kātibūna	,,	كَاتِبَاتٌ	kātibātun
,,	acc. gen.	كَاتِبِينَ	kātibīna	,,	كَاتِبَاتٍ	kātibātin.

After كَانَ the Participle expresses a condition in the past e.g. كَانَ زَيْدٌ كَاتِبًا kāna zaidun kātiban "Zaid was writing" thus having much the same meaning as كَانَ يَكْتُبُ (see Less. 13, 6).

6. There is no infinitive in the sense of the European languages in Arabic. The English infinitive is expressed by a sentence in Arabic e.g. يَقْدِرُ زَيْدٌ أَنْ يَعْمَلَهُ yaqdiru zaidun an yaʿmalahu "Zaid is able to do it"

The Verbal Noun.

7. Every verb in Arabic has a Verbal Noun (مَصْدَرٌ maṣdar). In the simple verb this may be of one or more of some 40 forms. Among the most common are فَعْلٌ faʿlun as قَتْلٌ qatlun "killing"; فَعَلٌ faʿalun (from verbs of the form فَعِلَ) as فَرَحٌ faraḥun "rejoicing" (from فَرِحَ); and فُعُولٌ fuʿūlun as دُخُولٌ dukhulun "entering", خُرُوجٌ khurūjun "going out", طُلُوعٌ ṭulūʿun "rising", نُزُولٌ nuzūlun "descending".

For details see Less. 34.

Vocabulary.

صَدَقَ	sadaqa(u) to tell the truth.	صَغِيرٌ	ṣaghīrun small.
سَكَتَ	sakata(u) to be silent.	لَبِسَ	labisa to put on (clothes).
سَكَنَ	sakana(u) to dwell.	ثَوْبٌ	thaubun (pl. ثِيَابٌ thiyābun) garment, clothes.
سَيِّدَةٌ	saiyidatun woman, mistress.		
فَعَلَ	faʿala to do.	وَسْطٌ	wasṭun middle, centre.

طَرَقَ	ṭaraqa to knock at.	أَجَابَ	ajāba to answer.
ظَرِيفٌ	zarīfun (plur. ظُرَفَاءُ zurafā'u) a witty person, wag.	فَإِنَّ	fa'inna for, (conjunction).

Exercise 31.

اِفْتَحِى ٱلْبَابَ يَا أُمِّى — يَا أَوْلَادُ لَا تَدْخُلُوا — اُصْدُقُوا
يَا تَلَامِذَةُ وَلَا تَكْذِبُوا — اُسْكُتْ يَا أَيُّهَا ٱلتِّلْمِيذُ وَٱجْلِسْ
عَلَى مَكَانِكَ — أَيْنَ هُمْ سَاكِنُونَ — كَانُوا سَاكِنِينَ فِى ٱلسُّوقِ
— يَا عَبْدَ ٱللّٰهِ ٱفْتَحْ بَابَ ٱلدَّارِ — يَا أَيُّهَا ٱلرِّجَالُ ٱمْنَعُوهُمْ
مِنَ ٱلدُّخُولِ عَلَيْنَا — اُنْظُرِى أَيَّتُهَا ٱلسَّيِّدَةُ مَا (what) فَعَلْتِ
— أَيْنَ أَنْتَ ذَاهِبٌ — أَنَا ذَاهِبٌ إِلَى ٱلسُّوقِ — كُنَّا
جَالِسِينَ أَمَامَ ٱلدَّارِ — وَجَدُوا ٱمْرَأَةً جَالِسَةً فِى غُرْفَةٍ صَغِيرَةٍ
— اِلْبَسُوا ثِيَابَكُمْ — اِطْلَعْ عَلَى هٰذَا ٱلْجَبَلِ يَا أَيُّهَا ٱلْوَلَدُ —
يَا صَاحِبَىَّ ٱجْلِسَا بِجَانِبِى — يَا بَنَاتُ ٱكْتُبْنَ مَكَاتِيبَكُنَّ —
طَرَقَ رَجُلٌ بَابَ أَحَدِ ٱلظُّرَفَاءِ فَقَالَ مَنْ هٰذَا أَجَابَهُ أَنَا فَقَالَ
لَهُ ٱذْهَبْ فَإِنِّى لَا أَعْرِفُ مِنْ أَصْحَابِى أَحَدًا ٱسْمُهُ أَنَا —

Exercise 32.

See, o boys, what you have done. — O friend, enter and sit by my side. — O scholar, open the door of the room. — I was going to the city. — Whither are you going? — We are going to the market. — O boy, come down from the mountain. — O you two scholars, write your two letters. — O girl, speak the truth and lie not. — Where is Mr. (سَيِّد) Hasan living? — He is living in the middle of the city. — What are you doing? — We are putting on our clothes. — I was writing a letter, when (فَ) our friend entered. — Do not prevent me from entrance to (عَلَى) you.

Seventeenth Lesson.

(اَلدَّرْسُ ٱلسَّابِعُ عَشَرَ)

The Passive.

1. The Active Voice is called in Arabic اَلْمَعْلُومُ almaʿlūm "the known" because the agent is known, when the active is used as in "Zaid struck him"; the Passive Voice is called اَلْمَجْهُولُ almajhūl "the unknown" because when the passive is used as in "Zaid is struck" the agent (the striker) is unknown.

The Passive is formed from the Active by change of vowels. In the perf. the 1st radical takes ـُ, the 2nd takes ـِ. In the imperf. the prefix takes ـُ, the 2nd radical takes ـَ. All the other vowels are as in the active e.g.

Perfect.

Sing.	3. masc.	ضُرِبَ	ḍuriba he was struck.
„	3. fem.	ضُرِبَتْ	ḍuribat she was struck.
„	2. masc.	ضُرِبْتَ	ḍuribta thou (m.) wast struck.
„	2. fem.	ضُرِبْتِ	ḍuribti thou (f.) wast struck.
„	1. m. a. f.	ضُرِبْتُ	ḍuribtu I was struck.

Imperfectum.

Sing.	3. masc.	يُضْرَبُ	yuḍrabu he is struck.
	3. fem.	تُضْرَبُ	tuḍrabu she is struck.
,,	2. masc.	تُضْرَبُ	tuḍrabu thou (m.) art struck.
,,	2. fem.	تُضْرَبِينَ	tuḍrabīna thou (f) art struck.
,,	1. m. a. f.	أُضْرَبُ	uḍrabu I am struck.

2. The Passive must not be used in Arabic when the agent is expressed; thus "Zaid has been struck by Omar" must be rendered by ضَرَبَ عُمَرُ زَيْدًا ḍaraba ʿumaru zaidan "Omar struck Zaid"

The Passive is often used impersonally e.g. ذُكِرَ dhukira "it has been mentioned", or "it is told"

Passive Participle.

3. The passive participle (إِسْمُ ٱلْمَفْعُولِ ism almafʿūl) is of the form مَفْعُولٌ mafʿūl e.g. مَكْتُوبٌ maktūbun "written". It is declined like other nouns and generally has the sound plural.

The Particle إِنَّ.

4. A Nominal sentence (جُمْلَةٌ إِسْمِيَّةٌ jumla ismīya see Less. 11, 6, b) is often introduced by the particle إِنَّ inna "verily", which is followed by the subject (ٱلْمُبْتَدَأُ almubtada') in the accus. and the predicate (ٱلْخَبَرُ alkhabar) in the nom. The predicate is often strengthened by the prefix لَ, e.g. إِنَّ زَيْدًا عَاقِلٌ inna zaidan ʿāqilun or إِنَّ زَيْدًا لَعَاقِلٌ inna zaidan laʿāqilun "verily Zaid is intelligent".

If the subject is a personal pronoun, it is attached as a suffix (see Less. 3) to إِنَّ e.g. إِنَّهُ innahu "verily he".

Note. Alternative forms are used with the 1st pers. pronoun i.e. إِنِّي innī and إِنَّنِي innanī "verily I"; إِنَّا innā and إِنَّنَا innanā "verily we".

The Particles أَنْ and أَنَّ.

5. The Conjunction "that" is expressed in Arabic:

a) By أَنْ an (see Less. 14, 3) with a Verbal sentence (Less. 11), the verb being either in the perf. (مَاض) or the imperf. subj. (مُضَارِعٌ مَنْصُوبٌ) e.g.

طَلَبَ ٱلْقَاضِي أَنْ يَحْضُرَ زَيْدٌ ṭalaba 'lqāḍī an yaḥḍura zaidun the judge required Zaid to be present (to appear).

سَمِعْتُ أَنْ ذَهَبَ زَيْدٌ samiʿtu an dhahaba zaidun I heard that Zaid had gone away.

If more than one verb is dependent on أَنْ, the imperf. subj. is used throughout and the أَنْ is not repeated e.g.

أَمَرَ ٱلْوَزِيرُ أَنْ يَحْضُرَ مُحَمَّدٌ وَيَجْلِسَ بِجَانِبِهِ amara 'lwazīru an yaḥḍura muḥammadun wayajlisa bijānibihi the vezir commanded Mohammed to be present and sit beside him.

b) By أَنَّ anna with a Nominal sentence, the noun immediately following the conjunction being put in the accus. (as with إِنَّ). If a pronoun follows it is added to أَنَّ as a suffix. With the 1st pers. pron. the double forms أَنِّي annī and أَنَّنِي annanī, أَنَّا annā and أَنَّنَا annanā are used.

If the predicate is a noun it is put in the nom., if it is a verb (see Less. 11, 6) it is put in the perf. or the imperf. indicative, e g.

بَلَغَنِي أَنَّ زَيْدًا عَاقِلٌ balaghanī anna zaidan ʿāqilun it has reached me (i.e. I have heard) that Zaid is intelligent.

أَعْلَمُ أَنَّ زَيْدًا يَحْضُرُ aʿlamu anna zaidan yaḥḍuru I know that Zaid will be present.

Vocabulary.

ذَكَرَ	dhakara to mention.	سِيرَةٌ	sīratun manner of life.
أَنِيسٌ	anīsun amiable.	خُسْرٌ	khusrun loss.
لِ	li for.	قَبِلَ	qabila to receive
شَجَاعَةٌ	shajāʿatun courage.	هَدِيَّةٌ	hadīyatun a gift, present.
ضَرَبَ	ḍaraba to strike, coin.	سُرُورٌ	surūrun joy.
سِكَّةٌ	sikkatun coin.	صَلَاحُ ٱلدِّينِ	ṣalāḥu ’ddīni Saladin.
اَلْقُسْطَنْطِينِيَّةُ	alqusṭanṭinīyatu Constantinople.	عَظِيمٌ	ʿaẓīmun powerful.
مَشْغُولٌ	mashghūlun busy.	مَجْهُولٌ	majhūlun unknown.
هَدَمَ	hadama to destroy.	غَلَبَ	ghalaba to conquer.
وَقْتٌ	waqtun time.	مُؤَرِّخٌ	muʾarrikhun historian (sound plur.).
خَطَرٌ	khatarun danger.	غَسَلَ	ghasala to wash.
خَوْفٌ	khaufun fear.	صَلَبَ	ṣalaba to crucify.

مُنَجِّمٌ	munajjimun astrologer.	رِفْعَةٌ	rif'atun lifting up, raising.
قِيلَ	qīla (passive of قَالَ qāla "to say").	وَلٰكِنَّ	walākinna but.
نَجْمٌ	najmun star.	خَشَبَةٌ	khashabatun a piece of wood.

Exercise 33.

ذُكِرَ أَنَّ حَسَنًا رَجُلٌ أَنِيسٌ — يُذْكَرُ ٱسْمُهُ لِشَجَاعَتِهِ —
ضُرِبَتْ هٰذِهِ ٱلسِّكَّةُ فِي ٱلْقُسْطَنْطِينِيَّةِ — هُدِمَتْ أَبْوَابُ ٱلْقَلْعَةِ
— إِنَّ زَيْدًا ٱلضَّارِبُ وَعُمَرُ هُوَ ٱلْمَضْرُوبُ — لَمْ نَعْرِفْ أَنَّكُمْ
مَشْغُولُونَ فِي هٰذَا ٱلْوَقْتِ — إِنَّا لِلّٰهِ وَإِنَّا إِلَيْهِ رَاجِعُونَ
(Koran, Sura 2, 151) — إِنَّنَا لَا نَعْرِفُ ٱلْخَطَرَ وَلَا ٱلْخَوْفَ —
هٰذَا مَعْلُومٌ عِنْدَنَا — إِنَّ هٰذِهِ ٱلْمَرْأَةَ كَانَتْ مَعْرُوفَةً عِنْدِي —
يُعْرَفُ ٱلْإِنْسَانُ بِسِيرَتِهِ — إِنَّ ٱلرَّجُلَ ٱلْمَذْكُورَ لَقَبِيحٌ — إِنَّ
ٱلْإِنْسَانَ لَفِي خُسْرٍ (Koran, Sura 103, 2) — صُلِبَ مُنَجِّمٌ
فَقِيلَ لَهُ هَلْ نَظَرْتَ هٰذَا فِي نَجْمِكَ فَقَالَ نَظَرْتُ رِفْعَةً وَلٰكِنْ لَمْ
أَعْلَمْ أَنَّهَا عَلَى خَشَبَةٍ —

Exercise 34.

The doors of the house were opened. — The present was received with (بِ) joy. — It is told that Saladin was a powerful sultan. — I did not know that you were busy today. — Was this news known to (عِنْدَ) you? — Truly this news is unknown to us. — I know that Hasan is the conqueror and that thou art the conquered. — Truly the men mentioned are my friends. — His courage has been mentioned by (عِنْدَ) the historians. — Your clothes were washed.

Eighteenth Lesson.

(أَلدَّرْسُ ٱلثَّامِنُ عَشَرَ)

Derived Forms of the Verb.

1. The Simple verb (which alone has been treated so far) is called فِعْلٌ مُجَرَّدٌ fiʿl mujarrad ("the naked verb"). From this is formed the derived verb (فِعْلٌ مَزِيدٌ فِيهِ fiʿl mazîd fîhi litterally "the verb in which is an increase"). There are 14 forms of this latter, each consisting of the three radicals of the Simple form with the addition of one or more letters and having a meaning which is a modification of that of the Simple form. These with the simple form are designated by the numbers 1 to 15. Of these the first 10 only are in common use, and the ten seldom occur from any one root. The forms of a root in actual use are given in the dictionaries.

2. General list of the Perfects in each of the 15 forms with its modification of the root meaning:

I. Simple form: فَعَلَ faʿala, فَعِلَ faʿila or فَعُلَ faʿula (see Less. 11).

Forms increased by one letter:

II. فَعَّلَ faʿʿala, (with doubling of the second radical).

Meaning: Intensive as قَطَعَ qaṭaʿa "to cut", قَطَّعَ qaṭṭaʿa "to cut to pieces"; or causative as عَلِمَ ʿalima "to know", عَلَّمَ ʿallama "to make to know, teach".

III. فَاعَلَ fāʿala (with introduction of an alif after the first radical).

Meaning: Relation of the action to a person as كَتَبَ kataba "to write", كَاتَبَ kātaba "to write to someone"; or Attempt to do the action as قَتَلَ qatala "to kill", قَاتَلَ qātala "to try to kill, fight".

IV. أَفْعَلَ afʿala (with prefixed هَمْزَةُ ٱلْقَطْعِ hamzat alqaṭʿ cf. Intro. § 10; the first radical losing its vowel).

Meaning: Causative as جَلَسَ jalasa "to sit", أَجْلَسَ ajlasa "to make to sit".

Forms increased by two letters:

V. تَفَعَّلَ tafaʿʿala (with prefixed تَ ta and doubling of the second radical).

Meaning: Reflexive of II. as قَلَّدَ qallada "to gird" تَقَلَّدَ taqallada "to gird oneself".

VI. تَفَاعَلَ tafāʿala (with prefixed تَ ta and alif introduced after the first radical).

Meaning: Reflexive of III. as قَاتَلَ qātala "to fight", تَقَاتَلَ taqātala "to fight one another".

VII. إِنْفَعَلَ infaʿala (with prefixed hamza and nūn the hamza here and in all the following forms being hamzat alwasl, cf. Intro. § 11).

Meaning: Originally Reflexive of I but generally used as a Passive as كَسَرَ kasara "to break" إِنْكَسَرَ inkasara "to be broken".

VIII. إِفْتَعَلَ iftaʿala (with prefixed hamzat alwaṣl and ت ta introduced after the radical, which loses its vowel).

Meaning: Reflexive of I as جَمَعَ jamaʿa "to collect, unite" إِجْتَمَعَ ijtamaʿa "to collect themselves, to assemble".

IX. إِفْعَلَّ ifʿalla (with prefixed hamzat alwaṣl, omission of the vowel of the first radical and doubling of the third radical).

Meaning: Used only for Colours and Defects as إِحْمَرَّ iḥmarra "to be red"; إِعْوَجَّ iʿwajja "to be crooked"

Forms increased by more than two letters:

X. إِسْتَفْعَلَ istafʿala (with prefixed إِسْتَ ista and omission of the vowel of the first radical).

Meaning: Properly Reflexive of IV as أَسْلَمَ aslama "to give up" إِسْتَسْلَمَ istaslama "to give oneself up".

XI. إِفْعَالَّ ifʿālla a rare secondary form of IX.

XII.	إِفْعَوْعَلَ	ifʿauʿala	rare forms occurring in certain verbs only with special meanings.
XIII.	إِفْعَوَّلَ	ifʿauwala	
XIV.	إِفْعَنْلَلَ	ifʿanlala	
XV.	إِفْعَنْلَى	ifʿanlā	

3. Any verb in the above list that has Reflexive meaning is called مُطَاوِعٌ muṭāwiʿ.

4. The imperfect of the derived forms is formed from the perfect according to the following rules:

a) The prefixes yā, tā, alif, nūn receive the vowel u if the verb is increased by one letter only (II, III, IV forms), otherwise a.

b) The second radical receives the vowel i except in the forms with prefixed ta (V and VI) when it receives a.

c) The first radical remains as in the perfect; the third radical receives the vowel of the mood — u for the indic., a for the subj., sukūn for the juss.

The hamza at the beginning of some forms in the perf. falls away in the imperf.

Thus the Imperfects are as follows:

	Perfect.	Imperfect.
II.	فَعَّلَ fa‘‘ala	يُفَعِّلُ yufa‘‘ilu
III.	فَاعَلَ fā‘ala	يُفَاعِلُ yufā‘ilu
IV.	أَفْعَلَ af‘ala	يُفْعِلُ yuf‘ilu
V.	تَفَعَّلَ tafa‘‘ala	يَتَفَعَّلُ yatafa‘‘alu
VI.	تَفَاعَلَ tafā‘ala	يَتَفَاعَلُ yatafā‘alu
VII.	إِنْفَعَلَ infa‘ala	يَنْفَعِلُ yanfa‘ilu
VIII.	إِفْتَعَلَ ifta‘ala	يَفْتَعِلُ yafta‘ilu
IX.	إِفْعَلَّ if‘alla	يَفْعَلُّ yaf‘allu
X.	إِسْتَفْعَلَ istaf‘ala	يَسْتَفْعِلُ yastaf‘ilu.

5. The Imperative is formed according to the general rule (Less. 16, 1) from the Jussive by the omission of the prefixes.

If the first radical thus becomes vowelless a hamza must be put before it (Intro. 13, 2). In the IV. form this is hamzat alqaṭ‘ (Intro. § 11) which receives the vowel a (fatha); in the other forms it is hamzat alwasl and receives i (kasra).

	Jussive.	Imperative.
II.	يُفَعِّلْ yufa‘‘il	فَعِّلْ fa‘‘il
III.	يُفَاعِلْ yufā‘il	فَاعِلْ fā‘il
IV.	يُفْعِلْ yuf‘il	أَفْعِلْ af‘il
V.	يَتَفَعَّلْ yatafa‘‘al	تَفَعَّلْ tafa‘‘al
VI.	يَتَفَاعَلْ yatafā‘al	تَفَاعَلْ tafā‘al
VII.	يَنْفَعِلْ yanfa‘il	إِنْفَعِلْ infa‘il
VIII.	يَفْتَعِلْ yafta‘il	إِفْتَعِلْ ifta‘il
IX.	يَفْعَلِلْ yaf‘alil	إِفْعَلِلْ if‘alil
X.	يَسْتَفْعِلْ yastaf‘il	إِسْتَفْعِلْ istaf‘il.

6. The Participles are formed from the Perfects by prefixing a mīm with the vowel u. The prefixed hamza is dropped. The second radical takes the vowel i in the Active, a in the Passive.

	Participle Active.	Participle Passive.
II.	مُفَعِّلٌ mufa‘‘ilun	مُفَعَّلٌ mufa‘‘alun
III.	مُفَاعِلٌ mufā‘ilun	مُفَاعَلٌ mufā‘alun
IV.	مُفْعِلٌ muf‘ilun	مُفْعَلٌ muf‘alun
V.	مُتَفَعِّلٌ mutafa‘‘ilun	مُتَفَعَّلٌ mutafa‘‘alun
VI.	مُتَفَاعِلٌ mutafā‘ilun	مُتَفَاعَلٌ mutafā‘alun
VII.	مُنْفَعِلٌ munfa‘ilun	مُنْفَعَلٌ munfa‘alun

	Participle Active.	Participle Passive.
VIII.	مُفْتَعِلٌ muftaʿilun	مُفْتَعَلٌ muftaʿalun
IX.	مُفْعَلٌّ mufʿallun	
X.	مُسْتَفْعِلٌ mustafʿilun	مُسْتَفْعَلٌ mustafʿalun.

7. The Verbal Noun (مَصْدَرٌ masdar) of the Derived forms is as follows:

from II.	فَعَّلَ faʿʿala:	تَفْعِيلٌ	tafʿīlun
„ III.	فَاعَلَ fāʿala:	فِعَالٌ	fiʿālun (more often مُفَاعَلَةٌ mufāʿalatun)
„ IV.	أَفْعَلَ afʿala:	إِفْعَالٌ	ifʿālun
„ V.	تَفَعَّلَ tafaʿʿala:	تَفَعُّلٌ	tafaʿʿulun
„ VI.	تَفَاعَلَ tafāʿala:	تَفَاعُلٌ	tafāʿulun
„ VII.	إِنْفَعَلَ infaʿala:	إِنْفِعَالٌ	infiʿālun
„ VIII.	إِفْتَعَلَ iftaʿala:	إِفْتِعَالٌ	iftiʿālun
„ IX.	إِفْعَلَّ ifʿalla:	إِفْعِلَالٌ	ifʿilālun
„ X.	إِسْتَفْعَلَ istafʿala:	إِسْتِفْعَالٌ	istifʿālun.

Note the introduction of an alif of prolongation before the last radical in all except II, V and VI.

Verbal nouns generally take the regular feminine plural.

Nineteenth Lesson.

(اَلدَّرْسُ اَلتَّاسِعُ عَشَرَ)

II. Form فَعَّلَ.

1. Conjugation of كَسَّرَ "to break to pieces, smash".

Perf.	Imperf. Indic.	Imperf. Subj.	Imperf. Juss.
كَسَّرَ	يُكَسِّرُ	يُكَسِّرَ	يُكَسِّرْ
كَسَّرَتْ	تُكَسِّرُ	تُكَسِّرَ	تُكَسِّرْ
كَسَّرْتَ	تُكَسِّرُ	تُكَسِّرَ	تُكَسِّرْ
كَسَّرْتِ	تُكَسِّرِينَ	تُكَسِّرِي	تُكَسِّرِي
كَسَّرْتُ	أُكَسِّرُ	أُكَسِّرَ	أُكَسِّرْ
etc.	etc.	etc.	etc.

Imperative

كَسِّرْ — Part. Active مُكَسِّرٌ

كَسِّرِي etc. — Part. Pass. مُكَسَّرٌ

Verbal noun تَكْسِيرٌ.

In some verbs there is a secondary form of the Verbal Noun of the form تَفْعَالٌ e.g. from رَحَّبَ "to welcome" تَرْحَابٌ.

The Passive is in the Perf. كُسِّرَ etc., in the Imperf. يُكَسَّرُ etc.

2. The form فَعَّلَ denotes:

a) A strengthening of the meaning e.g. كَسَرَ "to break", كَسَّرَ "to break into pieces, smash".

b) It has usually a Causative or Factitive meaning (like أَفْعَلَ) e.g. عَلِمَ "to learn" عَلَّمَ "to make to learn, teach".

Note. In these cases, if a verb is intransitive in the Simple form, it becomes transitive in II. e.g. كَثُرَ "to be numerous", كَثَّرَ "to make numerous, increase"; while if it is transitive in the Simple form, it becomes doubly transitive in II. e.g. بَلَغَ "to reach", بَلَّغَ "to make (something) reach (someone to transmit)".

c) Sometimes it has the meaning of thinking, esteeming e.g. كَذَبَ "to lie", كَذَّبَ "to esteem (someone) a liar", صَدَقَ "to be sincere" صَدَّقَ "to think (someone) sincere, believe".

d) It is often used to form verbs from nouns e.g. from جِلْدٌ "skin, leather" is formed جَلَّدَ "to skin, bind (books)"; from أَلسَّلَامُ عَلَيْكَ "peace be on thee" is formed سَلَّمَ عَلَيْهِ "he greeted him" i.e. said "peace be upon thee" to him.

III. Form فَاعَلَ.

3. Conjugation of كَاتَبَ "to write to":

Perf.	Imperf. Indic.	Imperf. Subj.	Imperf. Juss.
كَاتَبَ	يُكَاتِبُ	يُكَاتِبَ	يُكَاتِبْ
كَاتَبْتَ	تُكَاتِبُ	تُكَاتِبَ	تُكَاتِبْ

	Imperf.		
Perf.	Indic.	Subj.	Juss.
كَاتَبْتَ	تُكَاتِبُ	تُكَاتِبَ	تُكَاتِبْ
كَاتَبْتِ,	تُكَاتِبِينَ	تُكَاتِبِي	تُكَاتِبِي
كَاتَبْتُ	أُكَاتِبُ	أُكَاتِبَ	أُكَاتِبْ
etc.	etc.	etc.	etc.

Imperative

كَاتِبْ — Part. Active مُكَاتِبٌ

كَاتِبِي etc. — Part. Passive مُكَاتَبٌ

Verbal noun كِتَابٌ, more usually مُكَاتَبَةٌ

Passive, Perf. كُوتِبَ Imperf. Indic. يُكَاتَبُ

4. The form فَاعَلَ is used to express the relation of the action to a person e.g. كَتَبَ "to write", كَاتَبَ "to write to (someone), correspond with".

It also very often expresses an attempt to do something e.g. قَتَلَ "to kill", قَاتَلَ "to attempt to kill, to fight"; سَبَقَ "to precede", سَابَقَ "to try to precede, to compete with".

5. The فَاعَلَ form is always transitive and takes the Accus. of the Person e.g. كَاتَبَهُ "he corresponded with him", قَاتَلَهُ "he fought with him".

IV. Form أَفْعَلَ.

6. Conjugation of أَجْلَسَ "to make to sit".

	Imperf.		
Perf.	Indic.	Subj.	Juss.
أَجْلَسَ	يُجْلِسُ	يُجْلِسَ	يُجْلِسْ
أَجْلَسَتْ	تُجْلِسُ	تُجْلِسَ	تُجْلِسْ
أَجْلَسْتَ	تُجْلِسُ	تُجْلِسَ	تُجْلِسْ
أَجْلَسْتِ	تُجْلِسِينَ	تُجْلِسِي	تُجْلِسِي
أَجْلَسْتُ	أُجْلِسُ	أُجْلِسَ	أُجْلِسْ
etc.	etc.	etc.	etc.

Imperative

أَجْلِسْ — Part. Active مُجْلِسٌ

أَجْلِسِي etc. — Part. Passive مُجْلَسٌ

Verbal noun إِجْلَاسٌ

Passive, Perf. أُجْلِسَ — Imperf. Indic. يُجْلَسُ

7. The meaning of the أَفْعَلَ form is causative or factitive (cf. فَعَّلَ). It makes intransitive verbs transitive and transitive doubly transitive. حَضَرَ "to be present", أَحْضَرَ "to make to be present i.e. to bring, present"; جَلَسَ "to sit", أَجْلَسَ "to make to sit, seat".

Many verbs employ both the II. and IV. forms as causatives, sometimes with different shades of meaning, e.g. خَبَّرَ and أَخْبَرَ are both used to mean "to inform"; while عَلَّمَ means "to teach" and أَعْلَمَ "to inform".

The أَفْعَلَ form is often used to form verbs from nouns e.g. from صُبْحٌ "morning" أَصْبَحَ "to do in the morning"; from مَسَاءٌ "evening" أَمْسَى "to do in the evening"; from إِسْلَامٌ "Islam" أَسْلَمَ "to receive Islam, become a Moslem".

Vocabulary.

كَلَّمَ II. to speak to, address (acc.).	دَفَعَ III. to defend.
لَطَفَ III. to treat in a friendly way.	شَهِدَ to witness, III. to see.
قَبَّلَ II. to kiss.	نِصْفٌ half.
هَلَكَ IV. to destroy.	حَوْلَ around.
أَصْبَحَ to be (literally "to do in the morning").	إِلَّا if not, except.
	إِلَّا .... لَا only.
كَاسِرٌ ramping.	أُفُقٌ horizon.
	قَطَعَ III. to interrupt.
خَلَفَ III. to disobey.	كَلَامٌ speech.
أَمْرٌ pl. أَوَامِرُ command.	أَرْسَلَ to send.
أَمْرٌ pl. أُمُورٌ affair.	بَدْوٌ bedouin.
خَبَرَ IV. to inform (عَنْ "concerning").	قَدِمَ II. to bring.
وَالِدٌ father (literally "begetter").	حَضَرَ IV. to bring forward, present.
ظَلِمَ IV. to become dark.	بَلَغَ II. to cause to reach, convey.
شَاوَرَ to ask advice of.	لِصٌّ pl. لُصُوصٌ robber.
جَهَّزَ to equip.	هَجَمَ III. to attack.

بِلَادٌ	land.	حَالًا	immediately, (adverbial accus.).
عَنْ	from.	بَشَّرَ	II. to take good news to.
بُعْدٌ	distance.	خَلَطَ	to mix, III. to have intercourse with, (acc.).
فَتَّشَ	II. to seek.	عَشَرَ	III. to frequent the society of (acc.).
جَاوَرَ	to be neighbour to.	دَبَّرَ	II. to propose, manage.
جِوَارٌ	neighbourhood.	قَدَّرَ	II. to determine.
عَدِمَ	IV. to deprive, (with two accus.).	صَدَّقَ	II. to believe.
حَيَاةٌ	life, (see Intro. § 6, Note 3).	سَافَرَ	to travel.
رَقَبَ	III to watch, observe.	سَلَامٌ	peace, greeting.
غَمَرَ	to cover, overwhelm.	كَ	as, like.
لُطْفٌ	friendliness.	وَجَدَ	to find.
حَسَنَ	IV. to treat kindly.		

Exercise 35.

كَانَ ٱلْأَمِيرُ يُكَلِّمُ أَخَاهُ وَيُلَاطِفُهُ وَيُقَبِّلُهُ — إِنَّ ٱللُّصُوصَ
يُهَاجِمُونَ هٰذِهِ ٱلْبِلَادَ — قَدْ أَهْلَكَ مُحَمَّدُ عَلِي ٱلْمَمَالِيكَ —
أَصْبَحَ مَنْظَرُهُ كَٱلْأَسَدِ ٱلْكَاسِرِ — أُقَبِّلُ يَدَيْكَ يَا أَبِي وَلَمْ
أُخَالِفْ أَوَامِرَكَ — يَكُونُ ٱلْأَحْسَنُ أَنْ تَذْهَبُوا وَتُخْبِرُوا
وَالِدِى — كَانَ ٱللَّيْلُ قَدْ أَظْلَمَ فَشَاوَرَ ٱلشَّيْخُ رِجَالَهُ فِي
ٱلْأَمْرِ — جَهِّزُوا سِلَاحَكُمْ لِلدِّفَاعِ — ٱلْمُكَاتَبَةُ نِصْفُ ٱلْمُشَاهَدَةِ

— ثُمَّ لَا يُشَاهِدُونَ حَوْلَهُمْ إِلَّا أُفْقًا مُظْلِمًا — يَا وَلَدِي لَا
تُقَاطِعْ كَلَامِي — إِنِّي أُشَاهِدُ رَجُلًا عَنْ بُعْدٍ — إِنَّ ٱلرِّجَالَ
فَتَّشُوا تِلْكَ ٱلْجِوَارَ وَبَعْدَ ٱلتَّفْتِيشِ رَجَعُوا — إِرْجِعْ مِنْ عِنْدِكَ
يَا كَلْبَ ٱلْعَرَبِ وَإِلَّا أَعْدَمْتُكَ **(Perfect for the English Future)**
ٱلْحَيَاةَ — نَحْنُ مُجْتَهِدُونَ فِي ٱلتَّفْتِيشِ عَنْهُ — أَدْخَلَ ٱلضَّيْفَ
إِلَى خَيْمَتِهِ — رَاقَبْنَا حَرَكَاتِ ٱللُّصُوصِ — يَا صَاحِبَنَا غَمَرْتَنَا
بِلُطْفِكَ وَإِحْسَانِكَ — أَمَرَهُمُ ٱلشَّيْخُ أَنْ يَذْهَبُوا حَالًا لِتَبْشِيرِ
ٱلْأَمِيرِ — طَلَبَ زَيْدٌ أَنْ يُخْبِرُوا أَبَاهُ أَنَّهُ وَجَدَ ٱبْنَهُ وَأَنَّهُ
سَيَكُونُ عِنْدَهُ غَدًا — عَرَفَ ٱلشَّيْخُ أَنَّ ضَيْفَهُ خَالَطَ ٱلْبَدْوَ
وَعَاشَرَهُمْ — ٱلْإِنْسَانُ يُدَبِّرُ وَٱللّٰهُ يُقَدِّرُ (proverb) — نُرْسِلُ
لَهُ مَنْ يُخْبِرُهُ بِذٰلِكَ — أَخْبِرْنَا عَنِ ٱسْمِكَ —

Exercise 36.

O servant, bring us the coffee. — The judge commanded them to (that they should) bring forward the robber. — We kiss thy hands. — Convey to him my greeting. — I have commanded thee, o girl, to convey my greeting to them. — I informed him of (عَنْ) this affair, but he did not believe me. — Do not believe this boy, o girl. — The proposing is from men, the determining is from God. — I ask advice of my friends in anxiety. — Thou hast seen many cities and had intercourse with many peoples. — Send that man to me so that (لِ) I may treat him (أُنْيِهِ) kindly. — Do not disobey my commands. — Defence is the right of (the) man. — I bring thee the good news that we have conquered the robbers. — We have travelled to Damascus. — Bring in (cause to enter) the physician.

Twentieth . Lesson.

(اَلدَّرْسُ ٱلْعِشْرُونَ)

V. Form تَفَعَّلَ.

1. The تَفَعَّلَ form is the same as the فَعَّلَ with a prefixed تَ.

Conjugation of تَسَلَّمَ "to take over, receive":

Perf.	Imperf. Indic.	Imperf. Subj	Imperf. Juss.
تَسَلَّمَ	يَتَسَلَّمُ	يَتَسَلَّمَ	يَتَسَلَّمْ
تَسَلَّمْتَ	تَتَسَلَّمُ	تَتَسَلَّمَ	تَتَسَلَّمْ
تَسَلَّمْتَ	تَتَسَلَّمُ	تَتَسَلَّمَ	تَتَسَلَّمْ
تَسَلَّمْتِ	تَتَسَلَّمِينَ	تَتَسَلَّمِى	تَتَسَلَّمِى
تَسَلَّمْتُ	أَتَسَلَّمُ	أَتَسَلَّمَ	أَتَسَلَّمْ
etc.	etc.	etc.	etc.

Imperative

تَسَلَّمْ

تَسَلَّمِى etc.

Part. Active مُتَسَلِّمٌ

Part. Passive مُتَسَلَّمٌ

Verbal noun تَسَلُّمْ

Passive, Perf. تُسُلِّمَ Imperf. Indic. يُتَسَلَّمُ

2. The V. form تَفَعَّلَ is the Reflexive of the II. form فَعَّلَ e.g. فَرَّقَ "to separate", تَفَرَّقَ "to separate oneself to scatter"; عَلَّمَ "to teach" تَعَلَّمَ "to teach oneself i.e. to learn".

It is also used to form verbs from nouns e.g. from نَصْرَانِيٌّ "a Christian" is formed تَنَصَّرَ "to become a Christian"; from يَهُودِيٌّ "a Jew", تَهَوَّدَ "to become a Jew".

It often has the meaning "to think oneself, to represent oneself as", e.g. تَكَبَّرَ "to think oneself great, be haughty"; تَنَبَّأَ (from نَبِيٌّ "a prophet") "to represent oneself as a prophet".

VI. Form.

3. The VI. Form is the same as III. with a prefixed تَ.

Conjugation of تَقَاتَلَ "to fight with one another":

Perf.	Imperf. Indic.	Imperf. Subj.	Imperf. Juss.
تَقَاتَلَ	يَتَقَاتَلُ	يَتَقَاتَلَ	يَتَقَاتَلْ
تَقَاتَلْتَ	تَتَقَاتَلُ	تَتَقَاتَلَ	تَتَقَاتَلْ
تَقَاتَلَتْ	تَتَقَاتَلُ	تَتَقَاتَلَ	تَتَقَاتَلْ
تَقَاتَلْتِ	تَتَقَاتَلِينَ	تَتَقَاتَلِي	تَتَقَاتَلِي
تَقَاتَلْتُ	أَتَقَاتَلُ	أَتَقَاتَلَ	أَتَقَاتَلْ
etc.	etc.	etc.	etc.

Imperative

تَقَاتَلْ — Part. Active مُتَقَاتِلٌ

تَقَاتَلِى etc. — Part. Passive مُتَقَاتَلٌ

Verbal noun تَقَاتُلٌ

Passive, Perf. تُقُوتِلَ — Imperf. Indic. يُتَقَاتَلُ

4. The تَفَاعَلَ **form is the Reflexive of the III. form,** e.g. قَاتَلَ "to fight", تَقَاتَلَ "to fight with one another", therefore if the verb occurs in the Sing. its subject must be a Plural or a Collective, e.g. تَقَاتَلَ ٱلرِّجَالُ "the men fought with one another"; تَقَاتَلَ ٱلْقَوْمُ (قَوْمٌ is Collective) "the people fought with one another". This form is used more often than V. to mean "to represent oneself as", e.g. تَعَامَى "to pretend to be blind"; تَمَوَّتَ "to pretend to be dead".

Vocabulary.

كَلَّمَ	V. to speak.	جَمِيعًا	all (adv. accus.).
صَبَاحٌ	morning, acc. "in the morning".	أَيْضًا	also.
وَاجِبٌ	necessary, duty.	قَدِمَ	V. to come forward.
تَبِعَ	V. to follow.	فَرَقَ	V. to separate from one another, VI. to disperse.
أَثَرٌ	trace.	لَمَّا	when, after.
حَدَثَ	V. to narrate to one another, VI. to converse.	مِنْ عِنْدِ	from (the presence of . . .).
شَجُعَ	V. to show oneself brave.	جِهَةٌ	side, direction.

حُضُورٌ presenee, appearance.

شَكَرَ V. to be grateful.

عَاطِفَةٌ (plur. عَوَاطِفُ) tender feeling.

لَعِبَ VI. to play (بِ).

لَهِيبٌ flame.

ذَكَرَ V. to remember.

قَوْمٌ people.

مَهَلَ V. to be slow.

قَبِلَ VI. to meet one another.

جَسَرَ VI. to be bold.

عَجِبَ V. to wonder, be astonished.

غَايَةٌ extreme, extremity.

عَلِمَ to know, II. to teach, V. to learn.

طِبٌّ medicine.

كَذٰلِكَ thus, (literally "like that").

مَخْصُوصٌ appointed, specified.

شَرُفَ V. to have the honour.

نَصْرَانٌ or نَصْرَانِيٌّ (plur. نَصَارَى) Christian.

وَدَعَ V. to say farewell to one another.

Exercise 37.

هَلْ تَتَكَلَّمُ بِٱلْعَرَبِيِّ — نَعَمْ يَا سَيِّدِى أَنَا أَتَكَلَّمُ قَلِيلًا —
أَتَكَلَّمْتُمْ مَعَهُ — تَكَلَّمْنَا مَعَهُ صَبَاحًا — وَاجِبٌ عَلَيْنَا تَتَبُّعُ
أَثَرِهِمْ — ٱلْأَمِيرُ وَأَخُوهُ جَلَسَا يَتَحَدَّثَانِ فِى (about) ذٰلِكَ ٱلْأَمْرِ —
إِنَّنَا مُتَشَجِّعُونَ جَمِيعًا وَنَطْلُبُ إِلَيْكَ (from thee) أَنْ تَتَشَجَّعَ
أَيْضًا — تَقَدَّمَ ٱلشَّيْخُ وَقَبَّلَ يَدَىِ ٱلْوَزِيرِ — ٱلْأَحْسَنُ أَنْ
نَتَفَرَّقَ وَنَتَتَبَّعَ ٱلطَّرِيقَ — لَمَّا سَمِعَ ٱلرِّجَالُ ذٰلِكَ تَقَدَّمُوا
جَمِيعًا إِلَى جِهَتِهِ — كَانَتْ عَوَاطِفُهُ تَتَلَاعَبُ بِهِ تَلَاعُبَ ٱلرِّيحِ
بِٱللَّهِيبِ — هَلْ لَا تَتَذَكَّرِينَ مَا أَمَرْتُكِ يَا خَدَّامَةُ — يَا قَوْمُ

تَمَهَّلُوا لِنَتَقَابَلَ — أَتَجَاسَرُ أَنْ أَفْعَلَ هٰذَا — تَعَجَّبْنَا مِنْهُ غَايَةَ ٱلتَّعَجُّبِ (Less. 12, 5) — تَرَكْنَا ٱلْأَمِيرَ فِي خَيْمَتِهِ يَتَحَادَثُ هُوَ وَٱبْنُهُ فِي أَمْرِ أَخِيهِ —

Exercise 38.

Do you speak Arabic? — No, we do not speak Arabic. — They did not speak with us. — We conversed about this affair. — Hast thou learnt what thy teacher has taught thee? — Yes, I have learnt it. — These pupils learn the science of medicine. — Do not speak thus, o child. — They separated from one another that they might follow the way and meet at (فِي) an appointed place. — I was greatly astonished (I was astonished the extreme of astonishment) at (مِنْ) him. Truly we are exceedingly grateful (we are grateful the excess of gratitude). — The Moslems and the Christians fought with one another. — We said farewell to one another so that we might disperse.

Twenty-first Lesson.

(اَلدَّرْسُ ٱلْحَادِي وَٱلْعِشْرُونَ)

VII. Form.

1. Conjugation of إِنْكَسَرَ "to break" (intransitive):

Perf.	Imperf. Indic.	Imperf. Subj.	Imperf. Juss.
إِنْكَسَرَ	يَنْكَسِرُ	يَنْكَسِرَ	يَنْكَسِرْ
إِنْكَسَرْتَ	تَنْكَسِرُ	تَنْكَسِرَ	تَنْكَسِرْ

Perf.	Imperf. Indic.	Imperf. Subj.	Imperf. Juss.
إِنْكَسَرْتَ	تَنْكَسِرُ	تَنْكَسِرَ	تَنْكَسِرْ
إِنْكَسَرْتِ	تَنْكَسِرِينَ	تَنْكَسِرِى	تَنْكَسِرِى
إِنْكَسَرْتُ	أَنْكَسِرُ	أَنْكَسِرَ	أَنْكَسِرْ
etc.	etc.	etc.	etc.

Imperative

إِنْكَسِرْ — Part. Active مُنْكَسِرٌ

إِنْكَسِرِى etc. — Part. Passive مُنْكَسَرٌ

Verbal noun إِنْكِسَارٌ

Passive, Perf. أُنْكُسِرَ Imperf. Indic. يُنْكَسَرُ

2. The VII. form is originally the Reflexive of the Simple form, but generally it contains the idea of allowing some action to be done to one i.e. it has a Passive sense as كَشَفَ "to uncover", إِنْكَشَفَ "to be uncovered".

3. The VII. form is wanting in all verbs that begin with hamza, wāw, yā, rā, lām or nūn.

VIII. Form.

4. Conjugation of إِجْتَمَعَ "to assemble".

Perf.	Imperf. Indic.	Imperf. Subj.	Imperf. Juss.
إِجْتَمَعَ	يَجْتَمِعُ	يَجْتَمِعَ	يَجْتَمِعْ
إِجْتَمَعْتَ	تَجْتَمِعُ	تَجْتَمِعَ	تَجْتَمِعْ

Perf.	Imperf. Indic.	Subj.	Juss.
إِجْتَمَعْتُ	تَجْتَمِعُ	تَجْتَمِعَ	تَجْتَمِعْ
إِجْتَمَعْتِ	تَجْتَمِعِينَ	تَجْتَمِعِي	تَجْتَمِعِي
إِجْتَمَعْتُ	أَجْتَمِعُ	أَجْتَمِعَ	أَجْتَمِعْ
etc.	etc.	etc.	etc.

Imperative

إِجْتَمِعْ — Part. Active مُجْتَمِعٌ

إِجْتَمِعِي etc. — Part. Passive مُجْتَمَعٌ

Verbal noun إِجْتِمَاعٌ

Passive, Perf. أُجْتُمِعَ — Imperf. Indic. يُجْتَمَعُ

5. The *ta* introduced after the first radical undergoes certain changes:

a) If the first radical is one of the emphatic letters ص, ض, ط, ظ, the tā is changed into a ط; this is assimilated to a ط or ظ which is then written with tashdīd e.g. صَنَعَ "to make" forms إِصْطَنَعَ; ضَرَبَ "to strike" forms إِضْطَرَبَ; طَلَعَ "to rise" forms إِطَّلَعَ; ظَلِمَ "to be dark" forms إِظَّلَمَ and إِطَّلَمَ.

b) If the first radical is د, ذ or ز, the *tā* is softened to د; this is assimilated to a ذ, which is then written with tashdīd e.g. دَرَكَ forms إِدَّرَكَ; زَحَمَ forms إِزْدَحَمَ; ذَخَرَ forms إِذَّخَرَ and إِدَّخَرَ.

c) If the first radical is ث, it sometimes assimilates the ت e.g. ثَبَتَ forms إِثَّبَتَ or إِتَّبَتَ.

6. The VIII. form is like the VII. the Reflexive of the Simple verb e.g. from جَمَعَ "to collect" is formed إِجْتَمَعَ "to collect themselves, to assemble"; but has also the sense of doing a thing for oneself e.g. from كَسَبَ "to acquire" is formed إِكْتَسَبَ "to acquire for oneself". Sometimes it has a reciprocal meaning e.g. خَصَمَ "to strive", إِخْتَصَمَ "to strive with one another".

Vocabulary.

قَسَمَ to divide.

قِسْمٌ division, part.

قَرُبَ VIII. to approach (with مِن).

إِذَا see! behold!

عَدَدٌ number.

لَمَسَ VIII. to beseech (مِن someone).

عَفْوٌ excuse, pardon.

لَفَتَ VIII. to apply to.

حَامِلٌ a porter, bearer.

كِتَابٌ book, letter.

ضَرَبَ to strike, VIII. to be excited.

خَاطِرٌ plur. خَوَاطِرُ feeling.

سَمَاعٌ hearing.

خَبَرَ VIII. to be experienced.

خَلَطَ VIII. to be mingled.

مِثْلٌ plur. أَمْثَالٌ likeness.

كَثِيرًا (adv.), much, very.

فَطَرَ to cleave, rend.

ضَرِمَ to inflame.

شَرَحَ VII. (literally "to be widened" of the breast) to rejoice.

بَسَطَ VII. (literally "to extend itself"), to be pleased.

كَرُمَ V. with عَلَى to do a favour, to be generous to.

اَلْآنَ now.

نَظَرَ to look. VIII. to expect.

مُكَافَأَةٌ reward.

عَمَلٌ deed.

جَلَدَ to lash, flog.

سَوْطٌ a lash.

عَرَفَ { VIII. to confess (something بِ).

حَقِيقَةٌ truth.

قَدَمٌ foot.

رَجَفَ { I. and VIII. to tremble.

خَوْفٌ fear.

جَمِيعٌ whole, all.

شَابٌّ youth.

قُرْبٌ { nearness, neighbourhood.

جَيْشٌ army.

نَصَرَ { I. to help, VIII. to conquer (literally, "to be helped" by God).

فَكَرَ VIII. to think.

حَرَمَ VIII. to honour.

شَغَلَ { VIII. to busy oneself, work.

زَحَمَ { VIII. to crowd; verbal noun, "a crowd".

Exercise 39.

إِنْقَسَمَ ٱلْفَوَارِسُ قِسْمَيْنِ — لَمَّا ٱقْتَرَبُوا مِنْهُمْ إِذَا هُمْ قَلِيلُو
ٱلْعَدَدِ — ٱلْتَمِسْ مِنْكَ ٱلْعَفْوَ — إِلْتَفَتَ ٱلْأَمِيرُ إِلَى حَامِلِ
ٱلْكِتَابِ — إِضْطَرَبَ خَاطِرُ ٱلْوَلَدِ عِنْدَ سَمَاعِ ذٰلِكَ —
إِجْتَمَعَ ٱلْأَمِيرُ وَٱبْنُهُ فِي خَيْمَةٍ — إِخْتَلَطَتْ (Intro. § 9)
بِأَمْثَالِ هٰؤُلَاءِ ٱلْبَدْوِ كَثِيرًا فِي جِهَاتِ ٱلشَّامِ — تَقَدَّمَ إِلَيْهِ
رَجُلٌ مِنْهُمْ كَثِيرُ ٱلْاخْتِبَارِ — يَنْفَطِرُ قَلْبُهُ — إِضْطَرَمَ قَلْبِي
— تَكَلَّمْ مِنْ عِنْدِكَ وَلَا تَقْتَرِبْ إِلَيْنَا — جَلَسَ ٱلْمَلِكُ مَعَ

أَخِيهِ يَتَحَدَّثَانِ بِٱنْشِرَاحٍ — إِنْبَسَطْتُ غَايَةَ ٱلْأَنْبِسَاطِ أَنْ

تَكَرَّمْتُمْ عَلَيَّ — وَالِدُنَا ٱلْآنَ فِي ٱنْتِظَارِنَا — لَمْ أَنْتَظِرْ مُكَافَأَةً

هٰذَا ٱلْعَمَلِ — أَمَرَ ٱلْحَاكِمُ أَنْ يُجْلَدَ هٰؤُلَاءِ ٱلرِّجَالُ بِٱلسَّوْطِ

حَتَّى يَعْتَرِفُوا بِٱلْحَقِيقَةِ — تَقَدَّمَ وَاحِدٌ مِنْهُمْ وَقَبَّلَ قَدَمَيِ

ٱلْأَمِيرِ وَهُوَ يَرْتَجِفُ خَوْفًا ("from fear" adv. accus.) — فِي

ٱلصَّبَاحِ ٱجْتَمَعَ ٱلْجَمِيعُ فِي غُرْفَةِ ٱلشَّابِّ —

Exercise 40.

Do not approach us. — We assembled in the neighbourhood of the city. — Do not expect us. — We were exceedingly pleased that you were present with us. — The army of the Sultan was defeated (broken) and the Christians conquered. — Think not that thou hast conquered us. — Truly, he is honoured by all. — We are diligent and work much. — There was a great crowd in the streets. — The feelings of the men were stirred as they heard that. — Work and do not play, o children!

Twenty-second Lesson.

(أَلدَّرْسُ ٱلثَّانِي وَٱلْعِشْرُونَ)

IX. Form.

1. Through the meeting of two similar letters at the end of this form certain assimilations and contractions take place in the conjugation. The rules for these are given in Lesson 23.

Conjugation of إِحْمَرَّ "to be or become red".

Perfect.

	Sing.	Dual	Plur.
3. p. m.	إِحْمَرَّ	إِحْمَرَّا	إِحْمَرُّوا
3. „ f.	إِحْمَرَّتْ	إِحْمَرَّتَا	إِحْمَرَرْنَ
2. „ m.	إِحْمَرَرْتَ	إِحْمَرَرْتُمَا	إِحْمَرَرْتُمْ
2. „ f.	إِحْمَرَرْتِ		إِحْمَرَرْتُنَّ
1. „	إِحْمَرَرْتُ		إِحْمَرَرْنَا

Imperfect.	Indic.	Subj.	Juss.
Sing. 3. p. m.	يَحْمَرُّ	يَحْمَرَّ	يَحْمَرِرْ
„ 3. „ f.	تَحْمَرُّ	تَحْمَرَّ	تَحْمَرِرْ
„ 2. „ m.	تَحْمَرُّ	تَحْمَرَّ	تَحْمَرِرْ
„ 2. „ f.	تَحْمَرِّينَ	تَحْمَرِّي	تَحْمَرِّي
„ 1. „	أَحْمَرُّ	أَحْمَرَّ	أَحْمَرِرْ
Dual 3. „ m.	يَحْمَرَّانِ	يَحْمَرَّا	يَحْمَرَّا
„ 3. „ f.	تَحْمَرَّانِ	تَحْمَرَّا	تَحْمَرَّا
„ 2. „	تَحْمَرَّانِ	تَحْمَرَّا	تَحْمَرَّا
Plur. 3. „ m.	يَحْمَرُّونَ	يَحْمَرُّوا	يَحْمَرُّوا
„ 3. „ f.	يَحْمَرِرْنَ	يَحْمَرِرْنَ	يَحْمَرِرْنَ

	Imperfect. Indic.	Subj.	Juss.
Plur. 2. „ m.	تَحْمَرُّونَ	تَحْمَرُّوا	تَحْمَرُّوا
„ 2. „ f.	تَحْمَرِرْنَ	تَحْمَرِرْنَ	تَحْمَرِرْنَ
„ 1. „	نَحْمَرُّ	نَحْمَرَّ	نَحْمَرِرْ

Imperative.

Sing. 2. m. إِحْمَرِرْ Dual. 2. إِحْمَرَّا Plur. 2. m. إِحْمَرُّوا

„ 2. f. إِحْمَرِّي „ 2. f. إِحْمَرِرْنَ

Part. Active مُحْمَرٌّ

Part. Passive not used.

Verbal noun إِحْمِرَارٌ. Passive not in use.

2. The IX. form is used only for Colours and Defects (for the corresponding adjectives see Less. 10, 2), e.g.

إِسْوَدَّ to be or become black.

إِصْفَرَّ „ „ „ „ yellow, pale.

إِبْيَضَّ „ „ „ „ white.

إِحْمَرَّ „ „ „ „ red.

إِخْضَرَّ „ „ „ „ green.

إِعْوَجَّ „ „ „ „ crooked.

The very rare form XI. إِفْعَالَّ is according to some a stronger, according to others a weaker form of IX. e.g. إِحْمَارَّ "to be or become red".

X. Form.

3. Conjugation of إِسْتَحْسَنَ "to esteem beautiful":

Perfect	Imperfect Indic.	Subj.	Juss.
إِسْتَحْسَنَ	يَسْتَحْسِنُ	يَسْتَحْسِنَ	يَسْتَحْسِنْ
إِسْتَحْسَنْتَ	تَسْتَحْسِنُ	تَسْتَحْسِنَ	تَسْتَحْسِنْ
إِسْتَحْسَنَتْ	تَسْتَحْسِنُ	تَسْتَحْسِنَ	تَسْتَحْسِنْ
إِسْتَحْسَنْتِ	تَسْتَحْسِنِينَ	تَسْتَحْسِنِي	تَسْتَحْسِنِي
إِسْتَحْسَنْتُ	أَسْتَحْسِنُ	أَسْتَحْسِنَ	أَسْتَحْسِنْ
etc.	etc.	etc.	etc.

Imperative

إِسْتَحْسِنْ — Part. Active مُسْتَحْسِنٌ

إِسْتَحْسِنِي etc. — Part. Passive مُسْتَحْسَنٌ

Verbal noun إِسْتِحْسَانٌ

Passive, Perf. أُسْتُحْسِنَ Imperf. Indic. يُسْتَحْسَنُ

4. The X. form:

a) Is originally the Reflexive of IV. e.g. أَسْلَمَ "to give up" إِسْتَسْلَمَ "to give oneself up".

b) Denotes "to desire or ask for oneself" e.g. غَفَرَ "to pardon" إِسْتَغْفَرَ "to ask pardon".

c) Denotes "to esteem or think" e.g. حَسُنَ "to be beautiful" إِسْتَحْسَنَ "to think beautiful" قَبُحَ "to be disgraceful" إِسْتَقْبَحَ "to esteem (something) disgraceful, wrong".

d) Often has a Causative meaning, e.g. حَلَفَ "to swear", إِسْتَحْلَفَ "to make to swear"

Vocabulary

دُنْيَا world.	مَرْجٌ, plur. مُرُوجٌ meadow.
بَشَرَ X. to rejoice.	كَبُرَ to be big, X. to esteem great, important.
حَرَمَ X. to esteem forbidden.	وَاقِعَةٌ event.
رَأْيٌ opinion.	خَدَمَ to serve X. to take into ones service.
فَهِمَ X. to enquire.	حُكُومَةٌ government.
قَبِلَ X. to receive.	عَمِلَ X. to use.
	قَلَمٌ reed, pen.
مُسْتَقْبَلٌ future.	صَعْبٌ hard, difficult.
إِنْ شَاءَ ٱللهُ if God will.	خَبُرَ X. to enquire.

Exercise 41.

لَمَّا نَظَرَ ٱلْمَلِكُ ذٰلِكَ ٱسْوَدَّتِ ٱلدُّنْيَا فِي وَجْهِهِ
— يَا وَلَدُ لِمَا (لِمَ Lesson 9, 6) ٱصْفَرَرْتَ — نَظَرْنَا ٱلابْنَةَ
تَحْمَرُّ — نَظَرْتُ ٱحْمِرَارَ ٱلابْنَةِ — نَظَرُوا مِنْ بُعْدٍ فَوَارِسَ
فَٱسْتَبْشَرُوا — تَعْلَمُ أَنَّ هٰؤُلَاءِ ٱلْبَدْوَ لَا يَسْتَحْرِمُونَ عَمَلًا
— هَلْ تَسْتَحْسِنُونَ مَا فَعَلْنَا — لَمْ يَسْتَحْسِنِ ٱلْجَمِيعُ
هٰذَا ٱلرَّأْيَ — جَلَسَ يَسْتَفْهِمُ مِنْ ذٰلِكَ ٱلْفَارِسِ عَنْ حَقِيقَةِ

الأَمْرِ — اِسْتَقْبِلْنَا بِلُطْفٍ عَظِيمٍ — نَتَقَابَلُ فِي ٱلْمُسْتَقْبَلِ إِنْ
شَاءَ ٱللّٰهُ — أَسْتَغْفِرُ ٱللّٰهَ — اِخْضَرَّتِ ٱلْمُرُوجُ — لَمْ يَسْتَكْبِرِ
ٱلْوَاقِعَةَ — اِسْتَقْبَلَنَا ٱلسُّلْطَانُ ٱسْتِقْبَالًا عَظِيمًا (Less. 12, 5) —

Exercise 42.

Do not esteem this event important. — O girl, why hast thou become red? — I saw the men become pale (white). — Do you think right (beautiful) what he has done? — No, we think it disgraceful. — The plants have become green. — I have taken this slave into service. — He is taken into service by the government. — They have received this foreigner well (a great receiving). — Do you use this pen? — No, we do not use it, its use is difficult. — Do you think it right that I should take this man into service? — I think it wrong. — Enquire concerning (عَنْ) this matter. — He went out to the reception of the vezir.

Twenty-third Lesson.

(اَلدَّرْسُ ٱلثَّالِثُ وَٱلْعِشْرُونَ)

Classification of Verbs.

1. Verbs are divided by Arabian grammarians into:

a) Sound (فِعْلٌ سَالِمٌ).

b) Not sound (فِعْلٌ غَيْرُ سَالِمٍ).

These latter are again divided into:

I. فِعْلٌ صَحِيحٌ i.e. the Correct verb comprising (a) فِعْلٌ مُضَاعَفٌ "Doubled verb" i.e. the verb in which the 2nd and 3rd radicals are the same (b) فِعْلٌ مَهْمُوزٌ

"Hamzated verb" i.e. the verb in which one radical is a hamza.

II. فِعْلٌ مُعْتَلٌّ the "Weak" verb in which one of the radicals is a wāw or a yā.

Note. The terms سَالِمٌ and صَحِيحٌ are often used as identical. In this case the doubled verbs and hamzated verbs are regarded as Sound. The terms Regular and Irregular are sometimes used loosely for Sound and Not sound. This use should be avoided as all these verbs follow certain laws, though they suffer some changes of form due to the laws of contraction and assimilation.

Doubled Verbs.

2. The following rules govern the conjugation of verbs whose 2nd and 3rd radicals are the same letter:

I. These two identical radicals are written as one with tashdīd (or as the Arab grammarians say إِدْغَامٌ "assimilation" takes place):

a) When the 1st and 3rd radicals have vowels (are مُتَحَرِّكٌ "vowelled"), in which case the 2nd radical loses its vowel, e.g. دَلَّ from دَلَلَ; دَلَّتْ from دَلَلَتْ; دُلَّ from دُلِلَ (Pass. Perf.); دَلَّا from دَلَلَا (Dual Perf.); دَالَّ from دَالَلَ (III. form); دَالٌّ from دَالِلٌ (Part. Act.).

Exception: The Pass. Perf. of III. is دُولِلَ.

b) If the first radical is vowelless (سَاكِنٌ) and the 3rd radical has a vowel, in which case the 2nd radical gives up its vowel to the 1st, e.g. يَدُلُّ from يَدْلُلُ.

II. When the 3rd radical is vowelless, the 2nd retains its vowel and contraction (إِدْغَامٌ) does not take place, e.g. 2. Perf. Sing. Masc. Perf. دَلَلْتَ; Juss. يَدْلُلْ Imper. أُدْلُلْ.

Note 1. Doubled verbs of the فَعِلَ and فَعُلَ form are thus only distinguished from those of the فَعَلَ form in the uncontracted forms, e.g. مَلَّ (= مَلِلَ) forms in 2nd Sing. Masc. Perf. مَلِلْتَ.

Note 2. In the Jussive mood and in the 2nd Sing. Masc. Imperative contracted forms occur very often. In these cases, to prevent two vowelless letters coming together (Intro. § 13, 3) at the end, the doubled letter takes a vowel (either fatha or kasra, or damma when the Imperf. has damma), e.g.

Jussive: يَدُلَّ, يَدُلِّ and يَدُلُّ beside يَدْلُلْ.

Imperative: دُلَّ beside اُدْلُلْ.

The other forms of the Imper. are formed either from اُدْلُلْ as اُدْلُلِى, اُدْلُلَا, اُدْلُلُوا or from دُلَّ as دُلِّى دُلَّا دُلُّوا but always اُدْلُلْنَ.

III. When the 2nd radical is separated from the 3rd by a long vowel, no contraction can take place, e.g. Part. Pass. مَدْلُولٌ; Verbal noun of IV. إِدْلَالٌ.

3. Conjugation of دَلَّ "to show":

Perfect.

Sing. 3. m.	دَلَّ	Dual.	دَلَّا	Plur.	دَلُّوا
„ 3. f.	دَلَّتْ	„	دَلَّتَا	„	دَلَلْنَ
„ 2. m.	دَلَلْتَ	„	دَلَلْتُمَا	„	دَلَلْتُمْ
„ 2. f.	دَلَلْتِ			„	دَلَلْتُنَّ
„ 1.	دَلَلْتُ			„	دَلَلْنَا

Imperfect Indic.	Subj.	Juss.
يَدُلُّ	يَدُلَّ	يَدْلُلْ, also يَدُلَّ or يَدُلِّ
تَدُلُّ	تَدُلَّ	تَدْلُلْ or يَدُلُّ

Imperfect Indic.	Subj.	Juss.
تَدُلُّ	تَدُلَّ	تَدْلُلْ
تَدُلِّينَ	تَدُلِّي	تَدُلِّي
أَدُلُّ	أَدُلَّ	أَدْلُلْ
يَدُلَّانِ	يَدُلَّا	يَدُلَّا
تَدُلَّانِ	تَدُلَّا	تَدُلَّا
تَدُلَّانِ	تَدُلَّا	تَدُلَّا
يَدُلُّونَ	يَدُلُّوا	يَدُلُّوا
يَدْلُلْنَ	يَدْلُلْنَ	يَدْلُلْنَ
تَدُلُّونَ	تَدُلُّوا	تَدُلُّوا
تَدْلُلْنَ	تَدْلُلْنَ	تَدْلُلْنَ
نَدُلُّ	نَدُلَّ	نَدْلُلْ

Imperative.

أُدْلُلْ or دُلَّ دُلِّ دُلُّ

أُدْلُلِي or دُلِّي

أُدْلُلَا or دُلَّا

أُدْلُلُوا or دُلُّوا

أُدْلُلْنَ

Part. Active دَالٌّ Part. Passive مَدْلُولٌ

Passive.

Perf.	Imperf. Indic.	Juss.
دُلَّ	يُدَلُّ	يُدْلَلْ
دُلَّتْ	تُدَلُّ	تُدْلَلْ
دُلِلْتَ	تُدَلُّ	تُدْلَلْ
دُلِلْتِ	تُدَلِّينَ	تُدَلِّي
دُلِلْتُ	أُدَلُّ	أُدْلَلْ
etc.	etc.	etc.

Derived Forms.

	Perf.	Imperf.	Imper.	Part. Act.	Part. Pass.
II.	دَلَّلَ	يُدَلِّلُ	دَلِّلْ	مُدَلِّلٌ	تَدْلِيلٌ
III.	دَالَّ	يُدَالُّ	دَالِلْ	مُدَالٌّ	دِلَالٌ
(Passive	دُولِلَ	يُدَالُّ)			
IV.	أَدَلَّ	يُدِلُّ	أَدْلِلْ	مُدِلٌّ	إِدْلَالٌ
V.	تَدَلَّلَ	يَتَدَلَّلُ	تَدَلَّلْ	مُتَدَلِّلٌ	تَدَلُّلٌ
VI.	تَدَالَّ	يَتَدَالُّ	تَدَالَلْ	مُتَدَالٌّ	تَدَالٌّ
VII.	إِنْدَلَّ	يَنْدَلُّ	إِنْدَلِلْ	مُنْدَلٌّ	إِنْدِلَالٌ
VIII.	إِمْتَدَّ	يَمْتَدُّ	إِمْتَدِدْ	مُمْتَدٌّ	إِمْتِدَادٌ

(The VIII. form of مَدَّ "to stretch out" is given here, because in the VIII. form of دَلَّ there is assimilation = إِدَّلَّ (see Less. 21, 4, b.)

	Perf.	Imperf.	Imper.	Part. Act.	Part. Pass.
IX.	Seldom occurs.				
X.	إِسْتَدَلَّ	يَسْتَدِلُّ	إِسْتَدْلِلْ	مُسْتَدِلٌّ	إِسْتِدْلَالٌ

Vocabulary.

ثُمَّ then, thereupon.

مَدَّ (u) to stretch out, IV. to help, VIII. to extend.

سِمَاطٌ tablecloth.

كَ as (with genitive).

عَادَةٌ custom.

عَرَبٌ Bedouin.

قَصَّ (u) to narrate ("to" عَلَى).

قِصَّةٌ, حِكَايَةٌ narrative, story, history.

ضَمَّ (u) to collect, VII. to join (with مَعَ).

عَدَّ (u) to count IV. to prepare, X. to prepare oneself.

رَفِيقٌ, pl. رُفَقَاءُ companion.

رَحِيلٌ journey, start.

خَيْلٌ, pl. خُيُولٌ horses.

قَرَّ (i) to be settled.

قَرَارٌ determination.

وَجَهَ V. to go.

حَدٌّ, pl. حُدُودٌ boundary.

عَمٌّ uncle (on the father's side).

أَهْلٌ people.

حَرَبَ III. to make war.

فَرَنْسَوِيٌّ, pl. فَرَنْسَوِيَّةٌ Frenchman.

هَمَّ (i) to determine (with بِ).

اَلْقَاهِرَةُ Cairo.

ضَرَّ (u) to injure, VIII. to compel.

ظَنَّ (u) to think, believe, esteem.

دَهْرٌ time, fate.

صَفَا to be cheerful.

حَبَّ IV. to love.

رَحِبٌ extensive.

رَعِيَّةٌ subjects (of a kingdom).

حَلَّ (u) to loosen, VII. to become loose, slack, feeble.

يَدٌ, pl. أَيْدٍ hand.

مُمْكِنٌ possible.

سَرَّ (u) to rejoice.

مَنَعَ VIII. to refuse.

حَثَّ (IV.) to urge (upon عَلَى).

سُرُورٌ joy.

جَدَّ to be new, V. to be renewed.

أَمَلٌ, pl. آمَالٌ hope.

حَسَّ IV. to feel, perceive (with بِ).

بَرْدٌ cold.

وَادٍ valley.

حَفَّ to surround.

شَجَرٌ tree.

تُوتٌ mulberry (collective).

تِينٌ fig (collective).

كَرْمٌ vineyard.

جَنَّ to be mad.

مَجْنُونٌ, pl. مَجَانِينُ mad.

طَالَ (impf. يَطُولُ) to be long.

وَلٰكِنْ but.

عَاقِلٌ, pl. عُقَلَاءُ intelligent.

حَرٌّ heat.

مَرَّ (u) to pass by.

دَرَاهِم (plur. of دِرْهَمٌ "a dirham") money.

دَقَّ (u) to strike, knock, ring.

جَرَسٌ bell.

تَمَّ IV. to complete.

قَلَّ to be little, II. to make little.

شَدَّ to be strong, VIII. to strengthen oneself.

حَقَّ X. to deserve.

رَكِبَ to ride.

Exercise 43.

ثُمَّ مُدَّ ٱلسِّمَاطُ كَعَادَةِ ٱلْعَرَبِ — جَلَسَ ٱلرَّجُلُ يَقُصُّ
حِكَايَتَهُ عَلَيْهِ — رَجَعَ إِلَى مِصرَ لِيَنْضَمَّ مَعَ رُفَقَائِهِ — فِي لَيْلَةِ

ٱسْتِعْدَادِنَا لِلرَّحِيلِ أَعْدَدْنَا ٱلْخُيُولَ وَرَكِبْنَا — قَرَّ ٱلْقَرَارُ
عَلَى ٱلتَّوَجُّهِ إِلَى حُدُودِ مِصْرَ — أَخْبَرَنِي عَمِّي أَنَّ أَهْلَ مِصْرَ
يَسْتَعِدُّونَ لِمُحَارَبَةِ ٱلْفَرَنْسَوِيَّةِ — هَمَمْنَا بِٱلتَّوَجُّهِ إِلَى ٱلْقَاهِرَةِ —
أُضْطُرِرْنَا إِلَى مُخَالَفَتِهِ — ظَنَنْتُ أَنَّ ٱلدَّهْرَ قَدْ صَفَا لَنَا وَلَمْ
أَعْلَمْ بِمَا أَعَدَّ لَنَا ٱلدَّهْرُ — قَصَصْنَا عَلَيْهِ ٱلْقِصَّةَ — عَرَفْتُهُ
مُحِبًّا لِلْعَدْلِ — كَانُوا قَدْ أَعَدُّوا لَهُمْ مَنْزِلًا رَحِبًا — لَمْ تَكُنِ
ٱلرَّعِيَّةُ تُحِبُّهُ — إِنْحَلَّتْ أَيْدِيهِمْ — لَا أَظُنُّكَ تُخَالِفُنِي — هَلْ
تَظُنُّ ذٰلِكَ مُمْكِنًا — خَرَجَ ٱلْأَمِيرُ مَسْرُورًا (adverbial accus.) —
أَحَبَّ ٱلْوَلَدُ ٱلْاِمْتِنَاعَ فَأَلَحَّ عَلَيْهِ ٱلشَّيْخُ — سُرَّ لِذٰلِكَ سُرُورًا
عَظِيمًا — عَرَّفْتُكَ بِأَنْ أَكُونَ مُسْتَعِدًّا لِكُلِّ خِدْمَةٍ — لَمْ تُمِدَّانِي
بِرَأْيِكُمَا — تَجَدَّدَتْ آمَالِي — يَا بِنْتُ هَلْ أَحْسَسْتِ بِٱلْبَرْدِ
— لَمْ أُحْسِسْ بِهِ — هٰذَا ٱلْوَادِي مَحْفُوفٌ بِأَشْجَارِ ٱلتُّوتِ
وَٱلتِّينِ وَٱلْكَرْمِ ٱلْمُمْتَدِّ إِلَى ٱلْبَحْرِ — قِيلَ لِمَجْنُونٍ عُدَّ لَنَا
ٱلْمَجَانِينَ قَالَ هٰذَا يَطُولُ بِي وَلٰكِنْ أَعُدُّ ٱلْعُقَلَاءَ —

Exercise 44.

Have you felt the heat? — Yes, we have felt it. — Hast thou passed by this place? — I did not pass by it, but I will pass by it to-morrow, if God will. — Do you believe that he will appear before the judge? — We do not believe that. — The rich people count their money. — We have prepared ourselves for the journey. — Do you think him a brave man? — I thought him a brave man, but to-day I do not think him so (كَذٰلِكَ). — Thy presence rejoiced us. — We are glad (rejoiced) of it (بِهِ). — Ring the bell. — The boy did not complete his speech, when (فَ) his father entered. — Do not speak much (make little thy speech). — I loved her very much (a strong loving). — He loves her and she loves him. — The heat was too great for us (strengthened itself on us). — This city extends to the sea. — He deserves a great reward.

Twenty-fourth Lesson.

(أَلدَّرْسُ ٱلرَّابِعُ وَٱلْعِشْرُونَ)

The Hamzated Verbs.

(أَلْفِعْلُ ٱلْمَهْمُوزُ)

1. The Hamzated verbs are of three classes according to whether the hamza is the first radical as in أَخَذَ "to take"; or the second as in سَأَلَ "to ask"; or the third as in قَرَأَ "to read".

2. In the conjugation of these verbs the following rules are employed (cf. also Intro. 10):

a) At the beginning of a word the hamza is always written with alif e.g. أَخَذَ, Pass. Perf. أُخِذَ.

b) If it comes at the end of a syllable and has no vowel, it is written with alif after fatḥa, with yā after kasra, with wāw after ḍamma e.g.

يَأْخُذُ (Indic. Imperf. I.); يُؤْخَذُ (Indic. Imperf. Pass. I.); خُبِئْتُ (1. Sing. Perf. Pass. I. of خَبَأَ "to conceal"); قَرَأْتُ

(1. Sing. Perf. I. of قَرَأَ "to read"); مُؤْمِن (Part. Act. IV. of أَمِنَ "to be true, believing").

c) If it has kasra or ḍamma and follows fatḥa it is written with yā or wāw e.g. يَئِسَ "to despair"; بَؤُسَ "to be brave"

Exception. At the end of a word it is written with alif even when it follows fatḥa e.g. يَقْرَأُ (Imperf. Indic I. of قَرَأَ).

d) If it has fatha and follows kasra or ḍamma, it is written with' yā or wāw e.g. يُؤَلِّفُ (Imperf. Indic. II. of أَلِفَ); مُؤَلِّف (Part. Act.); دَنُؤَ (Perf. Act. I.).

e) If it has kasra or ḍamma and follows a vowelless letter, it is written with yā or wāw e.g. يَيْأَسُ or يَيْئِسُ (Imperf. Indic. of يَئِسَ); يَبْؤُسُ (Imperf. Indic. of بَؤُسَ); يُسَائِلُ (Imperf. Indic. III. of سَأَلَ); سَائِلٌ (Part. Act. I.).

f) If it has fatḥa and is followed by the alif that lengthens the vowel, the latter is written with madda (see Intro. § 12.) e.g. آخَذَ (Perf. III. of أَخَذَ); آخِذٌ (Part. Act. I. of the same). If however it has fatḥa and follows an alif that lengthens the vowel, it is written independently e.g. سَاءَلَ (Perf. III. of سَأَلَ).

g) If a hamza is prefixed to the first radical and that radical is a hamza, then two hamzas will come together, in which case alif with madda is written in place of both. The III. form and the IV. form will thus be identical in the Perf. e.g. آمَنَ (IV.) "to believe"; آخَذَ (III.) "to blame"

If the prefixed hamza has kasra or ḍamma, the hamza of the root is changed into the yā or wāw that lengthens the vowel e.g. إِيمَانٌ (Verbal noun of IV.); أُومُلْ (Imper. I. of أَمَلَ); إِيثِرْ (Imper. I. of أَثَرَ); إِيتَثَرَ (Perf. VIII. of أَثَرَ "to quote").

h) The **Verbal Noun** of the II. form takes the form تَفْعِلَةٌ in **verbs of which** the last radical is hamza e.g. تَقْرِئَةٌ (Verbal **noun** II. of قَرَأَ).

3. Peculiar forms of certain special Hamzated verbs:

a) The verbs أَخَذَ "to take", أَمَرَ "to command" and أَكَلَ "to eat" drop the first radical in the Imperative of the I. form e.g. خُذْ "take"; Fem. خُذِي, Dual خُذَا etc. مُرْ "command", كُلْ "eat".

b) The verb سَأَلَ has in the Jussive a regular form يَسْأَلْ (written also يَسْـَٔلْ) and a form يَسَلْ with omission of the hamza. So in the Imperative سَلْ (as well as إِسْأَلْ), Fem. سَلِي etc.

c) The verb أَخَذَ in the VIII. form assimilates the hamza to the following *ta* e.g. إِتَّخَذَ; Imperf. Indic. يَتَّخِذُ.

4. Conjugation of verb, the first radical of which is hamza:

أَلِفَ "to get accustomed to".

Perf.	Imperf. Indic.	Subj.	Juss.
أَلِفَ	يَأْلَفُ	يَأْلَفَ	يَأْلَفْ
أَلِفَتْ	تَأْلَفُ	تَأْلَفَ	تَأْلَفْ
أَلِفْتَ	تَأْلَفُ	تَأْلَفَ	تَأْلَفْ
أَلِفْتِ	تَأْلَفِينَ	تَأْلَفِى	تَأْلَفِى
أَلِفْتُ	آلَفُ	آلَفَ	آلَفْ
etc.	etc.	etc.	etc.

Imperative

إِيلَفْ — Part. Active آلِفٌ

إِيلَفِى etc. — Part. Passive مَأْلُوفٌ

Passive Perf. أُلِفَ Imperf. Indic. يُؤْلَفُ

أَمَلَ "to hope": Imperf. Indic. يَأْمُلُ Imper. أُومُلْ.

أَثَرَ "to quote": Imperf. Indic. يَأْثِرُ Imper. إِيثِرْ.

Derived Forms.

	Perf.	Imperf. Indic.	Imper.	Part. Act.	Verbal Noun.
II.	أَلَّفَ	يُؤَلِّفُ	أَلِّفْ	مُؤَلِّفٌ	تَأْلِيفٌ
III.	آلَفَ	يُوَالِفُ	آلِفْ	مُوَالِفٌ	إِلَافٌ or مُوَالَفَةٌ
IV.	آلَفَ	يُؤْلِفُ	آلِفْ	مُؤْلِفٌ	إِيلَافٌ
V.	تَأَلَّفَ	يَتَأَلَّفُ	تَأَلَّفْ	مُتَأَلِّفٌ	تَأَلُّفٌ

	Perf.	Imperf. Indic.	Imper.	Part. Act.	Verbal Noun.
VI.	تَآلَفَ	يَتَآلَفُ	تَآلَفْ	مُتَآلِفٌ	تَآلُفٌ
VII.	Wanting in all verbs beginning with hamza wāw, yā, rā, lām, nūn.				
VIII.	إِيتَلَفَ	يَأْتَلِفُ	إِيتَلِفْ	مُؤْتَلِفٌ	إِيتِلَافٌ
IX.	Wanting.				
X.	إِسْتَأْلَفَ	يَسْتَأْلِفُ	إِسْتَأْلِفْ	مُسْتَأْلِفٌ	إِسْتِئْلَافٌ

Vocabulary.

ظَهَرَ to appear, IV. to show.

أَنِسَ III. to be friendly with.

أَلِفَ III. to be intimate with.

أَمِنَ to be true, safe, IV. to believe (in religious sense).

مَلَكٌ properly مَلْأَكٌ (plur. مَلَائِكَةٌ) angel.

رَسُولٌ (plur. رُسُلٌ) apostle.

قِيَامَةٌ resurrection.

دِينٌ religion.

يَوْمُ ٱلدِّينِ the day of judgment.

سَفَرَ III. to travel.

أَخَذَ to take, III. to blame, VIII. to take for oneself.

مَالٌ wealth, possessions.

خُبْزٌ bread.

سَائِلٌ beggar.

شَبِعَ to be satisfied.

أَمَلَ to hope, V. to observe (with فِي of thing.

طَعَامٌ food.

طَرِيقَةٌ manner.

بَدَوِيٌّ bedouin (adjective).

حَرَكَةٌ (sound plur.) movement.

مَرِيضٌ sick, ill.

أَثَّرَ to make an impression, V. to be influenced, affected.

حَرَارَةٌ	heat.	قَتْلٌ	killing.
تَأَخَّرَ	(عَنْ) to be late.	مُنَجِّمٌ	astrologer.
دَعْوَةٌ	invitation.	أَجَرَ	IV. to let (for hire).
حَالَةٌ, حَالٌ	condition.	اِسْتَأْجَرَ	to hire.
أَذِنَ	to allow (something بِ or فِي), X. to ask for permission.	أَلْفٌ	thousand.
		قِرْشٌ	(pl. قُرُوشٌ) piastre
أَكَّدَ	to assure, V. to be assured, certain.	أَلَّفَ	to edit.
		حَارِسٌ	(pl. حُرَّاسٌ) watchman.
كَلِمَةٌ	word.	تَأَهَّبَ	to prepare oneself
قَامُوسٌ	dictionary.	مَسِيرٌ	way.
طَلَقَ	IV. to let loose, shoot.	مُضِرٌّ	injurious.
بَارُودٌ	powder, gun.	عَذَرَ	(i) to excuse.
أَهَّلَ	II. to greet.	أَدَّبَ	II. to discipline.
ظَنٌّ	(plur. ظُنُونٌ) thought.	وَاجِبٌ	duty (of عَلَى).
أَمِيرُ ٱلْمُؤْمِنِينَ	Commander of the Faithful, (title of the caliph).	عَدَمٌ	lack.
		أُجْرَةٌ	reward.

Exercise 45.

أَظْهَرَ ٱلشَّيْخُ لِلضَّيْفِ ٱلْمُوَانَسَةَ وَٱلْمُوَالَفَةَ — آمَنْتُ بِٱللّٰهِ وَبِمَلَائِكَتِهِ وَبِرُسُلِهِ وَبِكُتُبِهِ وَبِٱلْيَوْمِ ٱلْآخِرِ (Moslem creed.) —

يَقْتُلُ ٱللِّصُّ ٱلْمُسَافِرَ فِي ٱللَّيْلِ وَيَأْخُذُ مَالَهُ — خُذْ هٰذَا ٱلْخُبْزَ
يَا سَائِلُ لِتَأْكُلَهُ — كُلُوا وَٱشْرَبُوا حَتَّى تَشْبَعُوا — يَا بِنْتُ
مَا تَأْكُلِينَ — سَآخُذُ مِنْ هٰذَا ٱللَّحْمِ — أَمَّلْنَا أَنْ تُشَرِّفُونَا
بِحُضُورِكُمْ عِنْدَنَا — نَظَرْنَاهُمْ يَأْكُلُونَ — أَظُنُّ أَنْ تَكُونُوا لَمْ
تَأْلَفُوا ٱلطَّعَامَ عَلَى ٱلطَّرِيقَةِ ٱلْبَدَوِيَّةِ — نَحْنُ جَمِيعُنَا قَدْ أَلِفْنَا
هٰذِهِ ٱلْعَادَةَ — تَأَمَّلْنَا فِي حَرَكَاتِ ذٰلِكَ ٱلرَّجُلِ — كُنْتُ مَرِيضًا
مِنْ تَأْثِيرِ ٱلْحَرَارَةِ — تَأَخَّرْتُمْ عَنْ وَقْتِ ٱلدَّعْوَةِ — قَصَدْتُ أَنْ
آخُذَهَا مَعِي إِلَى مِصْرَ — تَأَمَّلِ ٱلْآنَ بِحَالَتِي — هَلْ تَأْذَنُ لِي
بِٱلدُّخُولِ عِنْدَكَ — أُؤَكِّدُ لَكَ أَنَّ ٱلْحَالَ كَذٰلِكَ — لَمْ يَأْخُذْ
مَعَهُ أَحَدًا — هٰذِهِ ٱلْكَلِمَةُ مَأْخُوذَةٌ مِنَ ٱلْقَامُوسِ — لَمْ يَتَأَثَّرِ
ٱلْوَزِيرُ مِنْ هٰذَا ٱلْكَلَامِ — أَطْلَقُوا لَهُ ٱلْبَارُودَ تَأْهِيلًا بِهِ
(adv. accus. "in order to") — ٱلشَّيْءُ لَا يُؤَكِّدُ ظُنُونَنَا —
تَقَدَّمَ سَعِيدٌ وَٱسْتَأْذَنَ ٱلْأَمِيرَ فِي ٱلْكَلَامِ فَأَذِنَ لَهُ — أَمَرَ أَمِيرُ
ٱلْمُؤْمِنِينَ بِقَتْلِ ٱلْمُنَجِّمِ — هَلِ ٱسْتَأْجَرْتَ هٰذِهِ ٱلدَّارَ —
نَعَمْ بِأَلْفِ غِرْشٍ — إِنَّ مُؤَلِّفَ هٰذَا ٱلْكِتَابِ رَجُلٌ ذُو عِلْمٍ —
لَا يَأْذَنُ ٱلْحُرَّاسُ لِأَحَدٍ بِٱلدُّخُولِ عَلَيْهِ — تَأَهَّبُوا لِلْمَسِيرِ — لَمْ
نَتَأَكَّدِ ٱلْخَبَرَ —

Exercise 46.

Have you taken the money? — No, we have not taken it, but we will take it now. — Eat and drink until thou art satisfied. — Take the reward of your work. — They both seated themselves to eat. — I think that I am affected by the heat. — He hopes that his father will command us to appear (that we appear). — Excuse us for our lateness. — We came forward to ask permission of the Commander of the Faithful to come in to him, and he allowed us that. — Truly this book is the work (editing) of the sheikh Mohammed. — Do not blame us. — Eat with us. — We discipline the lazy scholars. — The discipline of the lazy scholars is the duty of the teacher. — We do not blame (with us is lack of blaming). — We spoke pleasantly to him (we were friendly with him in speech). — He took (VIII.) a house.

Twenty-fifth Lesson.

(اَلدَّرْسُ ٱلْخَامِسُ وَٱلْعِشْرُونَ)

1. Conjugation of verb the second radical of which is hamza.

سَأَلَ "to ask".

Perf.	Imperf. Indic.	Subj.
سَأَلَ	يَسْأَلُ (also written يَسَلُ)	يَسْأَلَ (يَسَلَ)
سَأَلَتْ	تَسْأَلُ	تَسْأَلَ
سَأَلْتَ	تَسْأَلُ	تَسْأَلَ
سَأَلْتِ	تَسْأَلِينَ	تَسْأَلِى
سَأَلْتُ	أَسْأَلُ	أَسْأَلَ
etc.	etc.	etc.

Jussive.

يَسَلْ or (يَسْـَٔلْ) يَسْأَلْ

تَسَلْ ,, تَسْأَلْ

تَسَلْ ,, تَسْأَلْ

تَسَلِي ,, تَسْأَلِي

أَسَلْ ,, أَسْأَلْ

etc. etc.

Imperative.

سَلْ or (إِسْـَٔلْ also written) إِسْأَلْ

سَلِي ,, (إِسْـَٔلِي ,, ,,) إِسْأَلِي

etc. etc.

Part. Act. سَائِلٌ

Part. Pass. مَسْؤُولٌ (also written مَسْـُٔولٌ or مَسْئُولٌ)

Passive Perf. سُئِلَ, Imperf. Indic. يُسْأَلُ (also written يُسْـَٔلُ).

Example of the form فَعِلَ: كَئِبَ "to be cast down".

Imperf. Indic. يَكْأَبُ (also written يَكْـَٔبُ)

Imper. إِكْأَبْ (,, ,, إِكْـَٔبْ).

Example of the form فَعُلَ: بَؤُسَ "to be brave".

Imperf. Indic. يَبْؤُسُ

Imper. اُبْؤُسْ.

Derived Forms.

	Perf.	Imperf Indic.	Imper.	Part. Act.	Part. Pass.
II.	سَأَّلَ	يُسَئِّلُ	سَئِّلْ	مُسَئِّلٌ	مُسَأَّلٌ
III.	سَاءَلَ	يُسَائِلُ	سَائِلْ	مُسَائِلٌ	مُسَاءَلٌ
IV.	أَسْأَلَ	يُسْئِلُ	أَسْئِلْ	مُسْئِلٌ	مُسْأَلٌ
V.	تَسَأَّلَ	يَتَسَأَّلُ	تَسَأَّلْ	مُتَسَئِّلٌ	مُتَسَأَّلٌ
VI.	تَسَاءَلَ	يَتَسَاءَلُ	تَسَاءَلْ	مُتَسَائِلٌ	مُتَسَاءَلٌ
VII.	إِنْسَأَلَ	يَنْسَئِلُ	إِنْسَئِلْ	مُنْسَئِلٌ	مُنْسَأَلٌ
VIII.	إِلْتَأَمَ	يَلْتَئِمُ	إِلْتَئِمْ	مُلْتَئِمٌ	مُلْتَأَمٌ

(from لَأَمَ "to bind up a wound" as this form of سَأَلَ does not occur).

IX. does **not** occur.

X.	إِسْتَلْأَمَ	يَسْتَلْئِمُ	إِسْتَلْئِمْ	مُسْتَلْئِمٌ	مُسْتَلْأَمٌ

Verbal Noun.

II.	تَسْئِيلٌ	IV.	إِسْآلٌ	VI.	تَسَاؤُلٌ	VIII.	إِلْتِئَامٌ
III.	مُسَاءَلَةٌ	V.	تَسَؤُّلٌ	VII.	إِنْسِئَالٌ	X.	إِسْتِلْآمٌ

2. Example of verb, whose third radical is hamza: قَرَأَ "to read".

Perf.	Imperf. Indic.	Subj.	Juss.
قَرَأَ	يَقْرَأُ	يَقْرَأَ	يَقْرَأْ
قَرَأْتَ	تَقْرَأُ	تَقْرَأَ	تَقْرَأْ

Perf.	Imperf. Indic.	Subj.	Juss.
قَرَأْتَ	تَقْرَأُ	تَقْرَأَ	تَقْرَأْ
قَرَأْتِ	تَقْرَئِينَ	تَقْرَئِي	تَقْرَئِي
قَرَأْتُ	أَقْرَأُ	أَقْرَأَ	أَقْرَأْ
etc.	etc.	etc.	etc.

Imperative

إِقْرَأْ — Part. Active قَارِئٌ

إِقْرَئِي etc. — Part. Passive مَقْرُوءٌ

Pass. Perf. قُرِئَ — Imperf. Indic. يُقْرَأُ

قُرِئْتَ etc.

Conjugation of verbs which take kasra in the Imperf.: هَنَأَ "to be healthy", Imperf. Indic. يَهْنِئُ, Imperative إِهْنِئْ.

Conjugation of verbs of the form فَعِلَ: خَطِئَ "to sin".

Perf.	Imperf. Indic.	Imper.
خَطِئَ	يَخْطَأُ	إِخْطَأْ
خَطِئَتْ	تَخْطَأُ	إِخْطَئِي
خَطِئْتَ	تَخْطَأُ	etc.
خَطِئْتِ	تَخْطَئِينَ	
خَطِئْتُ	أَخْطَأُ	
etc.	etc.	

Conjugation of verbs of the form فَعُلَ: بَطُؤَ "to be slow"

Perf.	Imperf. Indic.	Imper.
بَطُؤَ	يَبْطُؤُ	أُبْطُؤْ
بَطُؤْتُ	تَبْطُؤُ	أُبْطُؤِي
بَطُؤْتَ	تَبْطُؤُ	etc.
etc.	etc.	

Derived Forms.

	Perf.	Imperf. Indic.	Imper.	Part. Act.	Part. Pass.
II.	قَرَّأَ	يُقَرِّئُ	قَرِّئْ	مُقَرِّئٌ	مُقَرَّأٌ
III.	قَارَأَ	يُقَارِئُ	قَارِئْ	مُقَارِئٌ	مُقَارَأٌ
IV.	أَقْرَأَ	يُقْرِئُ	أَقْرِئْ	مُقْرِئٌ	مُقْرَأٌ
V.	تَقَرَّأَ	يَتَقَرَّأُ	تَقَرَّأْ	مُتَقَرِّئٌ	مُتَقَرَّأٌ
VI.	تَقَارَأَ	يَتَقَارَأُ	تَقَارَأْ	مُتَقَارِئٌ	مُتَقَارَأٌ
VII.	إِنْقَرَأَ	يَنْقَرِئُ	إِنْقَرِئْ	مُنْقَرِئٌ	مُنْقَرَأٌ
VIII.	إِقْتَرَأَ	يَقْتَرِئُ	إِقْتَرِئْ	مُقْتَرِئٌ	مُقْتَرَأٌ
IX.	Does not occur.				
X.	إِسْتَقْرَأَ	يَسْتَقْرِئُ	إِسْتَقْرِئْ	مُسْتَقْرِئٌ	مُسْتَقْرَأٌ

Verbal Noun.

II.	تَقْرِئَةٌ	IV.	إِقْرَاءٌ	VI.	تَقَارُؤٌ	VIII.	إِقْتِرَاءٌ
III.	مُقَارَأَةٌ	V.	تَقَرُّؤٌ	VII.	إِنْقِرَاءٌ	X.	إِسْتِقْرَاءٌ

Vocabulary.

وَفِق	II. to help, give success (only of God).	جِدَارٌ	wall.
جرو	V. to dare.	وَتَدٌ	peg.
خَطَبَ	III. to address.	شَقّ	(u) to cleave.
حُلْمٌ	(plur. أَحْلَامٌ) dream.	عَنْ	of, about, concerning.
وَهْمٌ	(plur. أَوْهَامٌ) imagination.	خَيْرٌ	good (noun), better.
عَبَأَ	(pass.) to be regarded.	ثَمَنٌ	price.
كَفَأَ	III. to reward.	فَاكِهَةٌ	(plur. فَوَاكِهُ) fruit.
نَبَأَ	II. and IV. to announce (with accus. of person and بِ of thing).	حَاجَةٌ	need.
		غَفَرَ	(i) to pardon.
		ذَنْبٌ	guilt.
سَفِيرٌ	ambassador.	مَلَأَ	to fill.
لَجَأَ	VIII. to flee.	بِرْمِيلٌ	vat, cask.
سَعِيدٌ	Said (name of man).	تُفَّاحٌ	apples (collective).
هَنِئَ	to be enjoyable (of food), II. to congratulate.	حَالًا	immediately.
		بَدَأَ	VIII. to begin.
رُقَادٌ	sleep.	وُصُولٌ	arrival.
رُجُوعٌ	return.	قَدِمَ	II. to bring, V. to come forward.
فَيْلَسُوفٌ	philosopher.		
صَنَعَ	to make.	نَشَأَ	to grow up, rise, IV. to set up.
حَبَشِيٌّ	Abyssinian.	سَالِمٌ	sound, (adj.).
لَعَلَّ	(with pronominal suffix) perhaps.	مُرُورٌ	passing.

Exercise 47.

أَسَأَلْتُمُوهُمْ عَنْ حَالِهِمْ — سَأَلْنَاهُمْ عَنْهَا — أَسْأَلُ ٱللّٰهَ
أَنْ يُوَفِّقَكُمْ — لَمْ أَكُنْ أَتَجَرَّأُ عَلَى مُخَاطَبَتِهَا — إِنَّ ٱلْأَحْلَامَ
أَوْهَامٌ لَا يُعْبَأُ بِهَا — كَانَ مَقْصُودُنَا أَنْ نُكَافِئَهُ — أَنْبَأَنَا
ٱلسَّفِيرُ بِمُرُورِ ٱلْمَلِكِ — قَدْ عَرَفْنَا أَنَّ ٱلْأَمِيرَ مُلْتَجِئٌ إِلَى
قَبِيلَةٍ مِنَ ٱلْعَرَبِ — وَصَلَتْنَا تَنْبِئَةُ مُرُورِ ٱلْمَلِكِ — سَأَلْتُ
مُحَمَّدًا عَنْ أَوْلَادِهِ — يَسْتَحِقُّ مُكَافَأَةً كَبِيرَةً — يَكُونُ
ٱلْقَارِئُ قَدْ عَرَفَ ذٰلِكَ — سَلْ سَعِيدًا عَنْ رَأْيِهِ — لَمْ يَهْنَأْ
لَهَا طَعَامٌ وَلَا رُقَادٌ — أُهَنِّئُكَ بِرُجُوعِكَ سَالِمًا — نَظَرَ رَجُلٌ
إِلَى فَيْلَسُوفٍ يُؤَنِّبُ شَيْخًا فَقَالَ لَهُ مَا تَصْنَعُ قَالَ أَغْسِلُ حَبَشِيًّا
لَعَلَّهُ يَبْيَضُّ — قَالَ ٱلْجِدَارُ لِلْوَتَدِ لِمَ (Less. 9, 6) تَشُقُّنِي
قَالَ سَلْ مَنْ يَدُقُّنِي — إِسْأَلْ هٰذَا ٱلشَّيْخَ مِنْ أَيْنَ هُوَ —
ٱللّٰهُ يُكَافِئُكَ عَنِّي (for me) بِمَا هُوَ خَيْرٌ لَكَ مِنْ (than) مُكَافَأَتِي
— سُئِلَ عَنْ ثَمَنِ ٱلْفَوَاكِهِ —

Exercise 48.

Read this letter. — I have read it. — This woman seeks (قَصَدَ) me that (لِ) I may read her letter to her. — The people appeared asking (Imperf.) concerning my condition. — Ask me for what you want (ask me thy need). — I ask you to (that you) pardon my guilt. —

Have you filled this cask with apples? — We have filled it. — Fill it immediately. — O girl, read this book. — They began to read (that they read). — I know the beginning (Verbal Noun) of this book. — I have announced to them the arrival of the Emir. — Come forward that I may reward thee. — We bring thee congratulation (Verbal Noun). — We are beginners (Part.) in the Arabic language. — The Sultan set up a school.

Twenty-sixth Lesson.

(اَلدَّرْسُ ٱلسَّادِسُ وَٱلْعِشْرُونَ)

Weak Verbs.

1. The Weak verbs (فِعْلٌ مُعْتَلٌّ), in which one of the radicals is a wāw or a yā are divided into three classes:

A. Assimilated verbs (فِعْلٌ مِثَالٌ) whose first radical is wāw or yā.

B. Hollow verbs (فِعْلٌ أَجْوَفُ) whose second radical is wāw or yā.

C. Defective verbs (فِعْلٌ نَاقِصٌ) whose third radical is wāw or yā.

A. Assimilated Verbs.

I. Verbs whose first radical is و.

2. Verbs whose first radical is wāw have the following peculiarities:

a) Those that take kasra in the Imperf. lose their و in the Imperf. and Imper. e.g. from وَصَلَ "to arrive" Imperf. يَصِلُ Imper. صِلْ. Many also that take fatha in the Imperf. have the same peculiarity e.g.

Perf.		Imperf. Indic.	Imper.
وَضَعَ	"to place, put".	يَضَعُ	ضَعْ
وَسِعَ	"to be wide"	يَسَعُ	سَعْ
وَقَعَ	"to fall".	يَقَعُ	قَعْ
وَهَبَ	"to give".	يَهَبُ	هَبْ

Most verbs of the form فَعَلَ take kasra in the Imperf. (contrary to the rule in Less. 13, 3) e.g.

وَثِقَ	"to trust",	Imperf.	يَثِقُ	Imper.	ثِقْ
وَرِثَ	"to inherit"	"	يَرِثُ	"	رِثْ
وَرِمَ	"to be swollen"	"	يَرِمُ	"	رِمْ

The verbs which take ḍamma or fatha in the Imperf. and preserve their و are rare e.g.: وَجِلَ "to be afraid", Imperf. Indic. يَوْجَلُ, Imper. إِيجَلْ (for إِوْجَلْ see below).

Those which are also Doubled verbs retain their و in the Imperf: e.g. وَدَّ "to love", Imperf. Indic. يَوَدُّ.

Note. In the Imperf. of the Passive the و is retained, even when it is lost in the Active e.g.: وَجَدَ "to find", Imperf. Indic. Act. يَجِدُ, Pass. يُوجَدُ.

b) If the wāw is vowelless and preceded by a kasra it is changed into a yā e.g. إِيجَلْ (for إِوْجَلْ) Imper. from وَجِلَ, so from وَجَدَ the Verbal Noun IV. is إِيجَادٌ (for إِوْجَادٌ).

Vowelless wāw preceded by ḍamma becomes ū e.g. يُوجَدُ (for يُوْجَدُ) cf. Less. 27.

c) In the VIII. form the wāw is assimilated to the following *tā* e.g.

وَصَلَ "to join" VIII. إِتَّصَلَ, Imperf. Indic. يَتَّصِلُ.

II. Verbs whose first radical is ى.

3. These Verbs retain their yā in the Imperfect e.g. يَسِرَ "to be easy", Imperf. Indic. يَيْسِرُ.

يَئِسَ "to despair", " " يَيْأَسُ (see Less. 25).

If the yā is vowelless and follows ḍamma, it is changed into a wāw e.g. يَقِظَ "to be awake", Imperf. Indic. IV. يُوقِظُ (for يُيْقِظُ).

In the VIII. form the yā is assimilated to the following *tā* e.g. يَئِسَ VIII. إِتَّأَسَ.

4. Conjugation of the verb whose first radical is و

وَصَلَ "to arrive, join".

Perf.	Imperf. Indic.	Subj.	Juss.
وَصَلَ	يَصِلُ	يَصِلَ	يَصِلْ
وَصَلَتْ	تَصِلُ	تَصِلَ	تَصِلْ
وَصَلْتَ	تَصِلُ	تَصِلَ	تَصِلْ
وَصَلْتِ	تَصِلِينَ	تَصِلِي	تَصِلِي
وَصَلْتُ	أَصِلُ	أَصِلَ	أَصِلْ
etc.	etc.	etc.	etc.

Imperative

صِلْ Part. Act. وَاصِلٌ

صِلِي etc. Part. Pass. مَوْصُولٌ

Verbal Noun وَصْلٌ or وُصُولٌ or صِلَةٌ

Pass. Perf. وُصِلَ Imperf. Indic. يُوصَلُ

An example of those verbs, which retain their و in the Imperfect is وَجِلَ "to be afraid", Imperf. Indic. يَوْجَلُ Imper. إِيجَلْ.

Derived Forms.

	Perf.	Imperf. Indic.	Imper.	Part. Act.	Part. Pass.
II.	وَصَّلَ	يُوَصِّلُ	وَصِّلْ	مُوَصِّلٌ	مُوَصَّلٌ
III.	وَاصَلَ	يُوَاصِلُ	وَاصِلْ	مُوَاصِلٌ	مُوَاصَلٌ
IV.	أَوْصَلَ	يُوصِلُ	أَوْصِلْ	مُوصِلٌ	مُوصَلٌ
V.	تَوَصَّلَ	يَتَوَصَّلُ	تَوَصَّلْ	مُتَوَصِّلٌ	مُتَوَصَّلٌ
VI.	تَوَاصَلَ	يَتَوَاصَلُ	تَوَاصَلْ	مُتَوَاصِلٌ	مُتَوَاصَلٌ
VII.	إِنْوَصَلَ	يَنْوَصِلُ	إِنْوَصِلْ	مُنْوَصِلٌ	مُنْوَصَلٌ
VIII.	إِتَّصَلَ	يَتَّصِلُ	إِتَّصِلْ	مُتَّصِلٌ	مُتَّصَلٌ
IX.	Does not occur.				
X.	إِسْتَوْصَلَ	يَسْتَوْصِلُ	إِسْتَوْصِلْ	مُسْتَوْصِلٌ	مُسْتَوْصَلٌ

Verbal Noun.

II. تَوْصِيلٌ IV. إِيصَالٌ VI. تَوَاصُلٌ VIII. إِتِّصَالٌ

III. وِصَالٌ or مُوَاصَلَةٌ V. تَوَصُّلٌ VII. إِنْوِصَالٌ X. إِسْتِيصَالٌ

5. Conjugation of the verbs, whose first radical is ى:

يَبِسَ "to be dry".

Perf.	Imperf. Indic.	Subj.	Juss.
يَبِسَ	يَيْبَسُ	يَيْبَسَ	يَيْبَسْ
يَبِسَتْ	تَيْبَسُ	تَيْبَسَ	تَيْبَسْ
يَبِسْتَ	تَيْبَسُ	تَيْبَسَ	تَيْبَسْ
يَبِسْتِ	تَيْبَسِينَ	تَيْبَسِي	تَيْبَسِي
يَبِسْتُ	أَيْبَسُ	أَيْبَسَ	أَيْبَسْ
etc.	etc.	etc.	etc.

Imperative.

إِيبَسْ

إِيبَسِي etc.

Part. Act. يَابِسٌ

Part. Pass. مَيْبُوسٌ

Verbal Noun يَبْسٌ

Pass. Perf. يُبِسَ

Imperf. Indic. يُوبَسُ

Derived Forms.

	Perf.	Imperf. Indic.	Imper.	Part. Act.	Part. Pass.
II.	يَبَّسَ	يُيَبِّسُ	يَبِّسْ	مُيَبِّسٌ	مُيَبَّسٌ
III.	يَابَسَ	يُيَابِسُ	يَابِسْ	مُيَابِسٌ	مُيَابَسٌ
IV.	أَيْبَسَ	يُوبِسُ	أَيْبِسْ	مُوبِسٌ	مُوبَسٌ
V.	تَيَبَّسَ	يَتَيَبَّسُ	تَيَبَّسْ	مُتَيَبِّسٌ	مُتَيَبَّسٌ
VI.	تَيَابَسَ	يَتَيَابَسُ	تَيَابَسْ	مُتَيَابِسٌ	مُتَيَابَسٌ

	Perf.	Imperf. Indic.	Imper.	Part. Act.	Part. Pass.
VII.	إِنْيَبَسَ	يَنْيَبِسُ	إِنْيَبِسْ	مُنْيَبِسٌ	مُنْيَبَسٌ
VIII.	إِتَّبَسَ	يَتَّبِسُ	إِتَّبِسْ	مُتَّبِسٌ	مُتَّبَسٌ
IX.	Does not occur.				
X.	إِسْتَيْبَسَ	يَسْتَيْبِسُ	إِسْتَيْبِسْ	مُسْتَيْبِسٌ	مُسْتَيْبَسٌ

Verbal Noun.

II. تَيْبِيسٌ IV. إِيبَاسٌ VI. تَيَابُسٌ VIII. إِتِّبَاسٌ

III. مُيَابَسَةٌ V. تَيَبُّسٌ VII. إِنْيِبَاسٌ X. إِسْتِيبَاسٌ

Vocabulary.

رَبٌّ Lord (God).

يسر II. to make easy, V. to be made easy, possible.

عسر to be difficult, II. to make difficult.

تَمَّ II. to complete.

وقف to stay, remain, stand still, IV. to refrain from (with عَنْ), I. to learn, ascertain (with عَلَى).

كُرْسِيٌّ seat, throne.

ودع to lay down, to let, allow (only in Imperf. and Imper.).

اَلْإِسْكَنْدَرِيَّةُ Alexandria.

عَنْ قَرِيبٍ shortly.

وجه V. to betake oneself, go.

مُنْذُ since.

زَمَانٌ time.

ضرب VIII. to be disturbed, excited.

سَمْعٌ hearing.

وصل IV. to conduct, bring.

وَجَبَ to be necessary, incumbent (with عَلَى).

غَضَبٌ anger.

جِسْمٌ body.

وَفِقَ	III. to be suitable, to agree to (with عَلَى), VIII. come to an agreement.	حَبِيبٌ	friend, beloved.
		عَجِيبَةٌ	(pl. عَجَائِبُ) marvel.
مَنْزِلٌ	dwelling.	يَقِظَ	to be awake, X. to waken.
اَلَّتِي	who, which (fem.).	جَدَّ فِي ٱلْمَسِيرِ	(properly "to be violent in journeying") to hurry forward.
رِسَالَةٌ	(pl. رَسَائِلُ) message.		
وَرَدَ	(properly of a camel etc. to go down to a watering-place), to arrive.	كَلَمَ	III. to speak to, address.
		بِنَاءً عَلَى	on condition (that).
مُدِيرٌ	director, editor.	إِبْرَاهِيمُ بَاشَا	Ibrahim Pascha.
جَرِيدَةٌ	journal, newspaper.		
وَكَلَ	V. and VIII. to trust, rely.	قَدِمَ	V. to advance.
تَقْوَى	piety, fear of God.	بَرُّ ٱلْأَنَاضُولِ	Asia Minor.
سَرَّاءُ	joy.	سَلَامَةٌ	comfort.
ضَرَّاءُ	harm.	دُبٌّ	bear.
وَعَدَ	to promise (with accus. of person, بِ of thing).	جُبٌّ	cistern.
وَصَفَ	to describe.	حَرَكَ	V. to move (oneself).

Exercise 49.

يَا رَبِّي يَسِّرْ وَلَا تُعَسِّرْ تَمِّمْ بِٱلْخَيْرِ — ٱلْمَأْمُولُ أَنْ تَقِفُوا
عِنْدَنَا فِي ٱلشَّامِ — فَتَّشْنَا عَنْكُمْ وَلَمْ نَجِدْكُمْ — يَا أَيَّتُهَا
ٱلْبِنْتُ ضَعِي هٰذِهِ ٱلْأَشْيَاءَ عَلَى ٱلْكُرْسِيِّ — دَعُوهُ يَقِفُ —

تَعْنِي أَفْعَلُ كَذٰلِكَ — هَلْ تَصِلُونَ إِلَى ٱلْإِسْكَنْدَرِيَّةِ عَنْ قَرِيبٍ — إِنِّي تَوَجَّهْتُ إِلَى ٱلْقَاهِرَةِ — قَدْ وَصَلْتُ مُنْذُ زَمَانٍ — وَقَعَ سَعِيدٌ فِي ٱضْطِرَابٍ عَظِيمٍ مِنْ سَمْعِ ذٰلِكَ ٱلْخَبَرِ — يَا خَادِمُ أَوْصِلِ ٱلسُّفَرَاءَ إِلَى حُضُورِي — يَظْهَرُ أَنَّ ٱبْنَ سَيِّدِكَ لَمْ نَقِفْ لَهُ عَلَى أَثَرٍ — يَجِبُ عَلَيْكُمْ أَنْ تَدْفَعُوا مَالَنَا — ظَنَّ ٱلْوَلَدُ أَنْ يَقَعَ عَلَيْهِ غَضَبُ ٱلْوَزِيرِ — لَا أَعْرِفُ ٱلْأَهِنَّةَ لَا ٱسْمًا وَلَا جِسْمًا (in regard to . . .) فَأَنَا وَاثِقٌ أَنَّهَا تَكُونُ مُوَافِقَةً لِي كَثِيرًا — جَمِيعُ ٱلرَّسَائِلِ ٱلَّتِي تَرِدُ إِلَيْنَا يَجِبُ أَنْ تَكُونَ بِٱسْمِ مُدِيرِ ٱلْجَرِيدَةِ — تَوَكَّلْتُ عَلَى ٱللّٰهِ — عَلَيْكَ بِتَقْوَى ٱللّٰهِ وَٱلِٱتِّكَالِ عَلَيْهِ فِي ٱلسَّرَّاءِ وَٱلضَّرَّاءِ — وَعَدْتُمُونَا بِمُكَافَأَةٍ عَظِيمَةٍ — كَيْفَ أَصِفُ لَكَ يَا حَبِيبِي مَا نَظَرْتُ مِنَ ٱلْعَجَائِبِ — ثِقْ بِٱللّٰهِ وَٱلتَّوْفِيقُ مِنَ ٱللّٰهِ — إِتَّفَقْنَا أَنْ نَتَقَابَلَ غَدًا فِي هٰذَا ٱلْمَحَلِّ — إِسْتَيْقَظْنَا وَجَدْنَا فِي مَسِيرِنَا — لَا يَتَيَسَّرُ لَكَ مُشَاهَدَتُهَا وَمُكَالَمَتُهَا — إِنَّ ٱلْبَابَ ٱلْعَالِيَ لَمْ يُوَافِقْ عَلَى ذٰلِكَ إِلَّا بِنَاءً عَلَى إِيقَافِ إِبْرَاهِيمَ بَاشَا عَنِ ٱلتَّقَدُّمِ إِلَى بَرِّ ٱلْأَنَاضُولِ —

Exercise 50.

You have sought us and not found us. — Hast thou laid these books down on the seat? — I have not yet laid them down, but I will lay them down shortly. — Lay them down immediately. — Let us stay with you. — If God will, you will arrive at (إِلَى) Cairo in (the) comfort. — We have already arrived long ago (since a time). — He fled from the bear, he fell into the cistern. — O girl, do not fall. — O friends, lead us to the sheikh of the tribe. — This dwelling will be very suitable for us. — Stand still and do not move. — The entrance to (عِنْدَ) the Sultan was made possible for us. — It is our duty to bring you to the prince (the bringing you to). — Many marvels are found in Egypt. — I shall describe it to thee in this letter. — Your letter has not reached (وَرَدَ إِلَى) us. — We have fallen into great distress. — God will help (وفق, II) your affairs, for He (فَإِنَّهُ) is the Helper (Part.). — We have agreed that you shall stay with us for a long time (مُدَّةٌ Accus.).

Twenty-seventh Lesson.

(أَلدَّرْسُ ٱلسَّابِعُ وَٱلْعِشْرُونَ)

B. Hollow Verbs.

(فِعْلٌ أَجْوَفُ)

1. Hollow Verbs i.e. those, whose second radical is و or ى observe the following rules:

A. If the و or ى is vowelless and the third radical is also vowelless, then the و or ى is dropped to prevent the meeting of two vowelless letters (Intro. § 13, 3) e.g.

From قَامَ (for قَوَمَ) the Jussive should be يَقُومْ (see below, B, 1), but as the و and م are vowelless, the و is dropped and it becomes يَقُمْ; so Imper. قُمْ.

From بَاعَ (for بَيَعَ) the Jussive is يَبِعْ, the Imper. بِعْ.

From خَافَ (for خَوِفَ) the Jussive is يَخَفْ, the Imper. خَفْ.

If the third radical, by conjugation, receives a vowel, no elision takes place e.g. 2nd Sing. Fem. Juss. تَقُومِي, Plur. Masc. Imper. قُومُوا.

So also the *alif*, when it takes the place of و or ى, is dropped, whenever the third radical is vowelless by conjugation e.g.

From IV. أَقَامَ (for أَقْوَمَ) is formed 2nd Sing. Masc. أَقَمْتَ.

B. If the و or ى is vowelled, the following rules are observed:

1) If the first radical is vowelless, then the vowel of the و or ى is given to it, the و or ى thus becoming vowelless; *aw* is then changed to *a* and *iw* to *i*, e.g.:

From قَامَ (= قَوَمَ) is formed Imperf. Indic يَقُومُ (for يَقْوُمُ).

From بَاعَ (= بَيَعَ). Imperf. Indic. يَبِيعُ (for يَبْيِعُ).

From خَافَ (= خَوِفَ), Imperf. Indic. يَخَافُ (for يَخَوْفُ for يَخْوَفُ).

So also from قَامَ (= قَوَمَ) are formed Perf. IV. أَقَامَ for أَقْوَمَ for أَقْوَمَ); Imperf. Indic. IV. يُقِيمُ (for يُقْوِمُ for يُقْوِمُ); Part. Act. IV. مُقِيمٌ (for مُقْوِمٌ for مُقْوِمٌ); Part. Pass. IV. مُقَامٌ (for مُقْوَمٌ for مُقْوَمٌ).

2) If the first radical is vowelled.

a) Then if the third radical is also vowelled, α) *awa*, *awi*, *awu*, *aya*, *ayi*, *ayu* become *ā*, e.g. 3rd Sing. Perf. I. قَوَمَ becomes قَامَ, خَوِفَ becomes خَافَ, بَيَعَ becomes بَاعَ, طَوُلَ becomes طَالَ, هَيِبَ becomes هَابَ. VII. Form Perf. إِنْقَوَلَ becomes إِنْقَالَ and Imperf. Indic. يَنْقَوِلُ becomes يَنْقَالُ. β) *uwi*, *uyi* become *ī*, e.g. Pass. Perf. I. قُوِلَ becomes قِيلَ, صُيِرَ becomes صِيرَ.

Note. The rules α) and β) apply also to the VIII. form e.g. Perf. VIII. إِحْتَوَجَ becomes إِحْتَاجَ, Imperf. يَحْتَوِجُ becomes يَحْتَاجُ. Perf. إِمْتَيَزَ becomes إِمْتَازَ.

b) If the third radical is vowelless, elision takes place and

α) *awa* becomes *u*, *awi*, *aya*, *ayi* become *i*, e.g. 1st Sing. Perf. قَوَمْتُ becomes قُمْتُ, خَوِفْتُ becomes خِفْتُ, صَيَرْتُ becomes صِرْتُ, هَيِبْتُ becomes هِبْتُ;

β) *uwi* and *uyi* become *i*; e.g. 1st Sing. Perf. Pass. I. قُوِلْتُ becomes قِلْتُ, صُيِرْتُ becomes صِرْتُ.

2. The Verbal Nouns of IV. and X. drop the و and add *ta* after the third radical; e.g.

From أَقَامَ the Verbal Noun is إِقَامَةٌ; from إِسْتَقَامَ, it is إِسْتِقَامَةٌ.

3. In the Participle Active of the I. form the و and the ى are changed into hamza; e.g. قَائِمٌ (for قَاوِمٌ), صَائِرٌ (for صَايِرٌ).

4. In the Participle Passive of the I. form of verbs whose second radical is و one of the two *wāws* is dropped and *ḍamma* is written over the one left; e.g. from قَالَ the Part. Pass. I. is مَقُولٌ (for مَقْوُولٌ).

In the Pass. Part. of verbs whose second radical is ى the ى is dropped and *kasra* is written under the first radical; e.g. from بَاعَ (= بَيَعَ) the Pass. Part. I. is مَبِيعٌ (for مَبْيُوعٌ).

Note 1. A few verbs whose middle radical is و or ى of the form فَعِلَ preserve the و or ى and are conjugated as Sound verbs; e.g

عَوِرَ "to be one-eyed", Imperf. Indic. يَعْوَرُ etc.

Hollow verbs, which denote Colours or Defects, always retain the و or ى in the IX. form; e.g.

إِسْوَدَّ "to be or become black" Imperf. Indic. يَسْوَدُّ.

إِبْيَضَّ "to be or become white" „ „ يَبْيَضُّ.

The و is often retained in the X. form; e.g. إِسْتَصْوَبَ, Imperf. Indic. يَسْتَصْوِبُ.

Note 2. Hollow verbs, which have و or ى as third radical always retain their و e.g.

سَوِيَ "to be worth", Imperf. Indic. يَسْوَى.

Note 3. Those Hollow verbs which have *tā* or *nūn* as third radical assimilate it with a following *tā* or *nūn*; e.g.

From مَاتَ the 1st Sing. Perf. I. is مُتُّ (for مُتْتُ).

From كَانَ the 1st Plur. Perf. I. is كُنَّا (for كُنْنَا).

Conjugation of قام (= قَوَمَ) "to stand":

Perfect.

Sing.	قَامَ	Dual	قَامَا	Plural	قَامُوا
,,	قَامَتْ	,,	قَامَتَا	,,	قُمْنَ
,,	قُمْتَ	,,	قُمْتُمَا	,,	قُمْتُمْ
,,	قُمْتِ			,,	قُمْتُنَّ
,,	قُمْتُ			,,	قُمْنَا

Imperfect.

	Indic.	Subj.	Juss.
Sing. 3. m.	يَقُومُ	يَقُومَ	يَقُمْ
,, 3. f.	تَقُومُ	تَقُومَ	تَقُمْ
,, 2. m.	تَقُومُ	تَقُومَ	تَقُمْ
,, 2. f.	تَقُومِينَ	تَقُومِي	تَقُومِي
,, 1.	أَقُومُ	أَقُومَ	أَقُمْ
Dual 3. m.	يَقُومَانِ	يَقُومَا	يَقُومَا
,, 3. f.	تَقُومَانِ	تَقُومَا	تَقُومَا
,, 2.	تَقُومَانِ	تَقُومَا	تَقُومَا
Plur. 3. m.	يَقُومُونَ	يَقُومُوا	يَقُومُوا
,, 3. f.	يَقُمْنَ	يَقُمْنَ	يَقُمْنَ

	Indic.	Subj.	Juss.
Plur. 2. m.	تَقُومُونَ	تَقُومُوا	تَقُومُوا
„ 2. f.	تَقُمْنَ	تَقُمْنَ	تَقُمْنَ
„ 1.	نَقُومُ	نَقُومَ	نَقُمْ

Imperative

S. 2. m.	قُمْ		
„ 2. f.	قُومِى	Part. Act.	قَائِمٌ
D. 2.	قُومَا	Part. Pass.	مَقُومٌ
Pl. 2. m.	قُومُوا		
„ 2. f.	قُمْنَ		

Passive.

Perf.	Imperf. Indic.	Subj.	Juss.
قِيمَ	يُقَامُ	يُقَامَ	يُقَمْ
قِيمَتْ	تُقَامُ	تُقَامَ	تُقَمْ
قِمْتَ	تُقَامُ	تُقَامَ	تُقَمْ
قِمْتِ	تُقَامِينَ	تُقَامِى	تُقَامِى
قِمْتُ	أُقَامُ	أُقَامَ	أُقَمْ
etc.	etc.	etc.	etc.

Derived Forms.

	Perf.	Imperf. Indic.	Imper.	Part. Act.	Part. Pass
II.	قَوَّمَ	يُقَوِّمُ	قَوِّمْ	مُقَوِّمٌ	مُقَوَّمٌ
III.	قَاوَمَ	يُقَاوِمُ	قَاوِمْ	مُقَاوِمٌ	مُقَاوَمٌ
IV.	أَقَامَ	يُقِيمُ	أَقِمْ	مُقِيمٌ	مُقَامٌ

	Perf.	Imperf. Indic.	Imper.	Part. Act.	Part. Pass.
V.	تَقَوَّمَ	يَتَقَوَّمُ	تَقَوَّمْ	مُتَقَوِّمٌ	مُتَقَوَّمٌ
VI.	تَقَاوَمَ	يَتَقَاوَمُ	تَقَاوَمْ	مُتَقَاوِمٌ	مُتَقَاوَمٌ
VII.	إِنْقَامَ	يَنْقَامُ	إِنْقَمْ	مُنْقَامٌ	مُنْقَامٌ
VIII.	إِقْتَامَ	يَقْتَامُ	إِقْتَمْ	مُقْتَامٌ	مُقْتَامٌ
IX.	إِسْوَدَّ	يَسْوَدُّ	إِسْوَدِدْ	مُسْوَدٌّ	wanting
X.	إِسْتَقَامَ	يَسْتَقِيمُ	إِسْتَقِمْ	مُسْتَقِيمٌ	مُسْتَقَامٌ

Verbal Noun.

II.	تَقْوِيمٌ	V.	تَقَوُّمٌ	VIII.	إِقْتِيَامٌ
III.	مُقَاوَمَةٌ	VI.	تَقَاوُمٌ	IX.	إِسْوِدَادٌ
IV.	إِقَامَةٌ	VII.	إِنْقِيَامٌ	X.	إِسْتِقَامَةٌ

5. Conjugation of the form فَعِلَ.

خَافَ (for خَوِفَ) "to fear"

Perf.	Imperf. Indic.	Subj.	Juss.
خَافَ	يَخَافُ	يَخَافَ	يَخَفْ
خَافَتْ	تَخَافُ	تَخَافَ	تَخَفْ
خِفْتَ	تَخَافُ	تَخَافَ	تَخَفْ
خِفْتِ	تَخَافِينَ	تَخَافِي	تَخَافِي
خِفْتُ	أَخَافُ	أَخَافَ	أَخَفْ
etc.	etc.	etc.	

Imperative

خَفْ	Part. Act. خَائِفْ
خَافِي etc.	Part. Pass. مَخُوفْ

Passive.

Perf.	Imperf. Indic.	Subj.	Juss.
خِيفَ	يُخَافُ	يُخَافَ	يُخَفْ
خِيفَتْ	تُخَافُ	تُخَافَ	تُخَفْ
خِفْتَ etc.	etc.	etc.	etc.

Conjugation of the form فَعُلَ:

طَالَ (for طَوُلَ) "to be long".

Perf.	Imperf. Indic.	Subj.	Juss.	Imper.
طَالَ	يَطُولُ	يَطُولَ	يَطُلْ	طُلْ
طَالَتْ	تَطُولُ	تَطُولَ	تَطُلْ	طُولِي
طُلْتَ etc.	etc	etc.	etc.	etc.

6. Conjugation of verb, whose middle radical is ى:

صَارَ (for صَيَرَ) "to become"

Perfect.

Sing. 3. m.	صَارَ	Dual صَارَا	Plural صَارُوا
,, 3. f.	صَارَتْ	,, صَارَتَا	,, صِرْنَ
,, 2. m.	صِرْتَ	,, صِرْتُمَا	,, صِرْتُمْ
,, 2. f.	صِرْتِ		,, صِرْتُنَّ
,, 1.	صِرْتُ		,, صِرْنَا

Imperfect.

		Indic.	Subj.	Juss.
Sing.	3. m.	يَصِيرُ	يَصِيرَ	يَصِرْ
„	3. f.	تَصِيرُ	تَصِيرَ	تَصِرْ
„	2. m.	تَصِيرُ	تَصِيرَ	تَصِرْ
„	2. f.	تَصِيرِينَ	تَصِيرِى	تَصِيرِى
„	1.	أَصِيرُ	أَصِيرَ	أَصِرْ
Dual	3. m.	يَصِيرَانِ	يَصِيرَا	يَصِيرَا
„	3, f.	تَصِيرَانِ	تَصِيرَا	تَصِيرَا
„	2.	تَصِيرَانِ	تَصِيرَا	تَصِيرَا
Plur.	3. m.	يَصِيرُونَ	يَصِيرُوا	يَصِيرُوا
„	3. f.	يَصِرْنَ	يَصِرْنَ	يَصِرْنَ
„	2. m.	تَصِيرُونَ	تَصِيرُوا	تَصِيرُوا
„	2. f.	تَصِرْنَ	تَصِرْنَ	تَصِرْنَ
„	1.	نَصِيرُ	نَصِيرَ	نَصِرْ

Imperative

صِرْ

صِيرِى

صِيرَا

صِيرُوا

صِرْنَ

Part. Act. صَائِرٌ

Part. Pass. مَصِيرٌ

Passive.

Perf.	Imperf. Indic.	Subj.	Juss.
صِيرَ	يُصَارُ	يُصَارَ	يُصَرْ
صِيرْتَ	تُصَارُ	تُصَارَ	تُصَرْ
صِرْتَ	تُصَارُ	تُصَارَ	تُصَرْ
etc.	etc.	etc.	etc.

Derived Forms.

	Perf.	Imperf. Indic.	Imper.	Part. Act.	Part. Pass.
II.	صَيَّرَ	يُصَيِّرُ	صَيِّرْ	مُصَيِّرٌ	مُصَيَّرٌ
III.	صَايَرَ	يُصَايِرُ	صَايِرْ	مُصَايِرٌ	مُصَايَرٌ
IV.	أَصَارَ	يُصِيرُ	أَصِرْ	مُصِيرٌ	مُصَارٌ
V.	تَصَيَّرَ	يَتَصَيَّرُ	تَصَيَّرْ	مُتَصَيِّرٌ	مُتَصَيَّرٌ
VI.	تَصَايَرَ	يَتَصَايَرُ	تَصَايَرْ	مُتَصَايِرٌ	مُتَصَايَرٌ
VII.	إِنْصَارَ	يَنْصَارُ	إِنْصَرْ	مُنْصَارٌ	مُنْصَارٌ
VIII. (see Less. 21, 4a)	إِصْطَارَ	يَصْطَارُ	إِصْطَرْ	مُصْطَارٌ	مُصْطَارٌ
IX.	إِبْيَضَّ	يَبْيَضُّ	إِبْيَضِضْ	مُبْيَضٌّ	wanting.
X.	إِسْتَصَارَ	يَسْتَصِيرُ	إِسْتَصِرْ	مُسْتَصِيرٌ	مُسْتَصَارٌ

Verbal Noun.

II.	تَصْيِيرٌ	V.	تَصَيُّرٌ	VIII.	إِصْضِيَارٌ
III.	مُصَيرَةٌ	VI.	تَصَايُرٌ	IX.	إِبْيِضَاضٌ
IV.	إِصَارَةٌ	VII.	إِنْصِيَارٌ	X.	إِسْتِصَارَةٌ

Conjugation of the form فَعِلَ:

هَابَ (for هَيِبَ) "to fear".

Perf.	Imperf. Indic.	Subj.	Juss.	Imper.
هَابَ	يَهَابُ	يَهَابَ	يَهَبْ	هَبْ
هَابَتْ	تَهَابُ	تَهَابَ	تَهَبْ	هَابِى
هِبْتَ	تَهَابُ	تَهَابَ	تَهَبْ	etc.
etc.	etc.	etc.	etc.	

Vocabulary.

(The letter in brackets after a Hollow verb indicates the middle radical.)

قَامَ (و) I. to rise, IV. to set, place, stay.

خَافَ (خَوِفَ = و) to fear, II. to terrify.

فَرَّ (i) to flee.

رَاحَ (و) II. to give rest to, X. to rest.

مَاتَ (و) to die.

قَالَ (و) to say, (followed by إِنَّ and the exact words used; not by أَنَّ and indirect speech).

طَالَ (طَوُلَ = و) to be long II. and IV. to make long, lengthen.

بَقَاءٌ survival, life.

صَارَ (ى) to become; (with following Imperf.) to begin.

أَبَدًا (with negative) never.

سَارَ (ى) to go, journey.

سَيْرٌ way, journey.

عَادَ (و) to turn back, IV. to repeat, VIII. to be accustomed.

هَاجِسٌ (plur. هَوَاجِس) suggestion, agitation.

جَعَلَ to make; (with following Imperf.) to begin.

خَالَ (ى) V. to fancy, imagine.

صَابَ (و) IV. to come upon, afflict, X. to approve.

مَصِيبَةٌ misfortune.

طَعْنَةٌ thrust (of a lance).

فِيمَا while.

صَارَ (و) V. to imagine.

قَافِلَةٌ caravan.

غَدَاءٌ lunch.

نَالَ (و = نَوِلَ) to attain, III. to hand over (with double acc.).

بَاتَ (ى Imperf. يَبَاتُ and يَبِيتُ), to spend the night.

رَادَ (و) IV. to wish.

شِمَالٌ left side.

يَمِينٌ right side.

زَارَ (و) to visit.

رِفْقَةٌ company.

حَقٌّ right, truth.

حَقِيقِيٌّ true.

عُمُومِيٌّ public, general.

بَاعَ (ى) to sell.

إِشْتَرَى to buy.

جُنْدٌ (plur. جُنُودٌ) troop, army.

دَاخَ (و) to feel giddy, II. to make giddy.

زَادَ (ى) VIII. to increase.

كِبْرٌ pride.

طَاعَ (و) IV. to obey, X. to be able to (with accus. of the thing).

مَالَ (ى) to incline, bend.

غُرُوبٌ setting (of the sun).

لِسَانٌ tongue.

حَفِظَ to guard.

صَانَ (و) to protect.

خَانَ (و) to betray.

إِنْ, إِذَا if.

هَانَ (و) to be easy, IV. to insult.

طَاقَ (و) IV. to endure, suffer.

خَلَفَ III. to contradict, oppose.

نَقَمَ VIII. to take vengeance on (مِن).

اَلَّذِى who (masc. sing.).

عَانَ (ى) II. to determine, appoint.

عَانَ (و) II., III. and IV. to help.

جُمْعَةٌ Friday.

مَزَادٌ auction.

زَاجَ (و) II. to marry.

خَارَ (ى) VIII. to choose.

جَابَ (و) IV. to answer.

هَابَ (ى = هَيِبَ), to fear.

وَالِدَةٌ mother.

صَادَ (ى) VIII. to hunt.

جَارَ (و) III. to be neighbour to.

مَكَانٌ (plur. أَمَاكِنُ) place.

غَزَالٌ (plur. غِزْلَانٌ) gazelle.

شَاقَ (و) VIII. to yearn.

أَنِيسٌ amiable.

جَوَادٌ steed.

رَصَاصٌ lead.

رَصَاصَةٌ bullet.

دَفَعَ III. to defend.

رَاعَ (و) II. to terrify.

هَدَّ II. to threaten.

ضَابِطٌ officer.

سَاقَ (و) to lead.

شَرَرٌ sparks.

حَاجَ (و) VIII. to need (with إِلَى).

عَاشَ (ى) to live.

أَفَنْدِى sir.

أَفَنْدِينَا sire (used of Sultan or Khedive).

طَابَ (ى) to be good, quiet.

ضَاعَ (ى) IV. to lose.

سُوءٌ evil.

فَادَ (و) IV. to inform, benefit.

طَافَ (و) to go or wander round.

وَالٍ Governor.

صَاحَ (ى) to cry out.

دَامَ (و) to last.

وَاقِعَةٌ battle.

نَحْوَ towards, about.

مَيْلٌ inclination.

لَاقَ (ى) to be worthy, fitting.

زَوْجَةٌ wife.

فَائِدَةٌ advantage.

هُنَالِكَ there.

نَوْمٌ sleep.

غَابَ (ى) to be absent, go away.

بَيْضٌ eggs (collective).

نَامَ (و = نَوِمَ) to sleep.

حُكُومَةٌ government.

حِفْظٌ protection.

طَارَ (ى) to fly.

Exercise 51.

قُمْ يَا وَلَدِى وَدَعْنِى أَجْلِسُ — قِفْ وَلَا تَخَفْ — قُومُوا وَفِرُّوا مِنْ عِنْدِنَا — قُلْ لِى مَنْ أَنْتَ وَمِنْ أَيْنَ أَنْتَ — لَا تَقُلْ مِثْلَ ذٰلِكَ — قَالَ ٱلْحَكِيمُ إِنَّهُ سَيَمُوتُ عَنْ قَرِيبٍ — طَالَ ٱلزَّمَانُ عَلَيْنَا — أَطَالَ (Optative) ٱللّٰهُ بَقَاءَكُمْ — طَوِّلْ إِقَامَتَكَ عِنْدَنَا — هٰذَا لَا يَصِيرُ أَبَدًا — قَدْ سَارَ سَيْرًا سَرِيعًا — عَادَتْ إِلَيْهِ ٱلْهَوَاجِسُ وَجَعَلَ يَتَخَيَّلُ سَيِّدَهُ مُصَابًا بِطَعْنَةٍ وَفِيمَا هُوَ فِى هٰذِهِ ٱلتَّصَوُّرَاتِ وَقَفَتِ ٱلْقَافِلَةُ لِلْغَدَاءِ وَٱلِٱسْتِرَاحَةِ — جَلَسْنَا لِلِٱسْتِرَاحَةِ وَمُنَاوَلَةِ ٱلطَّعَامِ — لَمْ يَبِتْ فِى ٱلْقَرْيَةِ — أَرَدْتُ (Intro. § 9) ٱلسَّفَرَ فِى ٱلصَّبَاحِ — هَلْ أَنْتَ سَائِرٌ شِمَالًا أَوْ يَمِينًا — هَلْ تُرِيدُونَ أَنْ تَزُورُونَا غَدًا — هٰذَا غَايَةُ مُرَادِنَا — يَكُونُ صَاحِبِى قَدْ سَارَ إِلَى مِصْرَ — سِرْ يَابْنِى (= يَا ٱبْنِى) بِرِفْقَةِ هٰذَا ٱلرَّجُلِ — أَتُرِيدُ أَنْ أَقُولَ لَكَ ٱلْحَقَّ — ٱلْمُعْتَادُ فِى تِلْكَ ٱلْبِلَادِ أَنَّهُمْ يُقِيمُونَ فِى كُلِّ بَلْدَةٍ سُوقًا عُمُومِيًّا فَيَبِيعُونَ وَيَشْتَرُونَ فِيهِ — قِيلَ إِنَّ ٱلْجُنُودَ خَوَّفُوا

ٱلْبِلَادَ — يَزْدَادُ (Less. 21, 5, b) ٱلرَّجُلُ كِبَرًا ("as regards" . . .,
(see Less. 42, 2, f) — لَمْ يَكُنْ يَسْتَطِيعُ ٱلتَّقَدُّمَ إِلَى ٱلْمَجْلِسِ —
كَانَتِ ٱلشَّمْسُ قَدْ مَالَتْ إِلَى ٱلْغُرُوبِ — إِحْفَظْ لِسَانَكَ إِنْ
صُنْتَهُ صَانَكَ إِنْ خُنْتَهُ خَانَكَ (Proverb) — قَدْ نَظَرْتُمْ مَا أَصَابَنِي
فِي هٰذَا ٱلْيَوْمِ مِنَ ٱلْإِهَانَةِ (what . . . . of insult = what insult)
وَأَنْتُمْ تَعْلَمُونَ أَنَّ ٱلْإِهَانَةَ لَا تُطَاقُ فَهَلْ تُخَالِفُونَنِي إِذَا أَرَدْتُ
ٱلِٱنْتِقَامَ مِنَ ٱلرَّجُلِ ٱلَّذِي أَهَانَنِي — بِتُّ فِي ٱلْخَيْمَةِ تِلْكَ
ٱللَّيْلَةَ — إِنَّ ٱلتَّاجِرَ قَدْ عَيَّنَ نَهَارَ ٱلْجُمْعَةِ لِلْمَزَادِ ٱلْعُمُومِيِّ —
صَارَ يَخَافُ مِنَ ٱلْمَوْتِ — أَرَادَتِ ٱلِٱمْرَأَةُ أَنْ تُزَوِّجَ ٱبْنَهَا وَٱخْتَارَتْ
لَهُ ٱبْنَةً — لَمْ يُمْكِنْهُ إِجَابَةُ طَلَبِ ٱلْوَزِيرِ — قَاطَعَهَا ٱلْوَلَدُ
بِٱلْكَلَامِ قَائِلًا ٱنْظُرِي يَا وَالِدَتِي إِنِّي قَدْ صِرْتُ رَجُلًا — كَانَ
بَطَلًا عَظِيمًا تَهَابُهُ ("which the lions fear", see Less. 31, 4)
ٱلْأُسُودُ — قَالَ ٱلْوَلَدُ لِوَالِدَتِهِ مُرِينِي وَأَنَا وَلَدُكِ ٱلْمُطِيعُ —
كَانَ سَعِيدٌ يَصْطَادُ (Less. 21, 5, a) فِي جِوَارِ تِلْكَ ٱلْأَمَاكِنِ
مِنْ غِزْلَانِهَا — إِشْتَاقَتْ نَفْسِي إِلَى مُشَاهَدَتِكَ ٱلْأَنِيسَةِ —
أُصِيبَ جَوَادُهُ بِرَصَاصَةٍ — أَرَادَ ٱلدِّفَاعَ وَلَمْ يَسْتَطِعْ ذٰلِكَ —
أَتَظُنُّ أَنَّكَ تُرَوِّعُنِي بِهٰذَا ٱلتَّهْدِيدِ فَمَا أَنَا خَائِفٌ مِنَ ٱلْمَوْتِ

— تَقَدَّمَ ٱلضَّابِطُ لِيَسُوقَهُ إِلَى ٱلسِّجْنِ — أَرَدْتُ أَنْ أُعِيدَ ٱلسُّؤَالَ — يَطِيرُ ٱلشَّرَرُ مِنْ عَيْنَيْهِ — تَحْتَاجُونَ إِلَى طَعَامٍ — يَعِيشُ "as regards"...) أَفْدِينَا — طِبْ نَفْسًا (Optative) يَا عَزِيزِى (see Less. 42, 2, f — لَا تُضِعِ ٱلْوَقْتَ — ظَنَنْتُ أَنَّكَ أُصِبْتَ بِسُوءٍ — لَا يَا سَيِّدِى لَمْ أُصَبْ بِسُوءٍ — فِى ٱلْإِعَادَةِ إِفَادَةٌ (Proverb) — طُفْ فِى ٱلْبِلَادِ تَرْوِيحًا لِلنَّفْسِ (Less. 34, 6) — أَمَرَهُمْ أَنْ يَخْتَارُوا وَالِيًا عَلَيْهِمْ — ٱلْبِلَادُ قَائِمَةٌ عَلَيْنَا — إِسْتَصْوَبْنَا رَأْيَكُمْ — صَاحَ ٱلْفَارِسُ وَقَالَ مَنْ أَنْتَ يَا خَائِنُ فَلَمْ يُجِبْهُ — دَامَتِ ٱلْوَاقِعَةُ نَحْوَ نِصْفِ سَاعَةٍ — أَمَرَ ٱلْوَزِيرُ أَنْ يُطِيعُوا أَوَامِرَهُ — نَظَرْتُ ٱبْنَتِى تَمِيلُ إِلَيْكَ مَيْلًا حَقِيقِيًّا وَنَظَرْتُ أَنَّهَا تَلِيقُ أَنْ تَكُونَ زَوْجَةً لَكَ — خَرَجَ ٱلْوَلَدُ لِمُعَاوَنَتِى — أَسْتَقِيمُ طَوِيلًا فِى مِصْرَ — لَا أَظُنُّ لِى فَائِدَةً بِٱلْإِقَامَةِ هُنَالِكَ — أَفَدْتَنَا إِفَادَةً عَظِيمَةً — غِبْتُ عَنْ حَبِيبِى نَحْوَ سَنَةٍ — لَمْ يَنَامُوا فِى تِلْكَ ٱللَّيْلَةِ —

Exercise 52.

Rise O girl, and let us sit. — We wish to stay in this city half a year. — A great misfortune has come upon us. — You were afflicted by (بِ) a great misfortune. — O woman, go away and do not return. — What have you said? — We said, this is not fitting. — Do not say this. — Dost thou wish O girl, that I say to thee the truth? — It was said, the king had died. — He did not die and will live long. — Truly we yearn to see you (to your seeing). — I wished to visit you, but was not able to (that). — Go O my son, in the protection of God. — The merchant, who lives (Part. of أَقَامَ) in Cairo will visit us. — We wish that God may lengthen your life. — He fancied in (the) sleep that he was flying. — We flew from joy. — Eat and drink and rest. — They handed us the coffee and after the handing of the coffee we rested. — He wished to sell these eggs, but he was not able. — You have made us giddy with your speech. — Did you spend the night in Damascus? — No, we did not spend the night in that city. — The government appointed him governor. — Trust in God and fear not. — The coward (fearing) does not attain the reward. — Repeat your question. — I have already repeated it. — He will approve our opinion. — This stuff (قُمَاشٌ) will not last. -- (The) obedience (Verbal Noun of "obey") is our duty.

Twenty-eighth Lesson.

(أَلدَّرْسُ ٱلثَّامِنُ وَٱلْعِشْرُونَ)

C. Defective Verbs.

(فِعْلٌ نَاقِصٌ)

1. The Defective verbs, which have و or ى as third radical are conjugated according to the following rules:

A. If the و or ى is vowelless:

1. It is dropped, when nothing is added at the end, as in the Jussive and Imper. e.g.

From دَعَا (= دَعَوَ) "to call": Imperf. Indic. يَدْعُو, Juss. يَدْعُ, Imper. أُدْعُ.

From رَمَى (= رَمَيَ) "to throw": Imperf. Indic. يَرْمِي, Juss. يَرْمِ, Imper. إِرْمِ.

From لَقِيَ "to meet": Imperf. Indic. يَلْقَى, Juss. يَلْقَ, Imper. إِلْقَ.

So also in the II. form (and other Derived forms): دَعَّى forms Imperf. Indic. يُدَعِّي, Juss. يُدَعِّ, Imper. دَعِّ.

The elision takes place even when the Personal Pronoun is added as أُدْعُهُ "call him".

2. If there is an addition at the end:

a) *aw* becomes *au; ay* becomes *ai* e.g. 2nd Sing. Masc. Perf. I. of دَعَا is دَعَوْتَ; of رَمَى is رَمَيْتَ.

b) *iw* and *iy* become *ī*; *uw* becomes *ū*; e.g. 2nd Sing. Masc. Perf. I. of رَضِيَ is رَضِيتَ; of لَقِيَ is لَقِيتَ; of سَرُوَ "to be noble" is سَرُوتَ.

B. When the و or ى is vowelled:

1. If the second radical is vowelless, the و or ى is retained; e.g, Verbal Noun (of the form فَعْل) of غَزَا (= غَزَوَ) "to raid": غَزْو; of رَمَى: رَمْى.

2. If the second radical is vowelled, and

a) there is no addition at the end:

α) *awa* and *aya* become *ā*, this *ā* being written with *alif* when it is derived from *awa*, with *ya* when it is derived from *aya*; e.g 3rd Sing. Masc. Perf. I. of دَعَوَ is دَعَا, of رَمَيَ is رَمَى.

β) *iwa* becomes *iya*, *iya* remains; e g. رَضِوَ becomes رَضِيَ; Pass. Perf. I. دُعِوَ becomes دُعِيَ; لَقِيَ remains unchanged. So in Imperf. Subj. I. يَرْمِيَ remains unchanged.

γ) *uwa* remains; e.g. سَرُوَ, Imperf. Subj. يَدْعُوَ, (*uya* does not occur).

δ) *uwu* becomes *ū*; e.g. Imperf. Indic. I. يَدْعُوُ becomes يَدْعُو, (*uyu* does not occur).

ε) *iyu* becomes *ī*; e.g. Imperf. Indic. I. يَرْمِيُ becomes يَرْمِي, (*iwu* does not occur).

ζ) *awu* and *ayu* become *ā* (always written with ى); e.g. Imperf. Indic. I. يَرْضَوُ becomes يَرْضَى; يَرْعَيُ (from رَعَى "to pasture") becomes يَرْعَى.

The same changes take place in the Derived forms, where however ى always takes the place of و (see below rule 3); e.g. III. دَاعَيَ becomes دَاعَى; Imperf. Indic. يُدَاعِيُ becomes يُدَاعِي etc.

b) There is an addition at the end:

α) The و and ى are retained when immediately followed by an *alif* (in the Dual); e.g.:

3rd Dual, Perf. I. دَعَوَا, سَرُوَا, رَمَيَا, لَقِيَا.

3rd „ Imperf. يَدْعُوَانِ, يَسْرُوَانِ, يَرْمِيَانِ, يَلْقَيَانِ.

2nd „ Imper. اُدْعُوَا etc.

In these cases however *iwā* becomes *iyā*; e.g. رَضِوَا becomes رَضِيَا; Pass. Perf. دُعِوَا becomes دُعِيَا.

β) If *ū* or *ī* follows (as in Plur. Masc.; 2nd Sing. Fem. Imperf. and Imper.) the following changes take place:

awū and *ayū* become *au*, and so *awūna* and *ayūna* become *auna*: e.g. 3rd Plur. Masc. Perf. I. دَعَوُوا becomes دَعَوْا; 3rd Plur. Masc. Imperf. I. رَضَيُوا becomes رَضَوْا and يَرْضَوُونَ becomes يَرْضَوْنَ; يَلْقَيُونَ becomes يَلْقَوْنَ.

iwa, iya* and *uwa* become *ā and so *uwūna* and *iyūna* become *ana*; e.g. 3rd Plur. Masc. I. رَضُوُوا becomes رَضَوا; لَقِيُوا becomes لَقُوا; سَرُوُوا becomes سَرُوا; 3rd Plur. Masc. Imperf. يَرْمِيُونَ becomes يَرْمُونَ.

uwī and *iyī* become *ī*; e.g. 2nd Sing. Fem. Imperf. I. تَدْعُوِينَ becomes تَدْعِينَ; Juss. تَدْعُوِى becomes تَدْعِى and تَرْمِيِينَ becomes تَرْمِينَ.

ayī becomes *ai*; e.g. 2nd Sing. Fem. Imperf. I. تَلْقَيِينَ becomes تَلْقَيْنَ; Imper. Sing. Fem. إِلْقَيِى becomes إِلْقَىْ.

γ) When the ت of the 3rd Sing. Fem. Perf. is added, the *awa* and *aya* are first changed to *ā* and then, to prevent the meeting of two vowelless letters (see Intro. § 13, 3), the *alif* is dropped; e.g. دَعَوَتْ becomes دَعَاتْ then دَعَتْ; رَمَيَتْ becomes رَمَاتْ then رَمَتْ.

The Fem. of the Dual is (irregularly) formed by analogy from the Sing.: رَمَتَا, دَعَتَا.

The following forms are regular; رَضِيَتْ (since *iwa* changes into *iya*), Dual رَضِيَتَا; لَقِيَتْ لَقِيَتَا; سَرُوَتْ سَرُوَتَا.

Note. The ى as sign of *ā* at the end of a word is changed into ا whenever a suffix is added; e.g. رَمَاهُ "he threw him", (see Intro. § 6, Note 3).

2. In the Active Participle *iwun* and *iyun* are changed into *in*; e.g. دَاعِوٌ becomes دَاعٍ; رَامِيٌ becomes رَامٍ. These forms are declined like قَاضٍ in Less. 6, 3.

Singular.

Nom. Gen. دَاعٍ; with the Article اَلدَّاعِى (*iwu* and *iyu* become *ī*).

Accus. دَاعِيًا; with the Article اَلدَّاعِيَ (*iya* remains).

Dual.

Nom. دَاعِيَانِ; Gen. Accus. دَاعِيَيْنِ.

Plural.

Nom. دَاعُونَ (*uwu* and *iyu* become *u*), Gen. Accus. دَاعِينَ (*iwi* and *iyi* become *ī*).

In the Part. Pass. of verbs whose third radical is و the two *waws* are contracted into one written with *tashdīd*; e.g. مَدْعُووٌ becomes مَدْعُوٌّ.

In the verbs whose third radical is ى, the و of the form is changed to ى and this is assimilated to the ى of the root; e.g. مَرْمُوىٌ becomes مَرْمِيٌّ.

3. The verbs whose third radical is و are treated in the Derived forms as if their third radical were ى; e.g. from دَعَا: II. دَعَّى, III. دَاعَى, IV. أَدْعَى etc.

4. a) The Verbal Noun of the II. form is of the pattern تَفْعِلَةٌ (as in the case of the verbs whose third radical is *hamza*. See Less. 24, 2, h); e.g. تَسْمِيَةٌ from سَمَّى.

b) In the Verbal Noun of the III. form the *ya* is changed into *alif*; e.g. مُلَاقَاةٌ from لَاقَى "to meet".

c) In the Verbal Nouns of of the IV., VII., VIII. and X. forms, where the third radical follows an *alif*, the *yā* is changed into a *hamza* (without bearer); e.g.

IV. from أَلْقَى "to throw": إِلْقَاءٌ.

VII. from إِنْقَضَى "to come to an end": إِنْقِضَاءٌ.

VIII. from إِشْتَرَى "to buy": إِشْتِرَاءٌ.

X. from إِسْتَعْفَى "to ask forgiveness, abdicate": إِسْتِعْفَاءٌ.

d) In the Verbal Noun of the V. and VI. forms *uyun* becomes *in*, *uyu* becomes *ī*; e.g. تَلَقٍّ becomes تَلَقٍ; تَلَاقٍ becomes تَلَاقٍ; with the Article اَلتَّلَقِّي and اَلتَّلَاقِي.

5. In the Participles of the Derived forms *iyun* becomes *in*; *iyu* becomes *ī*; *ayun* becomes *an* (written with ى); *ayu* becomes *a* (also written with ى); e.g. مُلَقِّيٌ becomes مُلَقٍّ, with the Article اَلْمُلَقِّي; Part. Pass II. مُلَقَّيٌ becomes مُلَقًّى, with the Article اَلْمُلَقَّى etc.

Conjugation of the Defective Verbs.

a) Conjugation of the verbs whose third radical is و:

α) Of the form فَعَلَ:

دَعَا "to call".

Perfect.

Singular		Dual		Plural	
3. masc.	دَعَا	3. masc.	دَعَوَا	3. masc.	دَعَوْا
3. fem.	دَعَتْ	3. fem.	دَعَتَا	3. fem.	دَعَوْنَ
2. masc.	دَعَوْتَ	2.	دَعَوْتُمَا	2. masc.	دَعَوْتُمْ
2. fem.	دَعَوْتِ			2. fem.	دَعَوْتُنَّ
1.	دَعَوْتُ			1.	دَعَوْنَا

Imperfect.

	Indic.	Subj.	Juss.
Sing. 3. masc.	يَدْعُو	يَدْعُوَ	يَدْعُ
,, 3. fem.	تَدْعُو	تَدْعُوَ	تَدْعُ
,, 2. masc.	تَدْعُو	تَدْعُوَ	تَدْعُ
,, 2. fem.	تَدْعِينَ	تَدْعِي	تَدْعِي
,, 1.	أَدْعُو	أَدْعُوَ	أَدْعُ

	Indic.	Subj.	Juss.
Dual 3. masc.	يَدْعُوَانِ	يَدْعُوَا	يَدْعُوَا
„ 3. fem.	تَدْعُوَانِ	تَدْعُوَا	تَدْعُوَا
„ 2.	تَدْعُوَانِ	تَدْعُوَا	تَدْعُوَا
Plur. 3. masc.	يَدْعُونَ	يَدْعُوا	يَدْعُوا
„ 3. fem.	يَدْعُونَ	يَدْعُونَ	يَدْعُونَ
„ 2. masc.	تَدْعُونَ	تَدْعُوا	تَدْعُوا
„ 2. fem.	تَدْعُونَ	تَدْعُونَ	تَدْعُونَ
„ 1.	نَدْعُو	نَدْعُوَ	نَدْعُ

Imperative.

Sing. masc. أُدْعُ Dual أُدْعُوَا Plur. masc. أُدْعُوا

„ fem. أُدْعِي „ fem. أُدْعُونَ

Part. Active.

Sing. nom. masc. دَاعٍ (with Art. أَلدَّاعِي) fem. دَاعِيَةٌ

„ accus. „ دَاعِيًا („ „ أَلدَّاعِيَ) „ دَاعِيَةً

„ gen. „ دَاعٍ („ „ أَلدَّاعِي) „ دَاعِيَةٍ .

Dual. nom. masc. دَاعِيَانِ fem. دَاعِيَتَانِ

„ gen. accus. „ دَاعِيَيْنِ „ دَاعِيَتَيْنِ

Plur. nom. „ دَاعُونَ „ دَاعِيَاتٌ

„ gen. accus. „ دَاعِينَ „ دَاعِيَاتٍ

Part. Pass. مَدْعُوٌّ.

Passive Perfect.

			Dual		Plur.	
Sing. 3. masc.	دُعِيَ	Dual	دُعِيَا	Plur.	دُعُوا
,, 3. fem.	دُعِيَتْ	,,	دُعِيَتَا	,,	دُعِينَ
,, 2. masc.	دُعِيتَ	,,	دُعِيتُمَا	,,	دُعِيتُمْ
,, 2. fem.	دُعِيتِ			,,	دُعِيتُنَّ
,, 1.	دُعِيتُ			,,	دُعِينَا

	Pass. Imperf. Indic.	Subj.	Juss.
Sing. 3. masc.	يُدْعَى	يُدْعَى	يُدْعَ
,, 3. fem.	تُدْعَى	تُدْعَى	تُدْعَ
,, 2. masc.	تُدْعَى	تُدْعَى	تُدْعَ
,, 2. fem.	تُدْعَيْنَ	تُدْعَيْ	تُدْعَيْ
,, 1.	أُدْعَى	أُدْعَى	أُدْعَ
Dual 3. masc.	يُدْعَيَانِ	يُدْعَيَا	يُدْعَيَا
,, 3. fem.	تُدْعَيَانِ	تُدْعَيَا	تُدْعَيَا
,, 2.	تُدْعَيَانِ	تُدْعَيَا	تُدْعَيَا
Plur. 3. masc.	يُدْعَوْنَ	يُدْعَوْا	يُدْعَوْا
,, 3. fem.	يُدْعَيْنَ	يُدْعَيْنَ	يُدْعَيْنَ
,, 2. masc.	تُدْعَوْنَ	تُدْعَوْا	تُدْعَوْا
,, 2. fem.	تُدْعَيْنَ	تُدْعَيْنَ	تُدْعَيْنَ
,, 1.	نُدْعَى	نُدْعَى	نُدْعَ

β) Of the form فَعِلَ:

رَضِيَ "to be pleased".

Perfect.

			Dual		Plur.	
Sing. 3. masc.	رَضِيَ		رَضِيَا		رَضُوا	
„ 3. fem.	رَضِيَتْ	„	رَضِيَتَا	„	رَضِينَ	
„ 2. masc.	رَضِيتَ	„	رَضِيتُمَا	„	رَضِيتُمْ	
„ 2. fem.	رَضِيتِ			„	رَضِيتُنَّ	
„ 1.	رَضِيتُ			„	رَضِينَا	

	Imperf. Indic.	Subj.	Juss.
Sing. 3. masc.	يَرْضَى	يَرْضَى	يَرْضَ
„ 3. fem.	تَرْضَى	تَرْضَى	تَرْضَ
„ 2. masc.	تَرْضَى	تَرْضَى	تَرْضَ
„ 2. fem.	تَرْضَيْنَ	تَرْضَيْ	تَرْضَيْ
„ 1.	أَرْضَى	أَرْضَى	أَرْضَ
Dual 3. masc.	يَرْضَيَانِ	يَرْضَيَا	يَرْضَيَا
„ 3. fem.	تَرْضَيَانِ	تَرْضَيَا	تَرْضَيَا
„ 2.	تَرْضَيَانِ	تَرْضَيَا	تَرْضَيَا
Plur. 3. masc.	يَرْضَوْنَ	يَرْضَوْا	يَرْضَوْا
„ 3. fem.	يَرْضَيْنَ	يَرْضَيْنَ	يَرْضَيْنَ
„ 2. masc.	تَرْضَوْنَ	تَرْضَوْا	تَرْضَوْا
„ 2. fem.	تَرْضَيْنَ	تَرْضَيْنَ	تَرْضَيْنَ
„ 1.	نَرْضَى	نَرْضَى	نَرْضَ

Imperative.

Sing. masc.	إِرْضَ	Dual	إِرْضَيَا	Plur. masc.	إِرْضَوْا
„ fem.	إِرْضَيْ			„ fem.	إِرْضَيْنَ

Part. Act. رَاضٍ (أَلرَّاضِي) Part. Pass. مَرْضِيٌّ

Pass. Perf. رُضِيَ (s. دُعِيَ) Imperf. Indic. يُرْضَى (s. يُدْعَى).

Verbs of the form فَعُلَ (as سَرُوَ "to be noble") are rare.

b) Conjugation of verbs whose third radical is ى:

α) Of the form فَعَلَ;

رَمَى "to throw".

Perfect.

Sing.	3. masc.	رَمَى	Dual	رَمَيَا	Plur.	رَمَوْا
„	3. fem.	رَمَتْ	„	رَمَتَا	„	رَمَيْنَ
„	2. masc.	رَمَيْتَ	„	رَمَيْتُمَا	„	رَمَيْتُمْ
„	2. fem.	رَمَيْتِ			„	رَمَيْتُنَّ
„	1.	رَمَيْتُ			„	رَمَيْنَا

		Imperf. Indic.	Subj.	Juss.
Sing.	3. masc.	يَرْمِي	يَرْمِيَ	يَرْمِ
„	3. fem.	تَرْمِي	تَرْمِيَ	تَرْمِ
„	2. masc.	تَرْمِي	تَرْمِيَ	تَرْمِ
„	2. fem.	تَرْمِينَ	تَرْمِي	تَرْمِي
„	1.	أَرْمِي	أَرْمِيَ	أَرْمِ

	Imperf. Indic.	Subj.	Juss.
Dual 3. masc.	يَرْمِيَانِ	يَرْمِيَا	يَرْمِيَا
„ 3. fem.	تَرْمِيَانِ	تَرْمِيَا	تَرْمِيَا
„ 2.	تَرْمِيَانِ	تَرْمِيَا	تَرْمِيَا
Plur. 3. masc.	يَرْمُونَ	يَرْمُوا	يَرْمُوا
„ 3. fem.	يَرْمِينَ	يَرْمِينَ	يَرْمِينَ
„ 2. masc.	تَرْمُونَ	تَرْمُوا	تَرْمُوا
„ 2. fem.	تَرْمِينَ	تَرْمِينَ	تَرْمِينَ
„ 1.	نَرْمِي	نَرْمِيَ	نَرْمِ

Imperative.

Sing. masc. إِرْمِ	Dual	إِرْمِيَا	Plur. masc.	إِرْمُوا
„ fem. إِرْمِي			„ fem.	إِرْمِينَ

Verbal Noun رَمْيٌ

Part. Act. رَامٍ (اَلرَّامِي) Part. Pass. مَرْمِيٌّ

Pass. Perf. رُمِيَ Imperf. Indic. يُرْمَى

رُمِيتَ تُرْمَى

etc. = دُعِيَ etc. = يُدْعَى

3) Of the form فَعِلَ:

لَقِيَ "to meet" is conjugated like رَضِيَ.

c) **Conjugation of the Derived forms of all Defective verbs.**

	Perf.	Imperf. Indic.	Imper.	Part. Act.	Part. Pass.
II.	لَقَّى	يُلَقِّى	لَقِّ	مُلَقٍّ	مُلَقًّى
III.	لَاقَى	يُلَاقِى	لَاقِ	مُلَاقٍ	مُلَاقًى
IV.	أَلْقَى	يُلْقِى	أَلْقِ	مُلْقٍ	مُلْقًى
V.	تَلَقَّى	يَتَلَقَّى	تَلَقَّ	مُتَلَقٍّ	مُتَلَقًّى
VI.	تَلَاقَى	يَتَلَاقَى	تَلَاقَ	مُتَلَاقٍ	مُتَلَاقًى
VII.	إِنْلَقَى	يَنْلَقِى	إِنْلَقِ	مُنْلَقٍ	مُنْلَقًى
VIII.	إِلْتَقَى	يَلْتَقِى	إِلْتَقِ	مُلْتَقٍ	مُلْتَقًى
IX.	Wanting.				
X.	إِسْتَلْقَى	يَسْتَلْقِى	إِسْتَلْقِ	مُسْتَلْقٍ	مُسْتَلْقًى

Verbal Noun.

II.	تَلْقِيَةٌ	V.	تَلَقٍّ	VIII.	إِلْتِقَاءٌ
III.	مُلَاقَاةٌ and لِقَاءٌ	VI.	تَلَاقٍ	IX.	Wanting.
IV.	إِلْقَاءٌ	VII.	إِنْلِقَاءٌ	X.	إِسْتِلْقَاءٌ

Vocabulary.

بَكَى to weep. — جَرَى to run, flow, happen.

رَجَا to hope for. — نَسِيَ to forget.

عُذْرٌ excuse. — مَشَى to go, V. to wander about.

تَلَا to read. — عَجَلٌ (also عَجَلَةٌ) haste.

غَدَا V. to breakfast.

مَدَّ to stretch, V. to stretch oneself, rest.

عَشَا V. to take supper

عُشْب (plur. أَعْشَاب) herbs.

رَوِيَ I. and VIII. to be watered (sufficiently).

مَطَر rain.

زَمَن = زَمَان. time.

شِتَاء winter.

بَقِيَ to remain.

سَائِر rest, remainder.

فَصْل (pl. فُصُول) section, season.

رَعَى to pasture, feed on.

لَقِيَ I. and III. to meet, IV. to throw, VI. and VIII. to meet one another.

عَطَا IV. to give (with two accus.), VI. to give one another.

غَنَم sheep (collective).

بَدَل substitution, بَدَلاً مِنْ instead of.

حِنْطَة wheat.

تِبْن straw.

زُبْدَة butter.

تَمْر dried dates (collective).

تِبْغ tobacco.

مَضَى to go away, Part. Act. past, last.

دَعَا to call, to pray for, wish (with لِ of person, بِ of thing) VIII. (see Less. 21, 5, b) to claim, X. to summon.

بَائِع (plur. بَاعَة) seller.

حَرُمَ VIII. to honour.

دَنَا to approach.

حَيَّا (literally "to let live") to greet.

حَنَا to bend.

شَكَا to complain of (عَنْ).

قِصَر brevity.

كَفَى to be sufficient for, III. to reward.

جَمْع collecting.

قَدْر amount.

مَال wealth

بَلَا III. to be anxious (about بِ).

كَثُرَ to be much.
شَرَابٌ drink, wine.
هَمَّ to intend, determine (بِ).
نَدَا III. to call.
حِجْرٌ lap.
عَزِيَ II. to comfort.
قَسَا III. to endure.
خَلَقَ to create.
وَصَى II. to recommend, charge.
وَصِيَّةٌ recommendation, exhortation, charge.
فِرَارٌ flight.
نَجَا to escape.
رَهْنٌ pledge.
قَضَى to decide, VIII. to require, seek.
عَفَا to pardon (with عَنْ).
خَفِيَ to be hidden, concealed (from عَلَى).
بَنَى to build.
سَقَى to water.
جَوٌّ firmament.
صَفَا to be pure, clear.
شَيْطَانٌ Satan.

أَنَى V. to be slow.
اَلرَّحْمٰنُ the merciful = God.
غَشِيَ to cover.
غُشِيَ عَلَيْهِ he fainted.
غُشِيَ عَلَيْهَا she fainted.
مَشْيَةٌ walk, gait.
مَنَى V. to wish.
مَرْءٌ man.
دَرَكَ IV. to overtake, reach.
فَتَاةٌ girl.
رَبَا II. to train up.
قَضَاءٌ decision.
وَفَى V. (Pass.) to die.
فَضْلٌ goodness.
هَدَى to guide.
صِرَاطٌ path.
مُسْتَقِيمٌ straight.
بُكَاءٌ weeping.
مُرٌّ bitter.
رَضِيَ (بِ) to be content.
سَمَا II. to name, call.
شَهْرٌ month.

Exercise 53.

لِمَاذَا تَبْكِي يَا وَلَدِي — لَا تَبْكِ — رَجَوْنَا مِنْكُمْ ٱلْعُذْرَ — هَلْ تَلَوْتُمْ مَا جَرَى لَنَا — نَتْلُوهُ عَنْ قَرِيبٍ — نَسِيتُ ٱسْمَ ٱلْاِبْنَةِ وَلٰكِنْ لَمْ أَنْسَ ٱسْمَ أَبِيهَا — إِمْشِي بِٱلْعَجَلِ — تَغَدَّ تَمَدَّ (تَمَدَّدْ for) تَعَشَّ تَمَشَّ (Proverb) — إِنَّ هٰذِهِ ٱلْأَشْجَارَ وَٱلْأَعْشَابَ تَرْتَوِي مِنْ مَاءِ ٱلْمَطَرِ فِي زَمَنِ ٱلشِّتَاءِ وَتَبْقَى عَائِشَةً فِي سَائِرِ ٱلْفُصُولِ فَتَرْعَاهَا ٱلْجِمَالُ — كَانَ يَجِبُ أَنْ نَلْتَقِيَ بِهِ — ٱلرَّاعِي يُعْطِي ٱلْفَلَّاحَ غَنَمًا وَيَأْخُذُ بَدَلًا مِنْهَا حِنْطَةً أَوْ تِبْنًا أَوْ يُعْطِي زُبْدَةً وَيَأْخُذُ بَدَلًا مِنْهَا تَمْرًا أَوْ تِبْغًا — مَضَى سَعِيدٌ بَيْنَ ٱلْخِيَامِ مُدَّعِيًا أَنَّهُ أَحَدُ ٱلْبَاعَةِ — حَضَرْنَا لِمُلَاقَاةِ ٱلْبَاشَا — أَمَرَ رِجَالَهُ أَنْ يَبْقَوْا بَعِيدِينَ وَتَقَدَّمَ ٱحْتِرَامًا لِلْبَاشَا (Less. 34, 6) فَلَمَّا دَنَا مِنْهُ حَيَّاهُ حَانِيًا رَأْسَهُ — شَكَا ٱلْمَلِكُ مِنْ قِصَرِ ٱلْمُدَّةِ وَقَالَ لَا تَكْفِي لِجَمْعِ هٰذَا ٱلْقَدْرِ مِنَ ٱلْمَالِ — ثِقْ بِٱللّٰهِ وَلَا تُبَالِ — يَكْثُرُ تَعَاطِي ٱلشَّرَابِ — هَمَّ أَنْ يَتَنَحَّى مِنْ بَيْنِ (Less. 44, 5) ٱلنَّاسِ — أَرَادَ سَعِيدٌ أَنْ يُلْقِيَ بِنَفْسِهِ عَلَيْهِ وَنَادَاهُ — نَادَتِ ٱلْوَالِدَةُ ٱبْنَتَهَا إِلَى حِجْرِهَا لِتُعَزِّيَهُ — كَتَبَ لِي صَاحِبِي مَكْتُوبَ تَعْزِيَةٍ — وَرَدَ عَلَيْهِ كِتَابٌ مِنَ ٱلسُّلْطَانِ يَسْتَدْعِيهِ (Less. 31, 4) إِلَيْهِ — كَفَانِي مَا قَاسَيْتُ

قَبْلًا — إِنَّ ٱلرِّجَالَ خُلِقُوا لِمُقَاسَاةِ ٱلْحُرُوبِ — أُوصِيكَ وَصِيَّةً وَاحِدَةً وَأَرْجُو أَنْ لَا تَنْسَاهَا — أَرَادَ ٱلْفِرَارَ وَلَمْ يَنْجُ — سَتَبْقَى أَنْتَ عِنْدَنَا رَهْنًا (as pledge) حَتَّى يَقْضِيَ ٱللّٰهُ بَيْنَنَا — إِنَّهُمَا حَبِيبَانِ يَدْعُو كُلٌّ مِنْهُمَا ٱلْآخَرَ أَخًا — يَتَلَقَّاكَ ٱلْأَصْدِقَاءُ بِسَلَامٍ — دَنَوْا مِنَ ٱلْمَدِينَةِ — قَدْ عَفَوْنَا عَنْكَ — عَفَا (Optative: “May God pardon”, Less. 30, 6) ٱللّٰهُ عَنَّا وَعَنْكُمْ — لَا يَخْفَى عَلَيْنَا أَنَّ هٰذَا ٱلْجَامِعَ قَدْ بُنِيَ بِأَمْرِ ٱلسُّلْطَانِ — تِلْكَ ٱلْبَسَاتِينُ تُسْقَى مِنْ مَاءِ ٱلنَّهْرِ — قَدْ سَارَ سَعِيدٌ يَتَمَشَّى فِي تِلْكَ ٱلْبَسَاتِينِ — كَانَ ٱلْجَوُّ صَافِيًا — ٱلْجَوُّ صَافٍ — ٱلْعَجَلَةُ مِنَ ٱلشَّيْطَانِ وَٱلتَّأَنِّي مِنَ ٱلرَّحْمٰنِ (Proverb) — هٰذَا ٱلْوَلَدُ يُدْعَى مُحَمَّدًا — وَقَعَتِ ٱلْاِبْنَةُ مَغْشِيًّا عَلَيْهَا — قَضَوْنَا ذٰلِكَ ٱلنَّهَارَ بِٱلِٱنْشِرَاحِ — إِنَّ ٱلْجَوَادَ يَمْشِي بِٱلْفَارِسِ مَشْيَةَ ٱلْعَرُوسِ (Less. 34, 7) — لَا تُبَالِ بِهٰؤُلَاءِ ٱلْخَائِنِينَ — لَمَّا أَرَدْتُ سُؤَالَهُ عَنْ ذٰلِكَ لَمْ يُجِبْنِي بِشَيْءٍ فَٱقْتَضَيْتُ أَثَرَهُ — دَعَتْ لَهُ بِٱلسَّلَامَةِ — مَا كُلُّ مَا يَتَمَنَّى ٱلْمَرْءُ يُدْرِكُهُ (Proverb) — تَمَنَّ مَا تُرِيدُ — إِنَّ ٱلْفَتَاةَ مُرَبَّاةٌ أَحْسَنَ تَرْبِيَةٍ — مَا لَا تَقْدِرُ عَلَى قَضَائِهِ فَٱلْزَمْ مَنْ يَقْضِيهِ

بَقِيَتِ ٱلْأُمُورُ عَلَى — نُعِيتُ يَوْمًا إِلَى ٱلْأَمِيرِ — (Proverb)
حَالِهَا — قَدْ تُوُفِّيَ ٱلْأَمِيرُ — ٱلْمَرْجُوُّ مِنْ فَضْلِكَ أَنْ تُخْبِرَنَا
عَنْ حَالِكُمْ — إِهْدِنَا ٱلصِّرَاطَ ٱلْمُسْتَقِيمَ (Koran, Sura 1.) —

Exercise 54.

When was this house built? — It was (بُنِيَ) built (Part. Pass.) in the time (عَهْدُ) of the last Sultan. — Why did you weep O girls? — We beg your pardon (we hope from you the excuse). — I have read your letter. — Do not forget what I have said to thee O boy! — I have not forgotten it O my master. — Go slowly (with بِ slowness). — When will the time of our meeting be? — We shall give you what we ought (is necessary for us). — You have not given us our due (right). — Remain with us. — I heard a crier (Part. Act. III. of نَدَا) crying (he cries) in the market with a loud voice. — The girl wept bitterly (a bitter weeping). — We fell fainting. — What you wanted did not happen. — What you have said is sufficient for me. — Whither art thou going? — Wast thou content with what I said to thee? — I met a dog in the street. — What (how) is this called in Arabic? — I went from the house to meet them (to their meeting). — Do not be anxious about this man. — Spare me (make me remain II). — Hast thou watered the horses? — We have already breakfasted and, if God will, we shall shortly take supper. — Truly, the merchants buy and sell in the market. — Buy what is necessary for us. — If God will, we shall meet in the current (flowing) month.

Twenty-ninth Lesson.

(أَلدَّرْسُ ٱلتَّاسِعُ وَٱلْعِشْرُونَ)

Doubly weak Verb.

1. The most usual of the doubly weak **verbs** are of the following three classes:

A. Those in which one radical is **hamza,** while another is a weak letter.

B. Those in which two **radicals** are weak letters.

C. Those in which all three radicals are hamzas or weak letters.

A.

2. Verbs in which one radical is **hamza** and another a weak letter.

1) Those in which the first radical is hamza, the second و or ى; e.g.: آبَ "to return".

Perf.	Imperf. Indic.		Juss.
آبَ	يَؤُوبُ	(also written يَؤُبُ)	يَؤُبْ
آبَتْ	تَؤُوبُ		تَؤُبْ
أُبْتَ etc.	تَؤُوبُ etc.		تَؤُبْ etc.

Imper.

أُبْ	Part. Active	آئِبٌ
أُوبِي	Pass. Perf.	إِيبَ.

So too the rarer verbs:

آفَ (for أَوِفَ) "to injure".

آلَ (for أَوِلَ) "to come, return".

آدَ (for أَيِدَ) "to be strong". II. أَيَّدَ "to strengthen".

2) Those in which the first radical is hamza, the third و or ى; e.g. أَتَى "to come".

Perf.	Imperf. Indic.	Subj.	Juss.
أَتَى	يَأْتِي	يَأْتِيَ	يَأْتِ
أَتَتْ	تَأْتِي	تَأْتِيَ	تَأْتِ
أَتَيْتَ etc.	تَأْتِي etc.	تَأْتِيَ etc.	تَأْتِ etc.

Imper. { إِيتِ (from إِئْتِ) also shortened تِ
إِيتِي etc. }

Part. Active آتٍ (with Article اَلْآتِي)

Pass. Perf. أُتِيَ Imperf. Indic. يُؤْتَى.

Of this verb the IV. form is آتَى "to bring"; Imperf. Indic. يُؤْتِي; Juss. يُؤْتِ; Imper. آتِ; Pass. Perf. أُوتِيَ.

So also أَبَى "to refuse"; Imperf. Indic. يَأْبَى.

أَدَا "to pay"; II. أَدَّى (with same meaning); Verbal Noun تَأْدِيَةٌ.

3) Those in which the second radical is hamza, the first و or ى; e.g. يَئِسَ "to despair"; Imperf. Indic. يَيْأَسُ; Imper. إِيأَسْ etc.

4) Those in which the second radical is hamza, the third و or ى; e.g. رَأَى "to see". (Note that the hamza is dropped in the Imperf. and Imper. and in the IV. form).

Perfect.

			Dual		Plur.
Sing. 3. masc.	رَأَى		رَأَيَا		رَأَوْا
„ 3. fem.	رَأَتْ	„	رَأَتَا	„	رَأَيْنَ
„ 2. masc.	رَأَيْتَ	„	رَأَيْتُمَا	„	رَأَيْتُمْ
„ 2. fem.	رَأَيْتِ			„	رَأَيْتُنَّ
„ 1.	رَأَيْتُ			„	رَأَيْنَا

		Imperfect Indic.	Subj.	Juss.
Sing.	3. masc.	يَرَى	يَرَى	يَرَ
„	3. fem.	تَرَى	تَرَى	تَرَ
„	2. masc.	تَرَى	تَرَى	تَرَ
„	2. fem.	تَرَيْنَ	تَرَيْ	تَرَيْ
„	1.	أَرَى	أَرَى	أَرَ
Dual	3. masc.	يَرَيَانِ	يَرَيَا	يَرَيَا
„	3. fem.	تَرَيَانِ	تَرَيَا	تَرَيَا
„	2.	تَرَيَانِ	تَرَيَا	تَرَيَا
Plur.	3. masc.	يَرَوْنَ	يَرَوْا	يَرَوْا
„	3. fem.	يَرَيْنَ	يَرَيْنَ	يَرَيْنَ
„	2. masc.	تَرَوْنَ	تَرَوْا	تَرَوْا
„	2. fem.	تَرَيْنَ	تَرَيْنَ	تَرَيْنَ
„	1.	نَرَى	نَرَى	نَرَ

Imperative.

Sing.	رَ	Dual	رَيَا	Plur.	رَوْا
„	رَيْ			„	رَيْنَ

Verbal Noun رَأْيٌ

Part. Active رَاءٍ (with Article اَلرَّائِى)

Part. Pass. مَرْئِىٌّ

Pass. Perf. رُئِىَ Imperf. Indic. يُرَى.

When united with a suffix the forms used are رَآهُ "he saw him"; يَرَاهَا "he sees her" etc.

Of the Derived forms the following occur:

III. رَاءَى "to dissemble"; Imperf. Indic. يُرَائِي; Verbal Noun مُرَاءَاةٌ or رِئَاءٌ.

IV. أَرَى "to show"; Imperf. Indic. يُرِي; Juss. يُرِ; Imper. أَرِ; Verbal Noun إِرَاءٌ or إِرَاءَةٌ.

VI. تَرَاءَى "to look at one another".

VIII. إِرْتَأَى "to think".

5) Those in which the third radical is hamza, the first و or ى; e.g. وَطِئَ "to tread"; Imperf. Indic. يَطَأُ etc.

6) Those in which the third radical is hamza, the second و or ى, e.g. سَاءَ (for سَوَأَ) "to be bad".

Perf.	Imperf. Indic.	Juss.
سَاءَ	يَسُوءُ	يَسُؤْ
سَاءَتْ	تَسُوءُ	تَسُؤْ
سُؤْتَ	تَسُوءُ	تَسُؤْ
etc.	etc.	etc.

Imper.

سُؤْ — Verbal Noun سُوْءٌ

سُوئِي — Part. Active سَاءٍ (with Article اَلسَّائِي)

Pass. Perf. سِيءَ — Imperf. Indic. يُسَاءُ.

Of the Derived forms is IV. أَسَاءَ "to make bad"; [I]. Indic. يُسِيءُ; Imper. أَسِئْ; Verbal Noun إِسَاءَةٌ; Part. Act. مُسِيءٌ.

So from ضَاءَ (for ضَوَأَ) "to shine, be bright"; IV. أَضَاءَ "to light".

Conjugation of جَاءَ (for جَيَأَ) "to come".

Perf.	Imperf. Indic.	Juss.
جَاءَ	يَجِيءُ (also written يَجِئُ)	يَجِئْ
جَاءَتْ	تَجِيءُ	تَجِئْ
جِئْتَ etc.	تَجِيءُ etc.	تَجِئْ etc.

Imper.

جِئْ Verbal Noun مَجِيءٌ

جِيئِي etc. Part. Active جَاءٍ (with Article أَلْجَائِي)

Pass. Perf. جِيءَ.

So from هَاءَ (for هَيَأَ) II. form هَيَّأَ "to prepare"; Verbal Noun تَهْيِئَةٌ.

Conjugation of شَاءَ (for شَيِءَ) "to wish".

Perf.	Imperf. Indic.	Juss.
شَاءَ	يَشَاءُ	يَشَأْ
شَاءَتْ	تَشَاءُ	تَشَأْ
شِئْتَ etc.	تَشَاءُ etc.	تَشَأْ etc.

Imper. شَأْ Verbal Noun شَيْءٌ and مَشِيئَةٌ

Pass. Perf. شِيءَ Part. Act. شَاءٍ (with Article أَلشَّائِي).

B.

3. Verbs in which two radicals are weak letters.

1) Those in which the first and third radicals are weak letters. These follow the rules that govern the conjugation of the Assimilated and the Defective verbs; e.g.

Perf. وَقَى "to guard"; Imperf. Indic. يَقِى; Juss. يَقِ.

Imper. Masc. Sing. قِ; Fem. Sing. قِى; Plur. قُوا.

Part. Act. وَاقٍ (with Article أَلْوَاقِى).

VIII. form إِتَّقَى "to fear (God)".

Perf. وَفَى "to be complete, fulfil (a promise)".

IV. form أَوْفَى "to fulfil a vow"; Imperf. Indic. يُوفِى; Imper. أَوْفِ; Verbal Noun إِيفَاءٌ.

Perf. وَلِىَ "to be near"; Imperf. Indic. يَلِى; Juss. يَلِ; Imper. لِ.

2) Those in which the second and third radicals are weak letters. These retain the second radical (see Less. 27, 4, Note 2); e.g. رَوَى "to narrate".

Perf.	Imperf. Indic.	Juss.	Imper.
رَوَى	يَرْوِى	يَرْوِ	إِرْوِ.
رَوَتْ	تَرْوِى	تَرْوِ	إِرْوِى
رَوَيْتَ	تَرْوِى	تَرْوِ	etc.
etc.	etc.	etc.	

Part. Active رَاوٍ (أَلرَّاوِى) Part. Pass. مَرْوِىٌّ

Pass. Perf. رُوِىَ Imperf. Indic. يُرْوَى.

رَوِىَ "to be well watered" (of cattle, land, etc.).

Perf.	Imperf. Indic.	Juss.	Imper.
رَوِىَ	يَرْوَى	يَرْوَ	إِرْوَ
رَوِيَتْ	etc.	etc.	إِرْوَىْ
رَوِيتَ etc.			etc.

In the same way are conjugated سَوِيَ "to be worth": قَوِيَ "to be strong"

Conjugation of حَيِيَ also written حَيَّ (for حَيِوَ) "to live".

Perf. Imperf. Indic.

حَيِيَ يَحْيَى (also written يَحْيَا).

حَيِيْتَ

حَيِيتِ etc.

II. form حَيَّا "to let live, greet"; Verbal Noun contracted تَحِيَّةٌ.

X. form إِسْتَحْيَا "to spare alive"; in the sense "to be ashamed" generally written with one ى: Perf. إِسْتَحَى; Imperf. Indic. يَسْتَحِي.

C.

4. Verbs in which all three radicals are weak letters. The only verb of this class, which is in common use is أَوَى "to seek refuge"; Imperf. Indic. يَأْوِي; Juss. يَأْوِ; Imper. إِيوِ; Part. Act. آوٍ (with Article أَلْآوِي). II. form أَوَّى "to show hospitality to"; IV. form آوَى (with same meaning).

Vocabulary.

مَدْرَسَةٌ school.	دِرْهَمٌ (pl. دَرَاهِمُ) dirham, pl. money.
حَلَفَ to swear, X. to make to swear (by بِ).	بَطَلٌ hero.
أَتَى or جَاءَ بِ (literally "to come with"), to bring (with accus. of person).	إِنَّمَا only.
	حَاجَةٌ (plur. حَاجَاتٌ or حَوَائِجُ) need, affair.

مَأْكَلٌ food.	وُجُودٌ existence.
مَشْرَبٌ drink.	نُورٌ (plur. أَنْوَارٌ) light.
أَهْلٌ (plur. أَهَالٍ) people, inhabitants.	وَلَّى II. to flee.
طُولٌ length.	إِدْبَارٌ flight.
عُمْرٌ life, age.	جَيْشٌ (pl. جُيُوشٌ) army.
وِدَادٌ friendship.	جُمْعَةٌ week.
سَاءَ to injure.	الْأَسْتَانَةُ (Persian; literally "the threshold" i.e. of happiness) Constantinople.
أَخَّرَ V. to be late.	فِعْلٌ (plur. أَفْعَالٌ) deed.
سَلْمَى Salma (name of woman).	

Exercise 55.

إِنِّي آتٍ مِنَ ٱلشَّامِ وَمُتَوَجِّهٌ إِلَى ٱلْقَاهِرَةِ — هَلْ أَتَيْتَ مِنَ ٱلْبَيْتِ — لَا أَتَيْنَا مِنَ ٱلْمَدْرَسَةِ — فِي ٱلشَّهْرِ ٱلْآتِي نَلْتَقِي إِنْ شَاءَ ٱللّٰهُ — إِسْتَحْلِفِينِي بِمَا شِئْتِ أَنِّي آتِيكِ بِٱلدَّرَاهِمِ — جِئْنَا بِٱلْأَخْبَارِ إِلَى ٱلشَّيْخِ — إِنَّمَا مَنْ يَتَّقِي ٱللّٰهَ ٱلْبَطَلُ — يَأْتِي إِلَى ٱلسُّوقِ أَهْلُ ٱلْبَلْدَةِ جَاءَتْهُمُ ٱلنَّاسُ بِحَاجَتِهِمْ مِنَ ٱلْمَآكِلِ وَٱلْمَشْرَبِ وَجَاءَ كَثِيرُونَ مِنْ أَهَالِي ٱلْمَدِينَةِ — لَمْ أَرَ مِثْلَ هٰذِهِ ٱلْٱبْنَةِ طُولَ عُمْرِي — جَاءَتِ ٱلنَّاسُ لِيَرَوْا ذٰلِكَ — حَيَّا ٱلشَّيْخَ تَحِيَّةَ ٱلْوِدَادِ — سَاءَنِي كَثِيرًا أَنْ جِئْتَ مُتَأَخِّرًا —

نَرَى سَلْمَى قَدْ يَئِسَتْ مِنْ وُجُودِ زَوْجِهَا — قَدْ يَسُوءُ
ٱلصَّالِحُ (Proverb) — لَمَّا ضَاءَتْ أَنْوَارُ ٱلنَّهَارِ وَوَلَّتْ جُيُوشُ
ٱللَّيْلِ ٱلْإِدْبَارَ أَيْقَظَنِي خَادِمِي — ٱلشَّمْسُ تُضِيءُ ٱلْأَرْضَ —
تَجِيءُ مَتَى شِئْتَ — مَا رَأَيْتُ فِي مَجِيئِي خَيْرًا — رَأَيْتُمْ
تَهْيِئَةَ ٱلسَّفَرِ — مَا شَاءَ (Less. 47, 8) ٱللّٰهُ كَانَ وَمَا لَمْ يَشَأْ
لَمْ يَكُنْ — أَلَمْ يَأْتِكُمْ مَكْتُوبُنَا — رَآهُمْ يَأْكُلُونَ وَيَشْرَبُونَ
— لَمْ تَرَ مِثْلَ هٰذَا ٱلْكِتَابِ — هَلْ لَا تَسْتَحُونَ يَا أَوْلَادُ —
أَرِنَا أَيُّهَا ٱلْفَارِسُ أَفْعَالَكَ —

Exercise 56.

Have you seen us come (we come)? — We did not see you come. — I wished to see him, but he refused to see me. — You have come to us at a most seasonable time (the most blessed أَبْرَكُ of times). — In the coming week I will show you the goods I have (what is with me of goods). — We shall bring you what you wish. — After the greeting we inform you that we have come to (إِلَى) Constantinopie. — The physieian promised me that he would see me every day. — The master saw that I was ashamed (saw me I was ashamed). — Show me the books thou hast (what is with thee of books).

Thirtieth Lesson.

(أَلدَّرْسُ ٱلثَّلَاثُونَ)

Quadriliteral Verbs.

(فِعْلٌ رُبَاعِيٌّ)

1. The Quadriliteral verb is of the form فَعْلَلَ e.g. تَرْجَمَ "to translate".

Perf.	Imperf. Indic.	Juss.	Imper.
تَرْجَمَ	يُتَرْجِمُ	يُتَرْجِمْ	تَرْجِمْ
تَرْجَمْتُ	تُتَرْجِمُ	تُتَرْجِمْ	تَرْجِمِى
تَرْجَمْتَ	تُتَرْجِمُ	تُتَرْجِمْ	etc.
etc.	etc.	etc.	

Part. Active مُتَرْجِمٌ Part. Pass. مُتَرْجَمٌ

Verbal Noun تَرْجَمَةٌ

Pass. Perf. تُرْجِمَ Imperf. Indic. يُتَرْجَمُ.

Derived Forms.

a) تَفَعْلَلَ, e.g. from سَلْطَنَ "to appoint Sultan" تَسَلْطَنَ "to become Sultan".

Imperf. Indic. يَتَسَلْطَنُ Imper. تَسَلْطَنْ

Part. Active مُتَسَلْطِنٌ Verbal Noun تَسَلْطُنٌ.

b) إِفْعَلَلَّ, e.g. from طَمَانَ, إِطْمَأَنَّ "to be quiet".

Imperf. Indic. يَطْمَئِنُّ Imper. إِطْمَأْنِنْ

Part. Active مُطْمَئِنٌّ Verbal Noun إِطْمِئْنَانٌ.

There are numerous onomatopoetic quadriliteral verbs; e.g. زَلْزَلَ "to quake", تَزَلْزَلَ "to tremble", وَلْوَلَ "to howl (in mourning)", وَسْوَسَ "to whisper" etc.

The Verb لَيْسَ.

2. The Verb لَيْسَ "not to be" occurs in the Perfect only:

			Dual		Plur.	
Sing.	3. masc.	لَيْسَ	Dual	لَيْسَا	Plur.	لَيْسُوا
„	3. fem.	لَيْسَتْ	„	لَيْسَتَا	„	لَسْنَ
„	2. masc.	لَسْتَ	„	لَسْتُمَا	„	لَسْتُمْ
„	2. fem.	لَسْتِ			„	لَسْتُنَّ
„	1.	لَسْتُ			„	لَسْنَا

For the syntax of this verb see below § 12.

The Verbs نِعْمَ and بِئْسَ.

3. These are known as the Verbs of Praise (مَدْح) and Blame (ذَمّ) and occur in the 3rd Masc. and Fem. only: نِعْمَ, نِعْمَتْ "to be good"; بِئْسَ, بِئْسَتْ "to be bad".

The Verb عَسَى.

4. The Verb عَسَى followed by the conjunction أَنْ or أَنَّ means "it is possible that; it is to be hoped that; perhaps", e.g.

عَسَى أَنْ يَكُونَ ذٰلِكَ "Perhaps (or "it is to hoped") that will be".

The other Persons of the Perfect are rare.

Verbs of Surprise or Wonder.

(فِعْلُ ٱلتَّعَجُّبِ)

5. To express Surprise or Wonder two methods are employed:

a) The 3rd Sing. Masc. Perf. of the IV. form preceded by مَا "what" and followed by the Accusative; e.g. مَا أَحْسَنَ زَيْدًا "how beautiful is Zaid!" (literally "what has made Zaid beautiful").

b) The 2nd Sing. Masc. Imper. of the IV. form followed by a word with the Preposition بِ; e.g. أَحْسِنْ بِزَيْدٍ "how beautiful is Zaid!" (literally "make beautiful with Zaid").

The Optative.

6. The Optative is expressed by the Perfect at the beginning of a sentence; e.g.

رَحِمَهُ ٱللّٰهُ "may God have mercy upon him".

This Perfect may be preceded by لَا; e.g. لَا شُلَّتْ يَدَاكَ "may thy hands not grow dry!"

Note. In speech and in popular written language the Optative is expressed by a Nominal sentence with the verb in the Imperf. e.g.

ٱللّٰهُ يَرْحَمُكَ (pronounced allāh yarḥamak) "may God have mercy upon thee".

The Verb زَالَ.

7. The Verb زَالَ Imperf. يَزَالُ is used with the negative particles مَا, لَا and لَمْ (مَا زَالَ or لَا يَزَالُ or لَمْ يَزَلْ) with another verb or with an Accus. in the sense "is still" or "continues" e.g.

مَا زَالَ (لَمْ يَزَلْ) زَيْدٌ يَذْهَبُ (ذَاهِبًا) "Zaid did not cease to go i.e. goes still".

مَا زَالُوا (لَمْ يَزَالُوا) يُقَاتِلُونَ (مُقَاتِلِينَ) "they still fought".

لَا يَزَالُ حَيًّا "he is still alive".

Also:

مَا زَالَتِ (لَمْ تَزَلِ) ٱلْأُمُورُ عَلَى هٰذَا ٱلْحَالِ "matters were still in this condition".

The Verb عَادَ.

8. The Verb عَادَ, Imperf. يَعُودُ "to return" preceded by a negative and followed by another verb is used to express "not again", e.g.

مَا عَادَ (لَمْ يَعُدْ) يَرْجِعُ "he did not return again".

مَا عُدْنَا (لَمْ نَعُدْ) نَرْجِعُ "we did not return again"

Also in the Imperfect:

لَا تَعُدْ تَفْعَلْ كَذٰلِكَ "do not do so again".

لَا أَعُودُ أَفْعَلُهُ "I will not do it again".

Also with Accus. but without a second verb:

لَمْ يَعُدِ ٱلْمَسِيرُ مُمْكِنًا "the journey was no more possible".

The Verb كَادَ.

9. The Verb كَادَ, Imperf. يَكَادُ expresses the English "almost, nearly", e.g.

كَادَ يَفْعَلُهُ (أَنْ يَفْعَلَهُ) "he nearly did it".

أَنَا كِدْتُ أَمُوتُ (أَنْ أَمُوتَ) "I almost died".

The Verb دَامَ

10. The Verb دَامَ preceded by the Conjunction مَا "as long as" and followed by a verb in the Imperfect, or an Accusative is used to express "as long as, while", e.g.

مَا دَامَ يَقُومُ مَا دَامَ قَائِمًا	"as long as he stands".	مَا دُمْتُ أَقُومُ مَا دُمْتُ قَائِمًا	"as long as I stand".

The Verbs قَلَّ and طَالَ.

11 The Verb قَلَّ "to be little or rare" is used in the phrase قَلَّ مَا (also written قَلَّمَا) to express "seldom", e.g. قَلَّ مَا (قَلَّمَا) جِئْتَنَا "thou hast seldom come to us".

The verb طَالَ, Imperf. يَطُولُ "to be long" is used

in the phrase طَالَ مَا (also generally written طَالَمَا) to express "not for a long time", e.g.

طَالَمَا (طَالَ مَا) شَرَّفْتَنَا "thou hast not honoured us for a long time".

The Verb كَانَ and its Sisters.

12. The verb كَانَ used as a copula takes its predicate (خَبَرٌ) in the Accusative (see Less. 12, 4), e.g. كَانَ زَيْدٌ تَاجِرًا "Zaid was a merchant".

Certain other verbs known as the Sisters of كَانَ (أَخَوَاتُ كَانَ) have the same construction, e.g.

لَيْسَ "not to be" (see § 2), which may also take a predicate with بِ.

بَقِيَ to remain.

دَامَ to continue, last, (see § 10).

مَا زَالَ not to cease, (see § 7).

صَارَ (Imperf. يَصِيرُ) to become.
أَصْبَحَ to be or do in the morning.
أَمْسَى to be or do in the evening.
بَاتَ (ى) to be or do in the night.
} = to become.

e.g.

لَيْسَ سَعِيدٌ وَلَدًا (or بِوَلَدٍ) Said is not a boy.

لَيْسَ سَعِيدٌ مُجْتَهِدًا (or بِمُجْتَهِدٍ) Said is not diligent.

بَقِيتُ سَالِمًا I remained well.

{نَصِيرُ / نُصْبِحُ / نُمْسِي / نَبِيتُ} تَعْبَانِينَ we are getting (become) tired.

13. The verbs صَارَ "to become", أَخَذَ "to take", and جَعَلَ "to make" used before another verb in the Imperfect mean "to begin to" e.g.

أَخَذْنَا نَسِيرُ or صِرْنَا or جَعَلْنَا we began to travel.

Instead of the Imperfect of the verb the preposition فِي or بِ with the Verbal Noun may be used e.g.

أَخَذْنَا فِي ٱلْمَسِيرِ we began to travel.

Vocabulary.

فَضَلَ IV. to make excellent.
رَغِيفٌ loaf.
رَدُؤَ IV. to make bad, vile.
إِذْ since (conj.).
نَوْعٌ kind, sort.
طَرَقَ IV. to be silent with eyes cast down.
وِلَايَةٌ province.
بَرِيءٌ innocent.
حَدِيثٌ (pl. أَحَادِيثُ), narrative, story.
هَزِيعٌ part of the night.
دَوْلَةٌ kingdom.
اَلدَّوْلَةُ ٱلْعَلِيَّةُ the Turkish empire.
سَعَى to occupy oneself.

صَلُحَ IV. to reform.
أَرَبٌ aim.
وَطَنٌ home.
وَجِيزٌ small.
غَيْرٌ other than (followed by gen.). With following adjective = negative.
غَيْرُ قَادِرٍ incapable.
قَادِرٌ عَلَى able to.
حُصُولٌ attainment (w. عَلَى).
طَاقَةٌ power, ability.
طَالِعٌ star (in astrology).
لَامَ (ه) to blame.
قَطَّعَ II. to cut to pieces.
لَذَّ IV. to please.
تَمَرْمَرَ to murmur.
تَقَهْقَرَ to withdraw.

أَمَامَ before.

فَازَ (و) to attain (with ب).

غَلَبَة victory.

بِنَاء building.

حَدَثَ V. to converse.

مَشَقَّة misfortune.

خَامَ (ى), II. to pitch a tent.

سِتَار curtain.

حَالِك very black.

مَرْكَب ship.

بِدُونِ without.

دَفَّة rudder.

ظَاهِر outer, external

دَوَاء (plur. أَدْوِيَة) medicine.

بَطْن belly.

نَحْب death.

قَضَى نَحْبَهُ he died.

دَمْدَمَ to speak angrily.

وَلْوَلَ to wail.

قَضَّ VII. to rush.

كُفُؤ like, able, equal.

قَامَ III. to resist.

وَحْد loneliness (with suffix = alone).

وَحْدَهُ he alone.

عَانَ (و) II., III. and IV. to help.

هَمّ (pl. هُمُوم) care, anxiety.

صِنْف class, kind.

أَلْف thousand (plur. see Less. 32, 2).

حِين time.

فَرَج comfort, joy.

طَبِيعَة nature.

بَشَرِيّ human.

يَأْس despair.

نَظَرَ VIII. to expect.

نَوَال attainment.

رَغِبَ to wish.

سِوَى except.

قَبْر grave.

قَطَعَ طُرُقًا to commit highway robbery.

لَعَنَ to curse.

صَدْر (pl. صُدُور) breast.

قُمَاش (pl. أَقْمِشَة) goods.

ذَكَرَ to mention, remember.

فَضْلٌ goodness, nobility. مُعَسْكَرٌ camp.

كَأْسٌ cup. دَفَعَ III. to defend.

Exercise 57.

مَسَّاكَ ٱللّٰهُ بِخَيْرٍ — أَصْبَحَكُمُ ٱللّٰهُ بِخَيْرٍ — نِعْمَ هٰؤُلَاءِ ٱلْأَوْلَادُ
مَا أَفْضَلَهُمْ — بِئْسَ هٰذَا ٱلرَّغِيفُ مَا أَرْدَاهُ — لَمْ يَعُدِ ٱلْمَسِيرُ
مُمْكِنًا إِذِ ٱلْجِمَالُ لَيْسَتْ مِنْ نَوْعِ ٱلْجِمَالِ ٱلسَّرِيعَةِ — ٱلْعَرَبُ
لَيْسُوا سُودًا — لَمْ نَعُدْ نَرْجِعُ — كِدْنَا نَطِيرُ مِنَ ٱلْفَرَحِ —
سَيِّدُهُ كَانَ لَا يَزَالُ مُطْلَقًا — عَادَتِ ٱلْوِلَايَةُ إِلَيْهِ بَعْدَ أَنْ كَادَتْ
تَخْرُجُ مِنْ يَدِهِ — أَلَسْتَ ٱبْنَ ٱلْأَمِيرِ — إِنِّي لَا أُبَالِي بِٱلتَّهْدِيدِ
مَا نِمْتُ بَرِيئًا. — مُنْذُ نُزُولِنَا فِي مِصْرَ لَمْ أَعُدْ أُشَاهِدُكَ —
مَا زَالُوا فِي هٰذِهِ ٱلْأَحَادِيثِ حَتَّى ٱنْقَضَى هَزِيعَانِ مِنَ ٱللَّيْلِ —
إِنَّ ٱلدَّوْلَةَ ٱلْعَلِيَّةَ لَا تَزَالُ تَسْعَى فِي إِصْلَاحَاتِ ٱلْأَحْوَالِ — قَدْ
تَرَكْتُ تِلْكَ ٱلْبِلَادَ إِذْ لَيْسَ لِي فِيهَا أَرَبٌ وَلَيْسَتْ هِيَ وَطَنِي — هٰذِهِ
ٱلْمُدَّةُ لَيْسَتْ بِوَجِيزَةٍ — أَخَافُ أَنْ أُمْسِيَ غَيْرَ قَادِرٍ عَلَى ٱلْحُصُولِ
عَلَى مَطْلُوبِي — لَمْ يَعُدْ لِلْجَمَلِ طَاقَةٌ أَنْ يَجِدَّ ٱلْمَسِيرَ —
لَا نَزَالُ سَائِرِينَ — مَنْ عَسَى أَنْ يَكُونَ ذٰلِكَ ٱلرَّجُلُ — عَسَى
أَنْ يَكُونَ طَالِعُكَ سَعِيدًا — أَخَذْتُ أَلُومُ نَفْسِي — أَخَذْنَا
فِي تَقْطِيعِ مَا بَقِيَ لَنَا مِنَ ٱللَّحْمِ وَقُلْنَا مَا أَلَذَّ هٰذَا ٱلطَّعَامَ —

يَا فَتَاةُ كُونِي مُطْمَئِنَّةً — لَيْسَ ٱطْمِئْنَانُنَا كَامِلًا — أَخَذْنَا فِي ٱلْاِسْتِعْدَادِ لِلذَّهَابِ — هَلِ ٱلْأَعْدَاءُ لَا يَزَالُونَ بَعِيدِينَ عَنَّا — صَارَ ٱلنُّورُ فِي أَعْيُنِهِمْ ظَلَامًا وَأَخَذُوا يَتَمَرْمَرُونَ ثُمَّ تَقَهْقَرُوا مِنْ أَمَامِنَا — كِدْنَا نَفُوزُ بِٱلْغَلَبَةِ عَلَى ٱلْأَعْدَاءِ وَٱلْأَعْدَاءُ كَادُوا يُوَلُّونَ ٱلْإِدْبَارَ — أَخَذْنَا فِي بِنَاءِ ٱلْخَيْمَةِ فَصِرْنَا نَتَحَدَّثُ — كِدْتُ أَنْسَى مَشَقَّاتِي — خَيَّمَ ٱللَّيْلُ بِسِتَارِهِ ٱلْحَالِكِ فَأَصْبَحْنَا كَمَرْكَبٍ بِدُونِ دَفَّةٍ — قَالَ ٱلْأَمِيرُ أَبْقِ عِنْدَنَا طَبِيبًا مُكْرَمًا — رَأَى فَرَحِي لَيْسَ إِلَّا فَرَحًا ظَاهِرًا — لَمْ أَزَلْ أَضَعُ ٱلْأَدْوِيَةَ عَلَى بَطْنِهِ حَتَّى قَضَى نَحْبَهُ — قَدْ تَحَطَّمَتِ ٱلْفَوَارِسُ وَلَعِبَتِ ٱلسُّيُوفُ وَوَلْوَلَتِ ٱلنِّسَاءُ. فَٱنْقَضَّ عَلَيَّ فَارِسٌ مِنَ ٱلْأَعْدَاءِ وَرَفَعَ رُمْحَهُ لِيَطْعَنَنِي بِهِ ظَانًّا بِأَنِّي لَسْتُ كُفُوًا لِمُقَاوَمَتِهِ فَأَمْسَيْتُ وَحْدِي بِدُونِ مُعِينٍ وَلَا مُسَاعِدٍ — إِنَّ ٱلْجُوعَ وَٱلتَّعَبَ كَانَا قَدْ كَادَا يُهْلِكَانِهِمْ — لَيْسَ ٱلْهُمُومُ عَلَيَّ صِنْفًا وَاحِدًا عِنْدِي بِحَمْدِ ٱللهِ مِنْهُ أُلُوفٌ — مِنْ ذٰلِكَ ٱلْحِينِ لَمْ يَعُدْ يَرْجِعُ إِلَيْنَا وَلَمْ نَعُدْ نَسْمَعُ عَنْهُ شَيْئًا — عَسَى ٱللهُ أَنْ يَفْتَحَ لِي بَابَ ٱلْفَرَجِ — إِنَّ ٱلطَّبِيعَةَ ٱلْبَشَرِيَّةَ لَا تَيْأَسُ يَأْسًا تَامًّا وَلَا تَزَالُ تَنْتَظِرُ نَوَالَ ٱلْمَرْغُوبِ — لَيْسَ لِي حَبِيبٌ سِوَى ٱلْقَبْرِ —

أَظْلَمَتِ ٱلدُّنْيَا فِى وَجْهِى ,كِدتُ يُغْشَى عَلَىَّ — لَيْسَ مَنْ يَقْطَعُ طُرُقًا بَطَلاً —

Exercise 58.

The Emir died (Pass. V. of وَفَى), may God have mercy on him! — May God prolong your days! — May God reward you for (عَنْ) us! — The woman began to prepare the food. — God curse his father! — They almost died from fear (Adv. Accus.). — Satan whispers in the breasts of men. — O pupil, translate these words! — I have already translated them. — O boy, be quiet! — O boys, be quiet! — Good is this girl, how beautiful she is! — Bad are these goods, how vile they are! — Good morning (May God do to thee in the morning good), my master. — We still remember your kindness. — You are not (لَيْسَ) heros. — As long as we live, we shall remember your kindness. — Thanks to God we are still well (sound). — O boys, do not do this again! — We will not do it again. — I have not seen you for a long time. — We had almost drunk (جَرَعَ V.) the cup of death (مَنُونٌ). — They continued travelling until they arrived at the camp of the enemies. — We became (أَمْسَى) incapable of defending. — So long as we remained in this city, we continually saw wonders.

Thirty-first Lesson.

(أَلدَّرْسُ ٱلْحَادِى وَٱلثَّلَاثُونَ)

Relative Sentences.

1. The Relative Pronoun (أَلِاسْمُ ٱلْمَوْصُولُ) is:

Sing. Masc. أَلَّذِى, Fem. أَلَّتِى (in all cases), "who, which".

Dual Nom. Masc. أَللَّذَانِ Fem. أَللَّتَانِ

Gen. Accus. Masc. أَللَّذَيْنِ „ أَللَّتَيْنِ

Plural Masc. أَلَّذِينَ „ أَللَّاتِى or أَللَّوَاتِى
(in all cases).

Note. The pronoun أَلَّذِى is compounded of the Article أَلْ (therefore the hamza is a hamzat alwasl), the particle لَ and the Demonstrative ذَا, ذِى (see Less. 9, 1).

Notice that the common forms of the Sing. Masc. and Fem. and the Plur. Masc. are written with one lām, the other forms with two.

2. Other Pronouns used in Relative sentences are مَنْ "he who", مَا "that which, what", more rarely أَىّ Fem. أَيَّة (with following Gen.) "he who" and its compounds أَيُّمَنْ "whosoever" and أَيَّمَا "whatsoever".

The words مَنْ and مَا are always treated as nouns, أَلَّذِى usually as an adjective but sometimes as a noun, when it has the same meaning as مَنْ "he who" and مَا "what".

3. The Relative Pronoun is called أَلاِسْمُ ٱلْمَوْصُولُ and the following Relative Sentence أَلصِّلَةُ. This sentence is treated in Arabic as quite independent and as coordinate with the main sentence; e.g.

أَلرَّجُلُ ٱلَّذِى جَاءَ the man, who came (literally: The man — who — he came).

أَلرَّجُلُ ٱلَّذِى رَأَيْتُهُ the man, whom I saw (literally: The man — who — I saw him).

أَلرَّجُلُ ٱلَّذِى كَتَبْتُ لَهُ كِتَابًا the man to whom I wrote a letter (literally: The man — who — I wrote a letter to him).

أَلرَّجُلُ ٱلَّذِى رَأَيْتُ ٱبْنَهُ the man, whose son I saw (literally: The man — who — I saw his son).

The Relative Pronoun must always be caught up again in the Relative sentence by a Pronoun (called عَائِدٌ or رَاجِعٌ) either implied in the verb (as in the first sentence above) or manifest (as in the other sentences).

Note. After مَنْ and مَا the عَائِدٌ is often omitted; e.g. مَا رَأَيْتُ for مَا رَأَيْتُهُ "that, which I have seen".

4. If the noun to which the Relative sentence is attached is indefinite, the Relative pronoun is omitted. Such a sentence is called a صِفَةٌ; e.g.

لَقِيتُ رَجُلًا خَرَجَ مِنْ بَيْتِهِ I met a man, who had gone out from his house.

أَلشَّامُ مَدِينَةٌ فِيهَا عَجَائِبُ كَثِيرَةٌ Damascus is a city, in which are many marvels.

5. Certain constructions of the Participle Passive are to be explained as shortened Relative sentences; e.g.

أَلشُّهُودُ ٱلْمَذْكُورَةُ أَسْمَاؤُهُمْ أَدْنَاهُ the witnesses, whose names are mentioned below.

The Article here may be regarded as a shortened Relative pronoun, the following clause as a whole depending on it; e.g. "The witnesses, who (mentioned are their names)". The following phrases of a similar nature are much used:

أَلْمُومَا إِلَيْهِ or أَلْمُشَارُ إِلَيْهِ the above-mentioned.

أَلرَّجُلُ ٱلْمُشَارُ إِلَيْهِ
أَلرَّجُلُ ٱلْمُومَأُ إِلَيْهِ
} the man above-mentioned.

أَلْامْرَأَةُ ٱلْمُشَارُ (ٱلْمُومَأُ) إِلَيْهَا the woman above-mentioned.

أَلرِّجَالُ ٱلْمُشَارُ (ٱلْمُومَأُ) إِلَيْهِمْ the men above-mentioned.

Vocabulary.

جَبَلُ ٱلشَّيْخِ	Mt. Hermon.	سَمِعَ	I. and VIII. to hear.
دِمَشْقُ ٱلشَّامِ	Damascus.	لَحْنٌ	(pl. أَلْحَانٌ) melody.
أَعْلَى	(Elative of عَالٍ) highest, summit.	فَتَّ	II. to cut in pieces
		كَبِدٌ	(plur. أَكْبَادٌ) liver, (used metaphorically = heart).
نَكِرَ	IV. to deny.	لَانَ	(ى) II. to soften.
شَمِلَ	to embrace, surround.	جُلْمُودٌ	hard rock.
قَرِيبٌ	(pl. أَقْرِبَاءُ or أَقَارِبُ) relative.	رَقَّ	(i) to be tender, soft.
		جَبَّارٌ	giant.
جَوَابٌ	(plur. أَجْوِبَةٌ) answer.	عَنِيدٌ	obstinate.
بَارِدٌ	cold.	يَقِنَ	to be certain, V. to be convinced of.
عَدَلَ	III. to be like, correspond.	هُنَالِكَ	there.
رَخِيمٌ	tender.	حَطَمَ	(i) to break.
كَأَنَّ	as, as if.	عَزَمَ	to determine (on عَلَى).
بَلِيَّةٌ (pl. بَلَايَا) / دَاهِيَةٌ (pl. دَوَاهٍ)	misfortune.	نَقَذَ	IV. to deliver
		مَظْلُومٌ	oppressed.

لَمَّ IV. to seize (with بِ).
سَقَطَ to fall.
نِقَابٌ veil.
صَبِيحٌ fresh.
زَانَ (ى) II. to adorn.
وَرْدِيٌّ rosy.
بَهِيٌّ beautiful, shining.
ذَابِلٌ languid.
مَطَرَ IV. to rain (trans.).
لُؤْلُؤٌ pearl (collective).
حَرْقٌ inflaming.
خَرْقٌ piercing, splitting.
جَلِيلٌ exalted.
غِنَاءٌ song.
شَقِيٌّ (pl. أَشْقِيَاءُ) wretched.
شَدِيدٌ (pl. أَشِدَّاءُ) strong.
بَاسِلٌ brave.
مَفَرٌّ refuge, escape.
لَذِيذٌ delightful, agreeable.
طَلَقَ IV. to free.
أَطْلَقَ ٱلرَّصَاصَ to shoot.
مِيتَةٌ death.
صَرَخَ to cry.

صَرْخَةٌ cry.
قَلِقَ IV. to disturb.
وَحْشٌ (pl. وُحُوشٌ) wild beast.
ضَارٍ tearing, carnivorous.
أَثْنَاءٌ (pl. of ثِنْيٌ "fold") meantime.
قَبِلَ IV. to advance (to عَلَى).
زَادٌ provisions.
حَجَلٌ (pl. حِجْلَانٌ) partridge.
كَمِّيَّةٌ quantity.
غَابَ (ى) to be absent, distant.
صَنَعَ VIII. to prepare.
عَشَاءٌ supper.
أَوَّلَ أَمْسِ the day before yesterday.
كِفَاحٌ struggle.
فَقَدَ (pass.) to be lost.
مَعْرِكَةٌ battle.
سَكِرَ to be intoxicated.
جَرَيَانٌ flowing.
دَمٌ blood.
بَسَالَةٌ courage.

حَمَلَ to carry, induce to (عَلَى).

فَكَرَ V. and VIII. to consider (with فِي).

طَرِيقَةٌ method.

وَاسِطَةٌ means.

سُرْعَةٌ swiftness.

حُلُولٌ entrance, approach.

أَجَلٌ death.

رُقْعَةٌ letter, note.

غَيْبٌ hidden, absent.

عِدَّةٌ number.

كَبَدَ V. to endure.

كَالَ (ى) to measure.

كَيْلٌ measure.

عَائِلَةٌ family.

زَهْرٌ flowers (coll.).

بَسَمَ V. to smile.

رِسَالَةٌ (pl. رَسَائِلُ) message.

جَبَلُ لُبْنَانَ. Mt. Lebanon.

اَلْبَحْرُ ٱلْمُتَوَسِّطُ Mediterranean.

مَتَعَ V. to enjoy (بِ).

أَسِيرٌ (pl. أُسَرَاءُ) prisoner.

عَظْمٌ bones.

فَمٌ mouth.

مُشِيرٌ marshal.

أَخِيرٌ last.

Exercise 59.

إِنَّ جَبَلَ ٱلشَّيْخِ جَبَلٌ عَالٍ تَرَى دِمَشْقَ ٱلشَّامِ مِنْ أَعْلَاهُ — لَا أَقْدِرُ أَنْ أُنْكِرَ ٱلْمُؤَانَسَةَ وَٱللُّطْفَ ٱللَّذَيْنِ شَمِلَنِي بِهِمَا أَصْحَابُ صَدِيقِي وَأَقَارِبُهُ (Less. 7, 4) — فَرَأَيْتُهُ مِنَ ٱلْوَاجِبِ أَنْ أُجِيبَهُمْ بِأَجْوِبَةٍ بَارِدَةٍ تُعَادِلُ سُؤَالَاتِهِمْ — إِنِّي سَمِعْتُ صَوْتًا رَخِيمًا كَأَنَّهُ صَوْتُ مَنْ خَانَهُ ٱلدَّهْرُ وَرَمَاهُ فِي بَلِيَّةٍ أَوْ دَاهِيَةٍ

وَصِرْتُ أَسْتَمِعُ تِلْكَ ٱلْأَلْحَانَ ٱلْمُحْزِنَةَ ٱلَّتِي تُفَتِّتُ ٱلْأَكْبَادَ وَتُلَيِّنُ ٱلْجُلْمُودَ وَيَرِقُّ لَهَا كُلُّ جَبَّارٍ عَنِيدٍ فَتَيَقَّنْتُ أَنَّهُ يُوجَدُ هُنَالِكَ شَخْصٌ أَوْصَلَتْهُ ٱلْبَلَايَا إِلَى هٰذَا ٱلْمَكَانِ وَحَطَّمَتْهُ أَيْدِي ٱلزَّمَانِ فَعَزَمْتُ عَلَى إِنْقَاذِ هٰذَا ٱلْمَظْلُومِ مِنَ ٱلدَّاهِيَةِ ٱلَّتِي أَلَمَّتْ بِهِ فَوَجَدْتُهُ فَتَاةً وَافِرَةَ ٱلْجَمَالِ وَإِذْ سَقَطَ نِقَابُهَا ظَهَرَ مِنْ تَحْتِهِ وَجْهٌ صَبِيحٌ زَيَّنَهُ ٱللّٰهُ بِلَوْنٍ وَرْدِيٍّ بَهِيٍّ وَكَانَتْ عَيْنَاهَا ٱلذَّابِلَتَانِ تَمْطُرَانِ لُؤْلُؤًا جَعَلَهُ ٱللّٰهُ لِحَرْقِ ٱلْأَكْبَادِ وَخَرْقِ ٱلْفُؤَادِ فَقُلْتُ لَهَا مِنْ أَنَّى بِكِ أَيَّتُهَا ٱلسَّيِّدَةُ ٱلْجَلِيلَةُ إِلَى هٰذَا ٱلْمَكَانِ ٱلَّذِي لَا يَسْكُنُهُ إِنْسَانٌ فَقَالَتْ لَا تَسْأَلْ أَيُّهَا ٱلشَّابُّ ٱللَّطِيفُ عَنْ أَمْرِي فَإِنِّي أَسْمَعُ عَنْ بُعْدٍ صَوْتَ غِنَاءِ أُولٰئِكَ ٱلْأَشْقِيَاءِ ٱلَّذِينَ أَتَوْا بِي إِلَى هٰذَا ٱلْمَكَانِ فَقُلْتُ لَهَا كَمْ هُمْ وَمَنْ هُمْ وَهَلْ هُمْ مِنَ ٱلْأَشِدَّاءِ ٱلْبَسِلِينَ ٱلَّذِينَ لَا مَفَرَّ لَنَا مِنْ أَيْدِيهِمْ — أَلشَّخْصُ ٱلَّذِي قَدِمَ ٱلْآنَ هُوَ خَادِمِي فَوَصَلَ إِلَى ٱلْمَكَانِ ٱلَّذِي كُنَّا جَالِسِينَ فِيهِ — كَانَ لَدَيْنَا أَلَذُّ طَعَامٍ تَنَاوَلْنَاهُ فِي مُدَّةِ حَيَاتِنَا — أَطْلَقْتُ ٱلرَّصَاصَ عَلَى أُولٰئِكَ ٱلْأَشْقِيَاءِ ٱلَّذِينَ يَسْتَحِقُّونَ شَرَّ مِيتَةٍ فَصَرَخَ كَبِيرُهُمْ صَرْخَةً تُقْلِقُ ٱلْوُحُوشَ ٱلضَّارِيَةَ — فِي تِلْكَ ٱلْأَثْنَاءِ أَقْبَلَ حَسَنٌ وَمَعَهُ مِنَ ٱلزَّادِ مَا يَكْفِينَا

عَشَرَةَ أَيَّامٍ فَسِرْنَا فِي طَلَبِ صَيْدِ ٱلْحِجْلَانِ (Less. 44, 2 B 8) ٱلَّتِي يُوجَدُ مِنْهَا كَمِّيَّةٌ وَافِرَةٌ فِي ذٰلِكَ ٱلْجَبَلِ فَلَمْ نَغِبْ أَكْثَرَ مِنْ سَاعَةٍ حَتَّى ٱصْطَدْنَا حِجْلَانًا كَثِيرَةً فَرَجَعْنَا بِهَا ٱصْطَنَعْنَا لَنَا مِنْهَا عَشَاءً تَنَاوَلْنَاهُ بِسُرُورٍ لَا مَزِيدَ عَلَيْهِ — إِنَّنِي طَبِيبٌ أَجُولُ فِي ٱلْبِلَادِ وَقَدْ وَصَلْتُ أَوَّلَ أَمْسِ بَعْدَ نِصْفِ ٱللَّيْلِ إِلَى ٱلْقَبِيلَةِ ٱلَّتِي وَقَعَ ٱلْكِفَاحُ بَيْنَكُمْ وَبَيْنَهَا وَلَا يَخْفَى عَلَيْكَ أَيُّهَا ٱلْأَمِيرُ أَنَّ لِي أُخْتًا فُقِدَتْ فِي ٱلْمَعْرَكَةِ ٱلْمُشَارِ إِلَيْهَا — كُنْتُ كَمَنْ أَسْكَرَهُ مَنْظَرُ جَرَيَانِ ٱلدَّمِ — قَالَ ٱلْأَمِيرُ إِنَّ مَا رَأَيْتُهُ مِنْكَ مِنَ ٱلشَّجَاعَةِ وَٱلْبَسَالَةِ (Less. 44, 2 B 8) ٱللَّتَيْنِ أَظْهَرْتَهُمَا فِي ٱلْمَعْرَكَةِ ٱلْأَخِيرَةِ حَمَلَنِي عَلَى ذٰلِكَ — أَخَذْتُ أَتَفَكَّرُ فِي إِيجَادِ طَرِيقَةٍ تُمَكِّنُنِي مِنَ ٱلرُّجُوعِ إِلَى وَطَنِي ٱلَّذِي لَمْ أَكُنْ أَعْلَمُ مِقْدَارَ بُعْدِهِ عَنْ ذٰلِكَ ٱلْمَكَانِ — إِنَّ ٱلَّذِي كُنْتُ أُؤَمِّلُ أَنَّهُ يُخَلِّصُنِي مِنَ ٱلْهَلَاكِ كَانَ وَاسِطَةً لِسُرْعَةِ حُلُولِ أَجَلِي — وَرَدَتْنِي رُقْعَةٌ مَكْتُوبٌ فِيهَا مَا يَأْتِي — مَا مَضَى فَاتَ وَٱلْمُؤَمَّلُ غَيْبٌ وَلَكَ ٱلسَّاعَةُ ٱلَّتِي أَنْتَ فِيهَا — لَيْسَ ذٰلِكَ شَيْئًا يُذْكَرُ — صَرَفْنَا عِدَّةَ أَيَّامٍ أَنْسَتْنَا كُلَّمَا (all that) تَكَبَّدْنَاهُ — إِنَّ بِٱلْكَيْلِ ٱلَّذِي تَكِيلُونَ بِهِ يُكَالُ لَكُمْ —

Exercise 60.

Those men, who are in the market, buy and sell. — Those women, whom we have seen in the street, are of our family. — This is the boy to whom we have given the money. — He, whose tongue is long, his intelligence is small. — The girl, in whose hand (was) a flower, smiled. — I saw girls (بَنَاتٌ), in whose hands were flowers. — All letters, which come to us, must be addressed to (it is necessary that they be in the name of) the director of our journal. — This young man, whose father we know, is clever. — Mt. Lebanon, from the summit of which you see the Mediterranean, is a very high mountain. — After the enquiry concerning thy welfare (conditions) and the information concerning thee (thy informing) (as to) which I hope that thou art better than could be wished (thou art in excess of what is wished), I inform thee that thy friendly letter has reached me and I rejoice over (فِي) thy health and thy well-being (soundness), which mayest thou continually enjoy. — I saw soldiers, with whom (were) prisoners. — I inform you that I am still in the condition, which you know. — A dog met a dog, in whose mouth was a bone. — The above-mentioned Marshal is very renowned. — The above-mentioned persons are the owners of this house.

Thirty-second Lesson.

(اَلدَّرْسُ ٱلثَّانِي وَٱلثَّلَاثُونَ)

The Numerals.

(إِسْمُ ٱلْعَدَدِ)

A. The Cardinal Numbers.

1. The Cardinal Numbers are as follows:

a) From 1—10:

	masc.	fem.	Arabic Signs.
1.	وَاحِدٌ / أَحَدٌ	وَاحِدَةٌ / إِحْدَى	١
2.	إِثْنَانِ	إِثْنَتَانِ	٢
3.	ثَلَاثَةٌ (also written ثَلٰثَةٌ)	ثَلَاثٌ (also written ثَلٰثٌ)	٣
4.	أَرْبَعَةٌ	أَرْبَعٌ	٤
5.	خَمْسَةٌ	خَمْسٌ	٥
6.	سِتَّةٌ	سِتٌّ	٦
7.	سَبْعَةٌ	سَبْعٌ	٧
8.	ثَمَانِيَةٌ (also written ثَمٰنِيَةٌ)	ثَمَانٍ (also written ثَمٰنٍ)	٨
9.	تِسْعَةٌ	تِسْعٌ	٩
10.	عَشَرَةٌ	عَشْرٌ	١٠

b) From 11—19.

	masc.	fem.	
11.	أَحَدَ عَشَرَ	إِحْدَى عَشْرَةَ	١١
12.	إِثْنَا عَشَرَ	إِثْنَتَا عَشْرَةَ	١٢
13.	ثَلَاثَةَ عَشَرَ	ثَلَاثَ عَشْرَةَ	١٣
14.	أَرْبَعَةَ عَشَرَ	أَرْبَعَ عَشْرَةَ	١٤
15.	خَمْسَةَ عَشَرَ	خَمْسَ عَشْرَةَ	١٥
16.	سِتَّةَ عَشَرَ	سِتَّ عَشْرَةَ	١٦

	masc.		fem.		Arabic Signs.
17.	masc.	سَبْعَةَ عَشَرَ	fem.	سَبْعَ عَشْرَةَ	١٧
18.	„	ثَمَانِيَةَ عَشَرَ	„	ثَمَانِي عَشْرَةَ	١٨
19.	„	تِسْعَةَ عَشَرَ	„	تِسْعَ عَشْرَةَ	١٩

c) From 20—100.

20.	عِشْرُونَ	masc. and fem.	٢٠
21.	masc. أَحَدٌ وَعِشْرُونَ	fem. إِحْدَى وَعِشْرُونَ	٢١
22.	„ إِثْنَانِ وَعِشْرُونَ	„ إِثْنَتَانِ وَعِشْرُونَ	٢٢

etc.

30.	ثَلَاثُونَ	masc. and fem.	٣٠
40.	أَرْبَعُونَ	„ „ „	٤٠
50.	خَمْسُونَ	„ „ „	٥٠
60.	سِتُّونَ	„ „ „	٦٠
70.	سَبْعُونَ	„ „ „	٧٠
80.	ثَمَانُونَ	„ „ „	٨٠
90.	تِسْعُونَ	„ „ „	٩٠
100.	مِئَةٌ	(also frequently written مِائَةٌ, but the alif is not pronounced).	١٠٠

d) From 200 upwards.

200.	مِئَتَانِ (مِائَتَانِ)	٢٠٠

		Arabic Signs.
300.	ثَلَاثُ مِئَةٍ (also written ثَلَاثُمِائَةٍ or ثَلَاثُمِئَةٍ)	٣٠٠
400.	أَرْبَعُ مِئَةٍ	٤٠٠
500.	خَمْسُ مِئَةٍ	٥٠٠
600.	سِتُّ مِئَةٍ	٦٠٠
700.	سَبْعُ مِئَةٍ	٧٠٠
800.	ثَمَانِي مِئَةٍ	٨٠٠
900.	تِسْعُ مِئَةٍ	٩٠٠
1000.	أَلْفٌ	١٠٠٠
2000.	أَلْفَانِ	٢٠٠٠
3000.	ثَلَاثَةُ آلَافٍ	٣٠٠٠
	etc. to 10000.	
11000.	أَحَدَ عَشَرَ أَلْفًا etc.	١١٠٠٠
100000.	مِئَةُ أَلْفٍ	١٠٠٠٠٠
1000000.	أَلْفُ أَلْفٍ or مِلْيُونٌ, Plur. مَلَايِينُ	١٠٠٠٠٠٠

0. Zero, Nil صِفْرٌ

Declension of the Cardinal Numbers.

2. The Numerals from 1 to 10 are declined: a) إِثْنَانِ and إِثْنَتَانِ as Dual with Gen. Accus. إِثْنَيْنِ, إِثْنَتَيْنِ b) the others as Singulars, e.g.

وَاحِدٌ; Accus. وَاحِدًا; Gen. وَاحِدٍ

ثَلَاثَةٌ; „ ثَلَاثَةً; „ ثَلَاثَةٍ

Fem. ثَلَاثٌ; „ ثَلَاثًا; „ ثَلَاثٍ.

The Numeral ثَمَانٍ is declined like قَاضٍ.

11 is indeclinable (مَبْنِيٌّ).

12 forms Gen. Accus. إِثْنَيْ عَشَرَ; Fem. إِثْنَتَيْ عَشْرَةَ,

13—19 are indeclinable.

The Numerals 20—90 are declined as Sound Plurals; e.g.

Nom. عِشْرُونَ; Gen. Accus. عِشْرِينَ

The other Numerals are declined as follows:

Nom. مِئَةٌ; Accus. مِئَةً; Gen. مِئَةٍ

„ مِئَتَانِ; „ and „ مِئَتَيْنِ

„ أَلْفٌ; „ أَلْفًا; „ أَلْفٍ.

أَلْفٌ has two forms of the Plural: آلَافٌ and أُلُوفٌ, the latter being used for "thousands" in an indefinite sense.

The Cardinal numbers from 3 to 10 are used in the feminine form with masculine nouns and in the masc. with fem. nouns.

Formation of the Compound Numbers.

3. Compound numbers from 20 on are formed by joining the units, tens and hundreds by وَ.

The largest number is put first, but the units are put before the tens; e.g.

21 أَحَدٌ وَعِشْرُونَ ٢١

1896 أَلْفٌ وَثَمَانِي مِئَةٍ وَسِتَّةٌ وَتِسْعُونَ ١٨٩٦

Such an expression as eighteen hundred must be expressed by one thousand eight hundred.

In the compound numbers each numeral is declined: e.g. Accus. أَحَدًا وَعِشْرِينَ etc.

Syntax of the Numerals.

4. The Numerals are joined to the words they qualify according to the following rules:

a) The Numerals 1 and 2 are adjectives; e.g. قَلْبٌ وَاحِدٌ "one heart".

إِثْنَانِ is seldom used with a noun, because the Dual of the noun itself can be used, but when it is so used, the إِثْنَانِ loses its final nūn (see Less. 7, 1) and the noun follows in the Gen. Sing.

b) The Numerals 3 to 10 are Substantives and are followed by the noun in the Gen. Plur.: e.g.

ثَلَاثَةُ رِجَالٍ Three men. عَشْرُ نِسَاءٍ Ten women.

Note. They are more rarely placed after the noun in apposition to it; e.g.

رِجَالٌ ثَلَاثَةٌ, نِسَاءٌ عَشْرٌ.

c) The Numerals 11 to 99 are followed by the noun in the Accus. Sing.; e.g.

أَحَدَ عَشَرَ رَجُلًا Eleven men. عِشْرُونَ رَجُلًا Twenty men.

d) The Numerals from 100 on are Substantives and are followed by the noun in the Gen. Sing.; e.g.

ثَلَاثُ مِئَةِ رَجُلٍ Three hundred men. أَلْفُ لَيْلَةٍ A thousand nights.

e) After Compound Numerals the noun follows the laws regulating its relation to the last numeral mentioned; e.g.

مِئَةٌ وَثَلَاثَةُ رِجَالٍ A hundred and three men. (Rule b).

مِئَةٌ وَخَمْسَةٌ وَعِشْرُونَ رَجُلًا A hundred and twenty-five men. (Rule c).

5. The Indefinite Numeral "some", when it is used for a number between 3 and 10, is expressed by the substantive بِضْعٌ (later also بِضْعَةٌ) followed by the Genitive; e.g. بِضْعُ (بِضْعَةُ) أَيَّامٍ some days.

Note. This word must not be confused with the word بَعْضٌ, which means, "one of some, a certain" e.g. بَعْضُ ٱلشُّعَرَاءِ "Some poets" or "A certain poet".

An indefinite number over 10 is expressed by the word نَيِّفٌ; e.g.

مِئَةُ أَلْفٍ وَنَيِّفُ نَفْسٍ A hundred thousand and some (more) souls.

Method of denoting Hours and Days.

6. a) To express the Hour of the day the Ordinals are generally used (see Less. 33); e.g.

أَلسَّاعَةُ ٱلثَّالِثَةُ Three o'clock (the third hour).

فِي ٱلسَّاعَةِ ٱلثَّالِثَةِ At three o'clock (in the third hour).

But the Cardinal numbers are used predicatively; e.g.

أَلسَّاعَةُ ثَلَاثَةٌ It is three o'clock (the hour is three).

أَلسَّاعَةُ أَحَدَ عَشَرَ It is eleven o'clock.

Note. ثَلَاثُ سَاعَاتٍ would mean "3 hours"; أَحَدَ عَشَرَ سَاعَةً "11 hours".

"What time is it?" is expressed by كَمِ ٱلسَّاعَةُ or ٱلسَّاعَةُ كَمْ.

Note. The hours are counted in the East from sunset.

b) The times of day "in the morning", "in the evening", "at midday" are best expressed by the Accus., otherwise by the preposition فِي; e.g.

صَبَاحًا (فِي ٱلصَّبَاحِ) In the morning. مَسَاءً (فِي ٱلْمَسَاءِ) In the evening.

ظُهْرًا (فِي ٱلظُّهْرِ) At midday.

7. The names of the Days of the week are:

يَوْمُ (نَهَارُ) ٱلْأَحَدِ Sunday.

يَوْمُ (نَهَارُ) ٱلْاِثْنَيْنِ Monday.

يَوْمُ (نَهَارُ) ٱلثَّلَاثَاءِ (ٱلثَّلَثَاءِ) Tuesday.

يَوْمُ (نَهَارُ) ٱلْأَرْبِعَاءِ Wednesday.

يَوْمُ (نَهَارُ) ٱلْخَمِيسِ Thursday.

يَوْمُ (نَهَارُ) ٱلْجُمْعَةِ Friday.

يَوْمُ (نَهَارُ) ٱلسَّبْتِ Saturday.

The word يَوْمٌ or نَهَارٌ is often omitted; e.g. أَلثَّلَاثَاءُ Tuesday.

"The week" is أَلْجُمْعَةُ or أَلْأُسْبُوعُ.

The Months of the Christian year.

8. The Christian year is called أَلسَّنَةُ ٱلْمِيلَادِيَّةُ "the birth year" or أَلسَّنَةُ ٱلْمَسِيحِيَّةُ "the Messiah year" or أَلسَّنَةُ ٱلشَّمْسِيَّةُ "the sun year".

The twelve Months are named:

a) usually in Egypt:

يَنَائِرُ January.	يُولِيُو July (also لُولِيُو).
فِبْرَائِرُ February.	أَغُسْطُسُ August.
مَارْسُ March.	سِبْتَمْبِرُ September.
أَبْرِيلُ April.	أُكْتُوبِرُ October.
مَايُو May.	نُوفِمْبِرُ November.
يُونِيُو June.	دِيسِمْبِرُ December.

b) usually in Syria:

كَانُونُ ٱلثَّانِي January.	تَمُّوزُ July.
شُبَاطُ February.	آبُ August
آذَارُ March.	أَيْلُولُ September.
نِيسَانُ April.	تِشْرِينُ ٱلْأَوَّلُ October.
أَيَّارُ May.	تِشْرِينُ ٱلثَّانِي November.
حَزِيرَانُ June.	كَانُونُ ٱلْأَوَّلُ December.

B.C. is expressed in Arabic by قَبْلَ ٱلْمِيلَادِ (abbreviated ق م).

A.D. " " " " " بَعْدَ ٱلْمِيلَادِ (" ب م or simple م).

The Months of the Mohammedan Year.

9. The Mohammedan year is called أَلسَّنَةُ ٱلْهِجْرِيَّةُ "the flight year" (abbreviated after a date to ه) or أَلسَّنَةُ ٱلْقَمَرِيَّةُ "the moon year".

Dates are reckoned from 16th July 622 A.D., this being the day of the flight of Mohammed from Mecca to Medina.

Every year has 354 days.

The Mohammedan year 1327 began on 23rd Jan. 1909 A.D.

The year consists of the following twelve lunar months:

اَلْمُحَرَّمُ	رَجَبٌ
صَفَرٌ	شَعْبَانُ
رَبِيعُ ٱلأَوَّلُ	رَمَضَانُ (the month of fasting).
رَبِيعُ ٱلثَّانِي	شَوَّالٌ
جُمَادَى ٱلأُولَى	ذُو ٱلْقَعْدَةِ
جُمَادَى ٱلآخِرَةُ	ذُو ٱلْحِجَّةِ (Month of the حَجٌّ).

Some names of these months are often used with special attributive; e.g.

مُحَرَّمُ ٱلْحَرَامِ	صَفَرُ ٱلْخَيْرِ
رَجَبُ ٱلْفَرْدِ	شَعْبَانُ ٱلْمُعَظَّمُ
رَمَضَانُ ٱلْمُكَرَّمُ etc.	

Mohammedan Feasts.

The Mohammedans celebrate two chief festivals:

1) اَلْعِيدُ ٱلصَّغِيرُ "the small festival" at the beginning of the month شَوَّالٌ immediately after the end of the great fast in the month رَمَضَانُ.

2) اَلْعِيدُ ٱلْكَبِيرُ "the great festival" also called عِيدُ ٱلأَضْحَى "the sacrificial festival" on the 10th of the month ذُو ٱلْحِجَّةِ, when the pilgrims offer sacrifice in Mecca.

Method of indicating Date.

10. To indicate Date the Ordinal numbers are generally used. After the Ordinal is put the Name of the Month, with or without the word شَهْر before it, and after this the numbers indicating the Year with or without سَنَة before them, in the Genitive; e.g.

ثَالِثُ (شَهْرِ) ٱلْمُحَرَّمِ اَلْيَوْمُ ٱلثَّالِثُ مِنْ (شَهْرِ) ٱلْمُحَرَّمِ	the 3rd of Muḥarram.
أَوَّلُ (شَهْرِ) يَنَايِرَ (سَنَةَ) ١٨٩٦ اَلْيَوْمُ ٱلْأَوَّلُ مِنْ (شَهْرِ) يَنَايِرَ (سَنَةَ) ١٨٩٦	1st January 1896.

On such and such a date is expressed by the Accus. or the preposition فِي.

Indication of Age.

11. How old art thou? is expressed by:

عُمْرُكَ كَمْ سَنَةً literally "thy life (is) how many years?" or:

اِبْنُ كَمْ سَنَةً أَنْتَ literally "a son of how many years art thou?"

The answer to such a question would be of the form:

عُمْرِي عِشْرُونَ سَنَةً أَنَا ٱبْنُ عِشْرِينَ سَنَةً	"I am twenty years old".

Vocabulary.

دَقِيقَة	minute.	مَحَلّ	place.
أُهْبَة	equipment.	قِيمَة	value, price.
اَلْأَوَّل	the first.	شَرِكَ	VIII. to subscribe (to فِي).
مُضِيّ	expiration (of time).	فِرَانْك	franc.

جِهَةٌ direction, part (of the word).
ثَمَنٌ price.
نُسْخَةٌ copy.
غِرْشٌ (pl. غُرُوشٌ) piastre.
بَارَةٌ (pl. بَارَاتٌ) para.
أُجْرَةٌ reward, cost.
عَلَنَ IV. to advertise.
صَفْحَةٌ page (of a book).
سَطْرٌ line.
دَارَ (و) to revolve.
دَوْرَةٌ revolution.
مِحْوَرٌ axis.
دَائِرَةٌ (pl. دَوَائِرُ) circle.
قَسَمَ to divide, VII. to be divided.
دَرَجَةٌ degree.
ثَانِيَةٌ a second.
سَطْحٌ surface.
مِيلٌ (pl. أَمْيَالٌ) mile.
مُرَبَّعٌ square.
يَبَسٌ dry land.
نِسْبَةٌ relation.
عَالَمٌ world.
تَقْرِيبًا about.
مِنْطَقَةٌ (pl. مَنَاطِقُ) girdle, zone.
حَرٌّ heat.
حَارٌّ hot.
مُعْتَدِلٌ moderate, temperate.
اَلْقُطْرُ ٱلْمِصْرِيُّ the land of Egypt.
قِبْلِيٌّ southern.
اَلْوَجْهُ ٱلْقِبْلِيُّ Upper Egypt.
مُدِيرِيَّةٌ Mudirīya (a name given to some provinces of Egypt).
أَمَّا as for (see Less. 46, § 2 f).
عَدَا عَنْ beside.
مَرْكَزٌ (pl. مَرَاكِزُ) centre.
مُحَافَظَةٌ Muḥāfaẓa (a name given to some provinces of Egypt).
خَرَاجٌ tribute.
جِنِيهٌ guinea.
سَنَوِيٌّ yearly.

قَائِمَةٌ list, register.

مَكْتَبَةٌ library, bookshop.

عُنْوَانٌ title, address.

صَاغٌ (Turkish) of full weight or value.

رِوَايَةٌ narrative, play.

رِحْلَةٌ travel.

إِبْنُ بَطُوطَةَ Ibn Baṭûṭa, an Arabian traveller, who died 778 A.H. = 1377 A.D.

جِغْرَافِيَةٌ geography.

أَمِينْ بيك فِكْرِي Amin Bey Fikri (a modern Egyptian writer).

اَلْمُرْشِدُ ٱلْأَمِين "the trusty guide" (name of a book).

رِفَاعَة بيك Rifâ'at Bey, (modern Egyptian writer).

شَدٌّ packing.

جُمْلَةٌ total.

بَفْتَةٌ (Persian) thin cotton stuff.

بُوسْطَةٌ post.

إِسْكَنْدَرُ ٱلْأَكْبَرُ Alexander the great.

اَلْإِسْكَنْدَرِيَّةُ Alexandria.

رِيحٌ (pl. أَرْيَاحٌ) wind.

شَمَالٌ north.

جَنُوبٌ south.

شَرْقٌ east.

غَرْبٌ west.

عُلُوٌّ heighth.

كَرًى slumber.

صَرَفَ to spend (time).

شَدَّ VIII. to be strong.

غَسَّالَةٌ washerwoman.

قَمِيصٌ (pl. قُمْصَانٌ) shirt.

مِنْدِيلٌ (plur. مَنَادِيلُ) handkerchief.

أَخَرَ II. to lose (time), be slow (of a watch).

Exercise 61.

أَلسَّاعَةُ كَمْ — أَلسَّاعَةُ عِنْدِي أَحَدَ عَشَرَ وَعِشْرُونَ دَقِيقَةً — حَضَرْتُ أُهْبَةَ ٱلسَّفَرِ يَوْمَ ٱلثَّلَثَاءِ ٱلْأَوَّلِ مِنْ شَهْرِ تَمُّوزٍ فِي سَنَةِ أَلْفٍ وَثَمَانِي مِئَةٍ وَخَمْسَةٍ وَتِسْعِينَ — كَانَ عِنْدِي شَابٌّ

لَمْ يَبْلُغْ مِنَ ٱلْعُمْرِ أَكْثَرَ مِنْ سَبْعَ عَشْرَةَ سَنَةً — أَلْمَدِينَةُ تَبْعُدُ عَنَّا أَرْبَعَ سَاعَاتٍ — بَعْدَ مُضِيِّ خَمْسِ سَاعَاتٍ وَصَلْنَا إِلَى ٱلْمَحَلِّ ٱلْمَذْكُورِ — قِيمَةُ ٱلْاِشْتِرَاكِ فِي جَرِيدَتِنَا فِي بَيْرُوتَ وَلُبْنَانَ عَنْ (for) سَنَةٍ أَرْبَعَةَ عَشَرَ فِرَانْكًا وَفِي سَائِرِ ٱلْجِهَاتِ ثَمَانِيَةَ عَشَرَ فِرَانْكًا — ثَمَنُ ٱلنُّسْخَةِ ٱلْوَاحِدَةِ غِرْشٌ — أُجْرَةُ ٱلْإِعْلَانِ فِي ٱلصَّفْحَةِ ٱلْأَخِيرَةِ عَنْ كُلِّ سَطْرٍ غِرْشَانِ وَلِلْمُشْتَرِكِينَ سِتُّونَ بَارَةً وَفِي غَيْرِ ٱلصَّفْحَةِ ٱلْأَخِيرَةِ ثَلَاثَةُ غُرُوشٍ وَلِلْمُشْتَرِكِينَ نِصْفُ فِرَانْكٍ — ٱلْأَرْضُ تَدُورُ عَلَى مِحْوَرِهَا دَوْرَةً وَاحِدَةً كُلَّ أَرْبَعٍ وَعِشْرِينَ سَاعَةً — كُلُّ دَائِرَةٍ مِنْ دَوَائِرِ ٱلطُّولِ وَٱلْعَرْضِ تُقْسَمُ إِلَى ثَلَاثِ مِئَةٍ وَسِتِّينَ قِسْمًا يُقَالُ لَهُ دَرَجَاتٌ وَكُلُّ دَرَجَةٍ تُقْسَمُ إِلَى سِتِّينَ دَقِيقَةً وَٱلدَّقِيقَةُ إِلَى سِتِّينَ ثَانِيَةً — مَسَاحَةُ سَطْحِ ٱلْأَرْضِ تَبْلُغُ مِئَتَيْ مِلْيُونِ مِيلٍ مِنَ ٱلْأَمْيَالِ ٱلْمُرَبَّعَةِ وَهُوَ يَنْقَسِمُ إِلَى يَبْسٍ وَمَاءٍ وَنِسْبَةُ ٱلْيَبْسِ إِلَى ٱلْمَاءِ كَنِسْبَةِ ثَلَاثَةٍ إِلَى سَبْعَةٍ — عَدَدُ أَهْلِ ٱلْعَالَمِ أَلْفُ وَمِائَتَا مِلْيُونِ نَفْسٍ تَقْرِيبًا — سَطْحُ ٱلْأَرْضِ يُقْسَمُ أَيْضًا إِلَى خَمْسِ مَنَاطِقَ وَاحِدَةٌ حَارَّةٌ وَٱثْنَتَانِ مُعْتَدِلَتَانِ وَٱثْنَتَانِ بَارِدَتَانِ — إِنَّ ٱلْقُطْرَ ٱلْمِصْرِيَّ يَنْقَسِمُ إِلَى قِسْمَيْنِ جَنُوبِيٍّ وَشَمَالِيٍّ أَوْ قِبْلِيٍّ وَبَحْرِيٍّ فَيَنْقَسِمُ ٱلْوَجْهُ ٱلْقِبْلِيُّ

إلى سبع مديريات أما الوجه البحري فينقسم إلى ست مديريات وفي القطر المصري عدا عن هذه المديريات ستة مراكز يقال لها محافظات — إن حكومة مصر تدفع للباب العالي خراجا مقداره نحو سبعمئة ألف جنيه سنويا —

قائمة الكتب المطلوبة من المكتبة العمومية

غروش	صاغ	عدد	عنوان الكتب
٤٠		٤	الاربع روايات ب ١٠
٣٠		٢	رحلة ابن بطوطة ب ١٥
٣٠		١	جغرافية أمين بيك فكري
٢٥		١	المرشد الامين لرفاعة بيك
١٢٥		٨	الجملة
١٥			ثمن بفتة للدرد وأجرة البوسطة ومكتوب بيا
١٤٠			

مصر في أول شهر التوبر سنة ١٨٩٠

Exercise 62.

The earth revolves round (على) the sun once (one revolution) in 365 days and 6 hours. — The Moslems reckon from the Flight, which was (and it was) in the year 622 A.D. — Wilt thou honour us with a visit (thy coming) on Sunday? — I will visit you on Saturday. — Wilt thou come in the morning or the evening? —

I will come in the afternoon (after the midday), if God will. — Alexander the Great came to Egypt in the year 332 B.C. and built the city of Alexandria. — The number of its inhabitants is now 231 396 souls. — How old are you (two)? — I am 25 years old and my brother has not reached in age more than 9 years. — How old art thou O girl? — Next (on the coming) Wednesday I shall be (reach) 17. — The winds come to this mountain (Accus.) from the four directions, the North (and) the South (and) the East and the West, and its height is 11000 feet. — Truly, my eye has not tasted (ذَاقَ [u]) slumber for (since) four days. — We spend about three months in the mountains, for the heat is strong in the city. -- The washerwoman brought us six shirts and two nightshirts (shirts for the sleep نَوْم) and twelve handkerchiefs. — Hasan Pasha died in the year 1888, may God have mercy upon him! — What is the time? -- It is ten minutes past nine (nine and ten minutes). — Thy watch is slow, it will soon be ten. — How much (بِكَمْ) is this book? — Forty-five piastres, my master. —. This is dear (غَالٍ), I will give thee twenty. — Give me thirty, and enough! (وَٱلسَّلَامُ).

Thirty-third Lesson.

(أَلدَّرْسُ ٱلثَّالِثُ وَٱلثَّلَاثُونَ)

B. The Ordinal Numbers.

1. The Ordinals are generally formed from the Cardinals according to the type فَاعِل but with some exceptions:

أَلْأَوَّلُ	fem.	أَلْأُولَى	the first.
أَلثَّانِي	,,	أَلثَّانِيَةُ	the second.

أَلثَّالِثُ	fem.	أَلثَّالِثَةُ	the third.
أَلرَّابِعُ	„	أَلرَّابِعَةُ	the fourth.
أَلْخَامِسُ	„	أَلْخَامِسَةُ	the fifth.
أَلسَّادِسُ	„	أَلسَّادِسَةُ	the sixth.
أَلسَّابِعُ	„	أَلسَّابِعَةُ	the seventh.
أَلثَّامِنُ	„	أَلثَّامِنَةُ	the eighth.
أَلتَّاسِعُ	„	أَلتَّاسِعَةُ	the ninth.
أَلْعَاشِرُ	„	أَلْعَاشِرَةُ	the tenth.

All the above are declined fully.

The Ordinals from 11 to 19 are indeclinable:

أَلْحَادِى عَشَرَ	fem.	أَلْحَادِيَةَ عَشْرَةَ	the eleventh.
أَلثَّانِي عَشَرَ	„	أَلثَّانِيَةَ عَشْرَةَ	the twelfth.
أَلثَّالِثَ عَشَرَ	„	أَلثَّالِثَةَ عَشْرَةَ	the thirteenth etc.

For the higher numbers the Cardinals only are used; except that the Ordinals of the Units are used joined to the Cardinals of the Tens to express the Compound Ordinals. The Article must be attached to each numeral used.

أَلْعِشْرُونَ masc. and fem. the twentieth.

أَلْحَادِى وَٱلْعِشْرُونَ	fem.	أَلْحَادِيَةُ وَٱلْعِشْرُونَ	the twenty-first.
أَلثَّانِي وَٱلْعِشْرُونَ	„	أَلثَّانِيَةُ وَٱلْعِشْرُونَ	the twenty-second.
أَلثَّالِثُ وَٱلْعِشْرُونَ	„	أَلثَّالِثَةُ وَٱلْعِشْرُونَ	the twenty-third etc.

اَلْمِئَةُ masc. and fem. the hundredth.

اَلْآخِرُ	fem.	اَلْآخِرَةُ	the last.
اَلْأَخِيرُ	"	اَلْأَخِيرَةُ	

Note 1. For the use of the Ordinals in the indication of Dates and the Hours of the day see the previous lesson.

Note. 2. The Ordinals have the Sound Plural, e.g. اَلْأَوَّلُ Plur. اَلْأَوَّلُونَ

The word اَلْأَوَّلُ has also a Broken Plur. اَلْأَوَائِلُ meaning "the first parts" just as اَلْآخِرُ has a Plur. اَلْأَوَاخِرُ "the last parts", and اَلْأَوْسَطُ "the middle" has اَلْأَوَاسِطُ "the middle parts". These terms are sometimes used for the three decades of the month.

2. The Numeral Adverbs "firstly, secondly, thirdly" etc. are expressed by the Adverbial Accus. of the Ordinals, e.g.

أَوَّلًا, ثَانِيًا, ثَالِثًا, رَابِعًا, خَامِسًا etc.

3. The Numeral Adverbs "once, twice, three times" etc. are expressed usually by the word مَرَّةٌ in the Accus., e.g.

مَرَّةً "once", مَرَّتَيْنِ "twice", ثَلَاثَ مَرَّاتٍ "three times" etc.

(Once = "once upon a time, one day" is يَوْمًا or ذَاتَ يَوْمٍ).

Sometimes the occurrence of an action once or twice is expressed by the Verbal Noun with the ending ة (the so-called إِسْمُ مَرَّةٍ) e.g.

يَدُورُ دَوْرَةً أَوْ دَوْرَتَيْنِ "he turns round once or twice".

4. The Fractions (with the exception of "a half") are of the type فُعْلٌ or فُعُلٌ with the Plural أَفْعَالٌ:

$^1/_2$	نِصْفٌ				
$^1/_3$	ثُلْثٌ	or	ثُلُثٌ	Plur.	أَثْلَاثٌ
$^1/_4$	رُبْعٌ	,,	رُبُعٌ	,,	أَرْبَاعٌ
$^1/_5$	خُمْسٌ	,,	خُمُسٌ	,,	أَخْمَاسٌ
$^1/_6$	سُدْسٌ	,,	سُدُسٌ	,,	أَسْدَاسٌ
$^1/_7$	سُبْعٌ	,,	سُبُعٌ	,,	أَسْبَاعٌ
$^1/_8$	ثُمْنٌ	,,	ثُمُنٌ	,,	أَثْمَانٌ
$^1/_9$	تُسْعٌ	,,	تُسُعٌ	,,	أَتْسَاعٌ
$^1/_{10}$	عُشْرٌ	,,	عُشُرٌ	,,	أَعْشَارٌ

e.g. $^2/_3$ ثُلُثَانِ; $^3/_4$ ثَلَاثَةُ أَرْبَاعٍ.

If a whole and a fraction are united, they must be joined by وَ; e.g.

$4^5/_6$ = أَرْبَعَةٌ وَخَمْسَةُ أَسْدَاسٍ.

Note. $^1/_4$ is often written, ─; $^1/_2$, <; $^3/_4$, ≤.

5. The Multiplicative adjectives "twofold, threefold" etc. are of the form مُفَعَّلٌ: e.g. مُثَنًّى "twofold"; مُثَلَّثٌ "threefold (also = "triangle"); مُرَبَّعٌ "fourfold" (also = "square"). "Single, simple" is مُفْرَدٌ.

6. The Distributive adjectives "two by two" etc. are expressed

a) by repetition of the Cardinal number, or

b) by the forms فُعَالُ or مَفْعَلُ; e.g.:

جَاءُوا مَثْنَى or جَاءُوا اثْنَيْنِ اثْنَيْنِ they come two by two.

مَرَرْتُ بِقَوْمٍ مَثْنَى وَثُلَاثَ I passed by people (walking) in twos and threes.

7. Numeral adjectives expressing the number of parts of which anything is made, are of the form فُعَالِيٌّ, e.g.

ثُنَائِيٌّ Biliteral.

ثُلَاثِيٌّ Triliteral, or 3 cubits long, or high.

رُبَاعِيٌّ Quadriliteral, or 4 cubits high, or a quatrain.

Vocabulary.

تَعْلِيمٌ	doctrine, teaching.	شَرْقِيٌّ	eastern.
دَرْسٌ	lesson.	زَنْجِبَار	Zanzibar.
شَرِيفٌ	noble.	أَوْسَطُ	(fem. وُسْطَى) central, middle.
سُنَّةٌ	tradition (in Islam).	غَرْبِيٌّ	western.
شِيعَةٌ	Shiites, (a sect of Mohammedans).	جَنُوبِيٌّ	southern.
شَمَلَ	VIII. to comprise, contain.	رَأْسٌ	cape.
فَرْعٌ	(pl. فُرُوعٌ) branch.	تَبِعَ	to follow, belong.
مَغْرِبٌ	Maghrib.	قَارَّةٌ	continent.
اَلْجَزَائِرُ	Algeria.	أَرَّخَ	II. to date, (Verbal Noun = date, history).
مُرَّاكُش	Morocco.	وَفِقَ	III. to agree, correspond with.

شُرُوقٌ rising } of the sun.
غُرُوبٌ setting } of the sun.

إِفْرَنْجِيٌّ Frankish, European.

حَرْفٌ (pl. أَحْرُفٌ and حُرُوفٌ) letter, particle.

جُزْءٌ (pl. أَجْزَاءٌ) part.

سُورَةٌ sura, (chapter of the Koran).

ٱلْفَاتِحَةُ the Fatiha (name of the 1st sura).

إِسْمٌ (pl. أَسْمَاءٌ) noun.

فَسَدَ to be spoilt.

بَابٌ chapter.

إِبْتِدَاءٌ beginning.

فَصْلُ ٱلرَّبِيعِ Spring.

فَصْلُ ٱلْخَرِيفِ Autumn.

نَوْعٌ (pl. أَنْوَاعٌ) kind, class.

عَزِيزٌ noble.

Exercise 63.

تَعْلِيمُ أَسْمَاءِ ٱلْعَدَدِ يُوجَدُ فِي ٱلدَّرْسِ ٱلثَّانِي وَٱلثَّلَاثِينَ وَفِي ٱلدَّرْسِ ٱلثَّالِثِ وَٱلثَّلَاثِينَ مِنْ هٰذَا ٱلْكِتَابِ — دِينُ ٱلْإِسْلَامِ مَبْنِيٌّ عَلَى ٱلْقُرْآنِ ٱلشَّرِيفِ وَقَدِ ٱنْقَسَمَ أَصْحَابُهُ إِلَى قِسْمَيْنِ. ٱلْأَوَّلُ أَهْلُ ٱلسُّنَّةِ وَٱلثَّانِي أَهْلُ ٱلشِّيعَةِ — تُقْسَمُ أَفْرِيقِيَةُ إِلَى سَبْعَةِ أَقْسَامٍ. ٱلْأَوَّلُ يَشْتَمِلُ عَلَى ٱلْبِلَادِ ٱلَّتِي يَرْوِيهَا ٱلنِّيلُ وَفُرُوعُهُ وَفِيهَا مِصْرُ وَٱلثَّانِي بِلَادُ ٱلْمَغْرِبِ وَفِيهَا ٱلْجَزَائِرُ وَمَرَّاكِشُ وَٱلثَّالِثُ أَفْرِيقِيَةُ ٱلشَّرْقِيَّةُ وَفِيهَا زَنْجِبَارُ وَٱلرَّابِعُ أَفْرِيقِيَةُ ٱلْوُسْطَى وَٱلْخَامِسُ أَفْرِيقِيَةُ ٱلْغَرْبِيَّةُ وَٱلسَّادِسُ أَفْرِيقِيَةُ ٱلْجَنُوبِيَّةُ وَفِيهَا بِلَادُ ٱلرَّأْسِ وَٱلسَّابِعُ ٱلْجَزَائِرُ ٱلتَّابِعَةُ لِهٰذِهِ ٱلْقَارَّةِ — فِي

اَلسَّاعَةَ ٱلثَّامِنَةَ أَتَشَرَّفُ بِٱلْمَجِيءِ عِنْدَكُمْ — وَصَلَنَا كِتَابُكُمُ
ٱلْعَزِيزُ ٱلْمُوَرَّخُ بِيَوْمِ ٱلِاثْنَيْنِ ٣٠ كَانُونَ ٱلثَّانِي سَنَةَ ١٨٨٧ م ٱلْمُوَافِقُ
٢٧ رَبِيعٍ ٱلْأَوَّلِ سَنَةَ ١٣٠٥ هـ — يَكُونُ شُرُوقُ ٱلشَّمْسِ ٱلسَّاعَةَ ٢
وَ٤ دَقَائِقَ وَٱلظُّهْرُ ٱلسَّاعَةَ ٧ وَ٨ دَقَائِقَ وَٱلْغُرُوبُ ٱلْإِفْرَنْجِيُّ
ٱلسَّاعَةَ ٤ وَ٣٥ دَقِيقَةً — كُنْتُ فِي مَنْزِلِكَ ٱلسَّاعَةَ ٱلتَّاسِعَةَ
وَرُبْعٍ وَبَقِيتُ فِي ٱنْتِظَارِكَ نِصْفَ سَاعَةٍ وَٱلسَّاعَةَ ٱلتَّاسِعَةَ وَثَلَاثَةَ
أَرْبَاعٍ خَرَجْتُ مِنَ ٱلدَّارِ — قَدْ تَعَلَّمْنَا أَوَّلًا ٱلْأَسْمَاءَ ٱلْعَرَبِيَّةَ
وَثَانِيًا ٱلْأَفْعَالَ وَإِنْ شَاءَ ٱللّٰهُ نَتَعَلَّمُ ثَالِثًا ٱلْأَحْرُفَ فِي ٱلْجُزْءِ ٱلثَّانِي
مِنْ هٰذَا ٱلْكِتَابِ — إِنَّ ٱلسُّورَةَ ٱلْأُولَى مِنَ ٱلْقُرْآنِ ٱلشَّرِيفِ
ٱسْمُهَا ٱلْفَاتِحَةُ — خُذْ ثُلْثَيْنِ مِنْ هٰذَا ٱلرَّغِيفِ وَأَنَا آخُذُ
ٱلثُّلْثَ ٱلْآخَرَ — ٱلْعِيدُ ٱلصَّغِيرُ فِي أَوَائِلِ شَهْرِ شَوَّالٍ —

Exercise 64.

The date of this letter is: Tuesday the 1st July 1890, corresponding with the 13th Dhu'lqa'da 1307. — The 114th Sura of the noble Koran is called "The Sura of (the) men". — In the first days (ٱلْأَوَائِلُ) of the month of May you (sing.) will receive (will come to you) a letter from us and, if God will, you will send us the answer in the latter days of June. — In this night I have not slept a quarter of an hour. — I will return to your dwelling after three quarters of an (from the) hour. — Take seven eighths of this stuff and we will take the last eighth. — Two thirds of this food is spoilt — My servant was in the fifteenth year of his life. — Yesterday I read the first (and) second and third chapters of this book, and to-morrow I shall read the fourth (and) fifth and sixth. — How old art thou? — I am in the twenty-sixth year of my life, for I shall be twenty-six (reach the twenty-six) on the 29th January. — The beginning of Spring is on the 21st March, and the beginning of Summer on the 21st June, and (the beginning) of Autumn on the 21st September, and (the beginning) of Winter on the 21st December. — The doctrine of the Relative Pronoun is contained (is found) in the 31st Lesson of this book. — There are three kinds of words in the Arabic language: firstly the Noun, (and) secondly the Verb, (and) thirdly the Partiele.

END OF PART I.

Second Part.

Thirty-fourth Lesson.

(اَلدَّرْسُ اَلرَّابِعُ وَٱلثَّلَاثُونَ)

The Noun and its Derivation.

Nouns (إِسْمٌ Plur. أَسْمَاءٌ) are divided according to their Derivation into:

a) Primitive; e.g. رَأْسٌ "head". Such nouns are to be found in the dictionaries under the verbal stem, although in this case the verb رَأَسَ "to be at the head of a tribe, to strike on the head" is derived from the noun.

b) Derivative:

α) Derived from Verbs. Most nouns are of this class, e.g. قَتْلٌ "killing" from قَتَلَ; مَجْلِسٌ "session, council" from جَلَسَ "to sit"; كَبِيرٌ "great" from كَبُرَ "to be great"

β) Derived from Nouns; e.g. مَأْسَدَةٌ "a place in which there are lions" from أَسَدٌ "a lion"; إِسْلَامِيٌّ "Islamic" from إِسْلَامٌ "Islam".

2. The most usual nouns derived from the verb are:

a) The Verbal Noun (مَصْدَرٌ) which properly expresses the verbal idea in the form of a noun, but sometimes has a more remote meaning and is then known as the إِسْمُ مَصْدَرٍ.

b) The Active Participle (إِسْمُ ٱلْفَاعِلِ).

c) The Passive Participle (إِسْمُ ٱلْمَفْعُولِ).

These three forms have been treated in the first part of the grammar, but the following facts regarding the Verbal Noun of the Simple (I.) form of the verb should be noted:

a) The form فَعْلٌ occurs especially in transitive verbs of the form فَعَلَ and فَعِلَ; e.g. قَتْلٌ from قَتَلَ "to kill"; فَهْمٌ from فَهِمَ "to understand".

b) فَعَلٌ in intransitive verbs of the form فَعِلَ; e.g. فَرَحٌ "joy" from فَرِحَ.

c) فُعُولٌ in intransitive verbs of the form فَعَلَ; e.g. جُلُوسٌ from جَلَسَ "to sit".

d) فُعُولَةٌ and فَعَالَةٌ in verbs of the form فَعُلَ e.g. سُهُولَةٌ "smoothness" and سَهَالَةٌ "easiness" from سَهُلَ "to be smooth, easy".

e) فِعَالَةٌ especially in verbs denoting an Office or Trade; e.g. خِلَافَةٌ "Caliphate" from خَلَفَ "to follow"; خِيَاطَةٌ "tailoring" from خَاطَ "to sew".

f) Many verbs form their Verbal Noun with a prefixed mīm; e.g. مَقْصِدٌ "purpose" from قَصَدَ "to intend". This form of Verbal Noun is called مَصْدَرٌ مِيمِيٌّ

g) Other common forms of the Verbal Noun of the Simple verb are:

فَعْلٌ e.g. شَغْلٌ "business" from شَغَلَ "to occupy one in".

فِعْلٌ „ قِسْمٌ "part" „ قَسَمَ "to divide".

فِعَلٌ „ صِغَرٌ "smallness, youth" „ صَغُرَ "to be small".

فِعَالٌ e.g. لِقَاءٌ "meeting" from لَقِيَ "to meet".

فُعَالٌ „ سُؤَالٌ "question" „ سَأَلَ "to ask".

فَعَالٌ „ خَلَاصٌ "deliverance" „ خَلَصَ "to be delivered".

فَعْلَى „ دَعْوَى "call" „ دَعَا "to call".

فُعْلَانٌ „ غُفْرَانٌ "forgiveness" „ غَفَرَ "to forgive"

فِعْلَانٌ „ حِرْمَانٌ "privation" „ حَرَمَ "to deprive".

فَعَلَانٌ „ جَرَيَانٌ "flowing" „ جَرَى "to flow".

(rare)
فَعُولٌ e.g. قَبُولٌ "acceptance" „ قَبِلَ "to accept".

فَعِيلٌ „ رَحِيلٌ "journey" „ رَحَلَ "to journey"

فَعَالِيَةٌ „ كَرَاهِيَةٌ "hatred" „ كَرِهَ "to hate".

مَفْعَلَةٌ „ مَقَالَةٌ "treatise" „ قَالَ "to say".

Note. In the dictionaries the Verbal Noun is given for each verb Sometimes several forms are in use from the same verb, either with the same or different meanings; e.g. قَصْدٌ and مَقْصَدٌ "purpose" from قَصَدَ; وَصْفٌ "description" and صِفَةٌ "quality" from وَصَفَ "to describe

3. The Verbal Nouns of verbs whose 2nd and 3rd radicals are the same, of hamzated verbs and of weak verbs are of the same forms as above but subject to the rules for assimilation etc. given in the earlier lessons; e.g.

from ظَنَّ "to think": ظَنٌّ (for ظَنْنٌ) "opinion";

from قَامَ "to stand": قِيَامٌ (for قِوَامٌ) "standing";

from قَالَ "to say": مَقَالَةٌ (for مَقْوَلَةٌ) "treatise".

It should be noted that the verbs, whose first radical is و, which drop the و in the Imperf. (Less. 26, 2) have also a Verbal Noun without the first radical; e.g. from وَصَلَ "to unite": صِلَةٌ "tie" (beside وَصْلٌ); from وَصَفَ "to describe": صِفَةٌ "quality".

4. The Verbal Nouns of the Derived forms are given in Lesson 18, 7. In these forms the Part. Pass. is often used with the meaning of the Verbal Noun; e.g. اَلْمُقْتَضَى "that which is necessitated" instead of اَلْاِقْتِضَاءُ "necessity".

5. The meaning of the Verbal Noun is either Active or Passive. Often it is both; e.g. قَتْلٌ is "killing" or "being killed", sometimes it is only Passive; e.g. وُجُودٌ "being found i.e. existence" (Active only is وِجْدَانٌ "finding").

The meaning of the Verbal Noun is not in any way connected with the idea of time, e.g. قَتْلٌ means "killing" or "being killed" either in the past, present or future.

6. In its syntax the Verbal Noun partakes of the characteristics of the Noun and of the Verb. As a Noun it is followed by the Genitive, subjective or objective; e.g.

قَتْلُ زَيْدٍ may mean "Zaid's killing (someone)" or "the killing of Zaid" as in

أَمَرَ ٱلْمَلِكُ بِقَتْلِ زَيْدٍ "the king commanded that (someone) should kill Zaid".

If however the Verbal Noun has both a subject and an object, then the former is put in the Genitive and the latter in the Accusative or has the Preposition لِ; e.g.

قَتْلُ زَيْدٍ مُحَمَّدًا or لِمُحَمَّدٍ "the fact of Zaid's killing Mohammed".

So also حُبُّ ٱلْوَطَنِ "the love of (one's) country".

حُبُّ ٱلشَّابِ ٱلْوَطَنَ or لِلْوَطَنِ "the youth's love of (his) country",
and with a pronominal suffix:

قَتْلُهُ مُحَمَّدًا "his killing Mohammed".

حُبِّي لِلْوَطَنِ "my love of (my) country".

The preposition لِ is also used when the Verbal Noun is employed indefinitely with an adverbial meaning, e.g.

قُمْتُ إِكْرَامًا لِمُحَمَّدٍ "I rose in honour of Mohammed".

7. A verb can always be strengthened or specialised in meaning by the addition of a Verbal Noun (cf. Less. 12, ˉ). This (called in Arabic اَلْمَفْعُولُ ٱلْمُطْلَقُ "the absolute object") is usually derived from the same verb, e.g. فَرِحَ فَرَحًا عَظِيمًا "he rejoiced greatly". (In this case the absolute object is used "for distinguishing" لِلتَّمْيِيزِ): but may also be derived from another verb, e.g. فَرِحَ سُرُورًا عَظِيمًا "he rejoiced greatly".

It is also used with the Passive, e.g. ضُرِبَ ضَرْبًا شَدِيدًا "he was struck violently".

Sometimes the Verbal Noun is so used without an adjective, e.g. ضَرَبَ ضَرْبًا "he struck a striking". (In this case it is used لِلتَّأْكِيدِ i.e. for emphasising.)

Sometimes the Adjective alone is expressed and the Verbal Noun is understood, e.g. ضَرَبَ شَدِيدًا "he struck violently" for ضَرَبَ ضَرْبًا شَدِيدًا.

The Verbal Noun may be used thus with a Genitive, or a Suffix or a Demonstrative Pronoun or a Relative Sentence, e.g.

خِفْتَ خَوْفَ ٱلْجَبَانِ "thou fearest the fearing of the coward" i.e. like a coward.

ضَرَبْتُهُ هٰذَا ٱلضَّرْبَ "I struck him this striking" i.e. thus.

ضُرِبَ ضَرْبًا أَوْجَعَهُ "he was struck a striking which pained him".

8. The Active Participle (إِسْمُ ٱلْفَاعِلِ) may also be used as a Noun, in which case it is followed by a Genitive, or as a Verb when it is followed by an Accusative or the Preposition لِ, if it is used in the sense of the Imperfect, e.g.

قَاتِلُ ٱلنَّاسِ
قَاتِلُ ٱلنَّاسَ } "one, who kills men".

ٱلْقَاتِلُ ٱلنَّاسَ "he, who kills men".

ٱلطَّالِبُ لِلْعِلْمِ "he, who strives after knowledge".

But if it is used in the sense of the Perfect, it can have only the Genitive after it, e.g. قَاتِلُ ٱلنَّاسِ "he, who has killed men".

Exercise 65.

The words in the following exercises are to be found in the Vocabulary at the end of the book. The vowels of the Article and some common words are now omitted.

كُلُّ نَفْسٍ ذَائِقَةُ الْمَوْتِ — سِرْنَا سَيْرًا سَرِيعًا — كَانَ قَتْلُ الْخَلِيفَةِ جَعْفَرًا فى هذه السَّنَةِ — فَعَلَ زَيْدٌ هذا الفِعْلَ حُبًّا لِأَخِيهِ — قِيلَ حِينَ دُخُولِ الإِنْكلِيزِ بَرَّ مِصْرَ قَبْلَ مَسْكِهِمْ عَرَابِيًا. إِنَّ أَحَدَ جُنُودِ الإِنْكلِيزِ سَكِرَ سُكْرًا وفِيمَا هو فى هذا

الحَالِ مَرَّ بهِ ضَابِطٌ فقال له ما تَعْمَلُ هُنا فتَحَيَّرَ العَسْكَرِيُّ
حَيْرَةً ووَطِىءَ كأَنَّهُ يُرِيدُ أَنْ يَبْحَثَ عن شَيْءٍ وقال له إِنِّي
أَبْحَثُ عن عَرَابِيِّ فتَعَجَّبَ الضَابِطُ غايَةَ العَجَبِ من حُسْنِ
تَخَلُّصِهِ وتَرَكَهُ وانْصَرَفَ — إِنِّي تأَسَّفْتُ أَسَفًا عَظِيمًا لِعَدَمِ
رُؤْيَتِكُمْ بِالمَنْزِلِ عِنْدَ إِحْضَارِي الكُتُبَ التي طَلَبْتُمُوهَا فى المَكْتُوبِ
الذى أَرْسَلْتُمُوهُ إِلَيَّ البَارِحَةَ — قَدْ تَصَرَّحَ لِرَافِعِ هذهِ الرُخْصَةِ
بالتَفَرُّجِ على جُنَيْنَتَيِ الجَزِيرَةِ والجِيزَةِ — أَشْكُرُكَ شُكْرًا قَلْبِيًّا
مِنْ إِرْسَالِكَ لِي عُنْوَانَ صَاحِبِكَ — بَعْدَ إِهْدَائِكَ التَحِيَّةَ والسَلَامَ
أُخْبِرُكَ أَنِّي قد وَصَلْتُ بالسَلَامَةِ لمَدِينَةِ مصرَ مُنْذُ ثَلَاثَةِ أَيَّامٍ —
كان أَحْمَدُ يَنْظُرُ إِلى ذلكَ الغُلامِ ونَبَاهَتِهِ ولُطْفِهِ نَظْرَةَ المُعْجَبِ —

Exercise 66.

We rejoiced greatly, when we received the books you sent (your sending of the books). — The love of one's land is a part of (مِنْ) faith. — I praised this youth's love of his country. — We rose in honour of the prince. — They have done this deed from hatred of their enemies. — After bringing excess of greeting we inform you that the inducement to write it (i.e. this letter) is to ask concerning your health and your circumstances. — I shall leave the city (my leaving of the city will be) on the 15th of November of this year. — I rejoiced greatly that your Excellency has perfect health and security (I rejoice . . . . at your Excellency's possessing the perfection of etc.).

Thirty-fifth Lesson.

(أَلدَّرْسُ ٱلْخَمِسُ وَٱلثَّلَاثُونَ)

Nouns of Place and Time.

1. Nouns denoting the Time or Place of an action (إِسْمُ ٱلْمَكَانِ وَٱلزَّمَانِ), when derived from the Simple verb are of the forms مَفْعِلٌ, مَفْعَلٌ and مَفْعَلَةٌ, e.g.

from جَلَسَ "to sit": مَجْلِسٌ "place of sitting, assembly";

from كَتَبَ "to write": مَكْتَبٌ "office, school";

from قَبَرَ "to bury": مَقْبَرَةٌ "cemetery".

The Plural of these three forms is مَفَاعِلُ, e.g. مَجَالِسُ, مَكَاتِبُ, مَقَابِرُ.

Note 1. These nouns, when derived from verbs, which have kasra or fatha in the Imperf. are usually of the form مَفْعِلٌ; those from verbs with ḍamma in the Imperf. are of the form مَفْعَلٌ. But there are many exceptions such as

مَشْرِقٌ "place of sunrise, East", مَغْرِبٌ "place of sunset, West' مَسْجِدٌ "place of praying, mosque." مَسْكِنٌ "dwelling place", all from verbs, which have ḍamma in the Imperf.

Note 2. From some verbs more than one form is used e.g.

from كَتَبَ "to write": مَكْتَبٌ "office" and مَكْتَبَةٌ "library, book-shop";

from وَضَعَ "to place": مَوْضِعٌ and مَوْضَعٌ "place".

Note 3. A rarer form in use is مِفْعَالٌ (especially from verbs whose first radical is و or ى), e.g.

from وَلَدَ "to bear children": مِيلَادٌ (for مِوْلَادٌ) "time of birth";

from وَعَدَ "to promise": مِيعَادٌ (for مِوْعَادٌ) "time of fulfilling promise, term";

so also from the noun وَقْتٌ "time" مِيقَاتٌ (for مِوْقَاتٌ) "appointed time".

2. These nouns formed from verbs "not sound" (Less. 28, 1) are subject to the laws which control the forms of the verbs, e.g.

from قَرَّ "to settle: مَقَرٌّ (for مَقْرَرٌ) "abode";

from حَلَّ "to alight": مَحَلٌّ (for مَحْلَلٌ) "place" and مَحَلَّةٌ for مَحْلَلَةٌ) "city-quarter";

from قَامَ "to rise": مَقَامٌ (for مَقْوَمٌ) "place, position".

from رَعَى "to pasture": مَرْعًى "pasturage".

3. In the Derived forms of the verb the Part. Pass. is used for the Noun of Place and Time, e.g.

from اِلْتَقَى "to meet: مُلْتَقًى "place of meeting";

from اِسْتَنْقَعَ "to collect (of water)": مُسْتَنْقَعٌ "marsh";

from صَلَّى "to pray": مُصَلًّى "place of prayer".

Nouns of Instrument.

4. **Nouns which** denote the instrument used in an action (اِسْمُ الآلَةِ) are formed after the patterns: مِفْعَالٌ, مِفْعَلٌ **and مِفْعَلَةٌ**, e.g.

from فَتَحَ "to open": مِفْتَاحٌ "a key";

from كَنَسَ "to sweep": مِكْنَسَةٌ "a broom";

from وَزَنَ "to weigh": مِيزَانٌ (for مِوْزَانٌ) "a balance";

from رَقِيَ "to ascend": مِرْقَاةٌ (for مِرْقَيَةٌ) "a ladder".

The Plural of مِفْعَلٌ and مِفْعَلَةٌ is مَفَاعِلُ; of مِفْعَالٌ: مَفَاعِيلُ e.g. مَكَانِسُ, مَفَاتِيحُ.

The Diminutive.

5. The Diminutive (إِسْمُ ٱلتَّصْغِيرِ) is formed from triliteral nouns according to the pattern فُعَيْلٌ, e.g. كُلَيْبٌ "little dog" from كَلْبٌ.

In the case of words derived from Doubled or Weak verbs the usual changes take place, e.g. from ظِلٌّ "shadow": ظُلَيْلٌ;

from بَابٌ (for بَوَبٌ) "door": بُوَيْبٌ;

from فَتًى "youth": فُتَيٌّ.

From quadriliteral nouns the form of the Diminutive is فُعَيْلِلٌ, e.g.

from عَقْرَبٌ "scorpion": عُقَيْرِبٌ.

Or if there are more letters, **the form** فُعَيْلِيلٌ is used, e.g.

from عُصْفُورٌ "sparrow": عُصَيْفِيرٌ.

If the noun has a Feminine **ending, this ending** is attached to the Diminutive, e.g.

from قَلْعَةٌ "fortress": قُلَيْعَةٌ.

from سَلْمَى "Salma", (name of **a woman**): سُلَيْمَى.

The following Diminutives should be noted:

from أَبٌ (for أَبَوٌ) "father": أُبَيٌّ (for أُبَيْوٌ) "little father";

from أَخٌ (for أَخَوٌ) "brother": أُخَيٌّ (for أُخَيْوٌ) "little brother";

from أُخْتٌ "sister": أُخَيَّةٌ "little sister";

from إِبْنٌ (for بَنَوٌ) "son": بُنَيٌّ (for بُنَيْيٌ) "little son";

from إِبْنَةٌ or بِنْتٌ "daughter": بُنَيَّةٌ "little daughter";

from شَيْء "thing": شُوَيْء (for شُيَيْء) or more frequently شُوَيَّة "a little thing".

Note. The Diminutives are often used to express endearment or contempt. The form فَعُّول is often used with Proper names at the present time to express endearment, e.g. فَطُّوم from فَاطِمَة; قَدُّور from عَبْدُ ٱلْقَادِرِ; عَبُّود from عَبْدُ ٱللّٰهِ.

Exercise 67.

إِنِّي قَصَدتُّ السَّفَرَ فَوَصَلْتُ إِلَى بَلَدٍ لا أَعْرِفُ بِهِ أَحَدًا وجُلْتُ بها لَعَلِّي أَجِدُ بها مَأْوًى أَبِيتُ فيه تلك اللَّيْلَةَ — القاهِرَةُ عاصِمَةُ القُطْرِ المِصْرِيِّ وهي مَقَرُّ الجَنابِ العالِي الخِدِيوِيِّ ومَرْكَزُ حُكُومَتِهِ وفي أَيَّامِ المِصْرِيِّينَ القُدَماءِ عُرِفَ ذلك المَوْضِعُ بِمَنْف — أَطْلَقْتُ الرَّصاصَ على الظَّبْيِ فلَمْ يُصِبِ المَرْمَى — قد سَرَّحُوا الخَيْلَ لِلْمَرْعَى في تلك المَزارِعِ — إِنَّ الإِفْرَنْجَ يُسَمُّونَ مِقْيَاسَ الحَرارَةِ بِاسْمِ التِّرْمُومِتْرِ — المَسْجِدُ مَعْبَدُ المُسْلِمِينَ — عِيدُ مِيلادِ المَسِيحِ أَكْبَرُ أَعْيادِ النَّصارَى — مَحَلَّةُ الإِسْماعِيلِيَّةِ في مَدِينَةِ مِصْرَ كانت سابِقًا كُلُّها حَدائِقَ وبَساتِينَ ومُسْتَنْقَعاتٍ قَلَّما (Less. 30, 11) يُشاهَدُ فيها من المَساكِنِ والبُيُوتِ — يا عَيُّوشُ اِفْتَحِي البابَ بهذا المِفْتاحِ — يا عُبَيْدَ الله (Accus., Less. 16, 4) أَعْطِنِي شُوَيَّةً من هذا اللَّحْمِ — قال

هَلْ تَقْبَلُونَ دَعْوَتِي أَنْ تَتَنَاوَلُوا الطَّعَامَ عِنْدِي فِي مَنْزِلِي

فَدَخَلْنَا وَجَلَسْنَا على الْمُتَّكَآت فَقُدِّمَتْ لنا الْقَهْوَةُ ثُمَّ تَنَاوَلْنَا

الطَّعَامَ —

Exercise 68.

This little dog is very watchful. — This little man sweeps the room with the broom. — I went to my house and opened the door with the key — Beirut is the residence of the Wāli. — Boy, weigh the wheat in the balance. — The visiting of mosques and tombs is not allowed during the time of prayer. — I saw the horses in the pasturage. — O dear Fatima, give me a little of this bread. — The customs of the East and those (the customs) of the West are different. — When the king arrived, they fired the cannons. — O little son, I ask success from God. — I bought this book in the bookshop.

Thirty-sixth Lesson.

(اَلدَّرْسُ ٱلسَّادِسُ وَٱلثَّلَاثُونَ)

The Relative Adjective.

(إِسْمُ ٱلنِّسْبَةِ)

1. The ending ـِيٌّ attached to a noun denotes that a person or thing is related to, or connected with it, generally in respect to a tribe, land, city, business etc., e.g.

عَرَبٌ "Arabs" (collective); عَرَبِيٌّ "Arabian, an Arab";
مِصْرُ "Egypt, Cairo"; مِصْرِيٌّ "an Egyptian, a Cairene",
عِلْمٌ "science"; عِلْمِيٌّ "scientific";
يَوْمٌ "day"; يَوْمِيٌّ "daily".

If the noun has the feminine ending ة, this is dropped in the formation of the Relative Adjective, e.g.

طَبِيعَةٌ "nature"; طَبِيعِيٌّ "natural";
صِنَاعَةٌ "art"; صِنَاعِيٌّ "artificial";
مَكَّةُ "Mecca"; مَكِّيٌّ "Meccan".

Letters added to the radicals in the formation of the noun sometimes drop, e.g. مَدِينَةٌ "city"; مَدَنِيٌّ "pertaining to a city", but not always, e.g. حَدِيدٌ "iron" حَدِيدِيٌّ "iron" (adjective).

The words أَبٌ "father" and أَخٌ "brother", take back their original *wāw* again and so form أَبَوِيٌّ "fatherly", أَخَوِيٌّ "brotherly".

If a noun ends in *ā* or *an* (ـَا, ـَى, ـًا or ـًى), this is changed into *wāw* before the ـِيٌّ e.g. مَعْنًى "meaning" forms مَعْنَوِيٌّ "abstract"; دُنْيَا "world" forms دُنْيَوِيٌّ "worldly".

The same is the case with the *hamza* in the ending ـَاءٌ, e.g. سَمَاءٌ "heaven" forms سَمَاوِيٌّ "heavenly", but شِتَاءٌ "winter" forms شَتَوِيٌّ "wintry" (without *alif*).

From فَرَنْسَا "France" are formed فَرَنْسِيٌّ, فَرَنْسَوِيٌّ and فَرَنْسَاوِيٌّ "French".

The Plurals of these adjectives are usually regular, e.g. اَلْمِصْرِيُّونَ "the Egyptians".

2. The Feminine of the Relative Adjectives often adds to its ordinary meaning that of an abstract idea, e.g. إِنْسَانٌ "man", إِنْسَانِيٌّ "human", إِنْسَانِيَّةٌ "humanity".

إِلٰهٌ "God", إِلٰهِيٌّ "divine", إِلٰهِيَّةٌ "deity".

شَهْرٌ "month", شَهْرِيٌّ "monthly", شَهْرِيَّةٌ "monthly wages".

Adjectives.

3. The following forms of the Adjective (إِسْمُ صِفَةٍ) have been already mentioned (Less. 10):

a) فَاعِلٌ Active Participle.

b) فَعِيلٌ (sometimes also used in Passive sense, e.g: قَتِيلٌ "killed").

c) فَعُولٌ.

d) فَعْلَانُ.

e) أَفْعَلُ (for Colours and Defects).

f) مَفْعُولٌ Pass. Part. (Less. 17, 4).

4. The following forms are also of common occurrence:

g) فَعْلٌ especially from intransitive verbs of the form فَعُلَ, e.g. صَعْبٌ "difficult" from صَعُبَ "to be difficult".

h) فَعَلٌ, e.g. حَسَنٌ "beautiful" from حَسُنَ "to be beautiful"

i) فَعِلٌ especially from intransitive verbs of the form فَعِلَ, e.g. فَرِحٌ "joyful" from فَرِحَ "to be joyful".

j) فُعْلَانٌ, e.g. عُرْيَانٌ "naked".

k) فَعَّالٌ (intensive) e.g. كَذَّابٌ "addicted to lying" from كَذَبَ "to lie".

Note. The verbs whose second radical is و or ى change the form فَعِيلٌ into فَيْعِلٌ which becomes فَيِّلٌ, e.g.:

from جَادَ (و) "to be excellent" جَيِّدٌ (for جَوِيدٌ and جَيْوِدٌ) "excellent";

from طَابَ (ى) "to be good" طَيِّبٌ (for طَيِيبٌ and طَيْيِبٌ) "good".

5. The form فَعَّالٌ is also used to indicate one who exercises a trade or profession, e.g. حَمَّالٌ (from حَمَلَ "to carry") "a porter", and so خَبَّازٌ "a baker"; خَيَّاطٌ "a tailor"; سَقَّاءٌ "a water-carrier". These words use the Sound plural, e.g. خَبَّازُونَ, حَمَّالُونَ etc.

6. The Elative (إِسْمُ ٱلتَّفْضِيلِ see Less. 10, 3—7) is always formed from the three radicals, e.g. طَوِيلٌ (Root طول) "long"; أَطْوَلُ "longer"; جَيِّدٌ "excellent" (Root جود): أَجْوَدُ "more excellent".

Some adjectives, such as the Participles of the Derived forms and words of the form أَفْعَلُ cannot form Elatives. In these cases such phrases as the following are used:

مُجْتَهِدٌ "diligent" أَكْثَرُ ٱجْتِهَادًا "more diligent" lit. more as to diligence.

أَسْوَدُ "black" أَشَدُّ سَوَادًا "blacker" lit. stronger as to blackness.

7. If the second part of the comparison is not a noun but a whole sentence or an adverbial determination,

it is preceded by مِمَّا (for مِنْ مَا) with a verb or the Preposition مِنْ with a suffix of the Personal Pronoun, e.g. اَلْهَوَاءُ أَلْطَفُ ٱلْيَوْمَ مِمَّا كَانَ أَمْسِ "the weather is pleasanter to-day than it was yesterday" or: اَلْهَوَاءُ أَلْطَفُ ٱلْيَوْمَ مِنْهُ أَمْسِ lit. "than it yesterday".

Exercise 69.

فَرَسِى كَانَ مِنْ أَجْوَدِ ٱلْخَيْلِ — إِنَّهُ مِنْ أَرْدَإِ ٱلْعَوَائِدِ تَعَرُّضُ ٱلْإِنْسَانِ لِمَا لَا يَعْنِيهِ — بَلَدٌ فِيهَا أَتَعَيَّشُ فِي أَعْظَمِ مَوْطِنٍ وَقَوْمٌ أَكْرَمُونَا هُمُ ٱلْأَهْلُ (Proverb) — هٰذَا ٱلشَّارِعُ ٱلْآنَ أَعْرَضُ مِنْهُ سَابِقًا — ٱلرِّيحُ كَانَتْ أَشَدَّ أَمْسِ مِنْهَا ٱلْيَوْمَ — حَضَرَ أَحَدُ ٱلشَّامِيِّينَ إِلَى مِصْرَ وَدَخَلَ أَحَدَ ٱلْجَوَامِعِ لِيُصَلِّيَ وَفِيمَا هُوَ هُنَاكَ رَأَى رَجُلًا عَيَّانًا رَابِطَ رَأْسِهِ وَيَدَيْهِ وَرِجْلَيْهِ وَعَيْنَيْهِ وَيَطْلُبُ مِنَ ٱللّٰهِ قَائِلًا يَا رَبِّي ٱشْفِنِي يَا رَبِّي أَعْفُ عَنِّي وَخَلِّصْنِي مِنْ أَمْرَاضِي وَأَوْجَاعِي وَأَكْثَرَ مِنْ هٰذَا ٱلْكَلَامِ فَسَمِعَهُ ٱلشَّامِيُّ وَتَضَايَقَ وَنَظَرَ إِلَيْهِ وَقَالَ إِنْ خَلَقَ ٱللّٰهُ وَاحِدًا جَدِيدًا غَيْرَكَ كَانَ أَسْهَلَ لَهُ مِنْ أَنْ يَقْعُدَ يُرَقِّعُ فِيكَ فَلَمَّا سَمِعَهُ ٱلْمِصْرِيُّ شَتَمَهُ وَٱنْصَرَفَ — هٰذَا ٱلْحَمَّالُ أَكْثَرُ ٱجْتِهَادًا مِنْ ذٰلِكَ — ٱلسِّكَّةُ ٱلْحَدِيدِيَّةُ تُوصِلُ مِنَ ٱلْإِسْكَنْدَرِيَّةِ إِلَى مِصْرَ — إِنَّ ٱلْبَطَالَةَ وَٱلْكَسَلَ أَحْلَى مَذَاقًا مِنَ ٱلْعَسَلِ (Proverb) —

Exercise 70.

This water-carrier is more diligent to-day than he was yesterday. — My ink is blacker than yours (thy ink). — We arrived in Cairo by rail. — The Egyptian is cleverer than the Syrian. — If God will, the weather will be better to-morrow than it was yesterday. — This Englishman is prouder (stronger as to pride) than that Frenchman. — The porters are more diligent than the tailors. — The crowd at the festivities was greater than we thought. — We went further away than we intended. — This wine is excellent, it is more excellent than that, which we drank yesterday.

Thirty-seventh Lesson.

(اَلدَّرْسُ ٱلسَّابِعُ وَٱلثَّلَاثُونَ)

1. Words may be divided according to their meaning into: a) Class names (إِسْمُ ٱلْجِنْسِ): b) Proper names (اَلْعَلَمُ).

2. The Class names are divided into:

a) Concrete (إِسْمُ عَيْنٍ), whether Nouns as رَجُلٌ "man", فَرَسٌ "horse" or Adjectives as رَاكِبٌ "riding", جَالِسٌ "sitting".

b) Abstract (إِسْمُ مَعْنًى) whether Nouns as عِلْمٌ "science", جَهْلٌ "ignorance" or Adjectives as مَفْهُومٌ "understood", مُضْمَرٌ "concealed".

Abstract nouns when used in a general sense and without further determination always take the Article, e.g.

اَلشَّجَاعَةُ فَضِيلَةٌ "bravery is a virtue";

so also with names of material,. e.g.

اَلذَّهَبُ وَٱلْفِضَّةُ مَعْدِنَانِ "gold and silver are two metals".

Proper Names.

3. Proper names are always definite and so can be the subject of a Nominal sentence, e.g. زَيْدٌ رَجُلٌ "Zaid is a man".

Proper names are either Simple or Compound.

The Simple may consist of three or more radicals, e.g. زَيْدٌ Zaid; جَعْفَرٌ Ja'far.

The Compound may consist of:

a) Two names placed together, e.g. بَعْلَبَكُّ Ba'albek,

or b) A noun with a Genitive, e.g. عَبْدُ ٱللّٰهِ 'Abdallah, عَبْدُ ٱلرَّحْمٰنِ 'Abd-errahman, إِمْرُؤُ ٱلْقَيْسِ Imruulkais,

or c) A sentence, e.g. تَأَبَّطَ شَرًّا Ta'abbaṭa sharran (lit. he carried mischief i.e. a sword, under his armpits.

4. Personal names are of three kinds:

a) The Name in the strict sense (إِسْمٌ) as زَيْدٌ, جَعْفَرٌ.

b) The Kunya (كُنْيَةٌ) or name containing a term of relation such as "father, mother, brother etc.", e.g. أَبُو عَمْرٍو, أُمُّ كُلْثُومٍ, إِبْنُ بَطُّوطَةَ.

c) The Nickname (لَقَبٌ) usually given to a man, when he has grown up referring to some quality in him or event with which he has become associated etc., e.g. بَطَّةٌ (properly "a duck"), قُفَّةٌ (properly "a basket").

Note 1. Some Proper Names always have the Article as اَلْحَارِثُ (lit. the ploughman).

Note 2. The name 'Omar is distinguished from 'Amr by the fact that the latter has always an otiose و at the end in the Nom. and Gen., e.g. عَمْرٌو and عُمَرُ. The Accus. of both is عَمْرًا.

For the Declension of the Proper names and for exercises see Less. 41.

Thirty-eighth Lesson.

(اَلدَّرْسُ ٱلثَّامِنُ وَٱلثَّلَاثُونَ)

The Feminine.

1. For the formation of the Feminine see Less. 2. Certain Substantives are feminine without a special ending:

أَرْضٌ	earth, land.	عَصًا	staff.
أَفْعَى	viper.	عُقَابٌ	eagle.
بِئْرٌ	well.	عَقْرَبٌ	scorpion.
حَرْبٌ	war (sometimes masc.).	فَأْسٌ	axe.
دَارٌ	house.	فِرْدَوْسٌ	Paradise (masc. when it means "park").
دِرْعٌ	coat of mail (some times masc., always masc. when used in the meaning of "smock").	كَأْسٌ	cup.
		مَنْجَنِيقٌ	catapult (sometimes masc.).
دَلْوٌ	bucket (sometimes masc.).	مُوسَى	razor.
		نَارٌ	fire.
رَحًى	mill.	نَعْلٌ	sandal.
رِيحٌ	wind (sometimes masc.).	نَفْسٌ	soul (with the meaning "person" in counting, it is masc. نَفَسٌ "breath" is masc.).
شَمْسٌ	sun.		
ضَبُعٌ	hyena (sometimes masc.).		
عَرُوضٌ	foot (of verse).		

2. The following words are of Common Gender:

إِبْهَامٌ	thumb (usually masc.).	إِزَارٌ	veil.
أَرْنَبٌ	hare (usually fem.).	إِصْبَعٌ	finger.

بَشَرٌ man.
ثَدْيٌ breast.
ثَعْلَبٌ fox.
جَنَاحٌ wing (usually masc.).
حَالٌ condition (usually fem.).
حَانُوتٌ shop.
خَمْرٌ wine.
دُكَّانٌ shop.
رُوحٌ spirit.
سَبِيلٌ path.
سُرًى night journey.
سِكِّينٌ knife.
سِلَاحٌ weapon.
سُلْطَانٌ might (masc. with meaning "Sultan").
سِلْمٌ peace.
سُلَّمٌ ladder.
سَمَاءٌ heaven (masc. with meaning "roof").
سُوقٌ market.
شَعِيرٌ barley.
صَاعٌ a measure used for corn etc.
صِرَاطٌ way.
صُلْحٌ peace.
ضُحًى morning.
طِبَاعٌ natural disposition.
طَرِيقٌ way.
عُجُزٌ hinder part.
عُرْسٌ nuptials (masc. with the meaning "bridal feast").
عَسَلٌ honey.
عُنْقٌ or عُنُقٌ neck.
عَنْكَبُوتٌ spider (generally fem.).
فَرَسٌ horse.
فُلْكٌ boat.
قِدْرٌ kettle (generally fem.).
قَفًا neck.
قَوْسٌ bow.
قَوْمٌ people.
كَبِدٌ liver.
كُرَاعٌ shank.
لِسَانٌ tongue.
لَيْلٌ night (generally masc.).
مِسْكٌ musk (generally masc.).
مِعًى intestines (generally masc.).
مِلْحٌ salt (generally fem.).
نَاسٌ people (generally masc.).

3. Collectives denoting irrational living beings and from which nouns of unity ending in ة (Less. 2, 4) cannot be formed are Feminine, e.g. خَيْلٌ "horses" إِبِلٌ "camels".

4. Those Collectives from which nouns of unity can be formed are of Common gender, e.g. نَحْلٌ "bees", نَحْلَةٌ "a bee" etc. The names of the Letters of the alphabet are also of Common gender, but are generally used as Feminines, e.g. اَلْأَلِفُ الْمَقْصُورَةُ

5. The Feminine ending ـَى (the أَلِفٌ بِصُورَةِ الْيَاءِ or أَلِفٌ مَقْصُورَةٌ see Intro. § 6, Note 2) is used in the following cases:

a) Some Substantives have it,. e.g. ذِكْرَى "remembrance"; دُنْيَا "world" (properly fem. of the Elative of دَنِيٌّ "low"; اَلدُّنْيَا is used for "this present world" in contrast with اَلْآخِرَةُ "the future world").

b) Adjectives of the form فَعْلَانُ take as their Feminine فَعْلَى, e.g. غَضْبَانُ "angry", Fem. غَضْبَى (but not adjectives of the form فَعْلَانٌ (with nunation), e.g. نَدْمَانٌ "repentant", Fem. نَدْمَانَةٌ).

c) The Feminine of the Superlative is of the form فُعْلَى, e.g.

كَبِيرٌ "great"; اَلْأَكْبَرُ "the greatest" (masc.); اَلْكُبْرَى "the greatest" (fem.).

عَالٍ "high"; اَلْأَعْلَى "the highest" (masc.); اَلْعُلْيَا "the highest" (fem.).

d). The following should also be noticed:

Masc. اَلأَوَّلُ "the first"; Fem. اَلأُولَى.

„ اَلآخَرُ "the other"; „ اَلأُخْرَى.

أُنْثَى "feminine" } (no Masc.)
حُبْلَى "pregnant" }

6. The Feminine ending ـَاءُ (the so-called أَلِف مَمْدُودَة "the lengthened alif") is used:

a) with some Substantives, e.g. صَحْرَاءُ "desert", كِبْرِيَاءُ "greatness, pride".

b) with Adjectives of the form أَفْعَلُ denoting Colours or Defects (Less. 10 2), e.g. أَسْوَدُ "black", Fem. سَوْدَاءُ.

7. Some Adjectives have no special ending for the Feminine, e.g. those of the form فَعِيلٌ when they have a Passive meaning as إِبْنَةٌ قَتِيلٌ "a slain girl"; also those of the form فَعُولٌ when they have an Active meaning as إِبْنَةٌ صَبُورٌ "a patient girl"; also certain Adjectives which can only refer to women as حَامِلٌ "pregnant" مُرْضِعٌ "one who gives suck", عَاقِرٌ "barren".

Note. Foreign words are treated as Feminines, even when they were originally Masc., e.g. قُنْصُلَاتُو "consulate", پْرُتِسْتُو "protest" (legal).

Exercise 71.

قِفَا (يا خَلِيلَيَّ :supply) نَبْكِ (Less. 15, 3 a) مِنْ ذِكْرَى حَبِيبٍ (إِمْرُؤُ ٱلْقَيْسِ) — حَضَرَ رَجُلٌ بَيْنَ يَدَيْ بَعْضِ

المُلُوكِ فَأَغْلَظَ له السُّلْطَانُ فقال له الرَّجُلُ إِنَّمَا أَنْتَ كَالسَّمَاءِ إِذَا أَرْعَدَتْ وَأَبْرَقَتْ فَقَدْ قَرُبَ خَيْرُهَا فَسَكَنَ غَضَبُهُ وَأَحْسَنَ إليه — أَعْطُوهُ إِبِلًا كَثِيرَةً وَدِرْعًا ثَقِيلَةً — إِنَّ أَمِيرَ المُؤْمِنِينَ هَارُونَ الرَّشِيدَ خَرَجَ يَوْمًا مِنَ الأَيَّامِ هو وأَبُو يَعْقُوبَ النَّدِيمُ وجَعْفَرٌ البَرْمَكِيُّ وأَبُو نُوَاسٍ وساروا فى الصَّحْرَاء — خَرَجَ أَعْرَابِيٌّ قد وَلَّاهُ الحَجَّاجُ بَعْضَ النَّوَاحِي فَأَقَامَ بها مُدَّةً طَوِيلَةً فلمّا كان فى بَعْضِ الأَيَّامِ وَرَدَ عليه أَعْرَابِيٌّ من حَيِّهِ فَقَدَّمَ اليه الطَّعَامَ وكان إِذْ ذَاكَ جَائِعًا فَسَأَلَهُ عن أَهْلِهِ وقال ما حالُ ٱبْنِي عُمَيْرٍ قال على ما تُحِبُّ قد مَلَأَ الأَرْضَ والحَيَّ رجالًا ونساءً قال فما فَعَلَتْ أُمُّ عُمَيْرٍ قال صَالِحَةٌ أيضا قال فما حالُ الدارِ قال عَامِرَةٌ بِأَهْلِهَا قال وكَلْبُنَا إِيقَاعُ قال قد مَلَأَ الحَيَّ نَبْحًا قال فما حالُ جَمَلِي زُرَيْقٍ قال على ما يَسُرُّكَ قال فَٱلْتَفَتَ إلى خادمه وقال ٱرْفَعِ الطَّعَامَ فَرَفَعَهُ ولم يَشْبَعِ الأَعْرَابِيُّ ثُمَّ أَقْبَلَ عليه يَسْأَلُهُ وقال يا مُبَارَكَ النَاصِيَةِ أَعِدْ عَلَيَّ ما ذَكَرْتَ قال سَلْ عَمَّا بَدَا لَكَ قال فما حالُ كَلْبِي إِيقَاعٍ قال ماتَ قال فما الذى أَمَاتَهُ قال ٱخْتَنَقَ بِعَظْمَةٍ من عِظَامِ جَمَلِكَ زُرَيْقٍ فماتَ قال أَوَمَاتَ جَمَلِي زُرَيْقٌ قال نَعَمْ قال وما الذى أَمَاتَهُ قال كَثْرُ نَقْلِ

الماء إلى قَبْرِ أُمّ عُمَيْرٍ قال أَوماتَ أُمّ عُمَيْرٍ قال نَعَمْ قال وما

الذى أَماتَها قال كَثْرَةُ بُكائِها على عُمَيْرٍ قال أَوماتَ عُمَيْرٌ قال

نَعَمْ قال وما الذى أَماتَهُ قال سَقَطَتْ عليه الدارُ قال أَوَسَقَطَتْ

الدارُ قال نَعَمْ فقامَ له بِٱلْعَصَا ضارِبًا فَوَلَّى من بَيْنِ يَدَيْهِ هارِبًا —

Exercise 72.

When I went out of the city, I met two women, the one of them (was) white and the other black. — The lazy girl has not done what I commanded her. — This world is the house of transitoriness, and the other world is the house of eternity. — The sheikh gave me many horses. — The memory of the friend will be lasting. — No tree is found in the desert. — The condition of my friend is not (لَيْسَ) good. — My soul yearns to meet thee (for thy meeting). — Hind is a patient girl. — The pride of men will be punished. — The minister has received the highest grade of this order.

Thirty-ninth Lesson.

(أَلدَّرْسُ ٱلتَّاسِعُ وَٱلثَّلَاثُونَ)

Number.

1. For the three Numbers: Singular (مُفْرَدٌ), Dual (مُثَنًّى) and Plural (جَمْعٌ) see Lessons 3, 4 and 5.

2. The Sound Plural (جَمْعٌ سَالِمٌ) Masculine is used for:

1) Masculine Proper Names (except those which end in ة), e.g. زَيْدُونَ.

2) Diminutives of Proper Names and Class Names which indicate rational beings, e.g. عُمَيْرٌ (Dimin. of عُمَرُ), Plur. عُمَيْرُونَ; رُجَيْلٌ "little man", Plur. رُجَيْلُونَ.

3) Participles, which form their Fem. in ة, e.g. كَاتِبٌ "writer", Plur. كَاتِبُونَ; مَأْمُورٌ "official", Plur. مَأْمُورُونَ; مُؤْمِنٌ "believer", Plur. مُؤْمِنُونَ.

4) Nouns of the form فَعَّالٌ which denote workers at a trade or profession (Less. 36, 5), e.g. خَيَّاطٌ "tailor", Plur. خَيَّاطُونَ.

5) Relative Adjectives (Less. 36, 1), e.g. مِصْرِيٌّ "Egyptian", Plur. مِصْرِيُّونَ.

6) Adjectives of the form أَفْعَلُ denoting Elatives, e.g. أَكْثَرُ, Plur. الأَكْثَرُونَ.

The following Plurals should be noted:

إِبْنٌ son (for بَنَوٌ), Plur. بَنُونَ (also أَبْنَاءٌ)

عَالَمٌ world, " عَالَمُونَ

أَرْضٌ earth, " أَرَضُونَ (also أَرَاضٍ)

أَهْلٌ family, " أَهْلُونَ (also أَهَالٍ)

إِوَزٌّ goose, " إِوَزُّونَ

ذُو master, " ذَوُونَ

Also the Fem. سَنَةٌ "year", Plur. سِنُونَ (as well as سَنَوَاتٌ).

3. The Sound Plural Feminine is used for:

1. Feminine Proper Names, e.g. هِنْدٌ, Plur. هِنْدَاتٌ; also for Masculines ending in ة, e.g. طَرَفَةُ, Plur. طَرَفَاتٌ.

2) Many Class names ending in ة, e.g. حَارَةٌ "city-quarter", Plur. حَارَاتٌ.

3) The Feminines of Adjectives, whose Masc. takes the Sound Masc. Plur., e.g. كَاتِبَاتٌ "female writers", خَيَّاطَاتٌ "tailoresses", مِصْرِيَّاتٌ "Egyptian women".

4) Adjectives the Feminine of which end in ـَى or ـَاءُ (Less. 38, 5, 6), e.g. كُبْرَى "greatest" (fem.), Plur. كُبْرَيَاتٌ (rare); خَضْرَاءُ "green" (fem.), Plur. خَضْرَوَاتٌ.

5) Names of the Letters of the alphabet and of the months, e.g. أَلِفٌ "alif", Plur. أَلِفَاتٌ; مُحَرَّمٌ the month Muharram, Plur. مُحَرَّمَاتٌ.

6) Verbal Nouns of the Derived forms, e.g. تَأْلِيفٌ "written work", Plur. تَأْلِيفَاتٌ; تَصَرُّفٌ "disposal", Plur. تَصَرُّفَاتٌ.

But the Verbal Nouns of the II. and IV. forms have also Broken Plurals, e.g. تَصْوِيرٌ "picture", Plur. تَصَاوِيرُ; إِرْجَافٌ "false news", Plur. أَرَاجِيفُ.

7) Diminutives of words denoting things and irrational beings, e.g. كُلَيْبٌ "little dog", Plur. كُلَيْبَاتٌ.

8) Foreign words, even when they denote male persons, e.g. أَغَا (Turkish) "Aga", Plur. أَغَوَاتٌ; (خواجا) خَوَاجَةٌ (Persian) "Sir", Plur. خَوَاجَاتٌ; (بيك) بَكٌ (Turkish) "Bey", Plur. بَكَوَاتٌ.

Note. قُنْصُلَاتُو (Less. 38, 7, Note) makes Plur. قُنْصُلَاتَاتٌ. Another form is قُنْصُلِيَّةٌ, Plur. قُنْصُلِيَّاتٌ.

Note the two following words:

حَمَّامٌ "bath", Plur. حَمَّامَاتٌ; سَمَاءٌ "heaven", Plur. سَمَاوَاتٌ (or سَمٰوَاتٌ) cf. Less. 36, 1.

Note 1. The Sound Fem. Plural of the Participles (especially of the Pass. Part.) is often used with a Neuter meaning, e.g. كَائِنَاتٌ or مَوْجُودَاتٌ "existing things", مَخْلُوقَاتٌ "created things".

Note 2. Of words derived from verbs that end in و or ى typical Sound Fem. Plurals are: from صَلَاةٌ (also written صَلٰوةٌ cf. Intro. § 6, Note 3) "prayer", Plur. صَلَوَاتٌ; from فَتَاةٌ "young girl", Plur. فَتَيَاتٌ or فَتَوَاتٌ.

Broken Plurals.

4. The most frequently used forms of the Broken Plural (جَمْعٌ مُكَسَّرٌ) are:

A. From triliteral nouns.

1. فَعْلٌ (rare).

From فَاعِلٌ; e.g. صَاحِبٌ "companion", Plur. صَحْبٌ.

2. فُعْلٌ.

a) From أَفْعَلُ (adjectives denoting colours and defects), e.g. أَزْرَقُ "blue", Plur. زُرْقٌ; أَسْوَدُ "black", Plur. سُودٌ; أَبْيَضُ "white", Plur. بِيضٌ (for بُيْضٌ).

b) From فَعْلَاءُ (fem. of the preceding), e.g. زَرْقَاءُ "blue" (fem.), Plur. زُرْقٌ.

c) From فَعَلٌ, e.g. أَسَدٌ "lion", Plur. أُسْدٌ; دَارٌ (for دَوَرٌ) "house", Plur. دُورٌ, cf. Note to 5.

3. فِعَلٌ.

From فِعْلَةٌ (rarely فَعْلَةٌ), e.g. قِطْعَةٌ "piece", Plur. قِطَعٌ; مِلَّةٌ (for مِلْلَةٌ) "religion", Plur. مِلَلٌ; سِيرَةٌ "manner of life", Plur. سِيَرٌ; خَيْمَةٌ "tent", Plur. خِيَمٌ.

4. فُعَلٌ.

a) From فُعْلَةٌ, e.g. رُتْبَةٌ "rank", Plur. رُتَبٌ; قُبَّةٌ "dome", Plur. قُبَبٌ: صُورَةٌ "form", Plur. صُوَرٌ.

b) From فُعْلَى (cf. Less. 38, 5), e.g. أُخْرَى "other" (fem.), Plur. أُخَرُ (without nunation); اَلْكُبْرَى "the greatest" (fem.), Plur. اَلْكُبَرُ.

c From فَعْلَةٌ (especially from words with medial و or ى), e.g. دَوْلَةٌ "dynasty", Plur. دُوَلٌ; قَرْيَةٌ "village", Plur. قُرًى.

d) From فِعْلَةٌ (rare), e.g. لِحْيَةٌ "beard", Plur. لُحًى.

5. فُعُلٌ.

a) From فِعَالٌ (but not from words in which the second radical is doubled or from those that end in و or ى), e.g. كِتَابٌ "book", Plur. كُتُبٌ.

b) From فَعِيلٌ (but not from words, the third radical of which is و or ى), e.g. طَرِيقٌ "way", Plur. طُرُقٌ.

c) From فَعِيلَةٌ, e.g. مَدِينَةٌ "city", Plur. مُدُنٌ.

d) From فَعُولٌ, e.g. رَسُولٌ "messenger, ambassador", Plur. رُسُلٌ.

e) From فَعْلٌ or فَعَلٌ (rare), e,g. سَقْفٌ "roof", Plur. سُقُفٌ.

Note. فُعْلٌ is often met with beside فُعُلٌ (see 1), e.g. أَسَدٌ "lion", Plur. أُسُدٌ or أُسْدٌ.

6. فِعَالٌ.

a) From فُعْلٌ, e.g. كَلْبٌ "dog", Plur. كِلَابٌ; رُمْحٌ "lance", Plur. رِمَاحٌ; زِقٌّ "wine-skin", Plur. زِقَاقٌ; ثَوْبٌ "garment", Plur. ثِيَابٌ; رِيحٌ "wind", Plur. رِيَاحٌ.

b) From فَعُلٌ, e.g. رَجُلٌ "man", Plur. رِجَالٌ.

c) From فَعَلٌ and فَعَلَةٌ, e.g. جَبَلٌ "mountain", Plur. جِبَالٌ; رَقَبَةٌ "neck", Plur. رِقَابٌ; دَارٌ (for دَوَرٌ) "house", Plur. دِيَارٌ (with the meaning "land").

d) From فَعِيلٌ (but not when used with Passive meaning), e.g. كَرِيمٌ "generous", Plur. كِرَامٌ.

e) From فُعْلَةٌ, e.g. رُقْعَةٌ "piece of paper", Plur. رِقَاعٌ.

f) From فَعْلَةٌ, e.g. نَعْجَةٌ "sheep" Plur. نِعَاجٌ.

7. فَعِيلٌ.

a) From فَعْلٌ, e.g. عَبْدٌ "slave", Plur. عَبِيدٌ.

b) From فِعَالٌ, e.g. حِمَارٌ "ass", Plur. حَمِيرٌ.

8. فُعُولٌ.

a) From فَعْلٌ, e.g. قَلْبٌ "heart"; Plur. قُلُوبٌ; عِلْمٌ "science", Plur. عُلُومٌ; جُنْدٌ "troop", Plur. جُنُودٌ; حَقٌّ

"right", Plur. حُقُوق; رَأْس "head", Plur. رُؤُوس; بَيْت "house", Plur. بُيُوت.

b) From فَعَل, e.g. أَسَد "lion", Plur. أُسُود; مَلِك "king", Plur. مُلُوك.

c) From فَاعِل (but not when second radical is doubled, or the medial radical is و or ى), e.g. شَاهِد "witness", Plur. شُهُود.

9. فُعَّل.

From فَاعِل, e.g. حَاكِم "judge", Plur. حُكَّم; نَائِم "sleeper", Plur. نُوَّم.

10. فُعَّال.

Only from فَاعِل, e.g. كَاتِب "writer", Plur. كُتَّاب.

11. فَعَلَة.

Only from فَاعِل when it denotes rational beings and has not و or ى as third radical, e.g. كَاتِب "writer", Plur. كَتَبَة; بَائِع "seller", Plur. بَاعَة (for بَيَعَة).

12. فُعَلَة.

Only from فَاعِل when the third radical is و or ى and the word denotes rational beings, e.g. وَال "governor", Plur. وُلَاة (for وُلَيَة); قَاضٍ "judge", Plur. قُضَاة (for قُضَيَة).

13. فِعْلَة.

a) From فَعْل in words with medial و or ى, e.g. ثَور "ox", Plur. ثِيرَة.

b) From فَعَلٌ when the third radical is و or ى, e.g. أَخٌ (for أَخَوٌ) "brother", Plur. إِخْوَةٌ.

c) From فَعَالٌ, e.g. غَزَالٌ "gazelle", Plur. غِزْلَةٌ.

d) From فَعِيلٌ when the third radical is و or ى, e.g. صَبِيٌّ (for صَبِيوٌ) "boy", Plur. صِبْيَةٌ.

14. أَفْعُلٌ.

a) From فَعْلٌ, e.g. بَحْرٌ "sea", Plur. أَبْحُرٌ; عَيْنٌ "eye", Plur. أَعْيُنٌ.

b) From فِعْلٌ, e.g. رِجْلٌ "foot", Plur. أَرْجُلٌ.

c) From فُعْلٌ, e.g. قُفْلٌ "bolt", Plur. أَقْفُلٌ.

d) From Feminines, which do not end in ة, and which have a long vowel between the second and third radical, e.g. ذِرَاعٌ "arm", Plur. أَذْرُعٌ; يَمِينٌ "oath", Plur. أَيْمُنٌ.

15. فِعَالَةٌ (rare).

a) From فَعَلٌ, e.g. حَجَرٌ "stone", Plur. حِجَارَةٌ.

b) From فَاعِلٌ, e.g. صَاحِبٌ "friend, owner", Plur. صَحَابَةٌ (and صِحَابَةٌ).

16. فُعُولَةٌ (rare).

From فَعْلٌ when the second radical is doubled, e.g. عَمٌّ "uncle", Plur. عُمُومَةٌ.

17. أَفْعَالٌ.

a) From فُعْلٌ (فَعْلٌ especially, when the first radical is و or the middle radical is و or ى), e.g. شَخْصٌ "person",

Plur. أَشْخَاص; وَقْت "time", Plur. أَوْقَات; لَوْن "colour", Plur. أَلْوَان; يَوْم "day", Plur. أَيَّام (for أَيْوَام); شَيْء "thing", Plur. أَشْيَاء (without nunation, cf. Less. 41, 2 a); طِفْل "suckling", Plur. أَطْفَال; رُوح "spirit", Plur. أَرْوَاح.

b) From فَعَل, e.g. سَبَب "cause", Plur. أَسْبَاب; حَال (for حَوَل) "condition", Plur. أَحْوَال; إِبْن (for بَنَو) "son", Plur. أَبْنَاء.

c) From فَاعِل, e.g. صَاحِب "friend", Plur. أَصْحَاب.

d) From فَعِيل (not with Passive sense); e.g. شَرِيف "noble", Plur. أَشْرَاف; مَيِّت (for مَوِيت) "dead", Plur. أَمْوَات.

e) Note specially عَدُوّ "enemy", Plur. أَعْدَاء.

18. أَفْعِلَة.

a) From فِعَال, e.g. طَعَام "food", Plur. أَطْعِمَة; دَوَاء "physic", Plur. أَدْوِيَة; سِلَاح "weapon", Plur. أَسْلِحَة; إِمَام "Imam, leader of prayer", Plur. أَئِمَّة (for أَأْمِمَة); إِنَاء "vessel", Plur. آنِيَة; تُرَاب "dust", Plur. أَتْرِبَة.

b) From فَعِيل (especially with Adjectives, the second radical of which is doubled, or of which the third radical is و or ى), e.g. رَغِيف "loaf", Plur. أَرْغِفَة; دَلِيل "proof", Plur. أَدِلَّة (for أَدْلِلَة); عَزِيز "valuable, dear", Plur. أَعِزَّة (for أَعْزِزَة).

c) From فَعُول, e.g. عَمُود "column", Plur. أَعْمِدَة.

d) Note specially وَادٍ "valley", Plur. أَوْدِيَة.

19. أَفْعِلَاءُ.

From فَعِيلٌ (especially from roots with doubled second radical, or with final و or ى), when it refers to male persons, e.g. صَدِيقٌ "friend", Plur. أَصْدِقَاءُ; طَبِيبٌ "physician", Plur. أَطِبَّاءُ (for أَطْبِبَاءُ); غَنِيٌّ "rich", Plur. أَغْنِيَاءُ.

20. فَعْلَى.

a) From فَعِيلٌ usually with Passive meaning, e.g. قَتِيلٌ "slain", Plur. قَتْلَى; جَرِيحٌ "wounded", Plur. جَرْحَى; مَيِّتٌ (for مَوِيتٌ) "dead", Plur. مَوْتَى.

b) From فَعْلَانُ, e.g. كَسْلَانُ "idle", Plur. كَسْلَى.

21. فُعَلَاءُ.

a) From فَعِيلٌ (of male persons but not in words with doubled second radical or ending in و or ى), e.g. وَزِيرٌ "minister", Plur. وُزَرَاءُ; فَقِيرٌ "poor", Plur. فُقَرَاءُ.

b) From فَاعِلٌ, e.g. شَاعِرٌ "poet", Plur. شُعَرَاءُ.

c) Note specially خَلِيفَةٌ "Caliph", Plur. خُلَفَاءُ.

22. فِعْلَانٌ.

a) From فَعْلٌ (especially from words with medial و), e.g. نَارٌ (for نَوْرٌ) "fire", Plur. نِيرَانٌ; أَخٌ (for أَخَوٌ) "brother", Plur. إِخْوَانٌ.

b) From فُعْلٌ (medial و), e.g. حُوتٌ "large fish", Plur. حِيتَانٌ.

c) From فُعَالٌ, e.g. غَزَالٌ "gazelle", Plur. غِزْلَانٌ; غُلَامٌ "boy", Plur. غِلْمَانٌ.

d) From فعيلٌ, e.g. صَبِىٌّ "boy", Plur. صِبْيَانٌ.

e) From فاعلٌ, e.g. حَائِطٌ "wall", Plur. حِيطَانٌ.

23. فُعْلَانٌ.

a) From فَعَلٌ, e.g. بَلَدٌ "district", Plur. بُلْدَانٌ.

b) From فاعلٌ (used as substantive, but not medial و or ى), e.g. فَارِسٌ "rider", Plur. فُرْسَانٌ; شَابٌّ (for شَابِبٌ) "youth", Plur. شُبَّانٌ.

c) From فُعَالٌ, e.g. شُجَاعٌ "brave", Plur. شُجْعَانٌ.

d) From أَفْعَلُ (Colours and Defects), e.g. أَعْرَجُ "lame", Plur. عُرْجَانٌ.

Exercise 73.

قِيلَ إِنَّهُ كانَ لِأَحَدِ الأَغْنِيَاء راعٍ يَرْعَى غَنَمًا فى إِحْدَى البَرَارِىّ وكان قد عَيَّنَ له مَعَاشًا فيه شَىْءٌ من السَّمْنِ فكان الرَّاعِى يُبْقِى السَّمْنَ وِيَدَّخِرُهُ فى جَرَّةٍ له كانت مُعَلَّقَةً فى كُوخِهِ فَبَيْنَمَا هو ذاتَ يَوْمٍ جالِسٌ فى كُوخِهِ عند غُرُوبِ الشَّمْسِ وهو مُتَّكِئٌ على عَصاهُ أَخَذَ يَتَفَكَّرُ بِمَا يَعْمَلُهُ فيما ٱجْتَمَعَ من السَّمْنِ فقال فى نَفْسِهِ إِنِّى سَأَذْهَبُ بِهِ غَدًا إلى السُّوقِ وأَبِيعُهُ وأَشْتَرِى بِثَمَنِهِ نَعْجَةً حامِلًا (see Less. 38, 7) فَتَضَعُ لى نَعْجَةً أُخْرَى ثُمَّ تَكْبُرُ هذه وتَلِدُ لى مَعَ أُمِّها نِعاجًا أُخَرَ وهٰكَذا

إلى أَنْ يَصِيرَ عندى قَطِيعٌ كَبِيرٌ فأَرُدُّ ما عندى من الغَنَمِ إِلى

صاحِبِهِ وأَتَّخِذُ لى أَجِيرًا يرعَى غَنَمِي وأَبْتَنِي لى قَصْرًا عَظِيمًا

فأُزَيِّنُهُ بالمَفْرُوشَاتِ الحَسَنَةِ والآنِيَةِ المُرَصَّعَةِ والمَنْقُوشَاتِ البَهِجَةِ

ومَتَى بَلَغَ رُشْدَ وَلَدِى أُحْضِرُ له مُعَلِّمًا أَدِيبًا حَكِيمًا يُعَلِّمُهُ

الأَدَبَ والحِكْمَةَ وآمُرُهُ بِطَاعَتِي وٱحْتِرَامِي فإِنِ ٱمْتَثَلَ

(supply: "good!" Less. 47, 6) وَإِلَّا ضَرَبْتُهُ بهذه العَصَا

ورفعَ يَدَهُ بِعَصَاهُ فأَصابَتِ الجَرَّةَ فكَسَرَتْهَا فَسَقَطَ السَّمْنُ على

رأْسِهِ ولِحْيَتِهِ وثِيَابِهِ مُتَبَدِّدًا فى كُلِّ جِهَةٍ فَحَزِنَ لذلك حُزْنًا

عَظِيمًا قائِلًا لَعَلَّ هذا جَزاءُ مَنْ يُصْغِي الى تَخَيُّلاتِهِ —

Exercise 74.

The Commander of the Faithful sent ambassadors to the kings. — The governors are the officials of the Caliphs. — Praise (belongs) to God, the Lord of the worlds. — I have not seen my friends for (since) five years. — There were many vegetables in the market.

— We sat down to take (نَالَ VI.) the food and drink we had with us (what was with us of foods and drinks). — Five prayers on each day are incumbent on the Moslems. — The highway robber (cutter of the ways) demanded money from us. — The manner of life (Plur.) of the first (Plur.) will be a warning to the last (Plur.). — A preacher wished to say, "Improve your hearts", and he said, "Skin your dogs". — We said farewell to our (the) dear friends. — Kings have pages (youths) and slaves. — In Beirut there are many schools for boys.

Fortieth Lesson.

(اَلدَّرْسُ ٱلْأَرْبَعُونَ)

Broken Plurals of triliteral nouns continued.

24. فَوَاعِلُ.

a) From فَاعِلٌ, e.g. فَارِسٌ "rider", Plur. فَوَارِسُ; سَاحِلٌ "coast", Plur. سَوَاحِلُ.

b) From فَاعِلَةٌ, e.g. حَادِثَةٌ "novelty", Plur. حَوَادِثُ; خَاصَّةٌ (for خَاصِصَةٌ) "nobles", Plur. خَوَاصُّ (for خَوَاصِصُ); جَارِيَةٌ "slave-girl", Plur. جَوَارٍ (for جَوَارِيُ) cf. Less. 41.

25. فَعَائِلُ.

From Feminine nouns, which have a long vowel between the second and third radicals, e.g. عَجُوزٌ "old woman", Plur. عَجَائِزُ; رِسَالَةٌ "letter", Plur. رَسَائِلُ; عَجِيبَةٌ "wonderful thing", Plur. عَجَائِبُ.

Note specially ضَمِيرٌ "pronoun", Plur. ضَمَائِرُ;

26. فَعَالٍ (with Article أَلْفَعَالِى).

a) From فَعْلَاءُ, e.g. عَذْرَاءُ "maiden", Plur. عَذَارٍ (with Article أَلْعَذَارِى).

b) From فَعْلَى, e.g. فَتْوَى "legal decision", Plur. فَتَاوٍ.

c) Note specially لَيْلٌ "night", Plur. لَيَالٍ; أَهْلٌ "people, family", Plur. أَهَالٍ "inhabitants"; أَرْضٌ "earth", Plur. أَرَاضٍ "lands"

27. فُعَالَى.

a) Is used with 26 a, b; so عَذَارَى and فَتَاوَى.

b) From فُعْلَى (Feminine, but not that of the Superlative), e.g. حُبْلَى "pregnant", Plur. حَبَالَى.

c) From فَعْلَانُ, e.g. كَسْلَانُ "idle", Plur. كَسَالَى.

d) From فَعِيلَةٌ (with final و or ى), e.g. هَدِيَّةٌ "gift", Plur. هَدَايَا; مَنِيَّةٌ "fate, death", Plur. مَنَايَا; رَعِيَّةٌ "flock", Plur. رَعَايَا "subjects".

e) From فَاعِلَةٌ (with medial و and also final و or ى). e.g. زَاوِيَةٌ "corner", Plur. زَوَايَا.

B. Broken Plurals of quadriliteral nouns.

1. The three forms that occur have been mentioned already in Less. 5.

28. فَعَالِلُ.

كَوْكَبٌ "star", Plur. كَوَاكِبُ; قَنْطَرَةٌ "bridge", Plur. قَنَاطِرُ.

Nouns formed from triliteral roots by prefixing ت, م and أ take the same forms of Plural as quadriliterals, hence the forms: تَفَاعِلُ, مَفَاعِلُ and أَفَاعِلُ e.g. تَجْرِبَةٌ "experience", Plur. تَجَارِبُ; مَكْتَبٌ "school", Plur. مَكَاتِبُ; مَحَلٌّ (for مَحْلَلٌ) "place", Plur. مَحَالُّ (for مَحَالِلُ); الأكبر "the greatest", Plur. الأكابِرُ "the nobles".

29. فَعَالِيلُ.

From quadriliterals, which have a long vowel between the third and fourth radical, e.g. سُلْطَانٌ "Sultan", Plur. سَلَاطِينُ; قِنْدِيلٌ "lamp", Plur. قَنَادِيلُ; صُنْدُوقٌ

"coffer", Plur. صَنَادِيقُ; شُبَّاكٌ "window", Plur. شَبَابِيكُ; كُرْسِىٌّ "throne", Plur. كَرَاسِىُّ; بَرِّيَّةٌ "desert", Plur. بَرَارِىُّ.

So (as in 28) from triliterals with prefixes arise the forms تَفَاعِيلُ, مَفَاعِيلُ and أَفَاعِيلُ, e.g. تَصْوِيرٌ "picture", Plur. تَصَاوِيرُ (cf. Less. 39, 2); مِفْتَاحٌ "key", Plur. مَفَاتِيحُ; مَكْتُوبٌ "letter", Plur. مَكَاتِيبُ; إِكْلِيلٌ "crown", Plur. أَكَالِيلُ; إِرْجَافٌ "false news", Plur. أَرَاجِيفُ (cf. Less. 39, 2).

There is also a form فَوَاعِيلُ, e.g. جَامُوسٌ "buffalo", Plur. جَوَامِيسُ; قَانُونٌ "law", Plur. قَوَانِينُ.

Note specially: دِينَارٌ "dinar", Plur. دَنَانِيرُ; دِيوَانٌ "diwan, collection of poetry", Plur. دَوَاوِينُ.

30. فَعَالِلَةٌ.

a) From many Relative Adjectives (cf. Less. 36, 1), e.g. مَغْرِبِىٌّ "Moor", Plur. مَغَارِبَةٌ; أَرْمَنِىٌّ "Armenian", Plur. أَرَامِنَةٌ; بَغْدَادِىٌّ "man of Bagdad", Plur. بَغَادِدَةٌ.

b) From certain quadriliteral nouns indicating persons (whether with long vowel before the last radical or not), especially from Foreign words, e.g. جَبَّارٌ "giant", Plur. جَبَابِرَةٌ; أُسْتَاذٌ (Persian) "teacher", Plur. أَسَاتِذَةٌ; فَيْلَسُوفٌ "philosopher", Plur. فَلَاسِفَةٌ; أُسْقُفٌّ "bishop", Plur. أَسَاقِفَةٌ; مَلْأَكٌ "angel", Plur. مَلَائِكَةٌ.

Note 1. In nouns that contain more than four radicals the extra letters generally fall out, e.g. عَنْكَبُوتٌ "spider", Plur. عَنَاكِبُ, but not always, e.g. تُرْجُمَانٌ "interpreter", Plur. تَرَاجِمِينُ.

Note 2. Many nouns have different forms of Broken Plural with different meanings (see Less. 5, 3, Note 2), e.g. عَيْنٌ "eye, spring, notable person", Plur. أَعْيُنٌ and عُيُونٌ "eyes, springs", أَعْيَانٌ "notables"; عَبْدٌ "slave, servant", Plur. عَبِيدٌ and أَعْبُدٌ "slaves", عِبَادٌ "servants of God".

Note 3. From some Plurals a second Plural is formed, sometimes Sound, sometimes Broken, e.g. طَرِيقٌ "way", Plur. طُرُقٌ, Plur. of the Plur. طُرُقَاتٌ; يَدٌ "hand", Plur. أَيْدٍ, Plur. of Plur. أَيَادٍ; إِنَاءٌ "vessel", Plur. آنِيَةٌ, Plur. of Plur. أَوَانٍ.

2. In many Relative Adjectives the Feminine ending ة gives the sense of the Plural. (Properly it is an abstract Collective cf. Less. 36, 2), e.g. بَحْرِيٌّ "mariner", بَحْرِيَّةٌ "mariners"; صُوفِيٌّ "Sufi (mystic)", صُوفِيَّةٌ "Sufis".

In like manner the Feminine of some words of the form فَعَّالٌ is used, e.g. قَوَّاسٌ "bowman, Cawass", قَوَّاسَةٌ "bowmen, Cawasses".

3. The following Irregular Plurals should be noted:

أُمٌّ "mother", Plur. أُمَّهَاتٌ and أُمَّاتٌ.

فَمٌ "mouth" (cf Less. 7, 2), Plur. أَفْوَاهٌ.

مَاءٌ "water" (for مَاهٌ for مَوَهٌ), Plur. أَمْوَاهٌ and مِيَاهٌ (for مِوَاهٌ).

شَفَةٌ "lip" (for شَفْهَةٌ), Plur. شِفَاهٌ.

شَاةٌ "sheep" (for شَوَهَةٌ), Plur. شَاءٌ and شِيَاهٌ.

أَمَةٌ "maid-servant", Plur. إِمَاءٌ and أَمَوَاتٌ.

إِمْرَأَةٌ "woman", Plur. نِسَاءٌ and نِسْوَةٌ and نِسْوَانٌ.

إِنْسَانٌ "man", Plur. أُنَاسٌ usually نَاسٌ.

قَوْسٌ "bow", Plur. قِصِىٌّ and قُصِىٌّ.

Exercise 75.

حُكِىَ أَنَّ الرَّشِيدَ أَرِقَ ذَاتَ لَيْلَةٍ أَرَقًا شَدِيدًا فَٱسْتَدْعَى جَعْفَرًا وقال أُرِيدُ منك أَنْ تُزِيلَ ما بِقَلْبِى من الضَّجَرِ فقال الوَزِيرُ يا أَمِيرَ المُؤْمِنِينَ كَيْفَ يكون على قَلْبِكَ ضَجَرٌ وقد خَلَقَ الله أَشْيَاءَ كَثِيرَةً تُزِيلُ الهَمَّ عن المَهْمُومِ والغَمَّ عن المَغْمُومِ وأَنْتَ قَادِرٌ عليها فقال الرَّشِيدُ وما هِىَ يا جعفرُ فقال له قُمْ بِنَا الآنَ حَتَّى نَطْلُعَ الى فَوْقِ سَطْحِ هذا القَصْرِ حَتَّى نَتَفَرَّجَ على النُّجُومِ وٱشْتِبَاكِهَا وٱرْتِفَاعِهَا والقَمَرِ وحُسْنِ طَلْعَتِهِ فقال الرشيدُ يا جعفرُ ما تَهِمُّ نَفْسِى الى شَىْءٍ من ذلك فقال يا أَمِيرَ المومنينَ ٱفْتَحْ شُبَّاكَ القَصْرِ الذى يَطْلُعُ على البُسْتَانِ وتَفَرَّجْ على حُسْنِ تلك الأَشْجَارِ وٱسْمَعْ صَوْتَ تَغْرِيدِ الأَطْيَارِ وٱنْظُرْ الى هَدِيرِ الأَنْهَارِ وشُمَّ رَوَائِحَ تلك الأَزْهَارِ فقال يا جعفرُ ما تهمّ نفسى الى شىء من ذلك فقال يا أَمير المومنين ٱفْتَحِ الشُّبَّاكَ الذى يَطْلُعُ على دِجْلَةَ حتى نَتَفَرَّجَ على تلك المَرَاكِبِ والمَلَّاحِينَ فهذا يُصَفِّقُ وهذا يُنْشِدُ مَوَالِيَ فقال الرشيدُ ما تهمّ نفسى الى شىء من ذلك قال جعفرُ قُمْ يا امير المؤمنين

حتى نَنْزِلَ الى الإصْطَبْلِ الخاصّ ونَنْظُرَ الى الخيلِ العَرَبِيَّاتِ

ونَتَفرّجَ على حُسْنِ أَلْوانها ما بَيْنَ أَدْهَمَ كاللّيْلِ إذا أظْلَمَ

وأَشْقَرَ وأَشْهَبَ وكُمَيْتٍ وأَحْمَرَ وأَبيَضَ وأَخْضَرَ وأَبْلَقَ واصفر

وأَلْوانٍ تُحَيِّرُ العُقُولَ فقال الرشيد ما تهم نفسى الى شىء من

ذلك فقال جعفرُ يا امير المُومنين ما بَقِيَ إلّا ضَرْبُ عُنُقِ

مَمْلُوكِكَ جعفرٍ فإنّي قد عَجَزْتُ عن إزالةِ هَمِّ مَوْلانا فَضَحِكَ

الرَّشيدُ وطابَتْ نَفْسُهُ وزالَ عنه كَرْبُهُ — قال بعضُهُم اللّيالِي

حَبالَى تَلِدْنَ كُلَّ عَجِيبةٍ —

Exercise 76.

A certain philosopher had a slave (from the slaves), and one day the philosopher said to his slave, "I wish to go to one of the baths." — The soldiers bound the prisoners with (the) chains. — This man was one of the dearest of his friends. — Who will pay the expenses of the journey? — In this land I saw many schools, in which the scholars learn the sciences; and their teachers are of the learned. — Inform me soon of thy condition (Plur.), for thy friendship is dearer than all existing things. — Kiss the hands of the brothers and sisters. — The most honourable ruler and the most noble Sultan, possessor of the greatest happiness and of the highest (Superlative of سَامٍ) rank, God perpetuate his days and raise his standards! Amen. — All the travellers both men and women (what was between the men and the women) were smitten with seasickness. — The rains pour down like the mouths of the wine-skins.

Forty-first Lesson.

(اَلدَّرْسُ ٱلْحَادِي وَٱلْأَرْبَعُونَ)

Declension of the Noun.

(إِعْرَابُ ٱلِاسْمِ) see Lessons 6 and 7.

1. Nouns are either Indeclinable (مَبْنِيٌّ), e.g. حَذَارِ "Caution!", قَطَامِ "Qaṭām" (name of a woman), or Declinable (مُعْرَبٌ).

The Declinable are either Triptotes (مُنْصَرِفٌ) i.e. having three case-endings (Less. 6, 2 a). e.g. رَجُلٌ "a man", or Diptotes (غَيْرُ مُنْصَرِفٍ) i.e. with two case-endings only (Less. 6, 2 b and Note 1), e.g. كَسْلَانُ "idle", عُمَرُ "Omar".

2. The following are Diptote:

a) Broken Plurals of the forms أَفْعِلَاءُ, فُعَلَى, فُعَلَاءُ, فَوَاعِلُ, فَعَائِلُ, فَعَالَى, فَعَالِلُ and فَعَالِيلُ also the Plurals أُوَلُ (from أَوَّلُ "first"), أُخَرُ (from آخَرُ "other") and أَشْيَاءُ (from شَيْءٌ "thing").

b) The Feminine forms فَعْلَاءُ, فَعْلَى, فِعْلَى and فُعْلَى (Less. 38, 5, 6), e.g. صَحْرَاءُ "desert", بَيْضَاءُ "white", غَضْبَى "angry", ذِكْرَى "remembrance", كُبْرَى "greatest".

c) Nouns of the form أَفْعَلُ, the Feminine of which is فَعْلَاءُ or فُعْلَى (denoting colours, defects or elative), e.g. أَسْوَدُ "black", أَكْبَرُ "greater".

On the other hand أَرْمَلٌ "widower" makes a Feminine أَرْمَلَةٌ "widow".

d) Adjectives of the form فَعْلَانُ the Feminine of which is فَعْلَى, e.g. غَضْبَانُ (Fem. غَضْبَى) "angry".

On the other hand نَدْمَانٌ (Fem. نَدْمَانَةٌ) "companion at table".

e) The Numerals which end in ة when they stand alone as pure numbers, e.g. ثَلَاثَةُ نِصْفُ سِتَّةَ "three is the half of six".

f) Most Proper names (see Less. 37, 3, 4) including all that end in ة whether Masc. or Fem. e.g. طَرَفَةُ (masc.), فَاطِمَةُ, مَكَّةُ; all that end in ـَاءُ or ـَى e.g. زَكَرِيَّاءُ, يَحْيَى; those that end in ـَانُ, e.g. سُلَيْمَانُ, عُثْمَانُ; also the Proper names that correspond in form with a verbal form whether Perfect or Imperfect, e.g. شَمَّرُ (name of a tribe), أَحْمَدُ, يَزِيدُ; also many others as عُمَرُ, زَيْنَبُ (name of a woman). إِبْرٰهِيمُ.

Proper names on the other hand are Triptote when they are 1) of the forms فَعْلٌ, فِعْلٌ, فُعْلٌ, e.g. زَيْدٌ, "Zaid", عَمْرٌو "ʿAmr", نُوحٌ "Noah", هِنْدٌ (but also هِنْدُ and so with other names of women); 2) originally Participles or Adjectives, e.g. حَسَنٌ (properly "beautiful"). سَعِيدٌ (properly "happy"), مُرَادٌ (properly "desired"), مُحَمَّدٌ (properly "praised"); 3) certain single names as جَعْفَرٌ etc.

3. All Diptotes, when they are made definite by the Article or a Possessive suffix or a following Genitive are treated as Triptotes (see. Less. 6, 3), e.g.

مِنَ ٱلأَشْيَاءِ from the matters,

مِنْ أَشْيَائِهِ from his matters,

مِنْ أَشْيَاءِ ٱلْوَلَدِ from the boy's matters.

4. The nouns, which end in *in* ــٍ (arising from iwun, iyun and uyun) e.g. دَاعٍ (for دَاعِوٌ) "caller", قَاضٍ (for قَاضِيٌ), "judge", تَمَنٍّ (for تَمَنِّيٌ). "wish", change:

iwun, iwin, iyun, iyin, uyun, uyin into **in**,
iwū, iyū, uyū, into **ū**,
iwi, iyi, uyi, into **ī**,
iwu, iyu, uyu, iwi, iyi, and uyi into ī (cf. Less. 6, 3, Note 2 and Less. 28, 2) e.g.

قَاضٍ "judge" Nom. and Gen. Sing.

قَاضِيًا " Accus. Sing.

قَاضِيَانِ "two judges" Nom. Dual.

قَاضِيَيْنِ " " Gen. and Accus. Dual.

قَاضُونَ "judges" Nom. Plur.

قَاضِينَ " Gen. and Accus. Plur.

With Article: ٱلْقَاضِي "the judge" or "of the judge" Nom. and Gen. Sing.

ٱلْقَاضِيَ " " Accus. Sing.

The Broken Plurals, which are Diptotes and are derived from verbs whose third radical is و or ى, have as endings in the Nom. and Gen. *in*, in the Accus. *iya*, e.g. from جَارِيَةٌ "slave girl", Plur. Nom. and Gen. جَوَارٍ,

Accus. جَوَارِىَ; from فَتْوَى "legal decision", Plur. Nom. and Gen. فَتَاوٍ, Accus. فَتَاوِىَ.

5. Nouns, which end in *an* (written ـًا or ـًى) as عَصًا "stick" (for عَصَوٌ), هُدًى "guidance" (for هُدَىٌ), مُصْطَفًى "Mustafa" (for مُصْطَفَوٌ) are alike in all cases of the Singular; so also are the Diptotes as ذِكْرَى "remembrance", دُنْيَا "world".

6. The noun إِبْنٌ "son" drops its alif, when it comes between the name of the son and that of the father. The Proper name preceding it loses its nunation, e.g.

زَيْدُ بْنُ عَمْرٍو "Zaid the son of ʿAmr". But if the إِبْنُ happens to begin a new line the alif is retained. It is also retained if the word إِبْنٌ is used predicatively (cf. Intro. § 11, 4 b), e.g.

زَيْدٌ إِبْنُ عَمْرٍو "Zaid is the son of ʿAmr".

Exercise 77.

وَقَعَ بَيْنَ الوَلِيدِ بنِ عَبْدِ المَلِكِ وَبَيْنَ أَخِيهِ سُلَيْمَانَ كَلَامٌ فَعَجَّلَ عليه سليمانُ بِأَمْرٍ يَلْحَقُ أُمَّهُ فَفَتَحَ فاهُ (see. Less. 7, 2) لِيُجِيبَهُ وإِذَا بِجَنْبِهِ عُمَرُ بْنُ عَبْدِ العَزِيزِ فَأَمْسَكَ على فِيهِ وَرَدَّ كَلِمَتَهُ وقال يا آبْنَ عَبْدِ المَلِكِ أَخُوكَ وَآبْنُ أُمِّكَ وله السَّبْقُ عليك فقال يا أَبَا حَفْصٍ قَتَلْتَنِي قال وما صَنَعْتُ بِكَ قال رَدَدْتَ فى صَدْرِى أَحَرَّ من الجَمْرِ ومَالَ لِجَنْبِهِ فَمَاتَ —

كان الخَليفةُ المُسْتَعْصِمُ بَطَلاً شُجاعاً وفارِسًا صِنْدِيدًا لم يكن فى بَنِى العَبّاسِ أَشْجَعُ منه ولا أَشَدُّ قَلْبًا قال آبْنُ أَبِى دُاوُدَ كان المُسْتَعْصِمُ يَقُولُ لِى يا أَبا عبدِ اللهِ عَضَّ على ساعِدِى بِأَكْثَرِ قُوَّتِكَ فأَقُولُ واللهِ يا أَمِيرَ المُومنين ما تَطِيبُ نَفْسِى بذلك فَيَقُولُ إِنَّهُ لا يَضُرُّنِى فأَرُومُ ذلك فإذا هو لا تَعْمَلُ فيه الأَسِنَّةُ فَكَيْفَ تَعْمَلُ فيه الأَسْنَانُ —

Exercise 78.

Strike him with the stick. — Five is the half of ten. — The Caliph el-Muʿtaṣim was acquainted (كَانَ and Imperf.) with Ali, the son of el-Junaid el-Iskāfī and el-Muʿtaṣim said to the son of Ḥammād, "Go to the son of el-Junaid and tell him to prepare to be-a-guest to me" and he came to him and said to him, "Prepare to be-a-guest of the Commander of the Faithful, for to be a guest of Caliphs is a great thing (is great). — It was said to a boy, "Does not thy teacher clothe thee?" — And he answered, "Verily, if my teacher had a house filled with needles, and Jacob came and with him the prophets as intercessors and the angels as pledges, to borrow from him a needle with which to sew the garment of his son Joseph, which was torn, he would not lend (Perf.) him it; then how should he clothe me?"

Forty-second Lesson.

(اَلدَّرْسُ اَلثَّانِى وَالأَرْبَعُونَ)

The Use of the Cases.

(A word in the Nominative is called مَرْفُوعٌ, in the Accusative مَنْصُوبٌ, in the Genitive مَجْرُورٌ or مَخْفُوضٌ.)

1. The Nominative (رَفْعٌ) is used for:

a) The Subject in a Verbal sentence (فَاعِلٌ) and that of a Nominal sentence (مُبْتَدَأٌ). See Less. 11, 6.

b) The Predicate of the Nominal sentence (خَبَرٌ). See Less. 11, 6.

c) The word following the Particle of Address أَيُّهَا (always used with the Article) and after يَا (in the Sing. without nunation), when it is not made definite by a following word. See Less. 48.

d) The Attribute of, or word in Apposition to another word in the Nominative.

Note. The Predicate of sentences beginning with إِنَّ or the kindred particles (see below § 2 h) is put in the Nominative.

2. The Accusative (نَصْبٌ) is used for:

a) The Object (مَفْعُولٌ بِهِ), e.g.

ضَرَبْتُ زَيْدًا "I struck Zaid".

إِيَّاكَ نَعْبُدُ "Thee we serve".

ضَرَبْتُهُ "I struck him".

Note 1. In Arabic most verbs denoting "to come" are transitive. The transitive verb is called اَلْفِعْلُ ٱلْمُتَعَدِّي, the intransitive اَلْفِعْلُ ٱللَّازِمُ.

Note. 2. For the government of the Accus. by the Verbal Noun and the Participle see Less. 34, 6, 8.

b) The Absolute Object or Cognate Accusative (اَلْمَفْعُولُ ٱلْمُطْلَقُ) see Less. 34, 7.

c) Determinations of Time and Place (ظَرْفٌ) see Less. 45, 5, e.g. اَلْيَوْمَ "to-day", غَدًا "to-morrow", صَبَاحًا "in the morning", مُدَّةَ سَنَةٍ "(during) a whole year".

نَظَرَ يَمِينًا وَشِمَالًا "he looked right and left", سَافَرَ بَرًّا وَبَحْرًا "he travelled by land and sea".

To this class belong many words in the Accus. used as Prepositions, e.g. خَلْفَ "behind", فَوْقَ "above", تَحْتَ "under", etc.

d) Determinations of the Aim or Purpose, e.g. قُمْتُ إِكْرَامًا لَهُ "I rose to honour him" (cf. Less. 34, 6).

e) Determinations of Condition (حَالٌ) for which the Participle and Verbal Noun are used generally, e.g. جَاءَ رَاكِبًا "he came riding".

f) Specification (تَمْيِيزٌ) with the meaning "in regard to, in", e.g.

زَيْدٌ أَكْبَرُ عِلْمًا مِنْ عَمْرٍو "Zaid is greater in regard to knowledge than 'Amr".

طِبْ نَفْسًا "be good in regard to soul" i.e. "rejoice heartily".

g) The Predicate (خَبَرٌ) of كَانَ and its sisters (cf. Less. 30, 12), e.g.

كَانَ زَيْدٌ رَجُلًا "Zaid was a man".

h) The Subject after the following particles:

إِنَّ "truly", فَإِنَّ "for", لٰكِنَّ "but";

أَنَّ "that", لِأَنَّ "because", كَأَنَّ "as if";

لَيْتَ "O would that!", لَعَلَّ "perhaps"; e.g.

إِنَّ زَيْدًا قَائِمٌ or إِنَّ قَائِمٌ زَيْدًا "truly, Zaid is standing".

i) The noun after the لَا that denies absolutely (لَا لِنَفْيِ ٱلْجِنْسِ i.e. لَا for the denial of the class) cf.

Less. 45, 3 p 3. The noun loses its nunation, e.g. لَا مَفَرَّ "there is no escape", لَا شَكَّ "there is no doubt", لَا بُدَّ (لَا مَحَالَةَ or) مِن ٱلشَّيْء "there is no escape from the matter" i.e. "the matter is absolutely necessary".

j) The Noun after the Particle of Address يَا if it is followed by a Genitive, e.g. يَا عَبْدَ ٱللّٰهِ "O Abdallah", يَا أَمِيرَ ٱلْمُؤْمِنِين "O ruler of the Faithful!"

k) The Noun after the Conjunction وَ, when it means "with", e.g. زَيْدٌ وَأَخَاهُ "Zaid with his brother".

l) A word, which is an Attribute of, or in Apposition to another word in the Accus.

Note 1. Many verbs take two objects in the Accus. e.g. ظَنَنْتُ زَيْدًا حَكِيمًا "I thought Zaid (to be) a physician".

Note 2. The Accusative often stands in single expressions —especially Exclamations—, where a verb is to be supplied, e.g. أَهْلًا وَسَهْلًا "welcome!", where جِئْتَ is understood, i.e. "you have come to friends and an agreeable place"; مَهْلًا "slowly", where إِمْشِ "go" is understood.

3. The Genitive (جَرٌّ or خَفْضٌ) is used in the following:

a) A Noun which is connected with another by Annexation (إِضَافَةٌ), see Less. 6, 4.

Note. Arabian grammarians say that the إِضَافَةٌ, has the force of one of the prepositions لِ, مِنْ or فِي, e.g. غُلَامُ زَيْدٍ = أَلْغُلَامُ ٱلَّذِي لِزَيْدٍ "the boy who (belongs) to Zaid"; ثَوْبُ حَرِيرٍ = ثَوْبٌ مِنْ حَرِيرٍ "a garment of silk"; صَلٰوةُ ٱلْمَغْرِبِ = أَلصَّلٰوةُ فِي ٱلْمَغْرِبِ "the prayer of sunset".

b) A Noun after a Preposition (حَرْفُ ٱلْجَرِّ) see Less. 44.

c) A Noun which is an Attribute of or in Apposition to another in the Genitive.

In connection with a) it should be noted that some nouns combined with a Genitive in Arabic correspond to English Adjectives, Adverbs etc.:

1) كُلٌّ "whole", i.e. "all, every, the whole", e.g. كُلَّ يَوْمٍ "every day"; كُلُّ وَاحِدٍ "each"; كُلُّ ٱلْمَدِينَةِ "the whole city"; كُلُّ ٱلنَّاسِ "all men" (also ٱلنَّاسُ كُلُّهُمْ); كُلُّ مَنْ "everyone who"; كُلُّ مَا "all that (Rel.)".

Similarly جَمِيعٌ and كَافَّةٌ "whole" are used for "all", e.g. جَمِيعُ ٱلنَّاسِ or كَافَّةُ ٱلنَّاسِ "all men".

2) بَعْضٌ properly "a part", i.e. "one, some", e.g. بَعْضُ ٱلشُّعَرَاءِ "one of the poets" i.e. "a certain poet" or "some poets".

3) مِثْلٌ "likeness" corresponds to the English "as, like", e.g. مِثْلُ زَيْدٍ "like Zaid", مِثْلُهُ "like him", or "as he".

4) سِوًى properly "an other" means "except", e.g. سِوَى ٱلْعِلْمِ "except science"

5) غَيْرٌ properly "an other than" often corresponds to the prefixes non-, un-, im- etc., e.g. غَيْرُ ٱلْعَرَبِ "a non-Arab"; غَيْرُ مُمْكِنٍ "im-possible".

6)	كِلَانِ	Fem.	كِلْتَانِ	"both".
Gen. Accus.	كِلَيْنِ	Fem.	كِلْتَيْنِ	

E.g. كِلَا ٱلرَّجُلَيْنِ "both the men"; كِلَاهُمَا "they both" (cf. Less. 7, 1).

7) رُبَّ "a many of" i.e. "many a" always followed by an Indefinite Noun, e.g.

رُبَّ رَجُلٍ كَرِيمٍ قَدْ لَقِيتُ "many a noble man have I met".

Emphasis.

(اَلتَّوكِيدُ or اَلتَّأكِيدُ).

4. A noun can be emphasised by:

a) Repetition (اَلتَّأكِيدُ ٱللَّفظِيُّ "literal emphasis"), e.g.

جَاءَ رَاكِضًا رَاكِضًا "he came running (quickly)".

رَأَيْتُكَ إِيَّاكَ "I saw thee" (cf. Less. 43, 3).

b) The use of special words (اَلتَّأكِيدُ ٱلْمَعْنَوِيُّ "emphasis according to the sense"). Such words are: نَفْس (Plur. أَنْفُس) and عَيْن (Plur. أَعْيُن) "self", e.g.

جَاءَ زَيْدٌ نَفْسُهُ "Zaid himself came". One can also say بِنَفْسِهِ of بِعَيْنِهِ.

The words كُلّ, جَمِيع and كَافَّة are also used for Emphasis (see above § 3, 1).

The Permutative.

(اَلْبَدَلُ "the substitution")

5) The Permutative must follow immediately the word for which it is substituted (اَلْمُبْدَلُ مِنْهُ).

There are four kinds of substitution:

a) The substitution of the whole for the whole (بَدَلُ ٱلْكُلِّ مِنَ ٱلْكُلِّ) i.e. where the Permutative is exactly equivalent to the word for which it is substituted, e.g.

جَاءَ زَيْدٌ أَخُوكَ "Zaid, thy brother came";

جَاءَنِي قَوْمُ ٱلْمَدِينَةِ كِبَارُهُمْ وَصِغَارُهُمْ "the people of the city, the great and the small, came to me".

b) The part is substituted for the whole (بَدَلُ ٱلْبَعْضِ مِنَ ٱلْكُلِّ), e.g.

قَبِّلْهُ ٱلْيَدَ "kiss him the hand" i.e. "kiss his hand"; أَكَلَ ٱلرَّغِيفَ نِصْفَهُ "he ate the loaf, half of it" i.e. "he ate the half of the loaf".

c) A possession or quality is substituted for the name (بَدَلُ ٱلِاشْتِمَالِ i.e. Permutative of inclusion"), e.g. أَعْجَبَنِي زَيْدٌ ثَوْبُهُ "Zaid, his garment pleased me" i.e. "Zaid's garment pleased me"; مَدَحْتُ زَيْدًا حُسْنَهُ "I praised Zaid, his beauty" i.e. "I praised Zaid's beauty".

d) A word is used to correct the previous one (بَدَلُ ٱلْغَلَطِ "the Permutative of error"), e.g. مَرَرْتُ بِكَلْبٍ فَرَسٍ "I passed by a dog (no, I mean) a horse".

Exercise 79.

رَكِبْتُ قَاصِدًا جَبَلَ ٱلشَّيْخِ — سِرْنَا قَاصِدِينَ ٱلشَّامَ — مَسَاءً أَتَى أَقَارِبُ صَاحِبِ ٱلْمَحَلِّ لِيُسَلِّمُوا عَلَيَّ فَصَرَفْنَاهَا لَيْلَةً جَمِيلَةً فَجَلَسْتُ بُرْهَةً مَعَهُمْ ثُمَّ ٱسْتَأْذَنْتُ بِٱلذَّهَابِ وَلَمْ يَسْمَحُوا لِي بِذَلِكَ وَلَمَّا تَيَقَّنْتُ أَنَّهُ لَا بُدَّ مِنْ تَنْفِيذِ مَرْغُوبِهِمْ أَجَبْتُ سُؤَالَهُمْ — لَا بُدَّ دُونَ ٱلشَّهْدِ مِنْ إِبَرِ ٱلنَّحْلِ — رَأَيْتُ ظَبْيًا رَاكِضًا كَأَنَّهُ طَائِرٌ — كَانَ دَمُهُ يَجْرِي جَرْيًا

قَوِيًّا — هذا الجَبَلُ لا يَخْلُو من الثَلْجِ طُولَ مُدَّةِ السَنَةِ —
سَقَطَتِ ٱلٱبْنَةُ على وَجْهِهَا مَغْشِيًّا عليها — لا بُدَّ من الذَهَابِ
الآنَ بِأَسْرَعِ وَقْتٍ — الظَبْيُ كُلَّمَا ٱقْتَرَبْنَا إِليه كان يَزِيدُ نُفُورًا
وٱبْتِعادًا فلم نَزَلْ سائِرِينَ وراءَهُ مُدَّةً طَوِيلَةً ثُمَّ غابَ عن
نَظَرِنا — إِذْ كان قَلْبِي غائِصًا فى بِحارِ الهُمُومِ رَأَيْتُ سُعْدَى جادَّةَ
المَسِيرِ نَحْوِي فَقُلْتُ لها أَيْنَ كُنْتِ يا مُهْجَةَ الفُؤَادِ ويا قُرَّةَ
العَيْنِ فإِنَّ غِيابَكِ قد رَمانِي فى بِحارٍ من الأَحْزانِ والقَلَقِ —
إِنَّ اللُصُوصَ هَجَمُوا علىّ جَمِيعًا ظانِّينَ أَنَّنِي أُوَلِّي هارِبًا —
لَيْتَ كُلَّ الصُعُوباتِ كَهذه فإِنّه أَمْرٌ سَهْلٌ — لا شَىْءَ عندى
أَحَبُّ من ذلك — قَلْبِي كان مَمْلُوءًا ٱضْطِرابًا وحُزْنًا على فِراقِ
سُعْدَى — زادَ عند العَرَبِ ٱعْتِبارِي أَضْعافَ ما كان عليه —
قال لى الأَمِيرُ إِنَّ الجِراحَ التى أَصابَتْنِي أَمْسِ أَخَذَتْ فى أَنْ
تَزِيدَنِي أَلَمًا وسُهادًا فقُلْتُ له إِنّه لا بُدَّ لِكُلِّ إِنْسانٍ من أَنْ
يُصابَ بِأَوْجاعٍ — حَبِيبِي لم يُفارِقْ أَفْكارِي لا لَيْلًا ولا نَهارًا —
كان سَيْرُ المَرْكَبِ يُحاكِي هُبُوبَ الرِيحِ لِأَنَّ الهَواءَ كان مُوافِقًا له
— إِبْتَدَأَتْ عَيْنايَ تَقْطِرُ دُمُوعًا غَزِيرَةً وأَنا أَنْدُبُ سُوءَ حَظِّي
وأَقُولُ فى نَفْسِي يا لَيْتَ ذلك المَرْكَبَ لم يَأْتِ لِأَنّه أَغْرَقَ ما كان

سَبَبًا لِراحَتِى — أَشْهَدُ أَنْ لَا إِلٰهَ إِلَّا ٱللّٰهُ أَشْهَدُ أَنَّ مُحَمَّدًا رَسُولُ ٱللّٰهِ — كَبَا بِى ٱلْجَوادُ وَسَقَطْنَا كِلانا على الأَرْضِ — لا حَوْلَ ولا قُوَّةَ إِلَّا بِٱللّٰهِ ٱلْعَظِيمِ (used as an exclamation) — طِبْ نَفْسًا وَقِرَّ عَيْنًا (be comforted!) —

Exercise 80.

It is necessary to go away (there is no escape from going away). — It is necessary that I give thee what thou demandest. — The captain was extremely astonished at what (مِمَّا) had happened to me. — The sea was calm and the atmosphere clear and the weather still. — I travelled in the direction of (making for قَصَدَ Egypt and you travel in the direction of Syria. — I pray (سَأَلَ) God that he may bring you safe to your country. — We wept bitterly and that hour was a very grievous hour. — That man was intelligent, pious, of noble character, of noble soul. — Verily calamities do not cease following me, since I went out from the city. — She sighed in despair (the sigh of the despairing) and her sighing was increasing my pain and sorrow (me as to pain and sorrow). — I have no power to withstand calamities. — We have only death before us (there is not before us except death). — Throw us both into the sea, or preserve us both. — Since the main purpose (most important of purposes) of our high dynasty is the rooting out of the causes of encroachment and of evil by sea and land, we are legally and morally compelled to (that we) make war on all ships of the Corsairs.

Forty-third Lesson.

(اَلدَّرْسُ اَلثَّالِثُ وَالأَرْبَعُونَ)

Pronouns.

3. The Personal Pronoun (ضَمِيرٌ) is either Independent or Suffixed (cf. Less. 8, 1), and may be in the Nominative or the Accusative.

For the Independent Pronoun see Less. 3, 6.

Note. If the conjunctions وَ, فَ "and", لَ "verily" are prefixed to هُوَ or هِيَ the ه sometimes loses its vowel, e.g. وَهْوَ, فَهْيَ etc.

3. The Independent Pronoun in the Accusative is as follows:

3. Masc.	إِيَّاهُ	him.	إِيَّاهُمَا	them both	إِيَّاهُمْ	them.
3. Fem.	إِيَّاهَا	her.	إِيَّاكُمَا	you both	إِيَّاهُنَّ	,,
2. Masc.	إِيَّاكَ	thee.			إِيَّاكُمْ	you.
2. Fem.	إِيَّاكِ	,,			إِيَّاكُنَّ	,,
1.	إِيَّايَ	me.			إِيَّانَا	us.

4. The Independent Pronoun in the Accus. is used:

a) With a verb to emphasise the Pronoun, e.g. إِيَّاكَ نَعْبُدُ "Thee we serve".

b) If two Pronouns are Direct Objects of a verb, e.g. أَعْطَانِي إِيَّاهُ "he gave it (to) me"; but it is also possible to say أَعْطَانِيهِ. It is also used as the Object after a Verbal Noun, e.g. إِعْطَائِي إِيَّاهُ "my giving it (to) him".

c) Independently as a Warning, without a verb, e.g. إِيَّاكَ "take care!". see Less. 48, 2.

5. For the Suffixed Pronoun see Less. 8, 2, 3.

Note 1. The letter ى is often omitted in the cry رَبِّ, for رَبِّي "my Lord!" (cf. Less. 48, 1 Note), and in the Pronoun نِي, e.g. إِتَّقُونِ (for إِتَّقُونِي) "fear me".

Note 2. The Pronoun هُ often refers to a whole sentence and is then called a ضَمِيرُ ٱلشَّأْنِ; it is translated "it" or omitted in translation.

6. If the Personal Pronoun is to be emphasised it is repeated in the Independent form, whether it has already been contained in the verbal form or expressed as a Suffix, e.g. ضَرَبْتُ أَنَا "I struck", ضَرَبَنِي أَنَا "he struck me".

The Emphatic Pronoun "myself, himself" etc. is expressed by the use of نَفْسٌ (Plur. أَنْفُسٌ), عَيْنٌ (Plur. أَعْيُنٌ) or ذَاتٌ (Plur. ذَوَاتٌ) with the Pronominal suffixes (cf. Less. 42, 4 b), e.g. زَيْدٌ نَفْسُهُ or زَيْدٌ بِنَفْسِهِ "Zaid himself"; so also عَيْنُ ٱلشَّيْءِ "the matter itself, this same matter".

7. The Reflexive Pronoun in the Accus. is also expressed by نَفْسٌ, عَيْنٌ, ذَاتٌ (with their Plurals) and the Pronominal suffixes, e.g. قَتَلَ نَفْسَهُ "he killed himself".

If the Pronoun depends on a Preposition, it is enough to use the Pronominal suffix, e.g. أَخَذْتُ لِي شَيْئًا "I took something for myself".

8. The Reciprocal Pronoun "one another" is expressed by the use of بَعْضٌ "one, some", e.g. سَاعَدْنَا بَعْضُنَا بَعْضًا "we have helped one another".

After Prepositions the بَعْضٌ need not be repeated, e.g.

دَنَا ٱلْعَسَاكِرُ مِنْ بَعْضِهِمْ "the soldiers approached one another".

9. For the Demonstrative Pronoun and the Interrogative Pronoun see Less. 9; for the Relative Pronoun see Less. 31.

Exercise 81.

إِيَّاكَ نَعْبُدُ وَإِيَّاكَ نَسْتَعِينُ — جَمَعُوا إِبِلًا كَثِيرَةً وَأَعْطَوْهُ إِيَّاهَا — وَدَّعَنِي أَصْدِقَائِي قَبْلَ مُبَارَحَتِي إِيَّاهُمْ — لم أَقْدِرْ أَنْ أَمْنَعَ نَفْسِي عن أَنْ أَلُومَهم — سَأُكَابِدُ أَشَدَّ المَشَقَّاتِ وسَأُخَاطِرُ بِنَفْسِي حُبًّا بِصَدِيقِي — إِنَّ اللُّصُوصَ طَلَبُوا مِنَّا أَسْلِحَتَنَا فَسَلَّمْنَاهُمْ إِيَّاهَا — رَمَى الفَارِسُ بِذَاتِهِ عَلَيَّ لِيَأْخُذَنِي من أَيْدِيهِمْ — لَمَّا دَنَا الفَرِيقَانِ من بَعْضِهِمَا تَصَادَمَا — كُنَّا نَنْظُرُ إِلَى بَعْضِنَا من بُعْدٍ — رَأَيْتُ ذَاتِي مُبْتَعِدًا عن الأَوْطَانِ وَحِيدًا بَيْنَ أُولٰئِكَ العَرَبِ — لم يَعْلَمِ العَرَبِيُّ أَنِّي أَنَا الرَّجُلُ الذى يَطْلُبُهُ — أَخَذَ بَعْضُ أَفْكَارِي يُقَاوِمُ البَعْضَ — بَعْدَ أَنْ كِدْتُ أَتَجَرَّعُ كَأْسَ المَنُونِ فُزْتُ بِنَفْسِي — أَخَذْتُ فى تَعْزِيَةِ نَفْسِي وتَسْلِيَةِ هُمُومِي بِالأَلْعَابِ — أَيْنَ مَحْبُوبَتِي الآنَ وَمَنْ يُرِيهَا إِيَّايَ بَيْنَ هذه الأَمْوَاجِ ما العَمَلُ أَأُلْقِي بِنَفْسِي إِلَى البَحْرِ — قلتُ لها قُومِي وَٱسْتَفِيقِي الآنَ لِنَتَزَوَّدَ من بَعْضِنَا نَظْرَةً أَخِيرَةً —

Exercise 82.

You have struck us. — We ourselves have commanded this. — The beggar demanded an alms from us and we gave it him. — My giving it was (a) good. — You will offer yourselves to destruction. — You have demanded the same matter as we have demanded. — The two parties were entangled with one another. Those shepherds asked me if I was the person sought. — I began to comfort myself and cheer my spirit (raise myself) with vain hopes. — Truly, what has befallen me is by reason of my deceiving thee. — Let us throw ourselves into the sea and die at once. — The captain commanded a sailor to separate us from one another. — Remember my freeing thee from the hands of the robbers.

Forty-fourth Lesson.

(اَلدَّرْسُ ٱلرَّابِعُ وَالأَرْبَعُونَ).

Particles.

1. The Particles (حَرْفٌ) are divided into Prepositions, Adverbs, Conjunctions and Interjections.

Prepositions.

2. The Preposition is called حَرْفُ ٱلْجَرِّ, the word governed by a preposition is مَجْرُورٌ, and the preposition with its noun is اَلْجَارُّ وَالْمَجْرُورُ.

3. Prepositions are: A. Inseparable, consisting of one letter always attached to the following word; B. Separate, which stand alone and are either true particles or nouns in the Accus.

A. Inseparable Prepositions.

1) بِ "in, by. with" etc.

Verbs denoting "to adhere", "attach", "seize", "begin", are construed with بِ e.g. عَلِقَ "to hang on", بَدَأَ "to begin with".

"To believe in" is آمَنَ بِ, e.g. آمَنْتُ بِٱللّٰهِ "I believe in God".

"To swear by" is أَقْسَمَ بِ, e.g. أَقْسَمْتُ بِرَأْسِي "I swear by my head". Sometimes the verb is omitted.

After إِذَا "See! Behold!" بِ is used (but the noun alone in the Nom. may be used), e.g. إِذَا بِرَجُلٍ قَدْ أَتَى Behold a man came (or إِذَا رَجُلٌ).

In negative sentences, if the predicate is a noun, بِ is often prefixed to it, e.g.

لَيْسَ هُوَ بِفَارِسٍ he is not a rider (or فَارِسًا).

مَا هُمْ بِعَالِمِينَ they are not aware (or عَالِمُونَ).

Many intransitive verbs of motion become transitive, when they are followed by بِ and the object to which the motion refers, e.g. أَتَى بِشَيْءٍ he came with a thing, i.e. he brought it. (This ب is called بَاءُ ٱلتَّعْدِيَةِ.)

Note. The expression بِأَبِي أَنْتَ means "at the price of my father thou art to be redeemed", i.e. "thou art so dear to me, that I would redeem thee at the price of my father". (This is called بَاءُ ٱلتَّفْدِيَةِ, the *bā* of redemption.)

2) and 3) تَ and وَ "by" in an oath, e.g. تَٱللّٰهِ and وَٱللّٰهِ "by God". (تَ occurs only in this expression.) If however a verb is used in the oath, ب must be used.

4) لِ "for, to, because of".

لِ is used to express the Dative and denotes possession (= "have", see Less. 8, 5).

As a Conjunction (with the Subjunctive of the verb) it denotes "in order that, so that".

It denotes the English "of", when it follows an indeterminate noun, e.g. كِتَابٌ لِزَيْدٍ a book of (belonging to) Zaid": صَاحِبٌ لِي a friend of me i.e. one of my friends.

It is used especially for the editor of a book, e.g. قِصَصُ ٱلْأَنْبِيَاءِ لِلثَّعْلَبِيِّ The Stories of the Prophets of (i.e. written by) Thaʿlabī.

لِ also denotes "for the benefit of" (opposite of عَلَى) and so denotes a creditor (عَلَى the debtor), e.g. لِي عَلَيْكَ أَلْفُ دِرْهَمٍ thou owest me a thousand dirhams.

It is also used to denote the Purpose and the Cause, e.g.

قُمْتُ لِمُعَاوَنَتِهِ I rose to help him.

لِهٰذَا / لِذٰلِكَ } for this reason, therefore.

Note 1. قَالَ لِ "to say to" often means, especially in the Passive, "to call name", e.g. قِيلَ (يُقَالُ) لَهُ he was (is) called.

Note 2. لِ is changed to لَ before Pronominal suffixes (except with the 1st Pers.), e.g. لَهُ, لَهَا etc. It is also changed to لَ after the particle of address يَا e.g. يَا لَلْعَجَبِ "O wonder", يَا لَزَيْدٍ "O Zaid!" (i.e. come and help O Zaid!).

5) كَ "as, like" is usually counted among the prepositions, although it is really a noun meaning "similarity", e.g. كَزَيْدٍ "like Zaid".

It is not used with Pronominal suffixes.

B. Separate Prepositions.

1) إِلَى "to, unto, until".

Is nearly related in meaning to لِ and serves to express motion towards a place. e.g.

جَاءَ إِلَى ٱلْمَدِينَةِ he came to the city.

In relation to time it expresses continuance up to a certain point of time, e.g.

مِنَ ٱلِٱبْتِدَاءِ إِلَى ٱلِٱنْتِهَاءِ from beginning to end.

Notice specially إِلَى آخِرِهِ (abbreviated إِلخ, see Intro § 16) "and so forth", "et caetera".

With suffixes: إِلَيْهِ "to him", إِلَيَّ "to me", etc.

2) حَتَّى "up to, as far as".

Is not used with suffixes.

It is sometimes used to mean "even" and then exercises no influence on the case of the following word, e.g. أَكَلْتُ ٱلسَّمَكَةَ حَتَّى رَأْسَهَا "I ate the fish, even its head".

3) عَلَى "over, on, against".

With suffixes: عَلَيْهِ "on him"; عَلَيَّ "on me" etc.

Used of place. عَلَى ٱلطَّرِيقِ on the way.

جَلَسَ عَلَى ٱلْمَائِدَةِ he sat at table.

مَدِينَةٌ عَلَى نَهْرٍ a city on a river.

Notice specially:

تَفَرَّجَ عَلَى شَيْءٍ to look (with pleasure) at a thing.

إِطَّلَعَ عَلَى شَيْءٍ
وَقَفَ عَلَى شَيْءٍ } to examine into a thing.

غُشِيَ (أُغْمِيَ or) عَلَيْهِ he fainted (lit. it was made dark upon him).

اَلسَّلَامُ عَلَيْكُمْ Peace be on you! (the greeting of Moslems to one another, the answer being وَعَلَيْكُمُ ٱلسَّلَامُ).

رَحْمَةُ ٱللّٰهِ عَلَيْهِ God's mercy be upon him.

صَلَّى ٱللّٰهُ عَلَيْهِ وَسَلَّمَ God give him blessing and peace (see Intro. § 16).

Used in a hostile sense:

خَرَجَ عَلَيْهِ he went out (to war) against him.

So with verbs denoting anger:

غَضِبْتُ عَلَيْكَ I was angry with thee.

Used with Adjectives:

ذٰلِكَ صَعْبٌ (سَهْلٌ) عَلَيَّ that is too hard (easy) for me.

"To incite to" حَثَّ عَلَى; "to induce to" حَمَلَ عَلَى, e.g.

حَمَلْتُهُ عَلَى شَيْءٍ I have induced him to (do) something.

عَلَى is also used to indicate that a burden, duty or debt lies on one, e.g.

فَرْضٌ عَلَى إِنْسَانٍ a duty incumbent on a man.

يَجِبُ عَلَى فُلَانٍ it is the duty of such and such a one.

هٰذَا لِي عَلَيْكَ you owe me this (see A, 4).

فَضْلٌ عَلَى a preference over.

Common expressions with على are:

بِنَاءً عَلَى according to . . .

عَلَى أَنْ on the supposition that.

عَلَى قَدْرِ ٱلْإِمْكَانِ so far as possible.

عَلَيَّ بِهِ bring him here to me.

عَلَى ٱلرَّأْسِ وَٱلْعَيْنِ (lit. on the head and the eye) willingly, with pleasure.

بِٱللّٰهِ عَلَيْكَ I conjure thee by God.

4) عَنْ "from, instead of".

With suffixes: عَنْهُ "from him", عَنِّي "from me", عَنَّا "from us", etc.

Used of place = away from, and so is used with verbs denoting to flee, avoid, restrain oneself, forbid, hinder, defend (with many of these verbs مِنْ can be used), e.g.

مَنَعَ عَنْ (or مِنْ) to prevent from . . . .

إِجْتَنَبَ عَنْ (or مِنْ) to avoid . . . .

دَافَعَ عَنْ شَخْصٍ أَوْ شَيْءٍ to defend someone or something.

It is also used with verbs meaning to uncover, reveal, open and ask, e.g.

كَشَفَ عَنْ شَيْءٍ to uncover something.

سَأَلَ عَنْ شَخْصٍ أَوْ شَيْءٍ to ask about someone or something.

In the sense of the Latin de "concerning", e.g.

حُكِيَ عَنْ سُلَيْمَانَ it is told concerning Solomon.

To indicate the source of information, e.g.

حُكِيَ عَنِ ٱلشَّافِعِيِّ it is told on the authority of ash-Shāfiʿī.

It is sometimes used of time, e.g. عَنْ قَرِيبٍ "shortly, soon".

Notice specially:

رَضِىَ ٱللّٰهُ عَنْهُ May God be pleased with him (see Intro. § 16).

فَضْلاً عَنْ apart from.

5) فِى "in".

With suffixes: فِيهِ in him, فِىَّ in me etc.

It expresses rest in place or time and answers the questions "where?" and "when?", e.g. فِى ٱلدَّارِ in the house, فِى هٰذِهِ ٱلسَّنَةِ in this year.

Sometimes it expresses motion to a place, e.g. وَقَعَ فِى ٱلْجُبِّ he fell into the cistern.

It also denotes "among", e.g. مَنْ فِينَا who among us.

It is used with verbs of speaking and thinking:

تَكَلَّمَ فِى to speak about . . . .

إِفْتَكَرَ فِى to think over . . . .

تَأَمَّلَ فِى شَىْءٍ to consider something.

Also after the verbs of desiring: رَغِبَ فِى to wish for something; طَمِعَ فِى to yearn after.

"To multiply by" is ضَرَبَ فِى, e.g.

إِضْرِبْ ثَلَاثَةً فِى سَبْعَةٍ multiply three by seven.

6) لَدُنْ, لَدَى, لَدَا "with" (Latin "apud").

With suffixes لَدُنْهُ with him, لَدُنِّى with me etc.; لَدَيْهِ with him, لَدَىَّ with me; is rarer than عِنْدَ.

7) مَعَ (rarely مَعْ) "with".

With suffixes مَعَهُ with him, مَعِي with me etc.

It denotes association in place or connection in time, e.g.

سَارَ مَعِي he travelled with me.

جِئْتُكَ مَعَ طُلُوعِ ٱلشَّمْسِ I came to thee at sunrise.

It often means "to have something with one", e.g.

مَعِي سَاعَةٌ I have a watch with me.

It also translates the English "besides", e.g.

مَعَ كَوْنِهِ غَرِيبًا besides his being a stranger.

Notice specially:

مَعَ ذَلِكَ in spite of that.

مَعَ أَنَّ in spite of the fact that, although.

8) مِنْ "from".

With suffixes مِنْهُ from him, مِنَّا from us etc.

Used of place (often interchangeable with عَنْ):

خَرَجَ مِنَ ٱلْخَيْمَةِ he went out from the tent.

It is used with verbs denoting to go out, to free, to forbid:

أَعُوذُ بِٱللهِ مِنَ ٱلشَّرِّ I take refuge in God (to free me) from evil.

Used of time:

مِنَ ٱلصَّبَاحِ إِلَى ٱلْمَسَاءِ from morning to evening.

Sometimes used (like مُنْذُ) to mean "since".

مِنْ سَنَتَيْنِ since two years i.e. two years ago.

It is also employed witn verbs and nouns denoting nearness, as قَرُبَ دَنَا, e.g.

دَنَوْتُ مِنَ ٱلْعَدُوِّ I approached the enemy.

قَرِيبٌ مِنَّا near us.

Notice specially:

بَاعَ مِنْهُ he sold to him.

عَجِبَ (تَعَجَّبَ) مِنْ شَيْءٍ to wonder at something; so with other verbs of feeling:

فَرِحَ مِنْ to rejoice at . . . . .

مَبْسُوطٌ مِنْ pleased at . . . . .

The word "than" after a Comparative is expressed by مِنْ, e.g.

أَسْرَعُ مِنَ ٱلْكَلْبِ swifter than the dog.

"A certain" is often expressed by مِنْ preceded by a word indefinite in the Sing. and followed by the same word definite in the Plur. e.g.

تَاجِرٌ مِنَ ٱلتُّجَّارِ a certain merchant.

It is also used partitively (لِلتَّبْعِيضِ) followed by a definite noun in the Plur. to indicate an indefinite number or quantity, e.g.

قَدْ أَرَاكُمْ مِنْ آيَاتِهِ he has already shown you some of his signs, and to indicate material, e.g.

كُرْسِيٌّ مِنْ خَشَبٍ a chair of wood.

It is very often used after مَا to explain (لِلتَّبْيِينِ) what is intended by the particle, e.g.

مَا كَانَ عِنْدِي مِنَ ٱلْمَالِ what is with me in the way of wealth i.e. the wealth, which I have.

مَا عَمِلْتُمُوهُ بِنَا مِنَ ٱلْمَعْرُوفِ what you have done to us in the way of kindness i.e. the kindness, which you have done us.

9) مُنْذُ, مُذْ "since" (for مِنْ ذُو).

Is not used with suffixes.

It is sometimes followed by the Nominative, e.g.

مَا رَأَيْتُكَ مُنْذُ (مُذْ) يَوْمِ ٱلْأَحَدِ	I have not seen you since Sunday.
مَا رَأَيْتُكَ مُنْذُ (مُذْ) يَوْمُ ٱلْأَحَدِ	

Nouns used as Prepositions.

4. Of the Prepositions, which are really nouns in the Accusative (ظَرْفٌ), the following are the most common:

1) أَمَامَ "before, opposite" (of place):

أَمَامَ ٱلْقَصْرِ before, opposite the castle.

أَمَامَ ٱلْقَاضِي before the judge.

2) بَعْدَ "after" of time or rank (opposite of قَبْلَ):

بَعْدَ ٱلْمِيلَادِ after the birth (of Christ).

3) بَيْنَ "between".

When two words are dependent on بَيْنَ, then if both are substantives the بَيْنَ need not be repeated, but if one (or both) is a pronoun it is always repeated, e.g.

بَيْنَ زَيْدٍ وَعَمْرٍو between Zaid and ʿAmr.

بَيْنَكَ وَبَيْنَ أَخِيكَ between thee and thy brother.

بَيْنِي وَبَيْنَكَ between me and thee.

فِيمَا بَيْنَ and مَا بَيْنَ are often used with the same meaning as بَيْنَ.

بَيْنَ and مَا بَيْنَ sometimes mean "both — and" or "partly — partly":

جَاءَنَا مَا بَيْنَ فَقِيرٍ وَغَنِيٍّ both poor and rich came to us.

4) تُجَاهَ
5) تِلْقَاءَ } "opposite" (= حِذَاءَ).

6) تَحْتَ "under, below" of place or rank (opposite to فَوْقَ).

تَحْتَ شَجَرَةٍ under a tree.

تَحْتَ ٱلْمَلِكِ below the king (in rank).

7) حِذَاءَ "opposite":

حِذَاءَ ٱلدَّارِ opposite the house.

8) حَوْلَ "round about".

حَوْلَ ٱلْمَدِينَةِ round about the city.

9) خَلْفَ "behind":

خَلْفَ ظَهْرِي behind my back.

10) دُونَ "on this side of, under, without":

دُونَ ٱلنَّهْرِ on this side of the river.

دُونَ قَدَمِكَ خَدُّ عَدُوِّكَ may the cheek of the enemy be under thy feet.

With the meaning "without" بِدُونِ or مِنْ دُونِ may be used instead of دُونَ:

دُونَ (بِدُونِ or مِنْ دُونِ or) ذٰلِكَ without that.

Note. For the meaning of دُونَكَ and دُونَكُمْ see Less. 48, 2.

11) عِنْدَ "with, at":

Used of place:

جَلَسْتُ عِنْدَهُ I sat with (beside) him.

Used of time:

جَاءَ عِنْدَ طُلُوعِ ٱلشَّمْسِ he came at sunrise.

It is often used with the meaning "to have".

عِنْدِى (or لِى or مَعِى) مَالٌ I have wealth.

Note. عِنْدِى كَذَا means "according to my opinion it is so".

12) عِوَضَ (or عِوَضًا عَنْ) "instead of, in place of":

أَخَذْتُ هٰذَا عِوَضَ ذٰلِكَ I took this in place of that.

13) فَوْقَ "on, over, above": of place and rank (opposite of تَحْتَ):

فَوْقَ ٱلشَّجَرَةِ on the tree.

فَوْقَ ٱلْمَلِكِ above the king (in rank).

14) قَبْلَ "before" of time (opposite of بَعْدَ):

قَبْلَ ٱلْمِيلَادِ before the birth (of Christ).

15) قُدَّامَ "before" of place (more often أَمَامَ):

قُدَّامَ ٱلدَّارِ before the house.

16) نَحْوَ "towards":

نَحْوَ ٱلْغَرْبِ towards the West.

Note. نَحْوَ is used as a substantive in all Cases with a following Genitive in the sense of "like" or "about".

رَجُلٌ نَحْوُ زَيْدٍ a man like Zaid.

مَرَرْتُ بِنَحْوِ مِئَةِ رَجُلٍ I passed by about a hundred men.

17) وَرَاءَ "behind, on the far side of":

وَرَاءَهُمْ behind them.

وَرَاءَ ٱلْجِبَالِ behind (on the far side of) the mountains.

5. Two prepositions often occur together. In this case, if the second was originally a noun, it must be put in the Genitive, e.g.

مِنْ بَيْنِهِمْ from between them i.e. from the midst of them.

مِنْ فَوْقِ from over i.e. above.

مِنْ تَحْتِ from under i.e. underneath.

مِنْ عِنْدِ from with.

مِنْ عَلَى from on i.e. down from.

مِنْ دُونِ or بِدُونِ without.

مِنْ قَبْلِ before.

مِنْ بَعْدِ after.

Exercise 83.

قِيلَ إِنَّ رَجُلًا من التُّجَّارِ فُقِدَ منه كِيسٌ فيه مِائَةُ دِينارٍ فَأَرْسَلَ دَلَّالًا يُنادِى عليه فى الأَسْواقِ وَٱتَّفَقَ أَنَّ رَجُلًا كان قد وَجَدَهُ فَأَخَذَهُ الى بَيْتِهِ وَوَضَعَهُ فى صُنْدُوقٍ ثُمَّ خَرَجَ الى السُّوقِ يَتَجَسَّسُ خَبَرَهُ لَعَلَّ أَحَدًا يَسْأَلُ عنه فلمّا سَمِعَ المُنادِىَ تَقَدَّمَ اليه وقال إِنَّنِى وَجَدتُّ كِيسًا فَٱذْكُرْ لى عَلامَتَهُ لَعَلَّهُ هُوَ فَذَكَرَ له الدَّلَّالُ عَلامَتَهُ فَوَجَدَها مُطابِقَةً له فقال الرَّجُلُ نَعَمْ

هو فَٱذْهَبْ معى إلى دارى لِأُعْطِيَكَ إيّاه فذَهَبَ معه وفَتَحَ الرَجُلُ الصُنْدُوقَ وسَلَّمَهُ الكِيسَ فأَعْجَبَتِ الدلّالَ أَمانَتُهُ مع كَوْنِهِ فَقِيرًا وغَيْرَ مُتَّهَمٍ به فقال له يا رجلُ ٱذْهَبْ معى وسَلِّمْهُ إلى صاحِبِهِ وأَنا أَسْعَى لك عنده بحُلْوانٍ جَزِيلٍ فمَضَى مع الدلّالِ حتّى أَوْصَلَهُ الى صاحِبِ الكِيسِ وأَثْنَى بِكُلِّ جَمِيلٍ على هذا الرجلِ وقال إنّهُ يَسْتَحِقُّ حُلْوانًا جَزِيلاً فأَخَذَ الكِيسَ وٱفْتَقَدَ ما فيه من الدَنانِيرِ وكان بَخِيلاً جِدًّا فشَقَّ عليه الحُلْوانُ وأَرادَ أَنْ يَحْتالَ فى التَخَلُّصِ منه فٱدَّعَى على الرجلِ أَنّهُ قد أَخَذَ منه جانِبًا ويَكْفِيهِ أَنْ يُسامِحَهُ بما أَخَذَ منه وجَعَلَ يَشْتُمُهُ أَمامَ الناسِ فغَضِبَ الرجلُ وأَسْمَعَهُ كَلامًا جافِيًا فساقَهُ صاحِبُ الكِيسِ إلى دارِ الحُكُومَةِ وشَكاهُ إلى الحاكِمِ وأَعْلَمَهُ بِواقِعَةِ الحالِ وطلب منه أَنْ يُحَصِّلَ له ما أَخَذَهُ الرجلُ من الكِيسِ فٱسْتَنْطَقَ الحاكِمُ الرجلَ فحَدَّثَهُ بالقَضِيّةِ كما جَرَى وكان الحاكِمُ رجلاً ذَكِيًّا فعَلِمَ أَنَّ صاحِبَ الكِيسِ يُرِيدُ أَنْ يَتَجَنَّى عليه ظُلْمًا فقال له يا فُلانُ إنّنِى أَعْلَمُ أَنّكَ من أَكابِرِ الناسِ ولا أَشُكُّ فى صِدْقِ كَلامِكَ لِأَنَّكَ لا تَدَّعِى زُورًا ولا أَشُكُّ أَيْضًا فى أَمانَةِ هذا الرجلِ المِسْكِينِ لِأَنّهُ لَوْ أَرادَ أَنْ يَخُونَ لَكانَ أَخَذَ

الكيسَ بِرُمّتهِ ولا يَسْأَلْ عن صاحِبِهِ وعلى هذا أَرَى أَنَّ هذا
الكيسَ غَيْرَ كيسِكَ فأَرْجِعْهُ إلى الرجلِ لِيَحْفَظَهُ عنده إلى أَنْ
يَظْهَرَ صاحِبُهُ وأَنْتَ فَتِّشْ على كيسِكَ عند غَيْرِهِ فأَضْطَرَبَ
التاجِرُ وقال يا مَوْلاىَ قد سَمَحْتُ له بما أَخَذَ منه وإِنْ شِئْتَ
أُعْطِهِ فَوْقَهُ أَيْضًا فقال لا يُمْكِنُ هذا أَبَدًا لِأَنَّهُ لا يَجُوزُ أَنْ
تَأْخُذَ غَيْرَ مالِكَ فأَلَحَّ التاجِرُ عليه فى ذلك فغَضِبَ وأَمَرَ عليه
بِالضَّرْبِ وأَخَذَ الكيسَ منه وقال للذى وَجَدَهُ خُذْ هذا الكيسَ
وتَصَرَّفْ به حَلالًا ودَعْ هذا الخَبِيثَ يُفَتِّشُ على كيسِهِ الذى
أَعْلَمُ أَنَّهُ هذا بِعَيْنِهِ ولَكِنَّ الطَمَعَ قد أَضاعَهُ منه مَرَّةً ثانِيَةً —

Exercise 84.

I have (in) this day experienced (شاهَدَ) indescribable joy (what is not described in the way of joy). — I shall speak to thee about this matter (شأْن). — I was very disturbed on examining your letter which came (وَرَدَ Part. Act.) to his Excellency our lord and father (the excellency of our lord the father), may God protect him!, and although I almost turned away (in spite of my being I turned away) from the mind of his Excellency what disturbed him, yet I was not able to content my thoughts with the least (of what is) possible, and for this reason I find myself disturbed (of the mind), hoping that you will honour me (the being honoured — Verbal Noun of يَكَرَّم) by giving me information (إفادة); and we pray for you the continuance of health and wellbeing. — What I have learnt of thy indisposition has grieved me, and I have prayed God that He will clothe thee with the garment of recovery, for He can do all things (He over every thing is powerful). — Perhaps our lord will bring thee what will rejoice thee. — The sheikh was extremely astonished at our answer.

Forty-fifth Lesson.

(اَلدَّرْسُ ٱلْخَامِسُ وَٱلأَرْبَعُونَ)

Adverbs.

1. Adverbs are either 1) Particles, Inseparable or Separate, or 2) Nouns used only in the Nom. or Accus.

Inseparable Particles.

2. The Adverbs, which are Inseparable Particles are:

a) أَ a particle used to indicate a question (= هَلْ see Less. 2, 5) (called the حَرْفُ ٱلِاسْتِفْهَامِ); but only when no Interrogative pronoun occurs in the sentence, e.g.:

أَفَعَلْتَ (هَلْ فَعَلْتَ or هٰذَا) hast thou done this?

but مَنْ فَعَلَ هٰذَا who has done this?

أَ — أَمْ in a double question; see أَمْ.

b) سَ a particle used to give a Future meaning to the Imperfect (see Less. 13, 4). It is a shortened form of سَوْفَ "at the end".

سَأَفْعَلُهُ (سَوْفَ أَفْعَلُهُ) I shall do it.

c) لَ a particle used for Emphasis, "certainly, truly", often omitted in translation, e.g.:

لَفَعَلْتُهُ truly, I have done it.

Especially with the Modus Energicus (see Less. 15):

لَأَضْرِبَنَّكَ I shall certainly strike thee.

Also in an Oath:

لَعَمْرُكَ by thy life.

لَ is often used before the Predicate of a Nominal sentence, which begins with إِنَّ (see below 3 e).

It is often used to introduce the apodosis of a sentence beginning with لَوْ (see Less. 47, 5).

Separate Adverbial particles.

3. The most important separate particles are:

a) إِذَنْ and إِذًا (related to إِذَا, see Less. 46, 2 b) "in that case, then", e.g.:

نَرُوحُ إِذًا let us go then.

b) أَلَا (for أَ and لَا) "not" in an Interrogative sentence:

أَلَا أَفْعَلُهُ shall I not do it?

So أَلَمْ for أَ and لَمْ.

c) أَمْ "or" in a double question:

أَأَفْعَلُهُ أَمْ لَا shall I do it or not?

d) أَمَا (for أَ and مَا) "not" in an Interrogative sentence:

أَمَا فَعَلْتَهُ hast thou not done it?

e) إِنَّ "truly, certainly" (see Less. 17, 5).

إِنَّ introduces Nominal sentences, the subject following in the Accus., the Predicate often strengthened by لَ (see above 2 c) following in the Nom., e.g.:

إِنْ زَيْدًا عَاقِلٌ
إِنَّ زَيْدًا لَعَاقِلٌ } verily, Zaid is intelligent.

It may be used with Pronominal suffixes, the pronoun then being a subject, e.g. إِنَّهُ verily he, إِنِّي and إِنَّنِي verily I, إِنَّا and إِنَّنَا verily we.

f) إِنَّمَا (for إِنَّ and مَا) is always at the beginning of a sentence and limits the word or clause at the end of it by its meaning "only", e.g.:

إِنَّمَا ٱلصَّدَقَاتُ لِلْفُقَرَاءِ the alms are for the poor only.

g) أَيْ "i.e., that is" (= يَعْنِي).

h) أَيْنَ "where?"

مِنْ أَيْنَ "whence?"

إِلَى أَيْنَ "whither?"

أَيْنَمَا "wherever".

i) بَلْ "but rather, no on the contrary, but".

j) بَلَى "yes certainly" as answer to negative sentences.

k) ثَمَّ "there"

l) قَدْ before the Perfect expresses the completion or certainty of the action and can sometimes be translated "already", but is often to be left untranslated.

With the Imperfect it means "sometimes".

m) فَقَطْ "only" always placed after the word it modifies.

n) قَطُّ "never", follows a verb in the Perfect with a negative, e.g.:

مَا رَأَيْتُهُ قَطُّ I have never seen him.

o) كَلَّا "not at all, by no means".

p) لَا "not, no".

1) As particle of Denial (لَا لِلنَّفْيِ) before the Imperf. Indic. with Present or Future meaning:

لَا أَفْعَلُهُ I do it not (or I shall not do it).

2) As particle of Prohibition (لَا لِلنَّهْيِ) followed by the Jussive with the meaning of the Imperative:

لَا تَفْعَلْهُ do it not.

3) As particle of Complete Denial (لَا لِنَفْيِ ٱلْجِنْسِ) (see Less. 42, 2 i) "there is not (no)" It is followed by a noun in the Accus. without nunation:

لَا مَفَرَّ there is no escape (at all).

q) لَمْ "not" is used before the Jussive, which then has the meaning of the Past:

لَمْ يَفْعَلْ he did not.

r) لَمَّا followed by the Jussive means "not yet".

s) لَنْ "not" (see Less. 14, 3 Note) is followed by the Subjunctive, which then has the meaning of a Future:

لَنْ أَفْعَلَهُ I shall not do it.

t) مَا "not" is followed by either Perfect or Imperfect.

Note. For إِنْ as particle of Denial see Less. 46, 2 c) Note.

u) مَتَى "when" also used as a Conjunction.

v) نَعَمْ (rarely نَعِمْ) "yes" derived from نَعِمَ "(what you say) is agreeable".

w) هَلْ Particle of Interrogation (see Less. 2, 5).

هَلْ فَعَلْتَهُ hast thou done it.

In an indirect question it denotes "whether", e.g.: أَخْبِرْنِي هَلِ ٱنْتَظَرْتَنِي tell me whether thou hast expected me.

هَلَّا (for هَلْ and لَا) "not" in an Interrogative sentence.

x) هُنَا "here", or in a strengthened form هَاهُنَا (sometimes written هٰهُنَا).

y) هُنَاكَ and هُنَالِكَ "there"

Nouns used as Adverbs.

4. Many nouns, the Accusative of which are used as Prepositions, are used as Adverbs and are then Indeclinable ending always in u, e.g.:

بَعْدُ or مِنْ بَعْدُ "afterwards".	حَيْثُ "where.
مَا — بَعْدُ "not yet".	مِنْ حَيْثُ "whence".
قَبْلُ or مِنْ قَبْلُ "before".	إِلَى حَيْثُ "whither".
فَوْقُ " مِنْ فَوْقُ "above".	حَيْثُمَا "wherever".
تَحْتُ " مِنْ تَحْتُ "below".	غَيْرُ in the expression لَا غَيْرُ "nothing else, only this".

5. Most nouns used as Adverbs are employed in the Accusative (see Less. 42, 2, c, e), e.g.:

قَلِيلًا "little".	دَاخِلًا "inside".
قَلِيلًا مَا "seldom"	خَارِجًا "outside".
كَثِيرًا "much, very".	مَعًا "together".
كَثِيرًا مَا "often".	جَمِيعًا "altogether".
جِدًّا "very".	أَبَدًا "for ever" (with neg. "never").

يَوْمًا
يَوْمًا مَا
ذَاتَ يَوْمٍ } "one day, once".

نَهَارًا "by day".

يَمِينًا "on the right hand".

شِمَالًا "on the left hand".

اَلْيَوْمَ "to-day"

سَوْفَ (sign of Future tense).

غَدًا "to-morrow".

كَيْفَ "how".

دَائِمًا "always"

رُبَّمَا "often". (later "perhaps").

لَيْلًا "by night".

لَا سِيَّمَا (for لَا سِيَّ مَا "there is nothing like") "especially".

حِينَ (from the noun حِينٌ "time") in حِينَئِذٍ "then, at that time", so also وَقْتَئِذٍ "at that time".

أَلْبَتَّةَ "altogether".

تَارَةً — وَتَارَةً
تَارَةً — وَطَوْرًا
تَارَةً — وَأَحْيَانًا } at one time — at another time.

وَحْدَ "alone" is used with suffixes, e.g. وَحْدِى I alone, وَحْدَهُ he alone, etc.

Note. For some Verbs which are usually translated into English by Adverbs as عَسَى etc., see Less. 30.

عَلَّ and لَعَلَّ "perhaps" are often used with suffixes, e.g. لَعَلَّهُ perhaps he, لَعَلِّى (rarely لَعَلَّنِى) perhaps I.

لَيْتَ "would that" with suffixes لَيْتَهُ would that he, لَيْتَنِى (rarely لَيْتِى) whould that I.

Exercise 85.

يُقالُ إِنَّهُ انْقَطَعَ رَجُلٌ مِن قافِلَةِ الحاجِّ وغَلِطَ الطَّرِيقَ وَوَقَعَ
فِى الرِمالِ فَجَعَلَ يَسِيرُ إِلَى أَنْ وَصَلَ إِلَى خَيْمَةٍ فَرَأَى فِى الخَيْمَةِ
اِمْرَأَةً عَجُوزًا وعَلَى بابِ الخَيْمَةِ كَلْبًا نائِمًا فَسَلَّمَ الحاجُّ علَى العَجُوزِ
وطَلَبَ منها طَعامًا فقالَت العَجُوزُ اِمْضِ إِلَى ذلكَ الوادِى
وَاصْطَدْ من الحَيّاتِ بِقَدْرِ كِفايَتِكَ لِأَشْوِىَ لكَ منها وأُطْعِمَكَ
فقالَ الرجلُ أَنا لا أَجسرُ أَنْ أَصْطادَ الحَيّاتِ فقالَت العَجوزُ
أَنا أَصْطادُ معكَ فلا تَخَفْ فَمَضَيا وَتَبِعَهُما الكَلْبُ فَأَخَذا مِنَ
الحَيّاتِ بِقَدْرِ حاجَتِهِما فَأَتَت العَجوزُ وجَعَلَتْ تَشْوِى الحَيّاتِ
فلم يَرَ الحاجُّ بُدًّا من الأَكْلِ وخافَ أَنْ يَمُوتَ من الجُوعِ
والهُزالِ فأَكَلَ ثُمَّ إِنَّهُ عَطِشَ فَطَلَبَ منها الماءَ فقالَت دُونَكَ
العَيْنَ فَاشْرَبْ فَمَضَى الى العَيْنِ فَوَجَدَ الماءَ مُرًّا مالِحًا ولم
يَجِدْ من شُرْبِهِ بُدًّا فَشَرِبَ وعادَ إِلَى العَجوزِ وقالَ أَعْجَبُ منكِ
أَيَّتُها العَجوزُ ومن مُقامِكِ فى هذا المَكانِ واغْتِذائِكِ بهذا
الطَّعامِ فقالَت العَجوزُ كَيْفَ تَكُونُ بِلادُكُم فقالَ يَكُونُ فِى بِلادِنا
الدُّورُ الرَّحْبَةُ الواسِعَةُ والفَواكِهُ اليانِعَةُ والمِياهُ العَذْبَةُ والأَطْعِمَةُ
الطَّيِّبَةُ واللُّحُومُ السَّمِينَةُ والنَّعَمُ الكَثِيرَةُ والعُيُونُ الغَزِيرَةُ
فقالَت العَجوزُ وقد سَمِعْتُ هذا كُلَّهُ فَقُلْ لى هَلْ تكونون

تَحْتَ يَدَىْ سُلْطَانٍ يَجُورُ عليكم وإذا كان لكم ذَنْبٌ أَخَذَ

أَمْوالَكم وَٱسْتَأْصَلَ أَحْوالَكم وأَخْرَجَكم من بُيُوتِكم وأَمْلاكِكم

فقال قد يكونُ ذلك فقالت إذًا يَعُودُ ذلك الطَعامُ اللَطِيفُ

والعَيْشُ الظَرِيفُ والحَلْوَى العَجِيبَةُ مع الجَوْرِ والظُلْمِ سَمًّا ناقِعًا

وتَعُودُ أَطْعِمَتُنا مع الأَمْنِ دِرْيَاقًا نافِعًا أما سَمِعْتَ أَنّ أَجَلّ

النِعَمِ بَعْدَ نِعْمَةِ الهُدَى الصِحّةُ والأَمْنُ

(الغزالى)

Exercise 86.

Truly, he can both speak and write the Arabic language (he knows the Arabic language speaking and writing). — Permit me to see from time to time that trusty slave, nay rather the true friend Sa'īd. — You must have patience O my friend. — Jamīla said: Art thou trusting in that O Sa'īd? and he said Yes. — I hope that (Perhaps that) the journey will be pleasant to you, for the land of Egypt is a cheerful land especially in the winter season. — I beseech thee by the head of thy father, that thou deliver me from this trouble and command thy men to carry me from this place whither you wish. — He gave us permission to dwell, wherever we might wish. — One party of us travelled northwards and a party of us travelled southwards. — How can that be? — The prince said: Is she the princess Salma? — He said: Yes O prince. Then the prince turned pale (the paleness came upon عَلَا the face of the prince). — The best is that we return to where we were. — Bonaparte (بُونَابَرْت) journeyed from Egypt secretly to his country in the latter days of the year 1799 A. D., then the Mamlukes and the people of Egypt prepared together to fight the French, and they were not able only to drive them out of it. —

They two journeyed together to the place where he had prepared for them what was necessary. — Some of the inhabitants of the village came to us and began to ask us "Whence?" and "Whither?" — I alighted then from the back of my horse. — I said to her: What do you think? Shall we show enmity and resist them, or not? And she said: No, we shall not resist them. And I said: What shall we do (is the deed)? Shall I hand over to them my weapons and myself, that they may take me captive, and perhaps kill me?

Forty-sixth Lesson.

(اَلدَّرْسُ ٱلسَّادِسُ وَالْأَرْبَعُونَ)

Conjunctions.

1. The Conjunctions are either Inseparable of Separate.

The Inseparable are:

a) and b) وَ and فَ "and" (called in Arabic حَرْفُ عَطْفٍ "particle of union".

و joins two independent words or sentences, while

فَ, which usually joins sentences only, indicates a development in the narrative and may often be translated "and so" "and then". It is also generally used to join two sentences when there is a change of subject.

With a following verb in the Subjunctive فَ means "so that".

For فَ with the Predicate of Nominal sentences with أَمَّا see § 2 f.

For فَ in the Apodosis of Conditional sentences see Less. 47, 5.

فَإِنَّ with a following Nominal sentence or a Suffix means "for".

وَ between two sentences, of which the second is a Nominal sentence often means "while". Such a sentence introduced by وَ is called a جُمْلَةٌ حَالِيَّةٌ "sentence of condition", e.g.:

قَامَ زَيْدٌ وَهُوَ بَاكٍ قَامَ زَيْدٌ وَهُوَ يَبْكِي	Zaid stood up, while he wept (Zaid stood up weeping).

also with change of Subject:

ذَهَبَ زَيْدٌ وَعَمْرٌو بَاقٍ ذَهَبَ زَيْدٌ وَعَمْرٌو يَبْقَى	Zaid went away and ʿAmr remained (while ʿAmr remained).

The وَ is usually dropped, when a Verbal sentence follows:

جَاءَ زَيْدٌ يَضْحَكُ Zaid came, while he laughed (laughing).

The wāw of Condition (وَاوُ ٱلْحَالِ) is sometimes used before a Nominal sentence which has no Participle or Imperfect:

جَاءَ زَيْدٌ وَبِيَدِهِ سَيْفٌ Zaid came, and in his hand a sword (with a sword in his hand).

For وَ as Preposition with Accus. = "with" see Less. 42, 2 e.

For وَ with the Genitive see Less. 44, 3 A, 3.

c) لِ "so that" (for the Prep. لِ see Less. 44, 3 A, 4) with following Subjunctive:

جَاءَنِي لِيَطْلُبَ ٱلْمَالَ he came to me so that he might demand the wealth (to demand the wealth),

With the same meaning are used لِكَيْ, لِأَنْ; and negatively: لِئَلَّا, لِكَيْلَا "so that not".

لْ with the Jussive (nearly always in the 3rd Person) expresses a demand:

لِيَكْتُبْ let him write!

With the particle فَ the لْ loses its vowel: فَلْيَكْتُبْ (see Less. 14, 3).

2. The usual Separable Conjunctions are:

a) إِذْ "when, since, after, because" with following Nominal or Verbal sentence.

b) إِذَا "when, if" originally used of time, but often of condition (see Less. 47); in indirect questions = "whether".

إِذْ and إِذَا also mean "behold!", in which case the former is always followed by a Verbal sentence, the latter by a Nominal sentence in which the Subject is either in the Nominative or takes بِ (see Less. 44, 3 A, 1):

إِذْ أَتَى رَجُلٌ
إِذَا رَجُلٌ (بِرَجُلٍ) قَدْ أَتَى } behold, a man came!

إِذَامَا means "whenever" (see Less. 47).

c) إِنْ "if, whether" introduces Conditional sentences or indirect Questions (see Less. 47).

وَإِنْ means "and if, even if, although". لَئِنْ = "verily if".

Note. There is also a particle of Denial إِنْ, e.g.: إِنْ رَأَيْتُ مِنْهَا أَمْرًا أَغْمِصُهُ I have not seen anything of her, that I despise.

d) إِلَّا (for إِنْ and لَا) has the following meanings:

1) "if not", وَإِلَّا "and if not" i.e. "otherwise".

2) "except, only" preceded by a negative. (This إِلَّا is called a حَرْفُ الْإِسْتِثْنَاءِ i.e. "particle of exception"), e.g.:

لَا إِلٰهَ إِلَّا ٱللّٰهُ there is no god except God (Allah).

e) إِمَّا (for إِنْ and مَا) only in:

إِمَّا — أَوْ
إِمَّا — وَإِمَّا } "either — or"

f) أَمَّا "as for" with a following Nominative, the Predicate being always strengthened with a فَ, e.g.:

أَمَّا جَبَلُ ٱلشَّيْخِ فَهُوَ جَبَلٌ شَامِخٌ as for Mt. Hermon, it is a lofty mountain.

أَمَّا ٱلْكَلْبُ فَلَقِيتُهُ فِي ٱلطَّرِيقِ as for the dog, I met him on the road. (According to Arabian grammarians ٱلْكَلْبُ is the Subject, all the rest is Predicate.)

g) أَنْ "that" with following Verbal sentence, the verb being rarely in the Perf., nearly always in the Imperf. Subjunctive (cf. Less. 17, 6 a).

كَأَنْ = "as though"; لِأَنْ = "because".

With Negative: أَلَّا (for أَنْ and لَا) "that not"; لِئَلَّا "so that not".

h) أَنَّ "that" with a Nominal sentence, a later verb being in the Indicative.

With suffixes: أَنَّهُ "that he", أَنَّنِي or أَنِّي "that I", أَنَّنَا or أَنَّا "that we" etc.

In أَنَّهُ the suffix is often ضَمِيرُ ٱلشَّأْنِ (cf. Less. 43, 5, Note 2).

In compounds:

كَأَنَّ
كَأَنَّمَا } "just as if", "it is as if".

لِأَنَّ "because".

إِلَّا أَنَّ, غَيْرَ أَنَّ "except that, yet".

i) أَوْ "or"; أَوْ — إِمَّا "either -- or" (see above e).

With the Subjunctive أَوْ means "unless that, until that".

j) بَيْنَمَا (more rarely بَيْنَا) "while".

k) ثُمَّ "then, thereupon" often followed by إِنَّ.

l) حَتَّى "until" (= إِلَى أَنْ); with a Nominal sentence often حَتَّى أَنَّ.

m) كَيْ or لِكَيْ "in order that" with following Subjunctive.

With Negative كَيْلَا and لِكَيْلَا "in order that not".

n) لٰكِنْ and لٰكِنَّ "but", the former being followed by a verb or noun in the Nominative, the latter only by nouns in the Accusative or Pronominal suffixes: لٰكِنَّهُ "but he", لٰكِنَّنِي or لٰكِنِّي "but I", لٰكِنَّنَا or لٰكِنَّا "but we".

o) لَمَّا "when, after" with following Perfect to be translated usually by the Pluperfect.

p) لَوْ "if" in Conditional sentences referring to a mere supposition (see Less. 47).

لَوْ أَنَّ often with the meaning "would that!" before nouns and pronominal suffixes:

وَلَوْ = "although".

With Negative: لَوْمَا ;لَوْلَا ;لَوْ لَمْ "if not".

q) مَا "so long as" (مَا ٱلدَّيْمُومَةِ "the مَا of continuance"), is often used in compound Conjunctions:

بَعْدَ مَا "after".

بَيْنَمَا and فِيمَا "while".

قَبْلَ مَا "before" (always with the Imperf.).

It is often used also to generalise, e.g.:

إِذْمَا	"whenever".	مَتَى مَا	"whenever".
إِذَامَا	"if ever".	كُلَّمَا	"as often as".

In these cases it is followed by the Perf. or the Juss. in the sense of the Present.

r) مَتَى "when", مَتَى مَا "whenever".

s) مُنْذُ or مُذْ "since".

Exercise 87.

وَصَلَ بَعْضُ الْمُسَافِرِينَ لِقَصْدِ الْحَجِّ مَدِينَةً وَنَزَلَ عِنْدَ صَاحِبٍ لَهُ فَلَمَّا تَمَّتْ مُدَّةُ الْإِقَامَةِ وَعَزَمَ عَلَى الرَّحِيلِ أَخْبَرَ صَاحِبَهُ أَنَّ عِنْدَهُ أَمَانَةً وَهِيَ جُمْلَةٌ مِنَ النُّقُودِ وَالْجَوَاهِرِ وَيُرِيدُ أَنْ يُودِعَهَا عِنْدَ مُؤْتَمَنٍ إِلَى أَنْ يَرْجِعَ فَلَمَّا سَمِعَ مِنْهُ صَاحِبُهُ ذَلِكَ اسْتَحَى أَنْ يَقُولَ لَهُ ضَعْهَا عِنْدِي خَوْفًا مِنْ أَنْ يَظُنَّ أَنَّهُ طَامِعٌ فِيهَا فَأَشَارَ عَلَيْهِ أَنْ يَضَعَهَا عِنْدَ الْقَاضِي فَأَخَذَهَا وَذَهَبَ إِلَى الْقَاضِي وَقَالَ لَهُ إِنِّي رَجُلٌ غَرِيبٌ وَأُرِيدُ الْحَجَّ وَعِنْدِي أَمَانَةٌ قَدْرُهَا كَذَا مِنَ النُّقُودِ وَالْجَوَاهِرِ وَأُرِيدُ أَنْ أُسَلِّمَهَا لِحَضْرَةِ مَوْلَانَا الْقَاضِي لِيَحْفَظَهَا إِلَى أَنْ أَعُودَ مِنَ الْحَجِّ وَأَسْتَلِمَهَا فَقَالَ لَهُ الْقَاضِي نَعَمْ خُذْ هَذَا الْمِفْتَاحَ وَافْتَحْ هَذَا الصُّنْدُوقَ وَضَعْهَا فِيهِ وَأَغْلِقْ

الصُّنْدُوقَ جَيِّدًا فَفَعَلَ وَسَلَّمَ المفتاحَ إلى القاضى وسَلَّمَ عليه وتَوَجَّهَ فلمّا قَضَى حَجَّهُ ورَجَعَ ذَهَبَ الى القاضى لِيَطْلُبَ الأَمانَةَ فقال له إِنِّى لا أَعْرِفُكَ وأَنا عندى أَماناتٌ كثيرةٌ فمن أَيْنَ أَعْرِفُ أَنَّ لك أَمانَةً عندى وأَطالَ المُجادَلَةَ معه فٱنْصَرَفَ الرجلُ إلى صاحِبِهِ وأَعْلَمَهُ بذلك وعابَه فى هذه المَشُورَةِ فأَخَذَه وذَهَبَ إلى بَعْضِ الأُمَراءِ المُقَرَّبِينَ إلى المَلِكِ وأَخْبَرَه بتلك القَضِيَّةِ فأَوْعَدَهُم أَنَّهُ فى غَدٍ يَذْهَبُ إلى القاضى ويَجْلِسُ عنده ويُخْبِرُه بقَضِيَّةٍ أُخْرَى تَخُصُّهُ ويَدْخُلُ ذاك الشَّخْصُ صاحِبُ الأَمانَةِ عليهما ويَطْلُبُ أَمانَتَهُ من القاضى فلمّا كان الغَدُ ذَهَبَ ذلك الأَميرُ إلى القاضى وجَلَسَ بجانِبِهِ فلمّا ٱنْتَهَى تَعْظِيمُهُ وإِجْلالُهُ من القاضى على حَسَبِ مَقامِهِ قال له لَعَلَّ السَّبَبَ الذى أَوْجَبَكَ إلى تَشْرِيفِنا بقُدُومِكَ خَيْرٌ فقال له هو خَيْرٌ لك إِنْ شاءَ اللّهُ تَعالَى فقال ما هو فقال له الأَميرُ إِنِّى فى لَيْلَةِ أَمْسِ طَلَبَنِى المَلِكُ فذَهَبْتُ اليه فلمّا ٱنْتَهَى المَجْلِسُ وٱنْصَرَفَ الناسُ وأَرَدْتُّ أَنْ أَنْصَرِفَ وإِذا هو أَمَرَنِى أَنْ أَتَخَلَّفَ عنده فلمّا ٱخْتَلَيْنا أَشارَ إِلَىَّ أَنَّهُ يُرِيدُ أَنْ يَحُجَّ فى العامِ القابِلِ ويُرِيدُ أَنْ يُسَلِّمَ المَمْلَكَةَ جَمِيعَها لِمَنْ يَعْتَمِدُ ويُؤْتَمَنُ فى ذلك إِلَى أَنْ يَعُودَ بالسَّلامَةِ

فَٱسْتَشَارَنِى فى ذلك فَأَشَرْتُ عليه أَنْ يُسَلِّمَها لِجَنَابِك لِمَا نَعْهَدُ
عندك من الأَمانَةِ والعِفَّةِ والصَداقَةِ أَوْلَى من تَسْلِيمِها لِبَعْضِ
الذَوَاتِ فَرُبَّما يَعْمَلُ مُخالَفَةً أَوْ تَطْمَعُ نَفْسُهُ فى المَمْلَكَةِ فَيَعْمَلَ
فِتْنَةً أَوْ نَحْوَ ذلك فأَعْجَبَه ذلك الرَأْيُ وأَجْمَعَ أَنَّهُ بَعْدَ يَوْمَيْنِ
يَعْقِدُ مَجْلِسًا عامًّا ويَفْعَلُ بما أَشَرْتُ بِهِ عليه فَفَرِحَ القاضى بذلك
فَرَحًا شَدِيدًا وأَثْنَى عليه وإذا بصاحِبِ الأَمانَةِ داخِلٌ عليهما
وتَمَثَّلَ أَمامَ القاضى وسَلَّمَ وقال يا حَضْرَةَ مَوْلانا القاضى إِنَّ لى
أَمانَةً عندك وهى كَذا وكَذا وسَلَّمْتُها اليك وَقْتَ كَذا وكَذا
فما أَتَمَّ كَلامَهُ حَتَّى قال له القاضى نَعَمْ يا وَلَدِى وأَنَا تَذَكَّرْتُ
اللَيْلَةَ عند النَوْمِ وعَرَفْتُك وعَرَفْتُ أَمانَتَك فَخُذْ هذا المِفْتاحَ
وٱسْتَلِمْ أَمانَتَك فأَخَذَها وسَلَّمَ وٱنْصَرَفَ وٱنْصَرَفَ ذلك الأَمِيرُ
أَيْضًا فلَمّا مَضَى المِيعادُ الذى وَعَدَهُ القاضى ذَهَبَ إلى ذلك
الأَمِيرِ وسَأَلَهُ فى شَأْنِ المَمْلَكَةِ والمُلْكِ فقال له أَيُّها القاضى نَحْنُ
ما عَرَفْنا نُخَلِّصُ منك أَمانَةَ الرجلِ الغَرِيبِ الحاجِّ إِلّا لَمّا
مَلَّكْناك الدُنْيا بأَجْمَعِها فإذا مَلَّكْتُها بأَىِّ شَىْءٍ نُخَلِّصُها فعَرَفَ
أَنَّها حِيلَةٌ —

Exercise 88.

As for Jamīla, she went out of the hall into the inner court, and behold by the side of the door of the hall a large door. — No one sees him without being attracted to him (except, and he is attached by his love). — As for Sa'id, he was amazed at the prince, because he had not seen during his life a man like him. — And when the prince had determined to journey to Egypt, he called his two sons to accompany him. — And while they were so engaged (were in that), there was a knock at the door (the door was knocked) and behold the servant. — I have not seen any good in my coming that (فَ) I should return. — And the two, and those who were with them continued travelling, until they came to the pool of the Ezbekiya, and behold a park, which a canal encircled. — And it was, when he rode his steed, as though he and the saddle were one piece. — While I was examining one of the books, I lighted upon the following sentence. — After all had left, I went to my chamber. — I had not finished my speech, when (until) I heard the sound of the firing of a gun, and I prepared to defend myself as soon as I should see the first person of them, because it seemed to me that there was no deliverance possible (that there was not of anything which was possible to us in the way of deliverance) except that. — I do not permit that, so long as thou hast not said to me what thy name is. — Before I finished my speech, I saw my friend. — Inform me when thou hast returned hither. — Then I commanded Hasan to bring me large stones that we might build for us a fortress safe from the weapons of the enemies. — Joy came upon me until from the excess of what rejoiced me, it made me weep.

Forty-seventh Lesson.

(اَلدَّرْسُ السَّابِعُ وَالأَرْبَعُونَ)

Conditional Sentences.

Conditional sentences consist of a Protasis or sentence containing the condition (شَرْطٌ) and an Apodosis or main sentence (جَزَاءٌ or جَوَابٌ = "answer").

2. The Protasis is introduced by the Conjunction (حَرْفُ ٱلشَّرْطِ) إِنْ or إِذَا if the condition is regarded as possible or likely; by لَوْ if it is purely hypothetical or impossible.

3. In both parts of the Conditional sentence the perfect or the Jussive may be used in the sense of the English Present or Future.

There are thus four possible cases:

a) The perfect is used in both parts:

إِنْ ذَهَبَ زَيْدٌ ذَهَبْتُ مَعَهُ if Zaid goes I shall go with him.

b) The Jussive is used in the Protasis, the Perfect in the Apodosis:

إِنْ يَذْهَبْ زَيْدٌ ذَهَبْتُ مَعَهُ.

c) The Perfect is used in the Protasis, the Jussive in the Apodosis:

إِنْ ذَهَبَ زَيْدٌ أَذْهَبْ مَعَهُ.

d) The Jussive is used in both parts:

إِنْ يَذْهَبْ زَيْدٌ أَذْهَبْ مَعَهُ.

Note. After إِذَا in a Conditional sense the Jussive is scarcely ever used. With لَوْ the Perfect (rarely Imperf. Indic.) is used in both parts.

4. If the verb in a Conditional sentence is to express the meaning of the Past, it must be put in the Perfect and be preceded by كَانَ:

فَمَهِّدِ ٱلْعُذْرَ إِنْ كُنْتُ أَجْرَمْتُ excuse (me), if I have committed a crime.

The Perfect is used after لَوْ in the sense of the English Imperfect or Pluperfect Subjunctive or Potential. When it has the meaning of the Pluperfect كَانَ may be placed before it:

لَوْ شَاءَ رَبُّكَ لَجَعَلَ ٱلنَّاسَ أُمَّةً وَاحِدَةً if thy Lord had wished, He would have made men one people. (Koran 11, 120.)

5. If the Protasis begins with إِنْ, then the Apodosis must be introduced by فَ.

a) If it is a Nominal sentence:

إِنْ أَرَادَ ذٰلِكَ فَٱلأَمْرُ لَهُ if he wishes that, then the matter is his (i.e. to do as he likes).

b) If it is a Verbal sentence expressing a Wish, Command or Prohibition (the verb being in the Imperative or Jussive):

إِنْ رَأَيْتَ زَيْدًا فَقُلْ لَهُ if you see Zaid, tell him.

c) If it is a Verbal sentence which begins with one of the particles سَوْفَ (سَ), قَدْ, مَا (not), or لَنْ:

إِنْ يَسْرِقْ فَقَدْ سَرَقَ أَخٌ لَهُ مِنْ قَبْلُ if he steals, one of his brothers has already stolen before him (Koran 12, 77).

Instead of فَ the particles إِذْ or إِذَا "behold" sometimes occur.

If the Protasis begins with لَوْ, the Apodosis may be introduced by لَ:

لَوْ أَرَادَ أَنْ يَخُونَ لَكَانَ أَخَذَ ٱلْكِيسَ بِرُمَّتِهِ if he had wished to be treacherous, he would have taken the purse in its entirety.

6. Sometimes the Apodosis is omitted and must be supplied from the context:

إِنْ رَجَعْتَ عَنْ قَوْلِكَ وَإِلَّا أَمَرْتُ بِقَتْلِكَ if you go back on your word, (good); otherwise I command that you shall be killed.

7. "If not" is expressed by لَوْ لَا, إِنْ لَمْ, إِلَّا or لَوْ لَمْ.

If a Nominal sentence follows لَوْ, one can use لَوْ أَنَّ.

لَوْ is also used with the meaning "if only" to express a wish.

8. A sentence introduced by any of the following words is treated as a Protasis:

مَنْ "he who, if anyone".	حَيْثُمَا "wherever"
أَىّ "which, if any"	مَهْمَا "whatever"
أَيُّمَنْ "whoever".	مَتَى "when".
مَا "what, if anything"	مَتَامَا (مَتَى مَا) "whenever".
كُلَّمَنْ "everyone who".	أَيْنَ "where".
كُلَّمَا "whenever".	أَيْنَمَا "wherever".
حَيْثُ "where".	كَيْفَ "how".
	كَيْفَمَا "nowever".

when it has a general sense. In both parts of such sentences the Perfect or the Jussive is used in the sense of the English Present or Future:

مَنْ جَالَ نَالَ if anyone seeks, he attains (will attain).

Note. Sometimes an Imperative is used in a Conditional sense as a Protasis:

عِشْ قَنِعًا تَكُنْ مَلِكًا live contented (if thou livest contented), thou wilt be a king.

Exercise 89.

يَجِبُ أَنْ أُرَاعِيَ الجَارَ وَلَوْ جَارَ فَلْخَبَرْتُهم عن مُرادِى وَلَوْ

كان ذلك رَغْمًا عنى — قلتُ إِن ٱسْتَظْهَرْتُ على الأَعْدَاء كان

خَيْرًا وإِلَّا فالمَوْتُ أَحْلَى مِنْ حَيٰوةٍ مُرَّةٍ — دُخُولُكَ فِى بابِ
الهَوَى إِنْ أَرَدْتَهُ يَسِيرٌ ولٰكِنَّ الخُرُوجَ عَسِيرٌ — أَرْسَلْتُ حَسَنًا
إِلَى قِمَّةِ الجَبَلِ لِيُرَاقِبَ اللُّصُوصَ لِأَنَّهُ لَوْ لا ذٰلِكَ لَرُبَّمَا كَانَ
دَاهَمَنَا العَدُوُّ بَغْتَةً فَتَمَكَّنَ من أَسْرِنَا وقَتْلِنَا — ماذا تَفْعَلُونَ
إذا لَمْ نَدَعْكُم تَتَمَكَّنُونَ من ذلك — لا تَحْزَنِي عَلَيَّ أَيَّتُهَا
العَزِيزَةُ. إذا أَسْقَانِى هٰؤُلَاءِ الأَشْقِيَاءُ كَأْسَ المَنُونِ لِأَنَّنِى إِنْ مُتُّ
أَمُتْ شَرِيفًا أَمَامَ عَيْنَيْكِ وإِنْ قَسَمَ لِى اللهُ نَصِيبًا حَسَنًا فَأَنَا
لَكِ وأَنْتِ لِى — لَوْ لم نَعِدْ والِدَكَ الشَّيْخَ بِأَنَّنَا لا نُؤْذِيكُم
لَكُنَّا أَهْلَكْنَاكُم عن آخِرِكُم فَاذْهَبُوا بِسَلامٍ ويَجِبُ أَنْ تَتَأَكَّدُوا
أَنَّكُم إِنْ لم تَجِدُّوا المَسِيرَ تُعَرِّضُوا أَنْفُسَكُم للوَبَالِ — إِنْ
عَاهَدْتِنِى عَهْدًا صادِقًا بِأَنَّكِ تَقْتَرِنِينَ بِى أُرَافِقْكِ حَيْثُ تَشَائِينَ
— إِنْ شِئْتَ فَأَرْسِلْ أَحَدًا لِيَنْظُرَ إِذا كان أَحَدُ قَوْمِكُم رَآهَا
— قال الأَمِيرُ فَلْيَفْعَلِ البَارِئُ عَزَّ وَجَلَّ ما يَشَاءُ فَإِنْ شَفَى
جِرَاحِى وأَعَادَ صِحَّتِى إِلَيَّ حَمِدْتُهُ على ذلك وإِلَّا فَالأَمْرُ لَهُ
وإِنْ مُتُّ فَاسْتَلِمْ قِيَادَةَ هٰؤُلَاءِ العَرَبِ — إِنَّنِى وإِنْ أَكُنْ
بَعِيدًا عن وَطَنِكَ ومَدِينَتِكَ فَسَأَبْذُلُ جَهْدِى فِى إِيصالِكَ
إِلَيْهَا سالِمًا — إذا أَلَمَّ بالإِنْسانِ مُصِيبَتَانِ فالأَوْلَى أَنْ يَخْتَارَ أَسْهَلَهَا

-- إِنْ قَسَمَ لِى اللهُ نَصِيبًا لِلنَّجاةِ يَقْدِرُ أَنْ يُخَلِّصَنِى بِطُرُقٍ كَثِيرَةٍ وَإِنْ أَرادَ أَنْ يُهْلِكَنِي فِى وَسَطِ هذا البَحْرِ العَجّاجِ فَلا مَفَرَّ عَنِ المَوْتِ — القَلْبُ بَيْنَ الصَّحْبِ أَعْظَمُ شاهِدٍ يُرْضِى وَلَوْ كانت شَهادَةُ واحِدٍ — لَوْ لم تَكُنْ شَرًّا منهما لما تَخَلَّلْتَ بَيْنَهما — إِنْ مُتُّ فَإِنَّ عِظامِى تَصْرُخُ من قَبْرِى مُقِرَّةً لك بالجَمِيلِ والفَضْلِ — كان الرَّجُلُ يُحِبُّ الشَّرَفَ وَلَئِنْ يَكُنْ فارِغًا — إِنْ قَبِلْتَ (good) وإِنْ لم تَقْبَلْ فَأَنا أَقْبَلْ — مَنْ جَدَّ وَجَدَ — إِذا بَقِيتِ مُصِرَّةً على عِنادِكِ فَسَأُذِيقُكِ جَزاءَ عِصْيانِكِ إِلى يَوْمِ مَوْتِكِ — لَوْلا كَثْرَةُ الضّابِطِينَ الذين كانوا حَوْلَهُ لكان ذلك الجُمْهُورُ قَتَلَهُ فى الطَّرِيقِ —

Exercise 90.

If the matter is so, I will honour thee greatly and make thee chief over all my men. — If a man passes by you, tell me, and God will requite you with good. — I said to (in) myself: If God makes easy for me a way to escape, it is well; and if not, the matter is his and He will do what He pleases. — When the light of the morning had dawned, my spirit was refreshed, although I had despaired of deliverance. -- If I had known that I should happen to meet thee in this place, I would have expended all my energy in receiving thee. — If thou fulfillest my need, I shall be indebted to thee for such a pleasure, that the kings of the earth could not pay the weight of a grain of it; and if you reject my request, then thrust me into this sea. — If I demand thee (fem.) from thy father now, there is no doubt that he will send me back disappointed. — When (the) age thwarts us, then there is nothing for us but to take refuge in (the) fair patience and to rely on God. — When she shows rebellion, he shows stubbornness.

Forty-eighth Lesson.

(اَلدَّرْسُ ٱلثَّامِنُ وَٱلْأَرْبَعُونَ)

Interjections.

(حَرْفُ ٱلنِّدَاءِ)

1. The Vocative is expressed by the particles يَا and أَيُّهَا Fem. أَيَّتُهَا (but the Masc. is often used for the Fem.) or يَا أَيُّهَا.

أَيُّهَا and يَا أَيُّهَا are followed by the noun in the Nominative with the Article:

يَا أَيُّهَا ٱلتِّلْمِيذُ O scholar! (see. Less. 16, 4 and Less. 42, 1 c).

يَا is followed by the noun in the Nominative without Article (and without Nunation in the Sing.) if the person addressed is present and the noun is not determined by any following words, e.g.

يَا وَلَدُ O boy! يَا مُحَمَّدُ O Mohammed!

but يَا أَوْلَادُ O boys!

If the person addressed is absent or the noun is determined by some word or words after it, then the noun is put in the Accusative, e.g.:

يَا غَافِلًا O careless! (not addressed to any one particular person).

يَا طَالِعًا ٱلْجَبَلَ O thou, who climbest the mountain!

يَا عَبْدَ ٱللّٰه O Abdallah!

Note 1. يَا is sometimes written without alif, when the following word begins with alif, e.g.:

يَاخِي O my brother!. يَاهْلًا welcome!

Notice specially:

يَا أَبَتِ O my father! يَا أُمَّهْ O mother!

يَا رَبِّ O my Lord! (see. Less. 43, 4 Note 1).

Note 2. The noun that follows يَا often takes the Vocative ending ـَاهْ (see below on وَا).

Note 3. For يَا followed by لَ see Less. 44, 3 A 4 Note).

2. Some of the commonest Interjections are:

أَوَّاهْ, أَوْهْ, آهٍ, آهِ, آهْ, آ, أَ Ah!

وَا Oh! The following noun often has the ending ـَا oder ـَاهْ in pause, e.g.

وَا أَسَفَا or وَا أَسَفَاهْ O sorrow!

وَا حَسْرَتَا O grief!

وَيْ Alas! also with suffixes: وَيْكَ Alas for thee!

Notice also the Substantives وَيْبٌ, وَيْحٌ and وَيْلٌ used (also with suffixes) as Interjections, e.g.:

وَيْلَكَ Woe to thee. وَيْلٌ لِزَيْدٍ Woe to Zaid.

The form وَيْلَاهْ, with the Vocative ending may also be used.

هَا See there!

هُوَذَا See there he is!

هَيَّا Come! with the Preposition بِ: Come, let us go!

هَيْهَاتَ Far from it!

أُفٍّ, أُفَّ Fie!

بَخٍ and بَخْ بَخْ Bravo!

طُوبَى (Fem. of the Elative أَطْيَبُ "best") Hail!

طُوبَاكَ or طُوبَى لَكَ Hail to thee! هَلُمُّوا

هَلُمَّ also هَلُمَّ جَرًّا and in the Plural هَلُمُّوا "Hither!"

هَاتِ (properly the Imper. IV. of أَتَى "to come") "give, bring here!" also used in the Fem.

دُونَكَ and دُونَكُمْ "Beware!" (from Perf. دُونَ see Less. 44, 4).

إِيَّاكَ and إِيَّاكُمْ "Beware!" (see Less. 42, 2).

3. Certain nouns are used in the Accusative as Interjections (cf. Less. 42, 2 1, Note).

أَهْلًا وَسَهْلًا Welcome!

عَجَبًا Strange!

مَهْلًا Slowly!

مَرْحَبًا Welcome!

مَرْحَبًا بِكَ Welcome to thee!

سَمْعًا وَطَاعَةً (lit. "Hearing and obeying".) At your service!

تَبًّا لَكَ Alas for thee!

4. Many religious expressions are used interjectionally; e.g.:

أَللّٰهُ or يَا أَللّٰهُ or very Commonly أَللّٰهُمَّ O God!

وَاللّٰهِ بِاللّٰهِ تَاللّٰهِ By God!

اَلْحَمْدُ لِلّٰهِ	Thanks to God!
إِنْ شَاءَ ٱللّٰهُ	If God will!
بِسْمِ ٱللّٰهِ ٱلرَّحْمٰنِ ٱلرَّحِيمِ	In the name of God the Compassionate, the Merciful!
مَعَاذَ ٱللّٰهِ or أَعُوذُ بِٱللّٰهِ	God forbid! (lit. "I take refuge in God").
لَا حَوْلَ وَلَا قُوَّةَ إِلَّا بِٱللّٰهِ ٱلْعَظِيمِ	There is no might and no power, save in God the Mighty! (Expression of astonishment and alarm.)
مَا شَاءَ ٱللّٰهُ	What God will! (Astonishment.)
أَسْتَغْفِرُ ٱللّٰهَ	I ask pardon of God! (Used to decline a compliment.)

Praises constantly appended to the name of God:

تَعَالَى (Perf. IV of عَلَا) عَزَّ وَجَلَّ	He is exalted!
سُبْحَانَهُ	Praised be He!

Exercise 91.

أَمَّلْنَا بِبُلُوغِ ٱلْمَقْصُودِ عن قَرِيبٍ ولكِنَّ وا أَسَفَا فَإِنَّ سَهْمَنا وَقَعَ دُونَ ٱلْغَرَضِ (Proverb) — حالَمَا عَلِمَ ٱلعَرَبُ بِقُدُومِنا أَسْرَعُوا لِلِقائِنا فَرِحِينَ وَهُمْ يَصْرُخُونَ بِأَعْلَى أَصْواتِهِم يَا أَهْلًا بِٱلضَّيْفِ يَا أَهْلًا بِٱلضَّيفِ فقلتُ لهم إِنَّنِى نَزِيلُكم أَيُّها ٱلعَرَبُ فقالوا يَا أَهْلًا بكم يَا أَهْلًا بكم — قال ٱلأَمِيرُ هَيَّا بنا أَيُّها ٱلعَرَبُ فَإِنَّ بَنِى عَدْوانَ قد أَتَوْا لِغَزْوِنا وَهَلُمَّ جَرًّا من ٱلكَلام ٱلمُحَرِّضِ

على المُكافَحَةِ ودُونَكم هٰؤُلَاءِ الأَنْذَالَ الذين أَتَوا لِغَزْوِنا — قال

لى شُلَّتْ يَداكَ يأَنْذَلَ الرِجالِ بأَيَّةِ جَسارَةٍ تُذِيقُ وَلَدِى كَأْسَ

الحِمامِ فَهَيا وخُذْ جَزاءَ عَمَلِكَ — آوّاهْ قَدِ ٱقْتَرَبَ أَجَلِى —

يا لَلْعَجَبِ كَيْفَ قَدَرَ هذا الأَسِيرُ أَنْ يَفِرَّ من أَمامِ خَيْمَةِ الأَمِيرِ

— صَرَخْتُ بأَعْلَى صَوْتِى قائِلًا وَيْلاهُ ما هذا المُصابُ وما هذه

الداهِيَةُ — آهْ يا عَزِيزِى سأَمُوتُ مَسْرُورَةً لأَنّى رَأَيْتُكَ — سُبْحانَ

العَلِيِّ الجَبّارِ الذى فَرَّقَنا فى البَوادِى والقِفارِ وجَمَعَ شَمْلَنا فى

لُجَجِ البِحارِ — هاتِ ما بَدا لكَ — قال النُوتِيُّ الذى كانَ

مَرِيضًا يا لَيْتَنِى لم أُشْفَ لأَنَّ بالمَوْتِ راحَتِى وأَخَذَ بَقِيَّةُ

النُوتِيَّةِ يَقُولُونَ طُوبَى للقَبْطانِ الذى ٱرْتاحَ من هذه الأَتْعابِ

— أَوّاهْ واحَرَبا قد أَحاطَ بِىَ التَعْسُ مُنْذُ صِغَرِى — قالَتْ

آهْ ما حِيلَتِى وَيْلاهْ ما العَمَلُ ٱقْطِلى يا سَماءُ نُمُوعًا علينا وأَفِضْ

يا بَحْرُ أَمْواجَكَ وٱغْرِقْنا وأَرِحْنا من هذه العِيشَةِ النَكِيبَةِ فقلتُ

لها ٱنْهَضِى أَيَّتُها المَحْبُوبَةُ فإِنَّ اللهَ لم يَقْسِمْ لنا المَوْتَ هُوَذا

مَرْكَبٌ مُقْبِلٌ — يا لَيْتَنِى مُتُّ لَمّا كُنْتُ عائِمًا فى البَحْرِ —

فَلَمْ أَدَعْهُ يُتَمِّمُ كَلامَهُ وقلتُ لا حَوْلَ ولا قُوَّةَ إِلّا باللهِ العَظِيمِ

— إِذْ وَصَلْتُ إلى مَحَلِّ إِقامَتِى طَرَحْتُ نَفْسِى على سَرِيرِى

وَلَكِنْ تَبًّا لَهَا مِنْ لَيْلَةٍ لَمْ أَذُقْ فِيهَا ٱلْكَرَى دَقِيقَةً وَاحِدَةً — كَيْفَ أَقْدِرُ أَنْ أَسْلُوكِ وَقَدْ نَظَرْتُ دُمُوعَ ٱلْمَحَبَّةِ تَذْرِفُ مِنْ عَيْنَيْكِ ٱلنَّرْجِسِيَّتَيْنِ وَهَا أَنَا هَائِمٌ ٱلْآنَ فِي حُبِّكِ وَقَتِيلُ فِرَاقِكِ —

Exercise 92.

Hither, O Arabs, and follow (سَارَ) in the track of this bold man. — Come, let us take a walk in the garden! — Ah, O my God, what is this strange chance which has united me with my friend in this raging sea? — Woe, truly misfortunes come upon me and strike me; Ah, why dost thou threaten us, O sea? — O would that I had been slain among the Arabs! — Praised be the Exalted, the Mighty who has protected us from dangers and guarded us from troubles and brought us back to Beirut safe from harm (Plur.). — Ah, O my precious, who has brought thee to this place? — Alas for his (to him from) disturbing dream!

Forty-ninth Lesson.

(اَلدَّرْسُ ٱلتَّاسِعُ وَٱلْأَرْبَعُونَ)

Arabic Verse.

(عِلْمُ ٱلْعَرُوضِ)

1. Prose is called in Arabic نَثْرٌ ("scattering"), Poetry is نَظْمٌ ("ordering"). Rhymed Prose is سَجْعٌ.

2. Arabic Poetry (شِعْرٌ) has both Rhyme (قَافِيَةٌ) and Metre (وَزْنٌ or بَحْرٌ) the latter being quantitative.

An Open syllable is short, a closed syllable long (see Intro. § 13, 1).

Note. The Pronominal suffix ه and the second syllable in أَنَا may be either long or short.

3. Every Verse or Line (بَيْتٌ Plur. أَبْيَاتٌ) consists of two Half-verses (شَطْرٌ or مِصْرَاعٌ).

At the end of the Verse i.e. in Pause (وَقْفٌ) the Nunation is dropped and sometimes the vowel is omitted altogether.

In long poems the first half-verse must end in the rhyme of the poem.

Sometimes in poems in Rajaz metre (see below 5, b) there is no common rhyme, but the first half of each verse rhymes with the second.

4. The number of Feet in use is eight. They are indicated by means of the letters ف ع ل (as in the forms of the verb):

a) فَعُولُنْ ⏑ – –

b) فَاعِلُنْ – ⏑ –

c) مُسْتَفْعِلُنْ – – ⏑ –

d) مَفَاعِيلُنْ ⏑ – – –

e) فَاعِلَاتُنْ – ⏑ – –

f) مَفْعُولَاتُ – – – ⏑

g) مُفَاعَلَتُنْ ⏑ – ⏑ ⏑ –

h) مُتَفَاعِلُنْ ⏑ ⏑ – ⏑ –

These Feet are subject to certain changes, e.g.:

a) فَعُولُنْ ⏑ – – becomes فَعُولُ ⏑ – ⏑

b) فَاعِلُنْ – ⏑ – " فَعِلُنْ ⏑ ⏑ –

c) مُسْتَفْعِلُنْ — — u — becomes { مُتَفْعِلُنْ u u — — ; مُفْتَعِلُنْ — u u — ; مُتَعِلُنْ u u u — }

d) مَفَاعِيلُنْ u — — — „ { مَفَاعِلُنْ u — u — ; مَفَاعِيلُ u — — u }

e) فَاعِلَاتُنْ — u — — „ { فَاعِلَاتُ — u — u ; فَعِلَاتُنْ u u — — ; فَعِلَاتُ u u — u }

f) مَفْعُولَاتُ — — — u „ { مَفْعُلَاتُ — u — u ; فَعُولَاتُ u — — u }

g) مُفَاعَلَتُنْ u — u u — „ { مُفَاعَلْتُنْ u — — — ; مُفَاعَتُنْ u — u — (rare) }

h) مُتَفَاعِلُنْ u u — u — „ مُتْفَاعِلُنْ — — u —

If Catalexis (rejection of the last syllable) occurs at the end of a verse, then u — — is changed to u —; — u — to — — etc. These are also subject to the changes given above.

A verse is formed by repetition of the same foot or by a combination of several feet.

5. The sixteen Arabic Metres are:

a) أَلْمُتَقَارِبُ:

فَعُولُنْ فَعُولُنْ فَعُولُنْ فَعُولُنْ

فَعُولُنْ فَعُولُنْ فَعُولُنْ فَعُولُنْ

usually with Catalexis فَعُو in the second, sometimes also in the first half-verse:

أَلَا رُبَّ مَكْرُوهَةٍ قَدْ كَفَيْتَ

وَمُلْكٍ تَضَمَّنْتَهُ فَٱسْتَقَرْ

"How many an evil hast thou warded off, and how many a dominion hast thou protected so that it became firm."

b) أَلرَّجَزُ (especially in didactic poems; such a poem being called أُرْجُوزَةٌ):

مُسْتَفْعِلُنْ مُسْتَفْعِلُنْ مُسْتَفْعِلُنْ

مُسْتَفْعِلُنْ مُسْتَفْعِلُنْ مُسْتَفْعِلُنْ

e.g.:

قَالَ مُحَمَّدٌ هُوَ ٱبْنُ مَالِكِ

أَحْمَدُ رَبِّي ٱللّٰهَ خَيْرَ مَالِكِ

"Said Muhammad ibn Mālik: I praise my Lord God, the best Ruler."

(Beginning of the Alfiya of Ibn Mālik.)

In this metre Catalexis of the last foot (change ⏓ ⏓ ⏑ — to ⏓ ⏓ —) is very common. If there is no rhyme common to the whole poem, the first half-verse also has the Catalexis, e.g.:

يَقُولُ رَاجِى رَبِّهِ ٱلْغَفُورِ

يَحْيَى بْنُ مُعْطِ بْنِ عَبْدِ ٱلنُّورِ

"Says he, who hopes in his forgiving Lord, Yaḥyā ibn Muʿṭi Ibn ʿAbd-unnūr". (From Addurra al-Alfīyā by Yaḥyā Ibn ʿAbd al-Muʿti az-Zāwāwī).

c) اَلْهَزَجُ

مَفَاعِيلُنْ مَفَاعِيلُنْ

مَفَاعِيلُنْ مَفَاعِيلُنْ

e.g.:

فَقِيرٌ مَنْ لَهُ حِرْصٌ

غَنِيٌّ كُلُّ مَنْ يَقْنَعْ

"Poor is the greedy man, rich the contented."

d) اَلرَّمَلُ (usually with Catalexis in both half-verses):

فَاعِلَاتُنْ فَاعِلَاتُنْ فَاعِلُنْ

فَاعِلَاتُنْ فَاعِلَاتُنْ فَاعِلُنْ

e.g.:

إِطْرَحِ ٱلدُّنْيَا فَمِنْ عَادَاتِهَا

تَخْفِضُ ٱلْعَالِي وَتُعْلِي مَنْ سَفَلْ

"Thrust away the world, for it is of its customs to humble the exalted and to exalt him who is low."

e) اَلْوَافِرُ (almost always with Catalexis):

مُفَاعَلَتُنْ مُفَاعَلَتُنْ فَعُولُنْ

مُفَاعَلَتُنْ مُفَاعَلَتُنْ فَعُولُنْ

e.g.:

فَإِنْ تَفُقِ ٱلْأَنَامَ وَأَنْتَ مِنْهُمْ

كَأَنَّ ٱلْمِسْكَ بَعْضُ دَمِ ٱلْغَزَالِ

"When thou surpassest men of whom thou art, it is as if musk were a part of the blood of the gazelle."

f) أَلْكَامِلُ (also with Catalexis of the second half verse):

مُتَفَاعِلُنْ مُتَفَاعِلُنْ مُتَفَاعِلُنْ

مُتَفَاعِلُنْ مُتَفَاعِلُنْ مُتَفَاعِلُنْ

e.g.:

قَلْبِي يُحَدِّثُنِي بِأَنَّكَ مُتْلِفِي

رُوحِي فِدَاكَ عَرَفْتَ أَمْ لَمْ تَعْرِفِ

"My heart tells me that thou art my destroyer; my soul is thy ransom, whether thou knowest it or knowest it not." (Umar Ibn al-Fāriḍ.)

g) أَلطَّوِيلُ:

فَعُولُنْ مَفَاعِيلُنْ فَعُولُنْ مَفَاعِيلُنْ

فَعُولُنْ مَفَاعِيلُنْ فَعُولُنْ مَفَاعِيلُنْ

At the end of the first half-verse the مَفَاعِيلُنْ is usually changed to مَفَاعِلُنْ.

Catalexis may occur at the end of the second half-verse.

e.g.: قِفَا نَبْكِ مِنْ ذِكْرَى حَبِيبٍ وَمَنْزِلِ

بِسَقْطِ ٱللِّوَى بَيْنَ ٱلدَّخُولِ فَحَوْمَلِ

"Stay (both of you), let us weep over the memory of a beloved one and a place at the edge of the sand hill between ad-Dakhūl and Ḥaumal." (Imru'ulqais.)

h) أَلسَّرِيعُ (sometimes with Catalexis of the second half-verse):

مُسْتَفْعِلُنْ مُسْتَفْعِلُنْ فَاعِلُنْ

مُسْتَفْعِلُنْ مُسْتَفْعِلُنْ فَاعِلُنْ

e.g.: قَالَتْ لِيَ ٱلنَّفْسُ أَتَاكَ ٱلرَّدَى

وَأَنْتَ فِي دَارِ ٱلْمَعَاصِي مُقِيمْ

تَزَوَّدِ ٱلتَّقْوَى فَقُلْتُ ٱقْصِرِي

لَا يُحْمَلُ ٱلزَّادُ لِدَارِ ٱلْكَرِيمْ

"The soul said to me: death has come to thee, and thou abidest in the house of rebellion; provide thyself with piety; and I said: cease, provision is not taken to the house of the Generous." (Abū Nuwās.)

i) أَلْبَسِيطُ (often with Catalexis at the end of the second half-verse):

مُسْتَفْعِلُنْ فَاعِلُنْ مُسْتَفْعِلُنْ فَاعِلُنْ

مُسْتَفْعِلُنْ فَاعِلُنْ مُسْتَفْعِلُنْ فَاعِلُنْ

e.g.:

أَللَّيْلُ وَٱلْخَيْلُ وَٱلْبَيْدَاءُ تَعْرِفُنِي

وَٱلسَّيْفُ وَٱلضَّيْفُ وَٱلْقِرْطَاسُ وَٱلْقَلَمْ

"Night and the horses and the desert know me, also the sword and the guest and paper and the pen." (al-Mutanabbī.)

j) أَلْمُجْتَثُّ:

مُسْتَفْعِلُنْ فَاعِلَاتُنْ

مُسْتَفْعِلُنْ فَاعِلَاتُنْ

e.g.:

لَا تَحْسَبَنْ أَنَّ بِٱلشِّعْرِ

مِثْلَنَا سَتَصِيرُ

فَلِلدَّجَاجَةِ رِيشٌ

لٰكِنَّهَا لَا تَطِيرُ

"Imagine not that thou in the future wilt be in poetry as we; for the hen has feathers but it does not fly." (Ibn ad-Dahhān.)

k) أَلْمُنسَرِحُ:

مُسْتَفْعِلُنْ مَفْعُولَاتُ مُسْتَفْعِلُنْ

مُسْتَفْعِلُنْ مَفْعُولَاتُ مُسْتَفْعِلُنْ

As a rule the مَفْعُولَاتُ becomes مَفْعُلَاتُ, and the مُسْتَفْعِلُنْ at the end of each half-verse becomes مُفْتَعِلُنْ.

أَبْعَدُ نَأْيِ ٱلْمَلِيحَةِ ٱلْبَخَلُ

فِي ٱلْبُعْدِ مَا لَا تُكَلَّفُ ٱلْإِبِلُ

"The furthest distance of the fair maid is the miserliness (of her affection), which consists of a distance such as no camel can undertake to travel." (al-Mutanabbī.)

l) اَلْخَفِيفُ:

فَاعِلَاتُنْ مُسْتَفْعِلُنْ فَاعِلَاتُنْ

فَاعِلَاتُنْ مُسْتَفْعِلُنْ فَاعِلَاتُنْ

e.g.:

وَإِذَا خَامَرَ ٱلْهَوَى قَلْبَ صَبٍّ

فَعَلَيْهِ لِكُلِّ عَيْنٍ دَلِيلُ

"And when passion pervades the heart of a lover then every eye has a proof of it." (al-Mutanabbī.)

m) اَلْمَدِيدُ:

فَاعِلَاتُنْ فَاعِلُنْ فَاعِلُنْ

فَاعِلَاتُنْ فَاعِلُنْ فَاعِلُنْ

e.g.:

لِلْفَتَى عَقْلٌ يَعِيشُ بِهِ

حَيْثُ تَهْدِي سَاقَهُ ٱلْقَدَمُ

"The youth has intelligence wherewith to live, in so far as his foot guides his leg."

The other three metres اَلْمُضَارِعُ, اَلْمُتَدَارِكُ and اَلْمُقْتَضَبُ are not used by the older poets.

Exercise 93.

Examples of the more usual Metres.

اَلْمُتَقَارِبُ

فَوَاحَسْرَتَا مَا أَمَرَّ ٱلْفِرَاقَ

وَأَعْلَقَ نِيرَانَهُ بِٱلْكُبُودِ[1]

(اَلْمُتَنَبِّي)

---

[1] See Less. 30, 5.

ٱلرَّجَزُ

لَقَدْ رَأَيْتُ عَجَبَا[1] مُذْ أَمْسَا

عَجَائِزًا[2] مِثْلَ ٱلأَفَاعِي خَمْسَا

ٱلرَّمَلُ

لَيْسَ مَنْ يَقْطَعُ طُرْقًا بَطَلًا

إِنَّمَا مَنْ يَتَّقِي ٱللّٰهَ ٱلْبَطَلْ

ٱلْوَافِرُ

فَلَوْ بَرَزَ ٱلزَّمَانُ إِلَيَّ شَخْصًا

لَخَضَّبَ شَعْرَ مَفْرِقِهِ حُسَامِي

ٱلْكَامِلُ

فَٱقْنَعْ بِمَا قَسَمَ ٱلْمَلِيكُ فَإِنَّمَا

قَسَمَ ٱلْمَعَايِشَ بَيْنَنَا عَلَّامُهَا

إِنَّ ٱلْبِطَالَةَ وَٱلْكَسَلْ

أَحْلَى مَذَاقًا مِنْ عَسَلْ

ٱلطَّوِيلُ

إِذَا غَدَرَتْ حَسْنَاءُ وَفَّتْ بِعَهْدِهَا

فَمِنْ عَهْدِهَا أَنْ لَا يَدُومَ لَهَا عَهْدُ

(ٱلْمُتَنَبِّي)

---

[1] عَجَبًا used parenthetically "strange!"

[2] Used as a triptote by poetic license.

تَرُومِينَ إِدْرَاكَ ٱلْمَعَالِى رَخِيصَةً

وَلَا بُدَّ دُونَ ٱلشَّهْدِ مِنْ إِبَرِ ٱلنَّحْلِ

ٱلسَّرِيعُ

لَاعَبْتُ بِٱلْخَاتَمِ إِنْسَانَةً

كَمِثْلِ بَدْرٍ فِى ٱلدُّجَى ٱلنَّاجِمِ

وَكُلَّمَا حَاوَلْتُ أَخْذِى لَهُ

مِنَ ٱلْبَنَانِ ٱلْمُتْرَفِ ٱلنَّاعِمِ

أَلْقَتْهُ فِى فِيهَا[1] فَقُلْتُ ٱنْظُرُوا

قَدْ أَخْفَتِ ٱلْخَاتَمَ فِى ٱلْخَاتَمِ

ٱلْبَسِيطُ

فَارَقْتُكُمْ فَإِذَا مَا كَانَ عِنْدَكُمْ

قَبْلَ ٱلْفِرَاقِ أَذًى بَعْدَ ٱلْفِرَاقِ يَدُ

إِذَا تَذَكَّرْتُ مَا بَيْنِى وَبَيْنَكُمْ

أَعَانَ قَلْبِى عَلَى ٱلشَّوْقِ ٱلَّذِى أَجِدُ

مَا كُلُّ مَا يَتَمَنَّى ٱلْمَرْءُ يُدْرِكُهُ

تَجْرِى ٱلرِّيَاحُ بِمَا لَا تَشْتَهِى ٱلسُّفُنُ

ٱلْمُجْتَثُّ

[1] See Less. 7, 2.

(Riddle.)

إِسْمُ مَنْ هَاجَ خَاطِرِى

أَرْبَعٌ[1] فِى صُنُوفِهِ

فَإِنْ زَالَ رُبْعُهُ

زَالَ بَاقِى حُرُوفِهِ

(Solution: غَزَالٌ)

اَلْمُنْسَرِحُ

فَقُلْتُ إِنَّ ٱلْفَتَى شَجَاعَتُهُ

تُرِيهِ فِى ٱلشُّحِّ صُورَةَ ٱلْفَرَقِ

اَلشَّمْسُ قَدْ حَلَّتِ ٱلسَّمَاءَ وَمَا

يَحْجُبُهَا بُعْدُهَا عَنِ ٱلْحَدَقِ

اَلْخَفِيفُ

بِأَبِى[2] مَنْ وَدِدْتُهُ فَٱفْتَرَقْنَا

وَقَضَى ٱللّٰهُ بَعْدَ ذَاكَ ٱجْتِمَاعَا

فَٱفْتَرَقْنَا حَوْلًا وَلَمَّا ٱلْتَقَيْنَا

كَانَ تَسْلِيمُهُ عَلَيَّ وَدَاعَا

Exercise 94.

قِيلَ إِنَّ شاعِرًا كان له عَدُوٌّ فَبَيْنَمَا هو سائِرٌ ذاتَ يَوْمٍ فى بَعْضِ الطُّرُقِ إذا هو بِعَدُوِّهِ فعَلِمَ الشاعِرُ أَنَّ عَدُوَّهُ قاتِلُهُ لا مَحالَةَ فقال له يا هذا أنا أَعْلَمُ أَنَّ المَنِيَّةَ قد حَضَرَتْ ولكن سَأَلْتُكَ الله إذا أنتَ قَتَلْتَنِى ٱمْضِ إلى دارى وقِفْ بالبابِ وقُلْ

[1] A collection of four letters.

[2] See Less. 44, 3 A, 1. Note.

أَلَا أَيُّهَا ٱلْبِنْتَانِ إِنَّ أَبَاكُمَا

فقال سَمْعًا وطاعَةً ثُمَّ إِنَّهُ قَتَلَهُ فلمّا فَرَغَ من قَتْلِهِ أَتَى الى دارِهِ وَوَقَفَ بالبابِ وقال

أَلَا أَيُّهَا ٱلْبِنْتَانِ إِنَّ أَبَاكُمَا

وكان للشاعرِ ٱبْنَتَانِ فلمّا سَمِعَا ذلك منه أَجابَتَاهُ بِفَمٍ واحِدٍ

قَتِيلٌ خُذَا بِٱلثَّارِ مِمَّنْ أَتَاكُمَا

ثُمَّ تَعَلَّقَتَا بالرَجُلِ وَرَفَعَتَاهُ إِلى الحاكِمِ فَٱسْتَقَرَّهُ فَأَقَرَّ بِقَتْلِهِ فَقَتَلَهُ واللّه أعلم —

Supplement.

Selections.

From the Koran.

Sura 1.

سُورَةُ ٱلْفَاتِحَةِ

بِسْمِ ٱللّٰهِ ٱلرَّحْمٰنِ ٱلرَّحِيمِ

ٱلْحَمْدُ لِلّٰهِ رَبِّ ٱلْعَالَمِينَ ۝ ٱلرَّحْمٰنِ ٱلرَّحِيمِ ۝ مَالِكِ يَوْمِ
ٱلدِّينِ ۝ إِيَّاكَ نَعْبُدُ وَإِيَّاكَ نَسْتَعِينُ ۝ ٱهْدِنَا ٱلصِّرَاطَ ٱلْمُسْتَقِيمَ ۝
صِرَاطَ ٱلَّذِينَ أَنْعَمْتَ عَلَيْهِمْ ۝ غَيْرِ ٱلْمَغْضُوبِ عَلَيْهِمْ وَلَا ٱلضَّالِّينَ —

Sura 112.

سُورَةُ ٱلْإِخْلَاصِ

قُلْ هُوَ ٱللّٰهُ أَحَدٌ ۝ ٱللّٰهُ ٱلصَّمَدُ ۝ لَمْ يَلِدْ وَلَمْ يُولَدْ ۝
وَلَمْ يَكُنْ لَهُ كُفُوًا أَحَدٌ —

Sura 113.

سُورَةُ ٱلْفَلَقِ

قُلْ أَعُوذُ بِرَبِّ ٱلْفَلَقِ ۝ مِنْ شَرِّ مَا خَلَقَ ۝ وَمِنْ شَرِّ
غَاسِقٍ إِذَا وَقَبَ ۝ وَمِنْ شَرِّ ٱلنَّفَّاثَاتِ فِي ٱلْعُقَدِ ۝ وَمِنْ شَرِّ
حَاسِدٍ إِذَا حَسَدَ —

Sura 114

سُورَةُ ٱلنَّاسِ

قُلْ أَعُوذُ بِرَبِّ ٱلنَّاسِ ۞ مَلِكِ ٱلنَّاسِ ۞ إِلٰهِ ٱلنَّاسِ ۞
مِنْ شَرِّ ٱلْوَسْوَاسِ ٱلْخَنَّاسِ ۞ ٱلَّذِى يُوَسْوِسُ فِى صُدُورِ ٱلنَّاسِ ۞
مِنَ ٱلْجِنَّةِ وَٱلنَّاسِ —

Fables.

(from مجانى الأدب)

اَلنُّمُوسُ وَٱلدَّجَاجُ

بَلَغَ ٱلنُّمُوسَ أَنَّ ٱلدَّجَاجَ قَدْ مَرِضُوا فَلَبِسُوا جُلُودَ طَوَاوِيسَ وَأَتَوْا لِيَزُورُوهُمْ فقالوا لهم السَّلَامُ عليكم أَيُّهَا الدَّجَاجُ كَيْفَ أَنْتُمْ وَكَيْفَ أَحْوَالُكم فقالوا إِنَّا بِخَيْرٍ يَوْمَ لا نَرَى وُجُوهَكم (مَغْزَاهُ) أَنَّ كَثِيرًا يُظْهِرُونَ الْمَحَبَّةَ وَيُبْطِنُونَ البَغْضَاء

قِطَّتَانِ وَقِرْدٌ

قِطَّتَانِ ٱخْتَطَفَتَا جُبْنَةً وَذَهَبَتَا بها إِلى القِرْدِ لِكَيْ يَقْسِمَهَا بينهما فقَسَمَهَا إِلى قِسْمَيْنِ أَحَدُهما أَكْبَرُ من الثَّانِي وَوَضَعَهما فى مِيزَانِهِ فرَجَحَ الأَكْبَرُ فأَخَذَ منه شَيْئًا بِأَسْنَانِهِ وهو يُظْهِرُ أَنَّهُ يُرِيدُ مُسَاوَاتَهُ بالأَصْغَرِ ولكن إِذْ كان ما أَخَذَهُ منه هو أَكْثَرُ من اللَّازِمِ رَجَحَ الأَصْغَرُ ففَعَلَ بهذا ما فَعَلَهُ بذاكَ ثُمَّ فَعَلَ بذاك ما فعله بهذا وهكذا حَتَّى كادَ يَذْهَبُ بالجُبْنَةِ فقالت له القِطَّتَانِ نَحْنُ

رَضِينا بهذه القِسْمَةِ فأَعْطِنا الجُبْنَةَ فقال إذا كُنْتُما أَنْتُما رَضِيتُما فإِنّ العَدْلَ لا يَرضَى وما زالَ يَقْضَمُ القِسْمَ الراجِحَ منها كذلكَ حتّى أَتَى عليهما جميعًا فرَجَعَتِ القِطّتانِ بحُزْنٍ وخَيْبَةٍ وهما يقولانِ

وَمَا مِنْ يَدٍ إِلَّا يَدُ ٱللّٰهِ فَوْقَهَا وَلَا ظَالِمٌ إِلَّا سَيُبْلَى بِأَظْلَمِ

صَائِدٌ وعُصْفُورٌ

كان صائِدٌ يَصِيدُ العَصافِيرَ فى يَوْمٍ بارِدٍ فكان يَذْبَحُها والدُمُوعُ تَسِيلُ فقال عُصْفُورٌ لِصاحِبِهِ لا بَأْسَ عليكَ من الرَجُلِ أَما تَراه يَبْكِى فقال له الآخَرُ لا تَنْظُرْ دُمُوعَهُ وٱنْظُرْ ما تَصْنَعُ يَداهُ —

أَسْوَدُ

أَسْوَدُ فى فَصْلِ الشِتاء أَقْبَلَ يَأْخُذُ الثَلْجَ ويَفْرُكُ به بَدَنَهُ فقِيلَ له لِماذا ذلك فقال لَعَلِّى أَبْيَضُّ فقال له حَكِيمٌ يا هذا لا تُتْعِبْ نَفْسَكَ فرُبَّما ٱسْوَدَّ الثَلْجُ من جِسْمِكَ وهو باقٍ على حالِهِ (مَغزاهُ) أَنَّ الشَرِيرَ يَقْدِرُ أَنْ يُفْسِدَ الخَيِّرَ وقَلِيلًا ما يُصْلِحُهُ الخَيِّرُ

أَسَدٌ وثَعْلَبٌ وذِئْبٌ

وهُوَ مَثَلُ مَنِ ٱتَّعَظَ بِغَيْرِهِ وٱعْتَبَرَ بِهِ

أَسَدٌ وثَعْلَبٌ وذِئْبٌ ٱصْطَحَبُوا فخَرَجُوا يَتَصَيَّدُونَ فصادُوا حِمارًا وأَرْنَبًا وظَبْيًا فقال الأَسَدُ للذِئْبِ ٱقْسِمْ بيننا فقال الأَمْرُ بَيِّنٌ الحِمارُ للأَسَدِ والأَرْنَبُ للثعلبِ والظَبْيُ لى فخَبَطَهُ الأَسَدُ

فَطَارَ رَأْسَهُ ثُمَّ أَقْبَلَ على الثَّعْلَبِ وقال ما كان أَجْهَلَ صاحِبَكَ[1] بالغَنِيمَةِ هاتِ أَنتَ فقال يا أَبا الحارِثِ الأَمْرُ واضِحٌ الحِمارُ لِغَدائِكَ والظَّبيُ لِعَشائِكَ وتَخَلَّلْ بالأَرْنَبِ فيما بين ذلك فقال له الأَسَدُ ما أَقْضاكَ من عَلَّمَكَ هذا الفِقْهَ فقال رَأْسُ الذِّئْبِ الطائِرُ من جُثَّتِهِ —

ثَعلَبٌ وضَبُعٌ

حُكِيَ أَنَّ الثَّعْلَبَ اطَّلَعَ فى بِئْرٍ وهو عاطِشٌ وعليها رِشاءٌ فى طَرَفَيْهِ دَلْوانِ فقَعَدَ فى الدَّلْوِ العُلْيا فانْحَدَرَتْ فشَرِبَ فجاءَتِ الضَبُعُ فاطَّلَعَتْ فى البِئْرِ فأَبْصَرَتِ القَمَرَ فى الماء مُنْتَصِفًا والثعلبُ قاعِدٌ فى قَعْرِ البئرِ فقالت له ما تَصْنَعُ هُنا فقال لها إِنِّى أَكَلْتُ نِصْفَ هذه الجُبْنَةِ وبَقِيَ نِصْفُها لَكِ فانْزِلِى فكُلِيها فقالت وكيف أَنْزِلُ قال تَقْعُدِينَ فى الدَّلْوِ فقَعَدَتْ فيها فانْحَدَرَتْ وارْتَفَعَ الثعلبُ فى الدَّلْوِ الأُخْرى فلمّا الْتَقَيا فى وَسَطِ البئرِ قالت له ما هذا قال كذا التُّجارُ تَخْتَلِفُ فضَرَبَتْ بهما العَرَبُ المَثَلَ فى المُخْتَلِفِينَ —

حِكايَةُ الحِمارِ والثَّورِ مَعَ صاحِبِ الزَّرْعِ

(From أَلْفُ لَيْلَةٍ ولَيْلَةٍ).

قال انه كان لبعض التجار أَمْوال ومواشٍ وكان له زوجة وأَولاد وكان الله تعالى أَعطاه معرفة أَلسن الحيوانات والطير وكان مسكن

[1] See Less. 30, 5.

ذلك التاجر الأرياف وكان عنده فى داره حمار وثور، فأتى يومًا
الثور الى مكان الحمار فوجده مكنوسًا مرشوشًا وفى معلفه شعير
مغربل وتبن مغربل وهو راقد مستريح وفى بعض الأوقات يركبه
صاحبه لحاجة تعرض له ويرجع على حاله فلمّا كان فى بعض
الأيام سمع التاجر الثور وهو يقول للحمار هَنيئًا لك ذلك أنا
تعبان وأنت مستريح تأكل الشعير مُغربلًا ويخدمونك وفى بعض
الأوقات يركبك صاحبك ويرجع وأنا دائمًا للحرث والطحن
فقال له الحمار إذا خرجت إلى الغيط ووضعوا على رقبتك الناف
فارقد ولا تقم ولو ضربوك فإن قمت فارقد ثانيًا فإذا رجعوا بك
ووضعوا لك الفول فلا تأكله كأنّك ضعيف وامتنع من الأكل
والشرب يومًا أو يومين أو ثلاثة فإنّك تستريح من التعب والجهد
وكان التاجر يسمع كلامهما فلمّا جاء السوّاق إلى الثور بعلفه
أكل منه شيئًا يسيرًا فأصبح السوّاق يأخذ الثور إلى الحرث
فوجده ضعيفا فقال له التاجر خذ الحمار وأحرثه مكانه اليوم
كله فرجع الرجل وأخذ الحمار مكان الثور وأحرثه مكانه اليوم
كله فلمّا رجع آخر النهار شكره الثور على تفضلاته حيث
أراحه من التعب فى ذلك اليوم فلم يرد عليه الحمار جوابًا
وندم أشدّ الندامة فلمّا كان ثانى يوم جاء الزرّاع وأخذ
الحمار وأحرثه إلى آخر النهار فلم يرجع الحمار إلّا مسلوخ الرقبة
شديد الضعف فتأمّله الثور وشكره ومجّده فقال له الحمار كنت
مقيمًا مستريحًا فما ضرّنى إلّا فضولى ثم قال اعلم أنّى لك ناصح
وقد سمعت صاحبنا يقول إن لم يقم الثور من موضعه فأعطوه
للجزّار ليذبحه ويعمل جلده نطعًا وأنا خائف عليك ونصحتك

والسلام فلمّا سمع الثور كلام الحمار شكره وقال غد اسرح معهم ثم إن الثور أكل علفه بتمامه حتى لحس المذود بلسانه كل ذلك وصاحبهما يسمع كلامهما فلمّا طلع النهار خرج التاجر وزوجته إلى دار البقر وجلسا فجاء السوّاق وأخذ الثور وخرج فلمّا رأى الثور صاحبه حرّك ذنبه وضرط وبرطع فضحك التاجر حتى استلقى على قفاه فقالت له زوجته من أىّ شيء تضحك فقال لها شيء رأيته وسمعته ولا أقدر أن ابوح به فأموت فقالت له لا بدّ أن تخبرنى بذلك وما سبب ضحكك ولو كنت تموت فقال لها ما أقدر أن أبوح به خوفًا من الموت فقالت له أنت لم تضحك إلّا علىّ ثم إنّها لم تزل تلحّ عليه وتلجّ فى الكلام إلى أن غلبت عليه وتحيّر فأحضر أولاده وأرسل أحضر القاضى والشهود وأراد أن يوصى ثم يبوح لها بالسرّ ويموت لأنّه كان يحبّها محبّة عظيمة لأنّها بنت عمّه وأمّ أولاده وكان قد عمر من العمر مائة وعشرين سنة ثم إنّه أرسل أحضر جميع أهلها وأهل حارته وقال لهم حكايته وأنّه متى قال لأحد على سرّه مات فقال لها جميع الناس ممّن حضرها بالله عليك اتركى هذا الأمر لئلا يموت زوجك أبو أولادك فقالت لهم لا أرجع عنه حتى يقول لى ولو يموت فسكتوا عنها ثم إنّ التاجر قام من عندهم وتوجّه إلى دار الدواب ليتوضأ ثم يرجع يقول لهم ويموت وكان عنده ديك تحته خمسون دجاجة وكان عنده كلب فسمع التاجر الكلب وهو ينادى الديك ويسمّيه ويقول له أنت فرحان وصاحبنا رائح يموت فقال الديك للكلب وكيف ذلك الأمر فأعاد الكلب عليه القصة فقال له الديك. والله إن صاحبنا قليل العقل أنا لى

خمسون زوجة أرضى هذه واغضب هذه وهو ما له الّا زوجة واحدة ولا يعرف صلاح أُمره معها فما له لا يأخذ لها بعضًا من عيدان التوت ثم يدخل إلى حجرتها ويضربها حتّى تموت أو تتوب ولا تعود تسأله عن شىء قال فلمّا سمع التاجر كلام الديك وهو يخاطب الكلب رجع إلى عقله وعزم على ضربها ودخل عليها الحجرة بعد أن قطع لها عيدان التوت وخبأها داخل الحجرة وقال لها تعالى داخل الحجرة حتّى أقول لك ولا ينظرنى حد ثم أموت فدخلت معه ثم إنّه قفل باب الحجرة عليهما ونزل عليها بالضرب إلى أن أُغمى عليها فقالت له تبت ثم إنّها قبّلَتْ يديه ورجليه وتابت وخرجت هى وإياه وفرح الجماعة وأهلها وقعدوا فى أسرّ الأحوال إلى الممات —

القبطان والمحتال

(From قطائف اللطائف by Madame Rosa Ṣâhib.)

كان قبطان ساكنا فى الإسكندرية وكان كل يوم يشترى لوازم بيته من خضار ولحم وما أُشبه ذلك فاتفق أن يومًا ما بعد نزوله من البيت بنصف ساعة جاء شخص وطرق باب بيت هذا القبطان فسمع أهل البيت صوتا يقول خذوا اللحمة والخضار فنزلت الخادمة وأخذت اللحم والخضار وبعد ذلك قال الرجل للخادمة إن القبطان أوصانى أن تلموا كافة النحاس الموجود فى البيت لأجل أن آخذه عند المبيض وهو أعطانى هذه الحاجة ويرغب أن أوصّل له النحاس بالعجل فطلعت الخادمة وأخبرت سيدتها بذلك فأجابتها الستّ لمّوا كافة نحاس البيت بالعجل واعطيه هذا الرجل لربّما سيدك يكون مستعجلا ففعلت الخادمة حسب أمر

سيّدتها وملأت فردين كبيرين من النحاس كله فحمل الرجل
فردة منها وترك الثانية قائلًا لمّا أوصّل هذه الفردة أُرجع آخذ
الثانية ولما حمله وخرج أتى صاحب البيت حسب عادته ولوازم
البيت معه ونادى الخادمة وقال انزلى خذى العشاء فقالت له
هل عندنا اليوم عزومة حتّى أرسلت من ساعة كافة لوازم البيت
وأتيت الآن بخلافها فقال لها القبطان وما هى تلك الحاجة ومن
أتى بها أجابته الخادمة الذى أرسلته لأجل أُخذ النحاس للبياض
فقال صاحب البيت أنا ما أرسلت أحدًا مطلقًا وانّما هذا محتال
أخذ النحاس فقالت له الخادمة إنه لا شكّ يأتى الآن يا سيدى
حتّى يأخذ فردة النحاس الثانية فأجابها صاحب البيت متى
حضر لأخذها قولى له حاضر فأنزل أنا وأمسكه وبعد ذلك طلع
القبطان إلى فوق يخانق زوجته على قلّة عقلها ودخل يفكّ حصرًا
فاذا بالحرامى المحتال حضر ونادى الخادمة لأخذ الفردة الثانية
فخرج القبطان يجرى إلى الحوش بلباسه التحتانى فلمّا نظره
الحرامى فرّ هاربًا وصار يجرى والقبطان يجرى وراءه من عطفة
إلى عطفة ومن شارع إلى آخر وكان الحرامى اشد سرعة فى
الجرى من القبطان ولذلك زاغ من عينيه وتوجه أسرع من
البرق إلى بيت القبطان وصفّق على يديه وقال إنّ القبطان
يريد هدومه لأنّه مسك الحرامى وهو موجود فى الضابطية ويريد
أن ترسلوا له الهدوم لأنّه عائز يلبس بالعجل فقالت الستّ للخادمة
اسرعى بإعطائه الهدوم لأنّه لا يمكن سيّدك الرجوع قدام الناس
من غير لباسه فأخذت الخادمة ملابس سيّدها بالساعة وبكافة ما
كان فى جيوبه وأعطتها الرجل فأخذها المحتال وانصرف هاربًا

ولم تمض برهة وجيزة إلّا وحضر صاحب البيت ونادى على الخادمة بإحضار الملابس حتّى يمكنه التوجّه إلى الحاكم ويخبره بالقضية فأجابته الخادمة يا سيّدى أما،أنت أرسلت الآن شخصًا أخذ الهدوم ليوصّلها إليك فقال القبطان أنا ما بعثت أحدا مطلقًا وصار يلطم على وجهه ويقول أما كفاه أخذ النحاس ورجع وأخذ الحوائج أيضًا فأنت الآن أيّتها الامرأة طالقة وأنت أيّتها الخادمة مطرودة يا أولاد الكلب وبالحقيقة إنّ القبطان طلّق امرأته وطرد الخادمة وراحت عليه النحاس والهدوم فانظر هذا الحرامى المحتال —

Description of Kairo.

(From مختصر جغرافية مصر by جرجى زيدان)

يقطع القاهرة خليج يعرف بخليج مصر مارًّا من الجنوب إلى الشمال فيقسمها إلى قسمين متساويين تقريبًا.شرقى وغربى

وتقسم شوارع القاهرة إلى قسمين قديمة وحديثة فالشوارع القديمة يراد بها الشوارع التى فتحت قبل تبوّء العائلة المحمدية العلوية عرش الخديوية المصرية اى إلى سنة ١٨٠٥ ب والحديثة التى فتحت بعد ذلك وبما أن أقدم أجزاء القاهرة هو قسمها الشرقى كان أكثر الشوارع والبنايات القديمة واقعة فى تلك الجهة كما أن أشهر الشوارع والبنايات الحديثة واقع فى قسمها الغربى على الغالب ويمكن أن يقال أن الفاصل بين هذين القسمين خليج مصر

فأشهر الشوارع القديمة وهو بالحقيقة أطول شوارع القاهرة عموما شارع يخترق المدينة من الشمال إلى الجنوب فيبتدى

من باب الحسنية عند الزاوية الشمالية الشرقية وينتهى عند باب سعادة فى آخر حدود القاهرة جنوبا غير أن هذا الشارع الطويل لا يدعى كله باسم واحد بل كل جزء منه يعرف باسم خاص به كالحسينة والنحاسين والغورية وغيرها ويلى هذا الشارع شارع أقلّ منه طولًا يمرّ موازيًا له مرافقًا للخليج يبتدئ من جهة باب الشعرية شمالًا وينتهى عند باب السيدة زينب جنوبًا ومن أسماء أجزائه شوارع الشعراوى البرانى وبين السورين ومنصور باشا ودرب الجماميز آلخ[1] ومن الشوارع القديمة التى تمرّ من الشرق إلى الغرب شارع ممتدّ من باب البحر قرب شارع كلوت بك وينتهى فى شارع الجمالية ومن أسماء أجزائه شارع باب البحر وشارع سوق الزلط وشارع باب الشعرية وغيرها

ومن الشوارع الحديثة ما يخترق الشوارع القديمة كالسكة الجديدة التى باتصالها مع شارع الموسكى تقطع القاهرة من الغرب إلى الشرق يبتدئ الموسكى من ساحة الازبكية فى الغرب ثم يتّصل بالسكة الجديدة التى تنتهى خارج المدينة عند الجبل الشرقى

ومن الشوارع الحديثة شارع محمد على وهذا يبتدئ عند ابتداء الموسكى تقريبًا لكنه يسير نحو الشرق الجنوبى حتى ينتهى عند قلعة الجبل قرب الزاوية الشرقية الجنوبية للقاهرة

ومنها شارع كلوت بك وهذا يتّجه اتّجاه الشارع المتقدم ذكره لكنه يبتدئ من باب الحديد قرب الزاوية الشمالية الغربية للقاهرة وينتهى قرب الأزبكية وقد كان من مساعى الخديوى

---

[1] See Intro. § 17.

السابق الذى فتح هذا الشارع أن يجعله وشارع محمد على على استقامة واحدة مارًّا فى حديقة الأزبكية غير ان بعض أصحاب الأملاك التى لا بد له من هدمها فى فتح الشارع لم تتّفق معه على المبيع فاضطر أن يحرف الشارع عن استقامته كما هو الآن

وجميع الشوارع المتقدم ذكرها فتحت فتحا اى أنه كان فى مكانها مبان وهدمت من أجلها أمّا الشوارع الحديثة التى بُنِيت بناءً فكثيرة منها شارع فم الخليج وشارع المناخ وشارع الدواوين وغيرها كثير وجميع الشوارع المبنية حديثا تظللها أشجار من الجانبين

مبانى القاهرة وأشهر الأماكن فيها

إن الذى يجول فى هذه المدينة يرى فى بعض اقسامها أبنية فاخرة وقصورًا جميلة تحدق بها حدائق بهجة وتظلّل شوارعها أشجار غضة ويرى فى البعض الآخر بيوتًا وان ترآءى له على بعضها أثر النعمة الّا أنّه ينقبض لمنظرها وينطبق قلبه لما يرى فيها من دلائل الخراب كما هو الحال فى أكثر بنايات القسم الشرقى من المدينة وقد كانت تلك الأماكن فى أول أزمان القاهرة تُعدّ من أجمل المبانى المصرية وكان القسم الغربى إذ ذاك أرضًا قفرًا أو مستنقعًا لا يجف عنه الماء شتاءً ولا صيفا ولا يصلح للبناء أمّا الآن فقد انقلب الحال وأخذت القاهرة تغير مجدها إلى ما هو فى قسمها الغربى ولذلك ترى فى منتصف البلدة فى ما يقال له قسم الجمالية أو جهات باب الفتوح بيوتًا خربة ساقطة وليس مَن يرفع أنقاضها أو يرمها وقد أصبحت أثمان الأملاك

هناك بحسنة لا تقابل بما كانت عليه قبلًا وبضد ذلك القسم الغربى فإن الأملاك فيه تتحسن يومًا فيومًا

ومما يستحق الذكر فى القاهرة قلعتها التى عُرفت بقلعة الجبل وهى واقعة نحو الزاوية الجنوبية الشرقية فى سفح المقطّم بُنيت بأمر السلطان يوسف صلاح الدين الأيوبى فى الجيل السادس للهجرة وفيها بئر عجيبة عُرفت ببئر يوسف نسبة اليه وفى القلعة جامع عظيم يقال له جامع محمد على نسبة إلى محمد على باشا وفيه مدفنه

والأزبكية حديقة كبيرة واقعة فى قسم القاهرة الغربى تنظمت وبنيت على عهد العائلة المحمدية العلوية وقد كانت قبل ذلك بركة كبيرة يجرى اليها الماء أيام الفيضان ويبقى فيها مدار السنة

وفى القاهرة كثير من الجوامع المهمة القديمة والحديثة أقدمها جامع ابن طولون بُنِى فى منتصف القرن الثالث للهجرة فى الصليبية وهو خراب الآن واقدم من هذا جامع عمرو فى مصر القديمة يكاد يكون خرابًا وهذا أقدم جوامع القطر المصرى فقد بناه عمرو بن العاص فى الفسطاط عند فتح الديار المصرية

أمّا أهمّ جوامع القاهرة وأقدمها بعد المتقدم ذكرهما فالجامع الأزهر فهذا بُنى عند بناء القاهرة وفيه مدرسة جامعة تدرّس فيها العلوم الإسلامية والفقه وهى من أشهر المدارس الإسلامية فى العالم تعدّ تلامذتها بالآلاف وهناك جوامع أخرى بنيت بعد هذا بعضها خراب وبعضها لا يزال عامرا نذكرها بحسب قدمبتها وهى

جامع الحاكم عند باب الفتوح خراب وجامع الظاهر فى شارع الظاهر صار مخزنًا للأقوات وجامع قلاوون فى شارع النحاسين وجامع الناصرى فى القلعة وجامع السلطان حسن قرب القلعة وجامع المؤيّد وجامع الغورى فى شارع الغورية وجامع محمد على فى القلعة وغيرها

From the Romance المملوك الشارد by جرجى زيدان

سرّ عميق

وفى الصباح خرج الرهبان باكرًا كجارى العادة لجرف الثلوج التى تراكمت على أبواب الغرف وسطوحها تلك الليلة فلمّا كان الضحى استيقظ الضيوف وبعد تناول القهوة والطعام طلب العبد الانفراد برئيس الدير فى غرفة فانفردا

فقال العبد أعندكم للسرّ مكان قال الرئيس تكلم ولا تخف فاننا نحن جماعة الاكليروس قد عهد الينا فى حفظ أسرار الشعوب عندنا سرّ الاعتراف فقال العبد انى عالم بذلك وهذا هو داعى وثوقنا بك فاعلم يا حضرة الأب أننا لسنا من دمشق ولا من قراها وانما نحن من بلاد مصر وقد جئنا هذه البلاد فرارًا من القتل

قال الرئيس وكيف ذلك

قال العبد ان السيدة جميلة التى رأيتها هى زوجة أمير من أمراء المماليك الذين كانوا حكامًا فى مصر قبل ولاية الوالى الحالى المدعو محمد على باشا القوالى

فقاطعه الرئيس قائلًا وقد سمعنا ان محمد على باشا المشار

اليه قد ذبح أمراء المماليك السنة الماضية فى قلعة القاهرة بحيلة دعوتهم الى الاحتفال بخروج ابنه طوسون لمقاتلة الوهابيين

فقال العبد نعم يا سيدى وكان زوج هذه الأميرة فى جملة المدعوين الى ذلك الاحتفال وقد ذبح فى جملة من ذبح فاننا لم نسمع ان أحدًا منهم استطاع النجاة من تلك المذبحة فبعد ان قتل محمد على باشا هؤلاء الأمراء أباح لرجاله قتل كل من يلاقونه من أتباعهم فى كل جهات القطر فخرجت العساكر المصرية والأرناؤط والمغاربة وغيرهم على دور الأمراء وامعنوا فيها قتلًا ونهبًا وفتكًا بغير شفقة ولا حساب

وقد كنت فى بيت ذلك الأمير خصيًّا من خصيان قصره وكنت أحبّه حبًّا عظيمًا وكانت هذه الأميرة حاملًا ولها غُلام سنّه سبع سنوات وكان اسمه سليمًا فطلبت الىّ الفرار بها وبابنها من وجه الموت والعار وكنت عالمًا ان الصداقة وصدق الخدمة يظهران فى مثل هذه الحال فحملنا ما استطعنا حمله من خفيف الحمل وغالى الثمن وخرجنا من المدينة فى ظلام الليل على خيل الى خارجها وجددنا المسير مع صعوبة الركوب على تلك السيدة المنكودة الحظّ حتى بعدنا عن المدينة مسافة فوصلنا الى مكان اختبأنا فيه الى الصباح ثم سرنا فى الصباح التالى وما زلنا نجدّ السير ما استطعنا حتى دخلنا حدود سوريا ولا تسل عمّا قاسته هذه المسكينة من العذاب والمشقة وما ذرفته من الدموع السخينة

فنزلنا فى بلدة غزة فى بيت والناس هناك يسألون عنا فقلنا اننا من بلاد الترك نفيًا للشبهة وبعد بضعة أشهر آن وقت الولادة فوضعت هذا الغلام فدعوناه غريبا لانه ولد فى غربة

فلما تمت الولادة كما ذكرت اعملنا الفكرة فى وسيلة ننسى بها تلك المصائب ونعيش فى مكان يعزّى هذه الحزينة عن فقد زوجها فعلمنا بالاستقصاء أن جبل لبنان من أفضل ما خلق الله من الاماكن الجيّدة الهواء فتاقت نفسنا الى الإقامة فيه ولا سيما بعد ان سمعنا عن تيقظ أميره وتعهده راحة الرعية وسيادة الأمن فيهم وقد كنت فضلاً عن ذلك أرى فى سيدتى الأميرة ميلاً خصوصيًّا الى السكنى فيه لغير داعٍ أعلمه

فخرجنا من غزة فمررنا بيافا فاسترحنا فيها مدة ثم شددنا الرحال الى عكا وهناك أُصبنا بمصيبة لا تقلّ عن المصيبة الأولى بشىء

فأصاخ الرئيس أذنيه متلهفًا لما يقوله العبد وقد تأثر من حديثه تأثرًا أسقط عبراته لانه كان من ذوى الشفقة التى تكون على معظمها غالبًا فى من يعيشون عيش الفطرة بعيدًا من المدن

فأتم العبد كلامه قائلا تأمل أيها الأب المحترم بحظّ هذه المسكينة فانها بعد وصولنا الى عكا ببضعة أسابيع فقدت ابنها الأكبر بكيفية غريبة فقال الرئيس وكيف ذلك

فقال العبد اتّخذنا فى عكا مسكنًا منفردًا فى بعض المنازل على شاطئ البحر ترويحًا للنفس وتجنباً لانكشاف امرنا فكثنا فى تلك المدينة بضعة أسابيع نسأل عن أسهل السبل المؤدية الى لبنان وعن أفضل جهة من جهاته وكانت سيدتى الأميرة نظرًا الى شدة تعلقها بابنها سليم لانه مثال والده لا تردّ طلبه فى شىء فاتفق فى بعض الأيام انه رأى غلمان الحىّ ينزلون البحر بقارب صغير للنزهة فطلب الذهاب معهم فأبت والدته

خوفاً عليه من اللجج فألح عليها فأذنت له على أن أكون أنا برفقته فجرى بنا القارب فى البحر يسيرًا فسرّ سليم بذلك كثيرا ثم عدنا الى البرّ سالمين وقد لاحظت أثناء جرى القارب ان عينى الغلام لم تفارق النوتى لحظة بل كان يراقب حركاته وسكناته وكيفية استخدام المجذاف كأنه قد أحبّ مهنة الملاحة.

فلما وصلنا الشاطئ وجدنا هذه الوالدة فى انتظارنا فقبّلت الغلام وعدنا الى البيت ولكن لسوء الحظّ كان ذلك النوتى يرسو بقاربه بالقرب من منزلنا فيشده مساء فى صخر هناك ويذهب الى بيته فاذا عرض له ركّاب يأتى الى القارب فيحله ويذهب به ومتى انتهى منه يعود فيشده فى مكانه فبعد ذلك ببضعة ايام خرج الغلام يلعب خارج البيت كجارى العادة ونحن فى البيت ندبر بعض المهامّ لغريب فانشغلنا ساعتين ثم انتبهت والدته بغتة منادية أين سليم فقلت لها تركته يلعب أمام البيت ثم خرجنا نفتش عنه فلم نقف له على أثر فصاحت ويلاه قد فقد الولد فأخذت أناديه واستطلع أمره عبثا ثم نظرت الى البحر فلم ار القارب وقد كان منذ أيام لا ينفك مشدودًا بالشاطئ فقلت فى نفسى أظنّه ركب فيه يجرب نفسه فى مهنة الملاحة فقذفته الأمواج الى حيث لا نعلم

أمّا هذه الوالدة فأخذت تصيح وتندب نفسها وولدها وتقطع شعرها حتّى أُغمى عليها وأنا فى حيرة فأخذت فى تسكين روعها ثم سرت أفتش عن الغلام فى جوار المنزل وبعثت مناديًا

ينشده فى الأسواق فلم أقف له على خبر وبعد التفتيش عنه أربعة أيام يئسنا من لقائه فكرهنا البقاء فى تلك المدينة والمصيبة الكبرى أننا لم نكن نستطيع الظهور أمام الحكومة لنطلب إليها التفتيش عن الغلام بأكثر دقة خوفًا من كشف أمرنا وعود ذلك وبالًا علينا

فغادرنا عكا ونحن فى حالة يرثى لها من الحزن والكدر وهذه المسكينة لا تنفك عن البكاء لا ليلًا ولا نهارًا حتى أسقمت ولدها الآخر من إرضاعه لبان الهموم والأحزان قال ذلك وتساقطت العبرات من عينيه فبكى معه الرئيس ثم قال العبد فبالاختصار أيها الأب المحترم إننا وصلنا صيدا وهناك علمنا أن هذه الجهة من أفضل جهات لبنان فأخذنا فى المسير من قرية إلى أخرى وقد صممنا على الإقامة فى مكان منفرد فهدانا بعض العارفين إلى هذا الدير فسرنا صباح أمس على أمل الوصول اليكم عند الظهيرة ورافقنا رجل من بعض القرى معظم الطريق وكلما سألناه عن المكان المقصود يقول ها قد وصلنا فانه لا يبعد عنا أكثر من مرمى حجر أو طول رسن البغل أو مقدار شرب سيكاره أو غير ذلك ونحن قد أنهكنا التعب وتبللت ثيابنا من الأمطار وقاسينا من البرد أشد العناء ولم يكن يمكننا الركوب لوعرة الطرق فغربت الشمس فى مكان قيل لنا أنه قرية بيت الدين مسكن أمير هذه البلاد

فلما وصلنا إلى هناك أشار الرجل إلى مكان هذا الدير وقال اعذرانى إنى لا يمكننى الوصول معكما إلى هناك وودعنا ورجع كل ذلك والبرد شديد والثلوج متراكمة وقد لامنا كثيرون على

قدومنا إلى هذه الأماكن فى فصل الشتاء ولكن المقدر كائن لا ينمحى

وبعد أن فارقنا ذلك الرجل لقينا رجلًا متسربلًا بعباءة سوداء يظهر عليه أنه ليس من عامة الناس فسألنا عن جهة مسيرنا بكل لطف فاجبناه أن علينا نذرًا للدير الفلانى وقد أتينا الآن لوفائه فقال أتريدان أن أرافقكما إلى ذلك الدير لأنى أراكما غريبى الديار قلنا ولكم الفضل فلما وصلنا إلى باب الدير وقف بنا الرجل هنيهة ثم قال لنا هذا هو المكان فاقرعوه يفتح لكم ثم ودعنا وسار فشكرنا فضله وقرعنا باب الدير ودخلنا على ما رأيتمونا

فقلق الرئيس لئلا يكون ذلك الرفيق جاسوسًا من جواسيس الامير بشير ويكون قد سمع شيئًا ممّا قالوه ولكن تأثره من حكاية سعيد شغله عن الافتكار بغيرها

فالتفت الرئيس إلى سعيد قائلا طب نفسا يا ولدى وقرّ عينًا فقد حفظت كل مقالك فى صدرى سرًّا ونطلب من الله سبحانه وتعالى أن يعزّى هذه المسكينة ويهبها الصبر الجميل على أحزانها فإذا شئتما الإقامة عندنا فمرحبًا بكما فإنكما ستحلان الرحب والسعة وإلّا فانى مستعد لقضاء كل ما تحتاجون اليه ولا فرق عندى بين أن تكونا مسيحيين أو غير مسيحيين فاننا جميعا نعبد الاله الواحد القهار وفضلا عن ذلك فإن الديانة الإسلامية هى ديانة مولانا السلطان صاحب البلاد

Extracts from Journals.

1. From the Egyptian journal الأهرام.

خليفة البابا

تهتم الجرائد الألمانية فى هذه الأيام بمن سيكون خليفة البابا متى قضى الله أمره فيه وكلها تشكو الحكومة الفرنسوية بأنها ساعية فى أن يكون هذا الخلف كردينالًا فرنسويًا وقالت جريدة الطَجْبلاط فى برلين من مقالة عنوانها الحقيقة على الفاتيكان انه بالرغم عن صحة البابا وسلامته قد كثر الاهتمام فى خلافته وان مجمع الكردينالية القادم سيكون عظيمًا جدًا ويظهر انه يستحيل الاتفاق بينهم وان بعضهم يهتم فى ان يكون الكردينال لافيجرى هذا الخلف وهو معضد فى هذا الشأن بحزب عظيم من الكردينالية الأجانب وفى جملتهم بعض الكردينالية الألمانيين والنمسويين

ألمانيا

كان فى ٧ الجارى تذكار السنة لموت الامبراطورة أوغسطا وقد فتح فيه اكتتاب لإقامة تمثال لها فى برلين

اشتد البرد فى كل ألمانيا ولا سيما على شواطئها حتى تعذرت المواصلات وأصبح أكثرها صعبًا لكثرة الثلوج المتساقطة

الحمى فى فلورانسا

لا تزال الحمى التيفوسية تفتك فى هذه المدينة ولا يزال سكانها يهربون الى القرى وقد أُصيبت حاميتها بإصابات كثيرة وتحقق اليوم ان منشأها من سوء مياه الابار إذ قد ظهر من فحص مياه ١٠٠ بئر ان ٨٦ بئرًا منها حاوية جراثيم هذا

الداء وقد أمرت البلدية بسدّها وأخذت توزع على الأهالى ماء غالبًا ولا سيما للعساكر والمدارس والفقراء وقد بنيت عدة أفران خاصة لتطهر ببخارها بعض الموادّ المحتوية على هذا المرض

رسائل داخلية

شبين الكوم فى ١٥ لوكيلنا العام

قدم امس (الاربعا) الى بندرنا حضرة محمد بك وكيل تفتيش عموم السجون فقابله على المحطة حضرة حكمدار البوليس ومأمور السجن وقد تفقد سجون المديرية فسرّه ما رآه من انتظام حالتها وتعهد الاعمال الجارية فى بناء الليمان استنهض هموم العمال لانجازها

وورد اليوم بلاغ للمديرية مؤداه ان بعض اللصوص اعترضوا محمد أبو طبل ودرويش عبد الله القماشين فى منوف بينما كانا عائدين من سوق سرسنا الى بلدهما بالطريق المؤدية من السرساوية الى جنينة الدفراوى فى نحو الساعة الثانية عربية من ليل امس وسلبوا ما كان معهما من الانسجة وفرّوا لاجئين الى المزارع وقد توجه حضرة مأمور مركز منوف ومعاون بوليسه الى محل الحادثة واقتفيا اثر اللصوص حتى قبضا على ثلاثة منهم وهم من منوف وضواحيها وهى مأثرة لحضرة المامور والمعاون جديرة بالشكر نذكرها مضيفين اليها ما بلغنا من ان سعادتلو المدير قد كافأهما عن هذا العمل بان أرسل لهما كتابًا يشكرهما عليه ولا بدع فانهما أهل للثناء والمدح

نذكر حضرات المقاولين ولا سيما الوطنيين منهم بانه فى ٢٠ الجارى تفتح الطلبات المقدمة للمناقصة على مقاولة

الاعمال النيلية ونحثهم على تقديم طلباتهم عاجلاً لئلا تفوتهم الفائدة والله ولى التوفيق

بركة السبع .

فى ١٤ لمكاتبنا

توجهت اليوم لمركز السنطة فوجدت تلك النقطة آخذة أسباب التقدم لوجود المركز بها ولا سيما وان محطتها صارت منظمة للغاية لتصليحها فى هذا العام فضلاً عن زيادة ايراداتها عن العام الماضى الزيادة التى توجب لناظرها مزيد الشكر

ثم ان معاون محطتها الشاب النبيه حضرة محمد افندى ذكى من الذين تعلموا فى مدارسنا الاميرية وقد وجدت الجميع يثنون عليه كل الثناء ومسرورين من حسن استقامته فى الأشغال

حوادث محلية

غامت السماء يوم أمس واليوم ولم تمطر الّا قليلاً أما الهواء فساكن

بلغ عدد المواليد فى أتمّ مدن القطر فى الأسبوع الذى آخره ٨ ينائر الجارى ١٣٢٣ منها ٤٦١ فى العاصمة و٢٦٥ فى الاسكندرية وبلغ عدد الوفيات فى الأسبوع نفسه ٨٢٤ منها ٣٣٤ فى العاصمة و١٥٩ فى الاسكندرية والباقى فى سائر مدن القطر

وردت البراءة السلطانية من دار السعادة العلية الى حضرة الوجيه المسيو مرسيه مصدقة على تعيينه ويس قنصل لدولة

فرنسا الفخيمة فى دمنهور والعطف ايضًا .وقد بلغت حكومتنا بهذا الشأن الذى نعتبره فى محله لما نعهده فى حضرة من الاهلية والاستحقاق

اعلان

من محل تجارة جوانى زنانيرى التاجر

المشهور بالموسكى

محل جوانى زنانيرى التاجر المشهور بالموسكى الذى أُنشى من سنة ١٨٦٤ يعلن الجمهور وعلى الخصوص حضرات زبائنه المحترمين بانه اجابةً لطلب جملة من اصحابه العديدين الذين يعهدون به الامانة واتقان التفصيل على اخر موضة وانتقاء الاقمشة الجيدة النسيج والثابتة الالوان بان ورد له اخيرًا من اشهر اوريقات اوربا بفرنسا جانب عظيم من البدل الجاهزة للبس الرجال والاولاد والستات وجميع ذلك ملبوس فصل الشتاء والاعياد القابلة وايضًا قمصان ومناديل وشرابات وفانيلات .وجملة اصناف اخر ولاجل راحة الزبائن والاصحاب قد جعل الاثمان عن كافة البضائع فى غاية المهاودة حتى لا يمكن للغير ان يبيع بمثلها ومن شرف محله ينسرّ من حسن البضائع والوانها ومهاودة اسعارها والاعتناء بخدمة الزبائن

اعلان

ان محل سبانس وشركائه المشهور بالحسن المشروبات المرطبة يتشرف باعلان زبائنه العديدين انه يوجد فى محله اكثر من

٣٦ صنفا من تلك المشروبات مثل ماء الصوده والليموناده وشراب البرتقال والرمان والبيره وغيرها من المشروبات الطيبة المصطنعة بمزيد العناية والانتباه لحالة الاقليم المصرية ومحرمات السادة المسلمين ثم يوجد في المحل الواسع الشهير اجناس وافرة من الخمر والكنياك والعرق وسائر المشروبات الروحية المصنوعة فى أحسن المعامل فى اوربا ذلك فضلاً عن اجناس مختلفة من انواع المشروبات المصنوعة فى المحل نفسه

وان محله المدعو كران بار المشهور فى مصر بأسرها مستعد لان يفتح ليلًا ونهاراً لخدمة الجمهور من احسن جنس من المشروبات المثلجة وكذلك البوفه رستوران التابعة لهذا المحل المشهورة بحسن طبخها واتقان ماكلها ولذتها تعد العموم بانها تقوم بكامل خدمتهم من كل ما يطلبون مع النظافة واتقان الخدمة ومهاودة الاسعار فكل من شرفها يجد ما يسره باذن الله

الن والدرسن وشركاؤهم بالاسكندرية

توكيلهم محل بمصر بالازبكية بشارع وجه البركة بملك الخواجا مليكة شابى ووكيلهم الخواجا البرتو فانوتشة وهذا المحل هو من اشهر واسبق المحلات بالقطر المصرى فى مبيع جميع انواع الآلات البخارية ونوازمها وعلى استعداد تام فى تادية الطلبات باسرع ما يمكن

---

2. From the Syrian journal لسان الحال.

مراسلات

لبنان

فى ٦ الجارى

ليلة الخميس الواقعة فى ١٣ ت٢ بينما كان مارون يوسف البستانى وامرأته نائمين فى بيت الخواجا فضل الله بسترس الكائن على الرويسة بخراج قرية عيثات (حيث هو وكيل على لبيت المومأ اليه وبيت الخواجا خليل سرسق ايضا) واذا بشخص خارج البيت يقول يا صاحب البيت اعمل معروف ودلنا على طريق بيصور لاننى غريب المحل وخذ اجرتك ربع مجيدى فخرج مارون ليدله على الطريق واذا باشخاص ابتدروا مارون بالضرب فركضت امرأته لتستغيث فابتدرها احدهم ايضا بالضرب وهى تركض وتصرخ اما مارون فوقع على الارض مغشيا عليه وكان صوت الصراخ قد علا فحضر البعض الى مكان الحادثة فوجدوا مارون وامرأته طريحين على الارض فادخلوهما البيت واعلمت الكيفية لجناب رفعتلو محمد بك تلحوك مدير الغرب الذى كان وقتئذ فى الشويفات وراجعا الى عيثات ليلا فارسل حالا الضابطة للمحل المذكور وعمل جرنال الحادثة واخذ قرارات مارون وامرأته اللذين اوقعا التهمة على ستة اشخاص من قرية عيثات وما انبثق الفجر حتى صار الاشخاص المذكورون فى قبضة يده وكان قد استدعى حالا بالطبيب ليلا لروية مارون وأمرأته ومعالجتهما والحاصل انه احيا الليل بالقبض والتفتيش وعمل الجرنال الى

الصباح وارسل المتهمين تحت الحفظ لمركز القايمقامية وحينئذ بوقته وجد واحد المتهمين متغيباً عن المحل فوضعه تحت المراقبة الى ان القى القبض عليه فى الليلة الثانية عند منتصف الليل فما اجراه جناب البك المومأ اليه استوجب ممنونية الجميع ونهار السبت اى بعد الحادثة بثلاثة أيام حضر طبيب مركز المتصرفية لرؤية مارون وثانى يوم الاحد حضر مستنطق القضاء بصدد هذه الحادثة ايضاً اما مارون وامرأته فلله الحمد اخذا بالتقدم نحو الصحة

تلغرافات

رومية. حصل زلزال فى مدينة بازينسيانو من عمل كالابرا فدمرها وقد انتشل ٣٠ جثة من تحت الردم حتى الآن ولا يزال كثيرون مفقودين وقد امتد هذا الزلزال الى القرى المجاورة فالحق بها ايضاً اضراراً عظيمة

حوادث بلدية

مساء الجمعة قدم ثغرنا حضرة النشيط صاحب العزة محمد بك مدعى عمومى ولاية سورية قاصداً طرابلس الشام للنظر فى امور هامة فاستقبله فى الحازمية عدد من المامورين

تلقينا بمزيد السرور خبر توجيه النشان العثمانى من الصنف الرابع الى جناب صاحب العزة بشاره افندى سرمهندس الولاية لما اظهره من الهمة والنشاط فى اخراج آثار صيداء لا زالت احسانات الحضرة العلية السلطانية غامرة عبيدها الصادقين

اعلانات

ان الخواجا نخله كميد قد عين نهار الجمعة من بعد الظهر حتى غروب الشمس للمزاد العمومى على المفروشات الباقية عنده المعدودة للبيع الى الزايد الاخير وهى بيانو من الخشب الباليسندر وسجادات مفتخرة وطقم صالو من النسيج الفاخر وخزانة لوضع اوانى المائدة وطاولة سفرة وثريات وقناديل مختلفة الاشكال واشياء كثيرة خلافها لا يستغنى عنها فى البيوت كبيرة كانت ام صغيرة

اقلامنا الحديدية العربية

ان جودة هذه الاقلام قد اشتهرت لدى الجميع فى كل البلدان ومكاتب ومدارس شتى اختبرتها وعولت عليها ولما كان قد ورد لطرفنا اقلام تقليد اقلامنا هذه رأينا ان نحذر العموم بان اقلامنا مبصوم عليها اسمنا بالخط العربى فحذارِ حذار من التقليد. صاحبا المكتبة الجامعة. يطلب الى المكتبة الجامعة ولدًا بصفة خادم يحسن القراءة والكتابة والمخابرة فى ذلك مع صاحبيها

خليل وامين الخورى

وضع جناب رفعتلو الشيخ خطار افندى الدحداح كتابًا فى مبادىء القراءة الفرنسوية الحقه بنبذ منتخبة تنطوى على نكت ونصائح وامور من متعلقات الصناعة كالورق والحبر والاقلام والمطابع والمكينات البخارية وسكك الحديد. والمع عن سورية وما فيها من المدن والمحصولات والصنائع والسكان

وختمه بما يستولى على الانسان من الافراح والاحزان وبما لكلٍ من حواس الانسان فجاء كتاباً ابتدائيًا جلى العبارة حسن الاسلوب سهل الماخذ كبير الفائدة لمن يتعلم اللغة الفرنسوية يباع بمكتبة المطبعة الادبية وثمنه ثلاثة غروش

مدرسة البنات

ان مدرسة البنات فى سوق الغرب الكائنة بجانب بيت جناب الخواجا موسى سرسق المشتملة على عشر غُرَف وقطعة ارض فسيحة امامها مطروحة للمبيع فمن شاء شراءها والوقوف على كامل التفصيلات فليخابر جناب الخواجات هيلد وشركاه فى بيروت او الدكتور كارسلو رئيس المدارس الانكليزية اللبنانية فى الشوير

كاتبه

الدكتور كارسلو

ان كتاب الايضاحات الوفية فى قواعد اللغة العثمانية تأليف يوسف افندى حسنى الذى كان طبع قديمًا قد نفذ فاعيد طبعه الان بعد ان اضيف اليه افادات جمة وضُبِط بالشكل اللازم وطبع على ورق جيد باحرف جميلة وتسهيلاً للحصول عليه ورغبة فى زيادة انتشاره لتعميم فوائده عينا ثمن النسخة منه مجلدة ربع ريال مجيدى مع ان عدد صفحاته ٤٣٣ فمن رغب فى مشتراه[1] يطلبه من مكتبة المطبعة الادبية ومن مكاتب بيروت

[1] See Less. 34, 4.

اعلان

من مخزن البضائع الانكليزية

فى بيروت

اذا اردت الحصول على احسن انواع البضائع الانكليزية كالسكاكين والعويسيات وامواس الحلاقة والمقصات فعليك بمخزن البضائع الانكليزية فى سوق اياس فتشاهد جميع ما ترغبه من هذه الانواع وخلافها من البضائع المتقنة الصنعة الحسنة الجنس والبيع فيه بالمفرق وبالجملة باسعار موافقة للشارين الذين اختبروا لحد الآن حسن اجناس كل البضائع التى تباع فى المخزن المذكور

Letters.

Invitations.

الى جناب الاجل الاكرم

ارجو ان تشرف محلك هذا مع حضرة السيدة قرينتك المحترمة يوم الاحد القادم الساعة السادسة للغداء لنغتنم أُنس محاضرتكما لا زلتما على خير

الداعى
فلان

الجواب

سيدى كريم الشيم الخواجا فلان المحترم

قد تلقيت الدعوة بالطاعة وفى الوقت المعيّن نتشرف بالدار العامرة نقدم واجبات الثناء والاحترام ولا زالت بلابل الأُنس تغرد فى حديقة دارك بمنه ورحمته.

الداعى
فلان

الى حضرة الخواجا فلان الاكرم

ارجوك ان تتكرم فى الاحد الآتى بان تشرف للعشاء فى منزلك هذا احتفالًا بتذكار مولد صديقك

الداعى
فلان

الجواب

سيدى الاكرم

فى الطف ساعة وفدت علىّ الرسالة الكريمة التى تأمر بها ان اتشرف بدارك العامرة للعشاء وسنلبى امرك بالطاعة ونذهب بالوقت المعيّن نغتنم فرصة الأُنس ان شاء الله الداعى

فلان

سيدى الاخ الاعز الاكرم

اعرض انى منذ ساعة قد وصلت عائدًا من دمشق فان كانت الاشغال تسمح لسيدى الاخ ان يشرّفنى هنيهةً من الزمان فان عندى ما اخبره به ممّا يسرّ خاطره وانا فى البيت نهارى كله مستعدّ لتشريفه ساعة يريد لا عدمت وجوده

الداعى

فلان

جوابه

سيدى المحترم

سرّنى نبأُ عود سيدى من سفره سالمًا وسأذهب للتسليم عليه فى الساعة السبعة اطفاء لغليل الشوق بعذوبة مرآه اطال الله وجوده الداعى

فلان

Private letters.

عزيزى

ارجوك ان تنتظرنى فانى سآتى عن قريب لاتشرف بمقابلة حضرتكم فان انتظرت محسوبك فلك منه مزيد الشكر والثناء والا اذا لم تكن تريد الانتظار فعيّن لى وقتاً تاتى فيه الىّ باكر تاريخه فانى خرجت فى هذا الوقت لشغل ضرورى ومنى على جنابكم ازكى السلام الداعى

مصر فى ٧ سبتمبر ١٨٩٦ فلان

صديقنا الخواجا فلان العزيز

بعد السؤال عن خاطركم نرجو ان تكون بغاية الصحة والسلامة ثم اننا نقدم لك التهنئة بقدوم السنة الجديدة. هذا واننا مشتاقون كثيرًا لرؤياكم ومشاهدة برلين اللطيفة فى هذه الايام ايام عيد الميلاد. وساكتب لك ايها الصديق خطابا مطولا فى هذين اليومين لانى كنت مقصرًا كل التقصير. وسلم لنا على جميع الاحباب والسلام الصديق

مصر فى ٢٣ دسمبر ١٨٩٠ فلان

شقيقى الافخم

سررت جدًا من حيازة حضرتكم كمال الصحة والعافية وفرحت بمكافأة حضرتكم لى بالكتاب المشتمل على تصاوير واحيط شريف العلم ان العياط صار عندى مثل ابليس اللعين لا اتخذه خلّا وان شاء الله ساصرف فى ظل الحضرة الفخيمة الابوية ونفوس حضرتكم همتى ونشاطى فى علوم المدارس التجهيزية فى السنة القابلة للحصول على ما يسرك ثم انى تمت بوصية حضرتكم فقبلت ايدى والدى واقرأت اخوتى واخواتى السلام ولم اقدر على تقبيل الايادى والوجنات افندم كاتبه

فلان

Business letters.

عزيزنا الافخم وصديقنا الاكرم حضرة خليل افندى

دام بقاؤه

بعد اهداء مزيد السلام والاشواق نخبر حضرتكم ان الداعى لتحريره هو السؤال عن صحتكم واحوالكم حيث لم

يرد لنا منكم جواب من مدة طويلة نطمئنّ به عليكم فالامل ان تواصلونا بالمكاتبة فانها كما قيل نصف المشاهدة ونحن بغاية الصحة وسائر الاصحاب لا سيما صاحب الطرفين احمد افندى سالم يهدونكم ازكى السلام. هذا والرجاء من حضرتكم ان ترسلوا لنا عينة غطيان من شغل محلكم وستائر حيث انى اريد ان اعرضها على بعض محلات البيع حتى اذا استحسنوها نطلب من حضرتكم جملة من جنسها او خلاف ذلك وبلغوا سلامنا لحضرة اخيكم المحترم والعائلة الكريمة والانجال واقبلوا منى مزيد الاحترام

كاتبه
محبكم
على كمال
بمصر

فى ٣٦ يونيه ١٨٨٩

الى جناب الماجد المحترم حفظه الله

بعد اهداء السلام والاكرام اعرض انى قد فتحت مخزناً كبيراً وملأته من البضائع الباريزية الحسنة الجيدة الملائمة لمطاليب سكان البلاد فى مكثر ومقلّ ووسط وقد توسلت الى استجلابها باعظم ما يمكن من المراعاة فى السعر رغبةً فى مصلحتى ومصلحة الوطن وهذا المحلّ التجارى رهين امرك فما شئتَ من نسائجه وانواع بضائعه يرسل أقلّ من ثمن مثله هنا نظراً للوسيلة التى توصلت بها الى المراعاة فى امر السعر على ما تقدم

هذا ما دعت اليه الحال ور ى ان تشرفنى بكل خدمة تعرض للجناب وطال بقائك سيدى

الداعى
فلان

ايها السادة المحترمون

غب تأدية واجب الاحترام نعرض اننا تشرفنا بكتابكم الكريم الصادر بتاريخ كذا من الشهر الماضي وعلمنا منه طلبكم صورة الحساب فهى واصلة طيه لنا وقد اتخذنا هذه الفرصة وسيلة الى الشكر على جميع ما فعلتم معنا من الجميل اثناء هذه السنة راجين ان نبقى اهلاً لخدمتكم بما يلزم وسنفرغ الجهد فى كل ما تأمرون به واطال الله بقاءكم الداعى

فلان

جوابه

من فى سنة

بعد اداء ما يجب ويليق من السلام والاكرام اعرض ان قد وصلت الىّ رسالتك الكريمة المؤرخة بكذا وفى طيها صورة الحساب المطلوبة الّا انى اسفت لمجيئها غير منطبقة على ما فى دفاترى ولذا استنهض همتك الى مراجعة فحص الحساب بما ينبغى من التدقيق فقد وقعَ فيه خطاء صريح فى حساب الارباح فان مبلغ الميزانية فى حسابك كذا وكذا ليس غير والصحيح انه كذا وكذا هذا ما اعرضه الان مختومًا بتهنئتك باستهلال هذه السنة المباركة واطال بقاءك الداعى

فلان

Receipts, Leases etc.

تذكرة منصرفة مجاناً

رخصة

من ديوان عموم الاوقاف

قد تصرح لرافع هذه الرخصة مسيو فلان ومعه ثلاثة اشخاص بان يزور المساجد والمدافن والتكايا الشريفه بمصر

المحروسة والزيارة تكون فى غير اوقات الصلاة وهذا التصريح لا يتجاوز مدّة ثلاثة ايام من ابتداء تاريخه

تحريرًا ٢٣ اكتوبر سنة ١٨٩٧

وصول اقتراض

قروش

٣٠٠

فقط ثلاثمائة قرش لا غير

بتاريخه وصلنى من فلان مبلغ ثلاثمائة قرش وذلك بوجه القرض بلا فائض الى كذا يومًا واشعارًا بوصول المبلغ المرقوم الى يدى كاملًا كُتب هذا الوصل فى . . . سنة

كاتبه

فلان

وصول اجرة

بتاريخه وصلنى من فلان مبلغ مائة قرش وذلك اجرة محل سكن او حانوت عن ثلاثة اشهر مستحق وفاؤه فى كذا من شهر كذا وايذانًا بوصول المبلغ الى يدى كاملًا رقمت له هذا الوصل فى . . . سنة

كاتبه

فلان

كمبيالة

قروش

١٢٠٠

فقط الف ومائتا قرش لا غير

بعد مرور ثلاثة اشهر ندفع لامر فلان المبلغ المرقوم اعلاه قدره الف ومائتا قرش لا غير فضة وذهبًا على سعر نقود تجارة

بيروت والقيمة وصلت الى يدى منه ثمن بضاعة وللبيان كُتب
فى . . . سنة كاتبه
شهود الحـــال فلان

تحويل
قروش
٥٠٠
فقط خمسمائة قرش لا غير

ارجو من فلان ان يدفع لامر فلان لدى الاطلاع المبلغ المرقوم اعلاه وقدره خمسمائة قرش من النقود المتعارفة والقيمة ثمن كذا وللبيان كتب فى . . . سنة كاتبه
شهود الحـــال فلان

مبيع
الحمد لله وحده

انه فى . . . شهر . . . سنة . . . حضرت مجلس عقده هند بنت عمرو من البلد الفلانى فى صحة عقل وسلامة بدن وباعت من فلان وفلان ولدى فلان من البلد المذكور قطعة الارض الواقعة فى موضع يقال له كذا من اراضى البلد الموما اليه المشتملة على شجر توت المتصلة الى البائعة بالشراء الشرعى من زوجها فلان بموجب صك عليه تصديق محكمة القضاء والقطعة ممسوحة تحت عدد كذا محدودة قبلةً وغربًا بملك المشترين وشرقًا وشمالاً بملك البائعة والحد الفاصل حائط باعتهما اياه بيعًا باتًّا بجميع حقوق هذا المبيع واستحقاقه وطرقه وطرائقه وتوابعه ولواحقه ومضافاته ومشتملاته وبكل حق هو له

وفيه بثمن معجل قدره كذا . . . اقرّت البائعة المذكورة بقبضه
تماماً وكمالاً وانه لم يبق لها فى المبيع المذكور ولا فى ثمنه
ملك ولا شبهة ملك ولا حق ولا دعوى اصلاً ووالد المشترين
فلان قبل الشراء لولديه بمالهما لانفسهما فيما بينهما مناصفةً
على الوجه المذكور وبياناً لذلك كُتب الواقع بتاريخ اعلاه
المقرّ بما فيه

شهود الحـــال فلان

عدد . . . تصديق المحكمة

الحمد لله تعالى

انه فى . . . حضرت فلانة البائعة وفلان القابل الشراء بالوكالة ولديه فلان وفلان وتصادقا على مضمون هذا الصك

وللبيان سجل فى محكمة قضا . . . تطبيقاً للنظام العالى

(مكان الختم) الفقير اليه تعالى

قاضى قضاء فلان

ايجار دارٍ

وجه تسطيره

انه بتاريخه ادناه قد آجر فلان المعتبرة تصرفاته الشرعية فلاناً وكلاهما من المدينة الفلانية جميع داره الواقعة ضمن سور المدينة المشتملة على ستّ غرف سفلية ومطبخ وجنينة فيها بئر ماء نابع المحدودة شرقاً بدار فلان وغربا بدار فلان وشمالاً وجنوباً بملك الآجر المذكور ليسكنها سنة كاملة مبتداها تاريخ هذه الوثيقة بأجرة قدرها الف وخمسمائة

قرش من النقود الرائجة المتعامل بها فى هذه البلاد موزعةً على الاشهر او مقبوضة حالًا اجارةً صحيحة شرعية مشتملة على الايجاب والقبول مسبوقة بالرؤية التامة المعتبرة لمورد عقد الأجارة وسلّم الموجر الى المستاجر جميع الدار المستاجرة فارغةً غير مشغولة بما يمنع الانتفاع بها على ان يسلم اليه الاجرة موزّعة على الشهور كل شهر قسطه من الاجرة مائة قرش وخمسة وعشرون قرشًا وعلى هذا تراضيا بحضرة الشهود المذكورة اسماؤهم فيه واشعارًا بالواقع كتب فى . . . شهر . . . سنة

المقرّ بما فيه

شهود الحـــــال فلان

Vocabulary

of words (arranged according to roots) in the Exercises and Selections in Part II.

NB. The vowels in brackets after a verb indicate of the 2nd radical in the Imperf. vn. = verbal noun. n. pr. = proper name.

أ particle of interrogation.

أَبَدًا (with negative) never.

إِبْرَة plur. إِبَر needle.

إِبْرٰهِيم Ibrahim, Abraham.

إِبِل camel (coll.).

إِبْن son — إِبْنَة daughter, girl (see بنو).

أَب (ابو) father — أَبَوِيّ fatherly.

أَبُو نُوَاس n. pr. of the court-fool of Harûn Arrashîd.

أَبَى (a) to refuse.

أَتَى (i) to come — with بِ to bring — آتٍ following.

أَثَر II. to move — V. to be influenced — أَثَر plur. آثَار ruins, antiquities — مَأْثَرَة notable matter.

أَجَر IV. to let — X. to hire — أُجْرَة and إِجَارَة reward, price, hire — أَجِير hireling.

أَجَل period, death — لِأَجْلِ for (the sake of), that — مِنْ أَجْلِ for the sake of.

أَحَد fem. إِحْدَى one — نَهَارُ ٱلْأَحَدِ sunday.

أَخَذَ (u) to take, get — (with imperf.) to begin to — III. to blame — VIII. to take for oneself — vn. أَخْذ taking — مَأْخَذ conception.

أَخَّر V. to be late — آخَرُ fem. أُخْرَى plur. أُخَر other — آخِر and أَخِير last, end — عَنْ آخِرِهِمْ to the last man.

أخ (اخو) plur. إِخْوَة and إِخْوَان brother — أُخْت plur. أَخَوَات sister.

أدّب II. to discipline — أَدَب training — أَدِيب trained, cultured — أَدَبِيّ of good training.

أدّى II. and IV. to transmit, carry out, accomplish.

إِذْ when, since (conj.) — إِذْ ذَاكَ at that time.

إِذَا behold! — إِذَا when, if — إِذًا then.

أَذِنَ to permit (with بِ) — IV. to announce — X. to ask permission — إِذْن permission — أُذُن ear.

آذى IV. to injure — أَذًى damage.

أَرَب aim.

أرّخ II. to date.

أَرْض plur. أَرَاضٍ earth, land.

أَرِقَ (a) to be sleepless — vn. أَرَق.

أَرْنَاؤُد arnauts, albanians.

أَرْنَب hare.

أَسَد plur. أُسُود lion.

أَسْر captivity — بِأَسْرِهِمْ all, entirely — أَسِير prisoner of war.

أَسِفَ (a) to be afflicted — V. to vex oneself — أَسَف vexation.

اَلْإِسْكَنْدَرِيَّة Alexandria.

إِسْم plur. أَسْمَاء name, (see سمو).

اَلْإِسْمَاعِيلِيَّة the Ismailia (a quarter of Cairo).

إِصْطَبْل stall.

أصّل X. to root out — أَصْل origin — أَصْلاً altogether.

أُفُق horizon.

أَفَنْدِي (αὐθέντης) sir — أَفَنْدِيم my master.

أُكْتُوبِر october.

أكّد II. to assure — V. to be assured.

أَكَلَ (u) to eat — vn. أَكْل — مَأْكَل food.

إِكْلِيرُوس clerus.

أَلْ the definite article.

ٱلَّذِى fem. ٱلَّتِى plur. ٱلَّذِينَ who, which.

أَلِفَ (a) to become accustomed to — II. to edit — III. to be familiar with — أَلْفٌ plur. آلَافٌ and أُلُوفٌ thousand — تَأْلِيفٌ book.

أَلَمٌ pain.

أَلْمَانٌ a German — أَلْمَانِىٌّ German — أَلْمَانِيَا Germany.

إِلٰهٌ a god — أَللّٰهُ God, Allah.

إِلَى to — unto — إِلَى أَنْ until.

أَمْ or (in an alternative).

أُمٌّ mother — أَمَامَ before (prep.).

أَمَّا as for.

إِمْبَرَاطُورٌ emperor.

أَمَرَ (u) to command, (with accus. of the person and بِ of the thing) — أَمْرٌ plur. أَوَامِرُ command; plur. أُمُورٌ matter — أَمِيرٌ Emir, Prince — أَمِيرُ ٱلْمُؤْمِنِينَ Prince of the faithful — أَمِيرِىٌّ imperial — مَأْمُورٌ an official.

أَمْسِ yesterday.

أَمَلَ II. to hope — V. to consider — أَمَلٌ plur. آمَالٌ hope.

أَمِنَ (a) to be safe — IV. to believe (in بِ) — VIII. to rely on — أَمْنٌ safety — أَمَانَةٌ reliability, deposit — أَمِينٌ true, Emin (n. pr.) — مُؤْمِنٌ believer — مُؤْتَمَنٌ a reliable person.

أَنْ and أَنَّ that.

إِنْ if — إِلَّا if not, else — لَا — إِلَّا only — إِلَّا أَنَّ except that.

إِنَّ truly, verily — إِنَّمَا only.

أَنَا I.

بَرُّ ٱلْأَنَاضُولِ Anatolia, Asia Minor.

أَنْتَ fem. أَنْتِ thou — أَنْتُمَا you (dual) — أَنْتُمْ you (plur.).

أَنِسَ III. to be friendly — أُنْسٌ amiability — أَنِيسٌ amiable — إِنْسَانٌ plur. نَاسٌ man — إِنْسَانَةٌ woman.

إِنْكِلِيز English (coll.) — إِنْكِلِيزِيّ English (adj.).

أَنَّى V. to be slow — إِنَاءٌ plur. آنِيَة and أَوَانٍ vessel.

أَهَبَ V. to equip oneself — أُهْبَة equipment.

أَهَّلَ II. to greet — أَهْل plur. أَهَالٍ family, population, worthy — أَهْلًا welcome — أَهْلِيَّة ability, worthiness.

أَوْ or.

أُورُبَّا Europe.

أُورِيقَة factory.

إِوَزّ goose (coll.).

أُوغُسْطَا n. pr. Augusta.

آلَة instrument, machine — أَوَّل fem. أُولَى first, beginning — أَوَّلَ أَمْسِ the day before yesterday — ٱلْأَوَائِل the first parts.

آنَ (أون) to come (of time) — ٱلْآنَ now.

آهْ and أَوَّاهْ ah!

مَأْوَى place of refuge.

أَيْ that is, i.e.

آيَدَ (أيد i) II. to strengthen.

أَيْضًا also.

أَيْنَ where.

أَيّ fem. أَيَّة (with gen.) what . . .

إِيَّاهُ him (see Less. 43, 3).

أَيُّهَا oh!

أَيُّوبِيّ n. pr. Ayyubid.

بِ with, through, in — بِلَا without — بِمَا أَنْ since (conj.).

بَابَا pope.

بِئْر plur. آبَار well.

بَارَة para (a turkish coin.).

بَارِيز Paris.

بِئْسَ to be bad — بُؤْس misfortune.

بَاشَا Pasha.

بَتَّ (u) to decide.

بَثَقَ VII. to break out.

بَحَثَ (a) to seek (with عَنْ).

بَحْر plur. بِحَار and بُحُور sea, river (the Nile).

بُخَار steam — بُخَارِيّ steam-.

بَخْسٌ low (in price).

بُخْلٌ avarice — بَخِيلٌ avaricious.

بَدَّ V. to be scattered — بُدٌّ escape — لَا بُدَّ مِنْ it must be.

بَدَأَ VIII. to begin — مَبْدَأٌ beginning, elements — إِبْتِدَائِيٌّ elementary.

بَدَرَ VIII. to hasten to — بَدْرٌ full moon.

بِدْعٌ an extraordinary thing.

بَدَلٌ substitute — بَدَلًا مِنْ instead of — بَدْلَةٌ suit of clothes.

بَدَنٌ body.

بَدَا to appear, seem good — بَدْوٌ Bedouin (coll.) — بَدَوِيٌّ Bedouin (adj.) — بَادِيَةٌ plur. بَوَادٍ desert.

بَذَلَ (u) (أَلْجُهْدَ) to strive.

بَرٌّ land — بَرِّيَّةٌ plur. بَرَارِيُّ desert, plain — بَرَّانِيٌّ outward, external.

بَرَاءَةٌ diploma — بَارِئٌ creator — بَرِيءٌ innocent.

بُرْتُقَالٌ oranges (coll.).

بَرَحَ III. to leave — أَلْبَارِحَ yesterday.

بَرْدٌ cold — بَارِدٌ cold (adj.) — بَارُودٌ powder.

بَرَزَ (u) to come out.

بَرْطَعَ to move about, be restless.

بَرَقَ (u) to lighten — IV. to send forth lightning — بَرْقٌ lightning.

بَرَكَ III. to bless — بِرْكَةٌ pond.

بَرْلِين Berlin.

بَرْمَكِيٌّ n. pr. Barmecide.

بُرْهَةٌ space of time.

بُسْتَانٌ garden.

بَسَطَ VII. to take pleasure in — مَبْسُوطٌ contented.

بَسَالَةٌ courage — بَاسِلٌ brave.

بَشَرَ II. to bring good news — X. to rejoice — بَشِيرٌ and بِشَارَةٌ n. pr. — بَشَرِيٌّ human.

بَصُرَ IV. to see.

بَصَمَ (u) to stamp.

بِضْع some (3 to 10) — بِضَاعَةٌ plur. بَضَائِعُ wares.

بَطَل hero — بَطَالَةٌ idleness.

بطن IV. to conceal within — بَطْنٌ belly.

بَعَثَ (a) to send.

بَعُدَ (u) to be distant — VIII. to remove — بُعْدٌ distance — بَعِيدٌ far, distant — بَعْدَ after (prep.) — بَعْدَهُ afterwards — بَعْدَ أَنْ after (conj.).

بَعْضٌ one, some, another (see Less. 43, 8).

بَغْتَةً suddenly.

بَغْضَاءُ hatred.

بَغْلٌ mule (coll.).

بغا VII. to be desired.

بَفْتَةٌ (Persian) thin cotton material.

بَقَرٌ ox.

بَقِيَ (a) to remain. — IV. to retain — بَقَاءٌ stay, life — بَاقٍ and بَقِيَّةٌ remainder.

بكٌ Bey.

بَاكِرًا early, in the morning — أَبُو بَكْرٍ n. pr. Abu Bekr.

بَكَى (i) to weep (over مِنْ) — vn. بُكَاءٌ.

بَلْ but, rather.

بَلَّ V. to be wet through.

بُلْبُلٌ nightingale.

بَلَدٌ and بَلْدَةٌ district — بِلَادٌ plur. بُلْدَانٌ land — بَلَدِيٌّ native — اَلْبَلَدِيَّةُ the natives.

بَلَغَ (u) to reach — II. to make to reach — vn. بُلُوغٌ — بَلَاغٌ delivery — مَبْلَغٌ sum of money.

أَبْلَقُ piebald.

بَلَا (u) to put to the test — III. to be anxious about — بَلِيَّةٌ plur. بَلَايَا misfortune.

بَنَانٌ finger-tips.

بَنْدَرٌ seaport.

(بنو) إِبْنٌ plur. بَنُونَ and أَبْنَاءٌ son — إِبْنَةٌ and بِنْتٌ plur. بَنَاتٌ daughter, girl.

بَنَى (i) to build — VIII. to build for oneself — بِنَاءٌ plur. أَبْنِيَة, بِنَايَة and مَبْنًى building — بِنَاءً عَلَى on the ground of.

بَهِج cheerful.

بَهِيّ (بهو) fine, brilliant.

بَاءَ (بوء) V. to take possession.

بَاب (بوب) plur. أَبْوَاب door, gate.

بَاحَ (بوح u) to reveal — IV. to allow.

بُوسطَة post.

بُوفَة buffet, bar.

بُولِيس police.

بِيَانُو piano.

بَاتَ (بيت a and i) to spend the night — بَيْت plur. بُيُوت house.

إِبْيَضَّ to become white — أَبْيَض white — مُبَيِّض tinner — بَيَاض — tinning.

بِيرَة beer.

بَيْرُوت Beyrout.

بَاعَ (بيع) i) to sell — vn. بَيْع and مَبِيع — بَائِع plur. بَاعَة seller.

بيك (Turkish) Bey.

بَيَان explanation, proof — بَيِّن clear — بَيْنَ between —

بَيْنَمَا while.

تَبًّا لَكَ woe to thee!

تَبِعَ (a) to follow, belong to — V. to pursue — تَبَع plur. أَتْبَاع follower — تَابِع plur. تَوَابِع issue, consequence

تِبْغ tobacco.

تِبْن straw.

تِجَارَة business — تِجَارِيّ business (adj.) — تَاجِر plur. تُجَّار merchant.

تَحْتَ under (prep.) — تَحْتَانِيّ lower.

مُتْرَف soft, delicate.

تَرَكَ (u) to leave, give up — تُرْك n. pr. Turks.

تِرْمُومِتْر thermometer.

تَاسِع ninth.

تَعِبَ to become tired — IV. to weary — أَتْعَبَ تَعَب plur. أَتْعَاب weariness — تَعْبَان tired.

تَعْس misfortune.

إِتْقَان solidity — مُتْقَن solid, strong.

تَكِيَّة plur. تَكَايَا monastery of dervishes.

تِلِغْرَاف telegram.

تِلْمِيذ plur. تَلَامِذَة pupil, scholar.

تَلَا (u) to read — تَالٍ following.

تَمَّ (i) to be complete — II. and IV. to complete, finish — تَمَام perfection — تَامّ perfect, complete.

تَمْر dried dates (coll.).

تَمُّوز July.

تَهَمَ IV. to suspect — تُهْمَة suspicion.

تَابَ (توب u) to repent.

تُوت mulberry (coll.).

تَاقَ (توق u) to long for.

تِين fig (coll.).

ثَأْر revenge — أَخَذَ بِٱلثَّأْرِ مِن to take revenge on.

ثَابِت firm, sure.

ثُرَيَّا Pleiads (stars), candlestick.

ثَعْلَب fox.

ثَغْر boundary.

ثَقِيل heavy.

ثَلَاثَة fem. ثَلَاث three — ثَلَاثُون thirty — يَوْمُ ٱلثُّلَاثَاء Tuesday — ثُلْث a third — ثَالِث third.

ثَلْج plur. ثُلُوج snow — مُثَلَّج cooled with snow.

ثُمَّ then, thereupon.

ثَمَن plur. أَثْمَان price — ثَامِن eighth.

ثَنَى IV. to praise (عَلَى) — ثَنَاء praise — ثِنْي plur. أَثْنَاء fold, interval — فِي أَثْنَاء during — إِثْنَانِ two — ثَانٍ second — ثَانِيَة a second

ثَوْبٌ plur. ثِيَابٌ garment.

ثَوْرٌ ox.

جَبَّارٌ giant, powerful.

جَبَلٌ plur. جِبَالٌ mountain.

جُبْنَةٌ cheese.

جُثَّةٌ corpse.

جَدَّ (i) to be new, exert oneself — V. to be renewed — جَدٌّ grandfather - جِدًّا very — جَدِيدٌ new.

جِدَارٌ wall — جَدِيرٌ worthy.

مُجَادَلَةٌ strife.

مِجْذَافٌ oar.

جَرَّةٌ jar.

جَرُؤَ V. to dare.

جَرَبَ II. to tempt, try.

جُرْثُومَةٌ plur. جَرَاثِيمُ bud.

جِرَاحٌ wound.

جَرِيدَةٌ plur. جَرَائِدُ journal.

جَرَعَ V. to drink in draughts.

جَرْفٌ excavating.

جُرْنَالٌ journal, announcement.

جَرَى (i) to run, flow, happen — IV. to carry out — vn. جَرْيٌ and جَرَيَانٌ — جَارٍ current (month).

جُزْءٌ plur. أَجْزَاءٌ part.

جَزِيرَةٌ plur. جَزَائِرُ island (also n. pr. of a palace near Cairo) — اَلْجَزَائِرُ Algeria — جَزَّارٌ butcher.

جَزِيلٌ respectable.

جَزَاءٌ (جزى) reward, payment.

جَسَّ V. to acquire information — جَاسُوسٌ plur. جَوَاسِيسُ spy.

جَسَرَ (u) I. and VI. to dare — جَسَارَةٌ boldness.

جِسْمٌ body.

جَعْفَرٌ n. pr. Ja'far.

جَعَلَ (a) to make; (with following imperf.) to begin to.

جِغْرَافِيَّةٌ Geography.

جَفَّ (i) to dry.

جَافٍ (جفو) hard, rough.

جَلَّ (i) to be exalted — IV. to show honour — جَلِيلٌ exalted.

جَلَبَ X. to have a thing brought.

جَلَدَ (i) to lash — II. to bind (a book) — جِلْد plur. جُلُود skin.

جَلَسَ (i) to sit, seat oneself — مَجْلِس session.

جُلْمُود hard rock.

جَلِيّ clear.

جَمّ numerous.

جَمْر burning coal.

جُمَّيز plur. جَمَامِيز sycomore.

جَمَعَ (a) to gather — IV. to determine — VIII. to assemble, unite — جَمْع assembling — جُمْعَة week — نَهَار الْجُمْعَة Friday — جَمِيع totality, all — أَجْمَع whole — جَمَاعَة company — جَامِع plur. جَوَامِع mosque — مَجْمَع union, assembly.

جَمَل plur. جِمَال camel — جَمَال beauty — جَمِيلَة n. pr. — جُمْلَة sentence, sum total — بِالْجُمْلَة wholesale.

جُمْهُور crowd, public.

جِنّ and جِنَّة demon — جُنَيْنَة garden — مَجْنُون mad.

جَنْب V. to avoid — جَنْب and جَانِب side — بِجَانِب or بِجَنْب beside (prep.) — جَنَاب Majesty (title) — جَنُوب South — جَنُوبِيّ southerly — أَجْنَبِيّ plur. أَجَانِب strange.

جُنْد plur. جُنُود troop.

جِنْس plur. أَجْنَاس kind, class.

جِنِيه guinea (money).

جَنَى V. to charge falsely.

جَهْد zeal — إِجْتِهَاد industry — مُجْتَهِد industrious.

جَهَزَ to be ready — II. to equip, prepare — مَدْرَسَة تَجْهِيزِيَّة high school.

جَهِلَ (a) to be ignorant — جَهُول very ignorant.

جَوّ firmament.

جَابَ (جوب) IV. to answer,

correspond — جَوَابٌ plur. أَجْوِبَة answer.

جَوَاد steed — جَوْدَة excellence — جَيِّدٌ (elative أَجْوَد) — excellent.

جَارَ (جور u) to act wrongfully towards (عَلَى) — III. to be neighbour to — جَوْر tyranny — جَارٌ plur. جِيرَان neighbour — جِوَار neighbourhood.

جَازَ (جوز u) to be allowed — VI. to exceed.

جَاعَ (جوع u) to be hungry — جُوعٌ hunger — جَائِعٌ hungry.

جَالَ (جول u) to ramble about.

جَوْهَر Plur. جَوَاهِرُ jewel.

جَاءَ (جىء i) to come — vn. مَجِيء.

جَيْب plur. جُيُوبٌ pocket.

جِيزَة Gizeh (near Cairo).

جَيْش plur. جُيُوش army.

جِيلٌ century.

حَبَّ (i) IV. to love — vn. حُبّ and مَحَبَّة love — حَبِيب plur. أَحْبَابٌ friend, beloved (in the poets) — أَحَبُّ more loved — مَحْبُوبَة beloved (fem.).

حِبْر ink.

حَبَشِيّ Abyssinian.

حُبْلَى plur. حَبَالَى pregnant.

حَتَّى until, so that.

حَثَّ (u) to incite.

حَجَّ (u) to make the pilgrimage — vn. حَجّ — حَاجّ pilgrim — أَلْحَجَّاج n. pr. al-Hajjāj, governor for the Caliph ʿAbd al-Malik.

حَجَبَ (u) to conceal.

حَجَر stone — حِجْر lap — حُجْرَة room.

حَجَل plur. حِجْلَان partridge.

حَدَّ (u) to limit — حَدّ plur. حُدُود boundary — لِحَدِّ up to — حَدِيدٌ iron.

حَدَثَ II. to narrate to — V. to relate — VI. to converse — حَدِيث plur. أَحَادِيث

narrative, conversation — حَدِيث new — حَادِثَة plur. حَوَادِث event.

حَدَرَ VI. to come down.

حَدَقَ (i) to surround — حَدَق glance — حَدِيقَة plur. حَدَائِق park.

حَذَرَ II. to warn — حَذَارِ take care!

حَرَّ II. to write — حَرّ and حَرَارَة warmth, heat — حَارّ hot.

حَرَبَ III. to make war on — حَرْب plur. حُرُوب war — وَاحَرْبَا ah!

حَرَثَ IV. to cause to till — حَرْث tillage — اَلْحَارِثُ n. pr. — أَبُو ٱلْحَارِث name for a lion.

حَرَسَ (u) to guard — حَارِس plur. حُرَّاس watchman, watchful.

حَرَضَ II. to instigate.

حَرَفَ (i) to turn away — حَرْف plur. حُرُوف letter (of the alphabet), particle.

حَرْق burning.

حَرَّكَ II. to move — حَرَكَة movement.

حَرِمَ VIII. to honour — X. to esteem forbidden — حَرَامِيّ robber, thief — حُرْم forbidden (by religion).

حِزْب party.

حَزِنَ (a) to be sad — IV. to make sad — حُزْن plur. أَحْزَان sadness — حَزِين sad.

حَسَّ IV. to feel (بِ) — حَاسَّة plur. حَوَاسّ sense.

حِسَاب reckoning, regard — حَسَبَ ,عَلَى حَسَبِ and حَسَب in accordance with — مَحْسُوب friend.

حَسَدَ (i) to envy.

حَسْرَة sigh — وَاحَسْرَتَا alas!

حُسَام sword.

حَسُنَ IV. to be good to, to know — V. to improve — X. to approve, find pleasing — حُسْن beauty — حَسَن beautiful, also n. pr. — حَسْنَاء a beauty.

حَصْر anguish — فَكَّ حَصْرًا to make oneself comfortable.

حَصَلَ (u) to happen — IV. to get (money) — حُصُولٌ acquirement (عَلَى) — حَاصِلٌ result — مَحْصُولَاتٌ products.

حَضَرَ (u) to appear, come — II. to make ready — III. to converse with — IV. to bring — حُضُور presence — حَضْرَة presence (also used as a title) — حَاضِرٌ present, ready.

مَحَطَّةٌ railway station.

حَطَمَ (i) to smash.

حَظّ happiness.

حَفَّ (u) to surround.

أبو حَفْصٍ a name of the Caliph Omar.

حَفِظَ (a) to keep, guard — vn. حِفْظٌ — مُحَافَظَةٌ Muhāfaza (province of Egypt).

إِحْتِفَالٌ solemnity, festival.

حَقَّ V, to be verified — X. to deserve, be due — حَقّ plur. حُقُوق right, truth — حَقِيقَةٌ truth — حَقِيقِيّ real.

حِكْمَةٌ wisdom — حَاكِم plur. حُكَّام (حُكْمدار Persian) ruler, governor, judge — حُكُومَةٌ government, court — حَكِيمٌ physician, wise — مَحْكَمَةٌ court.

حَكَى (i) to relate — III. to imitate — حِكَايَةٌ narrative, story.

حَلَّ (u) to loosen, settle, inhabit — VII. to be loosed — حُلُولٌ entrance (of a period of time) — حَلَالٌ a thing allowed — مَحَلّ plur. مَحَلَّاتٌ place — مَحَلَّةٌ quarter (of a town) — مَحَلِّي belonging to a place.

حَلَفَ (i) to swear — X. to make to swear.

حِلَاقَةٌ shaving.

حَالِكٌ dark black.

حُلْم plur. أَحْلَام dream.

حُلْو sweet — حُلْوَانٌ present, gift — حَلْوَى sweetmeats.

حِمَامٌ death — حُمَّى fever — حُمَّى تَيْفُوسِيَّة typhoid fever.

حَمِدَ (a) to praise — vn. حَمْدٌ — أَحْمَدُ n. pr. — مُحَمَّدٌ n. pr. — مَحْمُودٌ n. pr.

إِحْمَرَّ to become red — أَحْمَرُ red — حِمَارٌ ass.

حَمَلَ (i) to carry, induce to (عَلَى) — vn. حَمْلٌ — حَامِلٌ bearer, pregnant — حَمَّالٌ porter.

حَمَى (i) to protect.

حَانُوتٌ wine shop.

حِنْطَةٌ wheat.

حَنَا (u) to bend.

حَاجَ (حوج) VIII. to need (إِلَى) — حَاجَةٌ plur. حَاجَاتٌ and حَوَائِجُ need, matter.

مِحْوَرٌ axis.

حِيَازَةٌ possession.

حَوْشٌ court-yard.

حَاطَ (حوط) IV. to surround — حَائِطٌ wall.

حَالَ (حول) III. to tempt — VIII. to be cunning — X. to be impossible — حَوْلٌ power, year — حَوْلَ (prep.) round about — حَالٌ plur. أَحْوَالٌ condition, state — حَالَةٌ condition — حَالًا (adv.) immediately — حَالَمَا as soon as — حَالِيٌّ present — حِيلَةٌ cunning — تَحْوِيلٌ exchange — مُحْتَالٌ artful — لَا مَحَالَةَ it is unavoidable.

حَوَى (i) I. and VIII. to contain.

حَيْثُ where, since.

حَارَ (حير) II. to confuse — V. to be confused — حَيْرَةٌ perplexity — حَارَةٌ quarter of a city.

حِينٌ time.

حَيِيَ II. to let live, greet — IV. to make to live — X. to be ashamed — حَيَاةٌ or حَيوةٌ life — حَيٌّ quarter (of city), settlement, tribe — حَيَّةٌ serpent — حَيَوَانٌ animal.

خَبَأَ (a) to conceal — VIII. to hide oneself.

خَبِيثٌ rascal.

خَبَرَ III. to get news — IV. to inform — VIII. to test — خَبَرٌ plur. أَخْبَارٌ news.

خُبْزٌ bread — خَبَّازٌ baker.

خَبَطَ (i) to strike, trample on.

خَتَمَ (i) to seal, close — خَتْمٌ seal — خَاتَمٌ seal-ring.

خَدَمَ (i. u) to serve — X. to take into service. — خِدْمَةٌ service — خَادِمٌ servant — خَادِمَةٌ maidservant.

خِدِيو (Persian) Khedive, prince — خِدِيوِى khedivial.

خَرَابٌ ruin — خَرِبٌ ruined.

خَرَجَ (u) to go out — IV. to bring out — vn. خُرُوجٌ — خَرَاجٌ tribute - خَارِجَ outside.

أَخْرَسُ dumb.

خَرَقَ VIII. to pierce, cut through — vn. خَرْقٌ.

خِزَانَةٌ cupboard — مَخْزِنٌ magazine, shop.

خُسْرٌ loss.

خَشَبٌ wood.

خَصَّ (u) to concern — خُصُوصِى special — عَلَى ٱلْخُصُوص specially. — خَاصٌّ special.

خَصَرَ VIII. to shorten — مُخْتَصَرٌ compendium.

خَصِىٌّ plur. خِصْيَانٌ eunuch.

خَضَبَ II. to dye.

إِخْضَرَّ to become green — أَخْضَرُ green — خُضَارٌ vegetables.

خَطٌّ line, writing.

خَطَأٌ and خَطِيئَةٌ fault.

خَطَبَ III. to address — خِطَابٌ letter.

خَطَرَ III. to risk (بِ) — خَطَرٌ danger — خَاطِرٌ plur. خَوَاطِرُ heart, condition.

خَطَفَ VIII. to snatch for oneself.

خَفِيف light (in weight).

خَفِيَ (a) to be hidden (from عَلَى) — IV. to hide.

خَلَّ V. to use a toothpick — خِلّ and خَلِيل friend, also n. pr.

خَلِيج canal.

خَلَصَ II. and IV. to free — V. to free oneself. — إِخْلَاص sincere worship — مُخْلِص honest.

خَلَطَ III. to have intercourse with — VIII. to be mingled.

خَلَفَ III. to disagree with, contradict — V. to remain behind — VIII. to go up and down — خِلَافَة succession — خَلِيفَة successor, Caliph — خَلَف successor — خِلَاف other than — مُخَالَفَة breach of law — مُخْتَلِف different.

خَلَقَ (u) to create.

خَلَا (u) to be empty — VIII. to be alone.

خَمْر wine.

خَمْس fem. خَمْسَة five — خَامِس fifty — خَمْسُون fifth — خَمِيس Thursday.

خَنَّاس he who holds back = Satan.

خَنَقَ III. to quarrel with — VIII. to choke (intrans.).

خَوَاجَا (Persian) sir (used of Christians).

خَافَ (خوف) (a) to fear — II. to frighten — خَوْف and مَخَافَة fear.

خَانَ (خون u) to betray, deceive.

خَيْبَة disappointment.

خَارَ (خير) VIII. to choose — خَيْر good, better.

خَيْط thread — خَيَّاط tailor.

خَالَ (خيل) V. to imagine — خَيْل plur. خُيُول horse (coll.).

خَامَ (خيم) II. to pitch a tent, to break (of night) — خَيْمَة plur. خِيَام tent.

دَابَّة plur. دَوَابّ beast of burden.

دَبَرَ II. to arrange — إِدْبَار flight.

دَجَاجٌ fowl (coll.).

دِجْلَةُ Tigris.

دُجًى darkness, night.

دَخَلَ (u) to enter — IV. to bring in — دُخُولٌ entrance — دَاخِلَ inside (prep.).

دُخَانٌ smoke, tobacco.

دَرْبٌ way.

دَرَجَةٌ degree.

دَرَسَ II. to teach — دَرْسٌ lesson — مَدْرَسَةٌ school.

دِرْعٌ coat of mail.

دَرَكَ IV. to overtake.

دِرْهَمٌ Dirham (coin or weight) — Plur. دَرَاهِمُ money.

دِرْيَاقٌ thyrine (ancient remedy against poison).

دِسِمْبِرُ December.

دَعَا (u) to call, name, pray (for لِ), wish بِ of thing) — VIII. to claim — X. to summon — دَعْوَى claim — دَعْوَةٌ invitation — دَاعٍ inducement — أَنْدَاعِي لَكُمْ yours obediently — مُدَّعٍ عُمُومِيٌّ Attorney-general.

دَفَّةٌ rudder

دَفْتَرٌ sheet (of paper), book.

دَفَعَ (a) to pay — III. to defend (عَنْ of person).

مَدْفِنٌ mausoleum.

دَقَّ (u) to knock — دَقَّةٌ and دَقِيقَةٌ, تَدْقِيقٌ exactness — دَقِيقَةٌ plur. دَقَائِقُ minute.

دَلَّ (u) to show — دَلِيلٌ plur. دَلَائِلُ proof, indication — دَلَّالٌ broker, auctioneer.

دَلْوٌ bucket.

دَهَمَ to rush upon.

دَمَرَ II. to destroy.

دِمَشْقُ ٱلشَّامِ Damascus.

دَمْعٌ plur. دُمُوعٌ tear.

دَمَنْهُورُ n. pr. of a city in Egypt.

دَمٌ (دمى) blood

دِينَارٌ plur. دَنَانِيرُ Dinar (a gold coin).

دَنَا (u) to approach — دُنْيَا world — أَدْنَى lowest.

دَهْرٌ time, fate.

دَهَمَ III. to crush — أَدْهَمُ dark-coloured.

دَاهِيَةٌ plur. دَوَاهٍ misfortune.

دَاءٌ (دوء) sickness

دَاوُدُ David.

دَارَ (دور) (u) to revolve — دَارٌ plur. دُورٌ house — plur. دِيَارٌ land — دَيْرٌ monastery — دَوْرَةٌ turn — دَائِرَةٌ plur. دَوَائِرُ circle — مَدَارٌ period. — مُدِيرٌ director, editor — مُدِيرِيَّةٌ Mudiriya (Egyptian province).

دَوْلَةٌ kingdom — اَلدَّوْلَةُ الْعَلِيَّةُ the Turkish Empire.

دَامَ (دوم u) to last — مَا دَامَ so long as — دَائِمًا always.

دُونَ on this side of, before, without (also بِدُونِ) — دُونَكَ beware!

دِيوَانٌ plur. دَوَاوِينُ Diwān, Divan.

دَوَاءٌ plur. أَدْوِيَةٌ medicine.

دِيكٌ cock.

دِينٌ and دِيَانَةٌ religion — يَوْمُ الدِّينِ the day of judgment.

ذِئْبٌ wolf.

ذَبَحَ (a) to slay — مَذْبَحَةٌ slaughter.

ذَابِلٌ languid.

ذَاكَ = ذٰلِكَ.

ذَخَرَ (a) to keep, save.

ذَرَفَ (i) to flow, shed (tears).

ذَكَرَ (u) to mention, remind — V. to remember — ذِكْرٌ and ذِكْرَى remembrance — تَذْكَارٌ remembrance — تَذْكِرَةٌ certificate, ticket.

ذَكِيٌّ (ذكو) aroused — also n. pr.

ذٰلِكَ fem. تِلْكَ plur. أُولٰئِكَ that, those.

ذَنْبٌ sin, fault — ذَنَبٌ tail.

ذَهَبَ (a) to go — vn. ذَهَابٌ — ذَهَبٌ gold.

ذو fem. ذَاتٌ master, possessor (with gen.) — ذَاتٌ plur. ذَوَاتٌ person — ذَاتَ يَوْمٍ one day.

مِذْوَدٌ stall.

ذَاقَ (ذوق u) to taste — IV. to make to taste — مَذَاقٌ taste.

رأس head, beginning, promontory — رَئِيس chief, captain.

رأى (يرى) to see, think good — IV. to show — VI. to appear — رؤيا and رؤية sight — رأى opinion — مرأى aspect.

رب lord — ربما perhaps.

رِبْح plur. أَرْبَاح gain.

رَبَطَ (u, i) to bind.

أربعة fem. أربع four — يوم الاربعاء Wednesday — رَابِع fourth — ربع plur. ارباع a fourth — الربيع الاول

n. pr. of a month — مربع square — ميل مربع a square mile.

ربا (ربو) II. to train up.

رَثَى (i) to lament.

رَجَحَ (a, i, u) to weigh more than.

رَجَعَ (i) to return, withdraw — III. to look through — IV. to give back — رُجُوع return.

رَجَفَ VIII. to tremble.

رِجْلٌ plur. رِجَالٌ man — رِجْلٌ foot.

رَجَا (u) to beg, hope — رَجَاء request.

رَحْب comfort — رَحْب and مَرْحَبًا spacious — رَحْب welcome!

رَحْلٌ plur. رِحَالٌ stage (of a journey) — رِحْلَة and رَحِيلٌ journey.

رحمة compassion - الرحمن الرحيم the all-compassionate i.e. God.

رُخْصَة permission, permit — رَخِيص cheap.

رَخِيم tender.

رَدَّ (u) to give back, answer, refuse.

رَدُؤَ IV. to make bad — رَدِىٌّ bad.

رَدْمٌ ruins.

رَسَلَ III. correspond with — IV. to send — رِسَالَةٌ plur. رَسَائِلُ message — رَسُولٌ plur. رُسُلٌ apostle.

رَسَنٌ halter.

رَسَا (u) to anchor.

رَشَّ (u) to sprinkle.

رُشْدٌ majority (of a child) — رَشِيدٌ upright — اَلرَّشِيدُ = Harūn ar-Rashid — مُرْشِدٌ one who leads aright.

رِشَاءٌ (رشو) rope.

رَصَاصٌ lead — رَصَاصَةٌ bullet.

رَصَعَ II. to set with precious stones.

رَضَعَ IV. to suck (of a child).

رَضِىَ (a) to be content — IV. to make contented, satisfy — VI. to come to terms with.

رَطَبَ II. refresh.

رَعَدَ I. and IV. to thunder.

رَعَى (a) to pasture — III. to pay attention to — رَاعٍ shepherd — رَعِيَّةٌ subjects (of a kingdom) — مَرْعًى pasturage.

رَغِبَ (a) to wish (for فِى) — رَغْبَةٌ wish.

رَغِيفٌ loaf.

رَغْمًا عَنْ (بِالرَّغْمِ) in spite of.

رَفَعَ (a) to lift up, take away — VIII. to raise oneself — رِفْعَةٌ a raising — رِفْعَتْلُو Turkish title — رَافِعٌ exalter, leader.

رَفَقَ III. to accompany — رِفْقَةٌ company — رَفِيقٌ plur. رُفَقَاءُ companion.

رَقَّ (i) to be tender, soft.

رَقَبَ III. to observe — رَقَبَةٌ neck.

رَقَدَ (u) to sleep, lie down — رُقَادٌ sleep.

رَقَعَ II. to patch — رُقْعَةٌ a note (short letter).

رَقَمَ (u) to write.

رَكِبَ (a) to ride — vn. رُكُوب — رَاكِب plur. رُكَّاب passenger — مَرْكَب ship.

مَرْكَز centre.

رَكَضَ (u) to run.

رَكَمَ VI. to be heaped up.

رُمَّة whole, totality.

رُمْح plur. رِمَاح lance.

رَمْل sand.

رُمَّان pomegranate (coll.).

رَمَى (i) to throw — مِرْمًى projectile.

رَاهِب plur. رُهْبَان monk.

رَهْن pledge — رَهِين pledged.

رَاجَ (روج u) to be current (coin).

رَاحَ (روح u) to go away or astray — II. and IV. to permit to rest — VIII. and X. to rest — رَاحَة rest, comfort — رِيح plur. رِيَاح wind — رَائِح about to (do something) — رَائِحَة plur. رَوَائِح smell, odour — رُوحِي spiritual.

رَادَ (رود) IV. to wish — يُرَادُ بِ it is understood among — مُرَاد wish, will.

رَاعَ (روع) II. to terrify — رَوْع terror.

رَامَ (روم u) to wish.

رُومِيَة Rome.

رَوِيَ (a) I. and VIII. to be sufficiently watered — رِوَايَة narrative, piece (in theatre).

رِيَالٌ مَجِيدِي Mejidi = 22 piasters 30 paras.

رِيف Plur. أَرْيَاف cultivated land.

زُبْدَة butter.

الأَزْبَكِيَّة the Ezbekiya a square in Cairo).

زُبُون plur. زَبَائِن customer.

زَرْع plantation — زَرَّاع sower, planter — مَزْرَعَة field.

أَزْرَق blue — زُرَيْق name of a camel.

زَعْلَان vexatious.

زَكِي (زكو) pure.

زَلْزَال earthquake.

زَمَن plur. أَزْمَان time — زَمَان time.

زهد modesty, asceticism.

زهر plur. أزهار flower — الجامع الازهر the Azhar mosque in Cairo.

زاج (زوج) II. to marry — زوج husband — زوجة wife.

زاد (زود) V. to take as provision — زاد provisions.

زار (زور u) to visit — زيارة visit — زور lie.

زال (زول a, u) to cease — IV. to make to cease.

زاوية corner.

زاد (زيد i) to increase — VIII. to increase — زيد n. pr. — زيادة increase — مزيد excess — زائد bidder — مزاد auction.

زاغ (زيغ i) to remove.

زان (زين) II. to adorn.

زينب n. pr. of a woman.

سأل (a) to ask (after عن), beg — سؤال question, request — سائل beggar.

سبب plur. أسباب cause.

نهار السبت Saturday.

سبتمبر September.

سبحانه praised be He (i.e. God).

سبع wild beast — سبعة fem.

سبع seven — سابع seventh — أسبوع plur. أسابيع week.

سبق (i, u) to precede — سبق precedence — سابقا earlier.

سبيل plur. سبل way.

ست (for سيدة) plur. ستات lady — ستة fem. ست six — ستون sixty.

ستار and ستارة plur. ستائر curtain.

سجادة prayer carpet — مسجد (small) mosque.

سجل II. to enter (in a register).

سجن plur. سجون prison.

سخين hot.

سد dam, stoppage.

سادس sixth.

سَرْ (Persian) head, chief.

سَرَّ (u) to rejoice — سُرُورٌ and سَرَّاءُ joy — سِرٌّ plur. أَسْرَارٌ secret — سَرِيرٌ couch — مَسْرُورٌ glad.

تَسَرْبَلَ to dress.

سَرَحَ (a) to go to pasture in the morning — II. to cause to go etc.

سِرَاطٌ street.

سَرُعَ IV. to hasten — سُرْعَةٌ haste — سَرِيعٌ swift.

سَطْحٌ plur. سُطُوحٌ roof.

سَطَرَ II. to write — سَطْرٌ line.

سَعَدَ III. to help — سَعَادَةٌ happiness — دَارُ ٱلسَّعَادَةِ Constantinople — سَعَادَتْلُو (Turkish) Your Excellency — سَعِيدٌ happy, also n. pr. — سُعْدَى n. pr. fem. — سَاعِدٌ fore-arm.

سِعْرٌ plur. أَسْعَارٌ current price, rate.

سَعَى (a) to exert oneself — مَسْعًى plur. مَسَاعٍ exertion.

سَفْحٌ foot (of a hill).

سَفَرَ III. to travel — سَفَرٌ journey — سُفْرَةٌ dining-table — سَفِيرٌ plur. سُفَرَاءُ ambassador.

سَفِيلٌ low, under (part.).

سَفِينَةٌ plur. سُفُنٌ ship.

سَقَطَ (u) to fall — IV. to make to fall — VI. to fall one after another.

سَقِمَ to be sick — IV. to make sick.

سَقَى (i) I. and IV. to give drink to. To water.

سِكَّةٌ coin, way — سِكَّةٌ حَدِيدِيَّةٌ railway.

سَكَتَ (u) to be silent.

سَكِرَ (a) to be drunken — vn. سُكْرٌ — IV. to intoxicate.

سَكَنَ (u) to dwell, be quiet — II. to quieten — سَكَنٌ and سُكْنَى dwelling, rest — سَكِينَةٌ to dwell — مَسْكِنٌ dwelling — سَاكِنٌ plur. سُكَّانٌ inhabitant, quiet — سِكِّين plur. سَكَاكِين knife.

سَلَبَ (u) to plunder, rob — أُسْلُوب method.

سِلَاح plur. أَسْلِحَة weapon.

سَلَخَ (u, a) to flay.

سُلْطَان plur. سَلَاطِين Sultan — سُلْطَانِيّ imperial.

سَلِمَ (a) to be sound — II. to hand over, greet (with عَلَى) — VIII. to take over — سَلَام peace, greeting — سَلَامَة good condition — إِسْلَام Islām — مُسْلِم Moslem — سَالِم safe, also n. pr. — سَلِيم n. pr. — سَلْمَى n. pr. fem. — سُلَيْمَان n. pr. Solomon.

سَلَا (u) to forget — II. to comfort.

سُمّ poison.

سَمَحَ (a) to permit — III. to make a generous present to.

سِمَاط table-cloth.

سَمِعَ (a) I. and VIII. to hear — IV. to cause to hear — vn. سَمْع and سَمَاع — سَمْعًا وَطَاعَةً at your service.

سَمْن butter — سَمِين fat (adj.).

سَمَّى II. to name — إِسْم plur. أَسْمَاء name, noun — سَمَاء heaven.

سِنّ plur. أَسْنَان tooth, age — سِنَان plur. أَسِنَّة point of lance — سُنَّة Sunna i.e. Moslem tradition.

سَنَة plur. سِنُون and سَنَوَات year — سَنَوِيّ yearly.

سُهَاد sleeplessness.

سَهَّلَ II. to make easy — سَهْل easy.

سَهْم arrow.

سَاءَ (سوء u) to be bad, injure (with accus.) — سُوء evil — سُوءُ الْحَظِّ misfortune.

سَاحَة square.

إِسْوَدَّ to become black — أَسْوَد black — plur. سُود — سَيِّد plur. سَادَة master — سَيِّدَة lady — سِيَادَة authority.

سُورٌ wall (of city) — **سُورَةٌ** Sura (of Koran).

سُورِيَا or **سُورِيَّةٌ** Syria.

سَوْطٌ lash.

سَاعَةٌ hour.

سَوْفَ particle indicating futurity — **مَسَافَةٌ** distance.

سَاقَ (**سوق** u) to drive (cattle), lead — **سُوقٌ** plur. **أَسْوَاقٌ** market — **سَوَّاقٌ** driver.

سَوِيَ III. to make equivalent — V. to be like — **سِوَى** beside, except — **لَا سِيَّمَا** specially.

سَائِحٌ (**سيح**) traveller — **مَسَاحَةٌ** extent.

سَارَ (**سير** i) to travel, go — **سَيْرٌ** and **مَسِيرٌ** way, journey — **سِيرَةٌ** manner of life — **سَائِرٌ** rest, remainder.

سَيْفٌ plur. **سُيُوفٌ** sword.

سِيكَارَةٌ cigar.

سَالَ (**سيل** i) to flow.

شَأْمٌ and **شَامٌ** Syria, Damascus — **شَامِيٌّ** Syrian.

شَأْنٌ condition — **فِي شَأْنِ** concerning.

شَابٌّ youth.

شَبِعَ (a) to be satisfied.

شَبَكَ VIII. to be entangled — **شُبَّاكٌ** window.

شَبَهَ IV. to resemble — **شُبْهَةٌ** doubt.

شَتِيتٌ plur. **شَتَّى** different.

شَتَمَ (u) to abuse.

شِتَاءٌ winter.

شَجَرٌ plur. **أَشْجَارٌ** tree (coll.).

شَجُعَ V. to take courage — **شَجَاعَةٌ** courage — **شُجَاعٌ** brave.

شُحٌّ avarice.

شَخْصٌ plur. **أَشْخَاصٌ** person.

شَدَّ (u) to strengthen, bind — VIII. to strengthen oneself — **شِدَّةٌ** violence — **شَدِيدٌ** plur. **أَشِدَّاءُ** violent, strong.

شَرٌّ evil — **شَرَرٌ** sparks — **شِرِّيرٌ** bad.

شَرِبَ (a) to drink, smoke — vn. شُرْبٌ — شَرَابٌ drink, wine — مَشْرَبٌ and مَشْرُوبٌ drink — شُرَابٌ plur. شُرَابَاتٌ stocking.

شَرَحَ VI. (literally to be wide of the breast) to rejoice.

شَرَدَ (u) to wander about.

شَرْطٌ plur. شُرُوطٌ condition.

شَارِعٌ plur. شَوَارِعُ street — شَرْعِيٌّ legal.

شَرَفَ II. to honour — V. to be honoured — شَرَفٌ honour — شَرِيفٌ noble, exalted.

شَرْقٌ east — شَرْقِيٌّ eastern — شُرُوقٌ sunrise.

شَرَكَ VIII. to subscribe to (with فِي) — شَرِيكٌ plur. شُرَكَاءُ companion.

شَرَى VIII. to buy — شِرَاءٌ purchase.

شَاطِئٌ plur. شَوَاطِئُ coast.

شَعْبٌ plur. شُعُوبٌ tribe, people.

شَعَرَ IV. to make known — شَعْرٌ hair — شَعِيرٌ barley — شَاعِرٌ poet.

شَغَلَ (a) to busy, occupy, distract from (عَنْ) — شُغْلٌ plur. أَشْغَالٌ business, work.

شَفَقَةٌ compassion.

شَفَى (i) to heal.

شَقَّ (u) to cleave, be unpleasant — شَقِيقٌ brother — مَشَقَّةٌ misfortune, hardship.

أَشْقَرُ reddish.

شَقِيٌّ (شقو) plur. أَشْقِيَاءُ miserable.

شَكَّ (u) to doubt — شَكٌّ doubt.

شَكَرَ (u) to thank — شُكْرٌ thanks.

شَكْلٌ plur. أَشْكَالٌ form, vowel-sign.

شَكَا (u) to complain (of عَنْ).

شَلَّ (pass.) to dry.

شَمَّ (u) to smell.

شَمْسٌ sun.

شَمَلَ (u) to embrace, surround — VIII. to contain (with عَلَى) — شَمْلٌ union — شَمَالٌ north

شَمَلِيٌّ — شِمَالٌ left side — northern.

أَشْهَب grey.

شَهِدَ (ε) to witness — III. to see, take into consideration — شَاهِدٌ evidence — شَهَادَةٌ witness — شُهُود plur. شَهْدٌ honey.

شَهَرَ VIII. to be renowned — شَهْرٌ plur. أَشْهُرٌ and شُهُور month — مَشْهُور and شَهِير renowned.

شَهَا VIII. to desire, wish.

شَارَ (شور) III. and X. to ask advice — IV. to indicate, advice — مَشُورَةٌ advice.

شَاقَ (شوق) VIII. to yearn — شَوْق plur. أَشْوَاق longing.

شَوَّال name of a month.

شَوَى (i) to roast.

شَاءَ (شىء a) to wish — شَيْءٌ plur. أَشْيَاءُ thing — شُوَيَّةٌ a little.

شَيْخ old man, sheykh — جَبَلُ ٱلشَّيْخِ mt. Hermon.

شَيْطَان satan, devil.

شِيعَةٌ the shiites.

شِيمَةٌ plur. شِيَم character.

صَالُو salon.

صَبَحَ IV. to be or do in the morning — صَبَاح morning — صَبِيح beautiful.

صَبْر patience.

صِحَّةٌ correctness, health — صَحِيح correct.

صَحِبَ VIII. to keep company with one another — صَاحِب plur. أَصْحَاب and صَحْب master, possessor, friend.

صَحْرَاء desert.

صَخْر rock, peak.

بِصَدَدِ concerning.

صَدَرَ (u, i) to go out from — صَدْر plur. صُدُور breast.

صَدَقَ (u) to be sincere — II. to confirm — VI. to unite — صِدْق sincerity — صَدَاقَةٌ sincerity, friendship — صَادِق sincere — صَدِيق plur. أَصْدِقَاء friend.

صدم III. and VI. to collide.

صرّ IV. to persist in.

صرّح II. to declare expressly — V. = *passive* — صَرِيحٌ obvious.

صَرَخَ (u) to cry out — صَرْخَةٌ and صُرَاخٌ cry.

صِرَاطٌ path.

صَرَفَ (i) to spend, use — V. to dispose of — VII. to remove — مُتَصَرِّفٌ Mutasarrif (a turkish official) — مُتَصَرِّفِيَّةٌ governmental district (in Turkey).

صَعْبٌ difficult — صُعُوبَةٌ difficulty.

صِغَرٌ youth, smallness — صَغِيرٌ small.

صغا IV. to hearken.

صَفْحَةٌ page (of a book)

إِصْفَرَّ to become yellow, pale — أَصْفَرُ yellow, pale.

صفّق II. to clap the hands.

صَفَا (u) to be pure, clear.

صَكٌّ deed (in law).

صَلَبَ (i) to crucify — صَلِيبَةٌ name of a street in Cairo.

صَلَحَ (u) to be sound — II. and IV. to repair, reform — صَالِحٌ adjustment — صُلْحٌ صَلَاحٌ — plur. صُلَحَاءُ honest — مَصْلَحَةٌ Saladin — صَلَاحُ ٱلدِّينِ interest.

صلّى II. to pray — صَلَاةٌ (or صَلٰوةٌ) prayer.

صمّم II. to determine.

صَمَدٌ eternal.

صِنْدِيدٌ strong, powerful.

صُنْدُوقٌ chest, box.

صَنَعَ (a) to make, prepare — VIII. to prepare — صُنْعَةٌ work — صِنَاعَةٌ plur. صَنَائِعُ art.

صِنْفٌ plur. أَصْنَافٌ and صُنُوفٌ class, genus.

صَابَ (صوب) IV. to hit — X. to approve — مُصِيبَةٌ plur. مَصَائِبُ misfortune — مُصَابٌ accident.

صَوْت plur. أَصْوَات voice.

صَاخَ (صوخ) IV. to listen to.

صَوْدَة soda.

صَارَ (صور) V. to imagine — صُورَة picture, copy — تَصْوِير picture.

صَاغ (Turkish) -- غِرْش صَاغ a gold) piastre.

صَانَ (صون u) to protect.

صَاحَ (صيح i) to cry out.

صَادَ (صيد i) I., V. and VIII. to hunt. — صَيْد hunt.

صَيْدَا Sidon.

صَارَ (صير i) to become, happen — (with imperf.) to begin to.

صَيْف summer.

ضَبَطَ (i, u) to correct — ضَابِط officer — ضَابِطَة and ضَابِطِيَّة police.

ضِبْع hyena.

ضَجَر unrest.

ضَحِكَ (a) to laugh - vn. ضِحْك.

ضُحَى (ضحو) afternoon — ضَاحِيَة plur. ضَوَاحٍ environs.

ضِدّ opposite.

ضَرَّ (u) to injure — VIII. to compel — ضَرَر plur. أَضْرَار injury — ضَرَّاء damage — ضَرُورِيّ necessary.

ضَرَبَ (i) to strike, coin — VIII. to be troubled — ضَرْب blow.

ضَرَطَ (i) to fart.

ضَرَمَ IV. to kindle.

ضَارٍ (ضرو) beast of prey.

ضَعِيف weakness — ضَعْف weak — ضُعْف plur. أَضْعَاف double.

ضَلَّ (i) to err, wander from path.

ضَمَّ (u) to gather — VII. to assemble.

ضِمْن interior — مَضْمُون contents.

ضَاءَ (ضوء u) to shine — IV. to light.

ضَاعَ (ضوع) IV. to lose.

ضَافَ (ضيف) IV. to add — ضَيْف plur. ضُيُوف guest.

ضَاقَ (ضيق) V. to feel oppressed — ضِيقٌ need.

طَبِيبٌ physician.

طَبْخٌ cooking — مَطْبَخٌ kitchen.

طَبَعَ (a) to print — vn. طَبْعٌ — طَبِيعَةٌ nature — مَطْبَعَةٌ printing office.

طَبَقَ III. to agree with — VII. to cover oneself, be shut — تَطْبِيقًا لِ in accordance with.

طَجْبلاط journal.

طَحْنٌ milling.

طَرَابُلُس Tripoli.

طَرَحَ (a) to throw down or out — طَرِيحٌ prostrate.

طَرَدَ (u) to chase away — طَرْدٌ parcel.

أَطْرَشُ deaf.

طَرَفٌ side, place.

طَرَقَ (u) to knock at — IV. to cast down the eyes — طَرِيقٌ plur. طُرُقٌ and طُرْقٌ way — طَرِيقَةٌ plur. طَرَائِقُ path, fashion.

طَعِمَ IV. to feed — طَعَامٌ plur. أَطْعِمَةٌ food

طَعَنَ (a) to pierce — طَعْنَةٌ thrust of a lance.

طَفِيَ IV. to extinguish.

طَقْمٌ uniform.

طَلَبَ (u) to require, seek — vn. طَلَبٌ and طِلْبَةٌ — مَطْلُوبٌ demand.

طَلَعَ (u) to mount, rise, go out to (with عَلَى) — VIII. to examine (with عَلَى) — X. to get information about — طَلْعَةٌ countenance — طَالِعٌ star (at birth).

طَلَقَ (i) to be repudiated (of a woman) — II. to repudiate — IV. to set free, shoot — مُطْلَقٌ absolute.

طَمْأَنَ to quieten oneself.

طَمِعَ (a) to desire — طَمْعٌ greediness.

طَهُرَ II. to purify, clean.

طَاوُوس plur. طَوَاوِيس peacock.

طَاعَ (طوع) IV. to obey — X. to be able to do (with accus.) — طَاعَة obedience — سَمْعًا وَطَاعَةً at your service — مُطِيع obedient.

طَافَ (طوف u) to go round.

طَاقَ (طوق) IV. to be able to do — طَاقَة power.

طَالَ (طول u) to be long — II. and IV. to lengthen — طُولٌ length — طَوِيلٌ long.

طَاوِلَة table.

طَوَى VII. to contain (with عَلَى) — طَيّ fold — طَيَّة enclosed.

طَابَ (طيب i) to be good, calm oneself — طَيِّب good — طُوبَى hail!

طَارَ (طير i) to fly — IV. to cause to fly — طَائِر and طَيْر plur. أَطْيَار bird.

ظَبْي gazelle.

ظَرِيف plur. ظُرَفَاءُ witty person, agreeable, comfortable.

ظَلَّ II. to give shade to — ظِلّ shade — مُظِلّ shady.

ظَلَمَ IV. to become dark — ظَلَامٌ darkness — ظُلْم oppression — ظَالِمٌ oppressor — مَظْلُومٌ oppressed

ظَنَّ (u) to think, believe, esteem — ظَنّ plur. ظُنُونٌ thought.

ظَهَرَ (a) to seem, appear — IV. to manifest, show — X. to get the upper hand — ظُهُور appearance — ظَهْر back — ظُهْر and ظَهِيرَة midday — ظَاهِر external.

عَبَأَ (a) *pass.* to be anxious about — عَبَاءَة woollen cloak.

عَبَثًا in vain.

عَبَدَ (u) to worship — عَبْد plur. عَبِيد slave — عَبْدُ ٱللّٰه n. pr. — مَعْبَد temple.

عَبَرَ VIII. to esteem, be experienced — عَبْرَة tears — عِبَارَة expression.

عَبَّاس n. pr. — بَنُو ٱلْعَبَّاسِ the Abbasids.

عُثْمَانِيّ Osman Turks.

عَجَّاج raging (of the sea).

عَجِبَ (a) I. and V. to be astonished at (with مِنْ) — IV. to please — عَجَبٌ astonishment — عَجَبًا adv. wonderfully — عَجِيبٌ wonderful — عَجِيبَةٌ plur. عَجَائِبُ wonderful matter.

عَجَزَ (i) to be unable to do (with عَنْ) — عَجُوزٌ plur. عَجَائِزُ old woman.

عَجِلَ II. to do quickly — X. to hurry — عَجَلٌ and عَجَلَةٌ haste — مُعَجَّلٌ paid beforehand — عَاجِلًا adv. quickly.

عَدَّ (u) to count, number — IV. to prepare — X. to prepare oneself — عَدَدٌ and عِدَّةٌ number — عَدِيدٌ numerous.

عَدَلَ III. to be equivalent to, correspond to — عَدْلٌ justice — عَادِلٌ just — مُعْتَدِلٌ temperate.

عَدِمَ (a) to cease to exist, be deprived — IV. to deprive of (with 2 accus.) — عَدَمٌ want.

عَدُوٌّ plur. أَعْدَاءٌ enemy — عَدَا عَنْ beside.

عَذْبٌ sweet (water) — عُذُوبَةٌ sweetness — عَذَابٌ anxiety.

عَذَرَ (i) to excuse — V. to be effaced — عُذْرٌ excuse.

عَرَبٌ arabs (coll.), bedouins — عِرَاقِيّ n. pr. أَعْرَابِيّ an arab, a bedouin.

عَرُوسٌ bride, young woman.

عَرْشٌ throne.

عَرَضَ (i) to offer, give over, communicate, happen to — V. to interfere in — VIII. to oppose — عَرْضٌ breadth — عَرِيضٌ broad.

عَرَفَ (i) to know — II. to inform — VI. to be recognised — VIII. to confess, grant (with بِ) — مَعْرِفَةٌ knowledge — مَعْرُوفٌ good, pleasure.

عَرَقٌ arak.

مَعْرِكَة battle.

عز (i) to be powerful — عِزّة power — عَزِيز dear, valuable.

عزم (i) to determine on (with على) — عَزُومَة dinner party.

عزى II. to comfort.

عسر II. to make difficult — عَسِير difficult.

عَسْكَر plur. عَسَاكِر army, troops — عَسْكَرِي soldier.

عَسَل honey.

عسى perhaps.

عُشْب plur. أَعْشَاب herb.

عشر III. to be in company with — عَشْر fem. عَشَرَة ten — عِشْرُون twenty.

عشا V. to eat in the evening. — عَشَاء evening meal-time.

عصفور plur. عَصَافِير sparrow.

عَاصِمَة chief city — المُعْتَصِم and المُسْتَعْصِم n. pr. of Caliphs.

عَصًا (عصو) stick — عِصْيَان rebellion.

عَضّ (a and u) to bite

عضد IV. to support.

عَطِش (a) to be thirsty.

عَطْفَة turn, side street — عَاطِفَة plur. عَوَاطِف tender feeling.

عطا IV. to give — VI. to give to one another — إِعْطَاء gift.

عظم II. to show honour to — عَظْم plur. عِظَام bone — عَظِيم excellent, extraordinary — مُعْظَم greater part.

عِفَّة chastity, trueness.

عفا (u) to pardon (with عَن) — عَفْو pardon — عَافِيَة good health.

عقد (i) to summon — عَقْد contract — عُقْدَة plur. عُقَد knot.

عَقْل plur. عُقُول intellect — عَاقِل plur. عُقَلَاء intellectual.

عَكَّا Acre.

عَلَّ and لَعَلَّ perhaps.

عَلَجَ III. to treat (a patient).

عَلَفَ (i) to feed — عَلَفٌ fodder — مَعْلَفٌ manger.

عَلِقَ II. to hang up — IV. to kindle — V. to hold fast to (with بِ), hang together, be dependent.

عَلِمَ (a) to know — II. to teach — IV. to inform — V. to learn — عِلْمٌ plur. عُلُومٌ science — تَعْلِيمٌ doctrine — عَلَامَةٌ mark — عَالِمٌ wise, learned — عَلَّامٌ very learned — مُعَلِّمٌ teacher.

عَالَمٌ plur. عَالَمُونَ world.

عَلَنَ IV. to advertise, inform.

عَلَا (u) to be high, loud — V. to come near — عَالٍ high — أَعْلَى highest, summit — عَلِيٌّ high, loud, Ali (n. pr.) — عُلْوِيٌّ exalted — تَعَالَى (God) is exalted — مَعْلَاةٌ plur. مَعَالٍ highest aim.

عَلَى on — عَلَى أَنْ on condition that.

عَمَّ II to make general or universal — عَمٌّ uncle (on the father's side) — بِنْتُ ٱلْعَمِّ cousin, wife — عُمُومٌ public, universality — عَامَّةُ ٱلنَّاسِ common people — عَامٌّ and عُمُومِيٌّ public, general — عُمُومًا generally.

عَمَدَ VIII. to rely on.

عَمَرَ (i) to live long — عُمْرٌ life, age — عُمَرُ Omar — عُمَيْرٌ diminutive of the preceding — عَمْرٌو Amr — عَامِرٌ flourishing.

عَمِيقٌ deep.

عَمِلَ (a) to do, have effect — IV. to hasten — VI. to transact business with one another — عَمَلٌ plur. أَعْمَالٌ action, deed, district — عَامِلٌ plur. عُمَّالٌ workman — مَعْمَلٌ manufactury

عَنْ from, instead of.

عِنْدَ with — عِنَادٌ obstinacy — عَنِيدٌ obstinate.

عُنُق neck.

عُنْوَان title, address (of a letter).

عَنَى (i) to concern, refer to — VIII. to care for — عَنَاءٌ pain — عِنَايَة anxiety.

عَهِدَ (a) to impose a condition, know — III. to make covenant — V. to care for — عَهْدٌ contract, epoch.

عَادَ (عود u) to return, become — IV to make to return, repeat — VIII. to be accustomed — عَوْدٌ return — عَادَة plur. عَوَائِدُ custom — عُودٌ plur. عِيدَانٌ aloe wood, stick.

عَاذَ (عوذ u) to take refuge (with بِ).

عَازَ (عوز u) to need, wish.

عُوَيْسِيَّة penknife.

عَالَ (عول) II. to put faith in — عَائِلَة family.

عَامَ (عوم u) to swim — عَامٌ year.

عَانَ (عون) III and IV. to help — X. to ask for help — مُعَاوِن helper.

عَابَ (عيب i) to blame.

عِيدٌ plur. أَعْيَادٌ feast — عِيدُ ٱلْمِيلَادِ Christmas.

عَارٌ (عير) shame, disgrace.

عَاشَ (عيش i) to live — V. to earn a living — عَيْشٌ and عِيشَة life — عَائِشَة (pet name عَيُّوش) Ayesha (n. pr. of woman) — مَعَاشٌ wages, plur. مَعَايِشُ provisions.

عِيَاطٌ cry, howl.

عَانَ (عين i) II. to determine — عَيْنٌ plur. أَعْيُنٌ and عُيُونٌ eye, spring — عَيِّنَة specimen, proof — عَيَّانٌ sick.

غِبَّ after.

غَدَرَ to deceive — III. to forsake.

غَدَا V. to breakfast — غَدَاءٌ breakfast — غَدٌ following day — غَدًا to-morrow.

غَذَا V. and VIII. to nourish oneself.

غَرَبَ (u) to set (of the sun) — غُرُوبٌ sunset — غَرْبٌ west — غَرْبِيٌّ western — غُرْبَةٌ foreign land — غَرِيبٌ plur. غُرَبَاءُ strange, extraordinary — مَغْرِبٌ Maghreb, western land — مَغْرِبِيٌّ plur. مَغَارِبَةٌ moor.

غَرْبَلَ to sift.

غَرِدَ I. and II. to twitter.

غِرْشٌ plur. غُرُوشٌ piastre.

غَرَضٌ aim.

غُرْفَةٌ plur. غُرَفٌ room.

غَرِقَ IV. to drown.

غَزَّةُ Gaza.

غَزِيرٌ abundant.

غَزَالٌ plur. غِزْلَانٌ gazelle.

غَزْوٌ raid — مَغْزًى meaning, moral.

غَسَقَ (i) to be dark.

غَسَلَ (i) to wash.

غَشِيَ to cover — غُشِيَ عَلَيْهِ he fainted.

غَضٌّ fresh.

غَضِبَ (a) to be or become angry — IV. to make angry — غَضَبٌ anger.

غِطَاءٌ plur. غِطْيَانٌ covering.

غَفَرَ X. to ask pardon.

غَفْلَةٌ carelessness.

غَلِيلٌ thirst.

غَلَبَ (i) to conquer — غَلَبَةٌ victory — غَالِبٌ usual.

غَلِطَ (a) to make a mistake, be deceived

غَلُظَ IV. to speak harshly.

غَلَقَ IV. to bolt (a door).

غُلَامٌ plur. غِلْمَانٌ youth.

غَالٍ (غلو) dear.

غَمٌّ anxiety — مَغْمُومٌ anxious.

غَمَرَ (u) to cover, overwhelm.

غُمِيَ عَلَيْهِ he fainted

غَنِمَ VIII. to seize an opportunity — غَنَمٌ sheep (coll.) — غَنِيمَةٌ booty.

غَنِىَ X. to esteem unnecessary — غِنَاءٌ song — غَنِىٌّ plur. أَغْنِيَاءُ rich.

غَاثَ (غوث) X. to call for help.

غَاصَ (غوص u) to plunge.

غَابَ (غيب) i I. and V. to be absent, depart — غِيَابٌ absence — غَيْبٌ distant, hidden — غَائِبٌ absent.

غَارَ (غير) II. to change — V. to be changed — غَيْرٌ other than, not — مِنْ غَيْرِ (بِغَيْرِ) without — غَيْرَ أَنَّ on the condition that.

غَيْطٌ garden, field.

غَامَ (غيم i) to be cloudy.

غَايَةٌ highest degree.

فَ and, and so, then — فَإِنَّ for.

فُؤَادٌ heart.

فَتَّ II. to crush.

فَتَحَ (a) to open — فَتْحٌ opening, capture — فُتُوحٌ capture — اَلْفَاتِحَةُ the first sura of the Koran — مِفْتَاحٌ key.

فَتَشَ II. to seek (with عَنْ or عَلَى), inspect.

فَتَكَ (u) to rage — فَتْكٌ act of violence.

فِتْنَةٌ sedition.

فَتًى youth — فَتَاةٌ (فتو) girl.

فَجْرٌ dawn.

فَحْصٌ scrutiny.

فَاخِرٌ and مُفْتَخِرٌ splendid.

فَخِيمٌ honoured.

فَرَّ (i) to flee — فِرَارٌ flight — مَفَرٌّ escape.

فَرَجَ V. to look with pleasure at (with عَلَى) — فَرَجٌ comfort, joy.

فَرِحَ (a) to rejoice — فَرَحٌ plur. أَفْرَاحٌ joy — فَرِحٌ and فَرْحَانُ glad.

فَرَدَ VII. to be single, alone — فَرْدٌ a piece, parcel.

فَرَسٌ plur. أَفْرَاسٌ horse, mare — فَارِسٌ plur. فَوَارِسُ rider.

مَفْرُوشَات (upholstered) furniture.

فُرْصَة opportunity.

فَرْع plur. فُرُوع branch, tributary (stream).

فَرَغَ to finish (with مِنْ) — IV. to empty out, (أَلْجُهْد) strive — فَارِغ empty.

فَرَّقَ II. to separate, isolate — III. to leave — V. and VIII. to separate — فَرْق difference — فَرَق fear — فِرَاق separation — فَرِيق party, division — مَفْرِق parting of the hair.

فَرَكَ (u) to rub.

فُرْن plur. أَفْرَان oven.

إِفْرِنْج Frank, European (coll.) — إِفْرِنْجِي Frankish, European.

فَرَنْسَوِي plur. فَرَنْسَوِيَّة french.

فِرَانْك franc.

فَسِيح roomy.

فَسَدَ IV. to corrupt.

فُسْطَاط old Cairo.

فَصَلَ (i) to divide — II. to isolate, cut out — فَصْل plur. فُصُول section, season — تَفْصِيل detail.

فِضَّة silver.

فَضَلَ IV. to make excellent — فَضْل plur. فُضُول excellence, grace — فَضْلًا عَنْ besides — تَفَضُّل kindness — فَاضِل excellent.

فَطَرَ (u) to cleave — فِطْرَة religious feeling.

فَاطِمَة n. pr. of woman.

فَعَلَ (a) to make, do — فِعْل plur. أَفْعَال deed, verb.

أَفْعَى plur. أَفَاعٍ viper.

فَقَدَ to lose — VIII. to seek something lost — فَقْد loss — مَفْقُود wanting, not on hand.

فَقِير plur. فُقَرَاء poor, needy.

فَقَطْ only.

فِقْه jurisprudence.

فَكَّ (u) to let loose.

فَكَرَ V. and VIII. to think, consider (with فِى) — فِكْر and فِكْرَة plur. أَفْكَار thought.

فَاكِهَة plur. فَوَاكِه fruit.

فَلَّاح peasant.

فَيْلَسُوف philosopher.

فَلَق dawn.

فُلَان a certain (person) — فُلَانِىّ a certain (adj.).

فَم mouth.

فِنْجَان cup.

فَهِمَ (a) to understand — X. to get information about.

فَاتَ (فوت u) to pass by, escape.

فَادَ (فود) IV. to benefit, inform — فَائِدَة plur. فَوَائِد profit.

فَازَ (فوز u) to acquire (with بِ) — (بِٱلنَّفْسِ) to save oneself.

فَاقَ (فوق) X. to wake up — فَوْق above, on.

فُول beans.

فُو (فوه) (only with genit. and suffixes) mouth.

فِى in — فِيمَا while.

فَاضَ (فيض) IV. to pour — فَيَضَان flood — فَائِض interest (on money).

قَبِيح bad, ugly.

قَبْر grave.

قَبَضَ (i) to seize (with عَلَى), receive money — VII. to shrink — قَبْض seizure, receiving of money — قَبْضَة handle.

قَبْطَان captain.

قَبِلَ (a) to receive, take up — II. to kiss — III. to correspond to, go to meet — IV. to advance to (with عَلَى) — VI. to meet one another — X. to receive — قَبُول reception — قِبْلَة south — قِبْلِىّ southern — ٱلْوَجْه ٱلْقِبْلِى upper Egypt — قَبِيلَة tribe (of Arabs) — قَبْلَ before (prep.) — قَبْلًا before (adv.) — قَابِل coming (month etc.) — مُسْتَقْبَل future.

قَتَلَ (u) to kill — III. to fight — قَتْل killing — قَتِيل killed.

قَدْ (particle of strengthening with the perf.) already — (with imperf.) sometimes.

قَدَرَ (i) to be able — II. to determine — قَدْر value — مِقْدَار amount — قَادِر able to do (with عَلَى).

قَدِمَ (a) to arrive — II. to offer, present — V. to come forward, advance, precede — قُدُوم arrival — قَدَم foot — قَادِم coming, next (month etc.) — قَدِيم plur. قُدَمَاء ancient — قُدَّام in front of.

قَذَفَ (i) to row.

قَرَّ (i) to persevere, be refreshed (of the eye) — IV. to confess (with بِ) — X. to lead to confess — قَرَار determination — قُرَّة ٱلْعَيْن consolation — بَرَّة dry land, continent — مَقَرّ residence.

قَرَأَ (a) to read — IV. to make to read, send (greeting) — vn. قِرَاءَة — قُرْآن reading, Koran.

قَرُبَ (u) to be near — VIII. to approach — قُرْب neighbourhood — قَرِيب near — قَرِيب عَنْ قَرِيبٍ shortly — plur. أَقْرِبَاء and أَقَارِب relative — قَارِب skiff — مُقَرَّب close to — تَقْرِيبًا about.

قِرْد ape.

قِرْش plur. قُرُوش (= غِرْش) piastre.

قَرْض and إِسْتِقْرَاض loan.

قَرَعَ (a) to knock (at a door).

قَرَنَ VIII. to marry — قَرْن century — قَرِينَة spouse.

قَرْيَة plur. قُرًى village.

قِسْط rate (of payment).

ٱلْقُسْطَنْطِينِيَّة Constantinople.

قَسَمَ (i) to divide, share — قِسْم plur. أَقْسَام part — قِسْمَة division.

قَسَا III. to endure.

قَصَّ (u) to narrate to (with عَلَى) — قِصَّة narrative, story — مِقَصّ scissors.

قَصَدَ (i) to aim at, make for, intend — قَصْد and مَقْصُود purpose, aim.

قَصُرَ II. to neglect — قِصَر shortness — قَصْر plur. قُصُور castle.

قَصَا X. to investigate.

قَضَّ VII. to rush.

قَضِمَ (a) to crunch, nibble.

قَضَى (i) to decide, be judge, spend, complete — VII. to pass away — VIII. to desire, seek — قَضَاء decision, accomplishment, settlement, Kaḍa (Turkish district) — قَضِيَّة affair — قَاضٍ judge.

قِطّ cat (coll.).

قَطَرَ IV. to make to drop — اَلْقُطْر الْمِصْرِى the land of Egypt.

قَطَعَ (a) to cut, cut through — قَطَعَ طُرُقًا to waylay — II. to cut to pieces — VII. to be cut off — قِطْعَة piece — قَطِيع flock, herd — قَاطِع cutting.

اَلْمُقَطَّم the muqaṭṭam hill (near Cairo).

قَعَدَ (u) to sit down — قَاعِدَة plur. قَوَاعِد rule.

قَعْر bottom (of the sea etc.).

قَفْر plur. قِفَار desert.

قَفَلَ (i) to shut — قَافِلَة caravan.

قَفَا VIII. to follow — قَفَا back of head, neck.

قَلَّ (i) to be less than (with عَنْ) — قَلَّمَا rarely — قِلَّة smallness — قَلِيل small, few — قَلِيلًا مَا seldom — مُقِلّ poor.

قَلَبَ VII. to revolve — قَلْب plur. قُلُوب heart — قَلْبِى cordial.

قَلَّدَ II. to imitate.

قَلْعَة fortress, citadel.

قَلِقَ (a) to be disturbed — IV. to disturb — قَلَقٌ unrest.

قَلَمٌ plur. أَقْلَامٌ reed, pen.

إِقْلِيمٌ zone.

قِمَّةٌ summit.

قَمَرٌ moon.

قَامُوسٌ dictionary.

قُمَاشٌ plur. أَقْمِشَةٌ cloth — قَمَّاشٌ dealer in cloth.

قَمِيصٌ plur. قُمْصَانٌ shirt.

قِنْدِيلٌ lamp.

قَنِعَ (a) to be content with (with بِ).

قَاهِرٌ conquering — أَلْقَاهِرَةُ Cairo — قَهَّارٌ conqueror.

تَقَهْقَرَ to withdraw.

قَهْوَةٌ coffee.

قُوتٌ plur. أَقْوَاتٌ provisions.

قِيَادَةٌ (قود) guidance.

قَالَ (قول u) to say — III. to get for oneself — قَوْلٌ and مَقَالٌ speech — مَقَالَةٌ article (in a journal etc.).

قَامَ (قوم u) to rise, occupy oneself with (with بِ), revolt against (with عَلَى) — قُمْ بِنَا let us rise! — III. to oppose — IV. to put up, establish, stay — X. to be straight — قَوْمٌ people — قِيَامَةٌ resurrection — قِيمَةٌ value, price — قَائِمَةٌ list, catalogue — إِقَامَةٌ and مُقَامٌ rank — مَقَامٌ sojourn — قَائِمَقَامٌ Kaimakam (Turkish official) — قَائِمَقَامِيَّةٌ district (governed by a Kaimakam) — إِسْتِقَامَةٌ straightness, uprightness — مُسْتَقِيمٌ straight.

قُوَّةٌ power, strength — قَوِيٌّ strong.

مِقْيَاسٌ measuring instrument.

كَ as (with genit.) — كَمَا as (with following sentence) — كَأَنَّ as though, as if — كَذَا and فَكَذَا and كَذٰلِكَ thus.

كَئِيبٌ sad.

كَأْسٌ cup.

كُبَّايَةٌ glass (for drinking).

كَبَدَ III. and V. to endure — كَبِدٌ plur. أَكْبَادٌ and كُبُودٌ liver, heart, interior.

كَبُرَ (u) to be or become large or great — X. to esteem great or important — كِبْرٌ pride — كَبِيرٌ plur. كِبَارٌ great.

كَبَا (u) to fall on the face.

كَتَبَ (u) to write — III. to write to, correspond with — VIII. to subscribe — كِتَابَةٌ writing — كِتَابٌ plur. كُتُبٌ book, letter — مَكْتَبٌ office — مَكْتَبَةٌ library, bookshop — مَكْتُوبٌ letter.

كَثُرَ (u) to be or become numerous — كُثْرٌ and كَثْرَةٌ abundance — كَثِيرًا — very — مُكْثِرٌ rich.

كَدِرَ II. to vex — كَدَرٌ trouble.

كَذَبَ (i) to lie.

كَرْبٌ grief.

كَرْدِينَالٌ cardinal.

كُرْسِيٌّ throne.

كَرُمَ IV. to honour (with عَلَى) — V. to do one a kindness — كَرْمٌ vineyard — كَرِيمٌ generous.

كَرِهَ (a) to hate.

كَرًى slumber.

كَسَرَ (i) to break — كَاسِرٌ beast of prey.

كَسَلٌ idleness — كَسُولٌ very idle.

كَشَفَ (i) to uncover, examine — كَشْفٌ uncovering.

كَافَّةٌ collection, all.

كَافَأَ III. to reward — كُفُوٌ a like, up to.

كَفَحَ III. to fight hand to hand.

كَفَى (i) to satisfy — كِفَايَةٌ satisfaction.

كُلٌّ every, all, whole — كُلَّمَا whenever.

كَلْبٌ plur. كِلَابٌ dog.

كَلَّمَ II. to speak to — III. to converse with — V. to speak — كَلَامٌ speech, controversy — كَلِمَةٌ word.

كِلَا both.

كُلُوتْ بَكْ n. pr. Clot Bey.

كَمْ how much? how many?

كَمْبِيَالَة bill of exchange.

كَمِّيَّة quantity, amount.

كُمَيْت reddish brown.

كُمَيْد n. pr.

كَمَال perfection, n. pr. — كَامِل perfect.

كَانُونُ ٱلثَّانِي January.

كَنَسَ (i) to sweep.

كُوخ hut.

كَادَ (كود a) almost to do.

كَانَ (كون u) to be — vn. كَوْن — مَكَان plur. أَمَاكِنُ place — مَكَانَهُ in his place.

كُونْيَاك cognac.

كِيس wallet, purse — كُوَيِّس pretty.

كَيْفَ how? — كَيْفِيَّة manner, contents.

كَالَ (كيل i) to measure — كَيْل measure.

لَ particle of emphasis — لَعَلَّ perhaps — لَئِنْ even if.

لِ (prep.) for, to — (conj.) so that, in order to — لِذَا or لِذٰلِكَ therefore — لِمَ, لِمَا and لِمَاذَا why? — لِكَيْ so that — لِأَنَّ because.

لَا not, no, there is not.

لَافِيجَرِي n. pr. Lavigerie.

لُؤْلُؤ pearl (coll.).

لَاءَمَ III. to suit, be adapted to.

لَبِسَ (a) to put on (clothes) — vn. لُبْس — لِبَاس clothes, trousers — مَلْبَس and مَلْبُوس clothes, clothing.

لَبَن plur. أَلْبَان milk.

لُبْنَان Lebanon.

لَبَّى II. to answer in the affirmative.

لَجَّ (a) to persevere in — لُجَّة plur. لُجَج depth (of the sea).

لَجَأَ VIII. to take flight.

لَحَّ IV. to oppress (with عَلَى).

لَحِسَ (a) to lick.

لَحَظَ III. to remark — لَحْظ glance — لَحْظَة moment.

لَحِقَ (a) to follow, concern — لَاحِقَةٌ plur. لَوَاحِقُ appurtenance.

لَحْمٌ plur. لُحُومٌ meat — لَحْمَةٌ a piece of meat.

لَحْنٌ plur. أَلْحَانٌ melody.

لِحْيَةٌ beard.

لَدَى at.

لَذَّ IV. to make (sensuously) pleasant — لَذَّةٌ pleasure — لَذِيذٌ pleasant.

لَزِمَ (a) to be necessary — لَازِمٌ necessary — لَازِمَةٌ plur. لَوَازِمُ need.

لِسَانٌ plur. أَلْسُنٌ tongue, language.

لِصٌّ plur. لُصُوصٌ robber.

لَطَفَ III. to treat in a friendly way — لُطْفٌ friendliness — لَطِيفٌ friendly, pleasant.

لَطَمَ (i) to slap.

لَعِبَ (a) I. and VI. play — III. to jest with — لَعِبٌ plur. أَلْعَابٌ play.

لَعِينٌ cursed.

لُغَةٌ (لغو) language.

لَفٌّ fold — لَفًّا included.

لَفَتَ VIII. to turn to.

لُقْمَةٌ bit, piece.

لَقِيَ (a) I. and III. to meet — IV. to throw — V. to receive — VI. and VIII. to meet — X. to fall on the back —

لِقَاءٌ meeting.

لٰكِنْ and لٰكِنَّ and وَلٰكِنْ and وَلٰكِنَّ but.

لَمْ (with imperf. in sense of perf.) not.

لَمَّا when, since.

لَمَّ to collect — IV. to haunt, infest (with بِ).

لَمَسَ VIII. to beseech (with مِنْ)

لَمَعَ (a) to flash — IV. to cause to shine, deal with.

لَهِيبٌ flame.

لَهِفَ V. to sigh.

لَوْ if (of a pure supposition) — وَلَوْ even if.

لَامَ (لوم u) to blame.

لَوْنٌ plur. أَلْوَانٌ colour.

لَيْتَ would that!

لَيْسَ not to be.

لَاقَ (ليق i) to be fitting, worthy.

لَيْلٌ plur. لَيَالٍ night (coll.).

لِيمَانٌ house of correction.

لِيمُونَادُو lemonade.

لَانَ (لين) II. to soften.

مَا and مَاذَا what? — مَا what, that.

مَا not.

مِئَةٌ (or مِائَةٌ) hundred.

مَتَى when?

مَثَلَ V. to appear (before a court) — VIII. to obey — مَثَلٌ resemblance, fable — مِثْلٌ plur. أَمْثَالٌ like, as — مِثَالٌ pattern — تِمْثَالٌ statue.

مَجَدَ (u) to be renowned — II. to praise — مَجْدٌ glory — مَاجِدٌ noble — مَجِيدِيٌّ (رِيَالٌ مَجِيدِيٌّ) mejidi (money worth 22 piastres and 30 paras).

مَجَّانًا gratis, free of charge.

مَحَا (u) to blot out, efface.

مَدَّ (u) to stretch, lengthen — IV. to help, reinforce — V. to stretch oneself, rest — VIII. to be stretched, prolonged — مُدَّةٌ respite, space of time — مَادَّةٌ plur. مَوَادُّ material — مَدِيدٌ extended.

مَدْحٌ praise.

مَدِينَةٌ plur. مُدُنٌ city.

مُذْ since.

مَرَّ (u) to pass by — IV. to make bitter — مُرُورٌ passing by, course — مَرَّةٌ time — مَرَّةً once — مُرٌّ bitter.

مَرْءٌ man — إِمْرَأَةٌ or مَرْأَةٌ plur. نِسَاءٌ woman.

مَرْجٌ plur. مُرُوجٌ meadow.

مِرْسِيه n. pr. Mercier.

مَرِضَ (a) to be or become sick — مَرَضٌ plur. أَمْرَاضٌ sickness — مَرِيضٌ sick.

مَرَّاكِش Morocco.

تَمَرْمَرَ to murmur.

مَسَحَ (a) to enter (in a catalogue etc.) — أَلْمَسِيحُ the messiah, Christ — مَسِيحِيٌّ a Christian, christian (adj.).

مَسَكَ (i) to seize — IV. to hold back — مَسْكٌ seizure — مِسْكِينٌ poor.

مسى II. to wish good evening — IV. to be or remain in the evening — مَسَاءٌ evening.

مُسِيُو monsieur.

مَشَى (i) to go, walk — V. to walk about — مِشْيَةٌ gait — مَاشِيَةٌ plur. مَوَاشٍ cattle.

مِصْرُ Egypt, Cairo — مِصْرِيٌّ Egyptian, Cairene.

مَضَى (i) to go away, be lost — مُضِيٌّ course (of time) — مَاضٍ past, last.

مَطَرَ (u) I. and IV. to rain — مَطَرٌ plur. أَمْطَارٌ rain.

مَعَ with, in spite of — مَعَ أَنَّ although.

مَعَنَ IV. to be zealous.

مَكَثَ (u) to tarry, stay.

مَكُنَ IV. to enable, be possible — V. to be enabled to (with مِنْ) — مُمْكِنٌ possible.

مَكِينَةٌ machine

مَلَأَ (a) to fill.

مَالِحٌ salted — مَلَّاحٌ sailor — مِلَاحَةٌ navigation.

مَلَكَ (i) to possess — II. to give possession of — مِلْكٌ and مُلْكٌ plur. أَمْلَاكٌ possession, property — مَلِكٌ plur. مُلُوكٌ king — مَلَكٌ (مَلْأَكٌ) plur. مَلَائِكَةٌ angel — مَالِكٌ and مَلِيكٌ ruler — مَمْلَكَةٌ kingdom — مَمْلُوكٌ mamluke, white slave.

مِلْيُونٌ million.

مَنْ who? he who.

مِنْ of, from, than.

مَنّ favour — مَنُونٌ death — مَمْنُونِيَّةٌ obligation, thanks.

مُنْذُ since.

مَنَعَ (a) to prevent — VIII. to refuse.

مَنْفُ Memphis.

مَنُوفُ Manuf (a city in Egypt).

مَنَى V. to wish — مَنِيَّةٌ fate, death.

مُهْجَةٌ blood.

مَهَلَ V. to be slow.

مِهْنَةٌ profession, trade.

مَاتَ (موت u) to die — IV. to kill — مَوْتٌ and مِيتَةٌ and مَمَاتٌ death — مَيِّتٌ dead.

مَوْجٌ plur. أَمْوَاجٌ wave.

الْمُوسْكِي the Muski (a street in Cairo).

مُوسَى (colloquially مُوس) plur. أَمْوَاسٌ razor — مُوسَى Moses.

مُوضَةٌ mode, fashion.

مَالٌ (مول) plur. أَمْوَالٌ wealth, capital — مَوَالِيَا (or مَوَالِي) a kind of poetry.

مَاءٌ (موه) plur. مِيَاهٌ water.

مَائِدَةٌ (ميد) table

مَالَ (ميل i) to incline, bend — مَيْلٌ inclination — مِيلٌ plur. أَمْيَالٌ mile.

نَبَأَ II. and IV. to announce to (with accus. of person and بِ of thing) — نَبَأٌ news.

نَبْحٌ barking.

نُبْذَةٌ plur. نُبَذٌ article (in a journal etc.).

نَبَعَ (a, i, u) to spring up (of water).

نَبَهَ VIII. to pay attention, notice — نَبَاهَةٌ wakefulness — نَبِيهٌ awake, clever.

نَجَّارٌ joiner.

نَجَزَ IV. to complete.

نَجْلٌ plur. أَنْجَالٌ offspring, son.

نَجْمٌ plur. نُجُومٌ star — مُنَجِّمٌ astrologer — نَاجِمٌ clear.

نَجَا (u) to escape — نَجَاةٌ escape, deliverance.

نَحْبٌ death — قَضَى نَحْبَهُ he died.

نُحَاسٌ copper — نَحَّاسٌ coppersmith.

نَحْلٌ bees (coll.).

نَحْنُ we.

نَاحِيَةٌ (نحو) plur. نَوَاحٍ district — نَحْوَ towards, about.

نَخَبَ VIII. to choose.

نَخْلَةٌ n. pr.

نَدَبَ (u) to bewail.

مِنْدِيلٌ pockethandkerchief.

نَدِمَ (a) to repent — نَدَامَةٌ repentance — نَدِيمٌ confidant.

نَدَا III. to call, summon.

نَذْرٌ vow.

نَذْلٌ plur. أَنْذَالٌ vile, simpleton — نَذِيلٌ abject.

نَرْجِسِيٌّ narcissue-like.

نَزَلَ (i) to descend, dismount — vn. نُزُولٌ — نَزِيلٌ guest — مَنْزِلٌ dwelling.

نُزْهَةٌ pleasure.

نِسْبَةٌ relation.

نَسِيجٌ plur. أَنْسِجَةٌ and نَسَائِجُ textile fabric, tissue.

نُسْخَةٌ copy.

نِسَاءٌ (plur. of إِمْرَأَةٌ) women.

نَسِيَ (a) to forget — IV. to cause to forget.

نَشَأَ IV. to found — مَنْشَأٌ origin.

نَشَدَ (u) to announce — IV. to quote, recite.

نَشَرَ VIII. to spread.

نَشَاطٌ liveliness, zeal — نَشِيطٌ lively.

نَشَلَ (u) to take away.

نِشَانٌ order, badge of an order.

نَصِيبٌ lot, happiness.

نَصَحَ (a) to advise well — نَصِيحَةٌ plur. نَصَائِحُ good advice — نَاصِحٌ adviser.

نَصْرَانٌ and نَصْرَانِيٌّ plur. نَصَارَى Nazarene = Christian.

نَصَفَ III. to divide into halves — VIII. to be divided into halves — مُنْتَصَف half — نِصْف middle.

نَاصِيَة (نصو) fore-lock..

نَطْع leather mat.

نَطَقَ X. to hear a case (of a judge) — مُسْتَنْطِق examining judge — مِنْطَقَة zone.

نَظَرَ (u) to see — VIII. to expect — نَظَر and نَظْرَة glance, look — نَظَرًا إِلَى in regard to — نَاظِر inspector — مَنْظَر appearance.

نَظَافَة cleanness, purity — نَظِيف clean, pure.

نَظَمَ II. to put in order — V. and VIII. to be put in order — نِظَام order, law.

نَعْجَة plur. نِعَاج sheep.

نَعَمَ IV. to be kind to (with عَلَى) — نَعِمَ to be good — نَعَم cattle (coll.) — نَعْمَة well-being — نِعْمَة plur. نِعَم benefit — نَعَمْ yes — نَاعِم tender.

نَفَّاث blower.

نَفِدَ (a) to be out of print.

نَفَذَ II. to fulfil (a wish etc.).

نُفُور flight.

نَفْس plur. أَنْفُس and نُفُوس soul, self — نَفِيس precious.

نَفَعَ VIII. to use — نَافِع useful

نَفْي expulsion.

نِقَاب veil.

نَقْد plur. نُقُود cash, ready money.

نَقَذَ IV. to deliver

مَنْقُوشَات sculpture.

مُنَاقَصَة lowest tender.

نَقْض plur. أَنْقَاض ruins.

نُقْطَة point.

نَاقِع penetrating, deadly (poison) — مُسْتَنْقَع marsh.

نَقْل transport.

نَقَمَ VIII. to take revenge on (with مِنْ).

نَقِي VIII. to choose.

نُكْتَة witticism.

مَنْكُودُ ٱلْحَظِّ unhappy.

نَكِرَ IV. to deny.

نِمْس plur. نُمُوس ichneumon.

ٱلنِّمْسَا Austria — نِمْسَاوِيّ Austrian.

نَهْب plundering.

نَهْر plur. أَنْهُر and أَنْهَار river — نَهَار day.

نَهَضَ (a) to rise — X. to stir up to.

نَهِكَ IV. to weaken.

نَهَا VIII. to be finished.

نُوتِيّ sailor.

مُنَاخ climate.

نُور plur. أَنْوَار light — نَار plur. نِيرَان fire.

نَوْع plur. أَنْوَاع kind, sort.

نَالَ (نول a) to attain — III. to hand over to (with two accus.) — V. to take for oneself — نَوَال attainment.

نَامَ (نوم a) to sleep — نَوْم sleep.

نَاف (نيف) yoke.

نِيل Nile.

هَا behold! — هٰكَذَا thus.

هَاتِ come!

هَارُون n. pr.

هُبُوب blowing (of wind).

ٱلْهِجْرَة the flight of Mohammed from Mecca to Medina (622 A.D.).

هَاجِس plur. هَوَاجِس unrest, disturbance.

هَاجَمَ III. to assail, assault.

هَدَّ II. to threaten.

هَدِير murmur (of water).

هَدَمَ (i) to destroy — vn. هَدْم — هُدُوم (plur.) clothes.

هَدَى (i) to guide — IV. to bestow, present — هُدًى guidance, way of salvation.

هٰذَا fem. هٰذِهِ plur. هٰؤُلَاءِ this.

هَرَبَ (u) to flee.

هَرَم plur. أَهْرَام pyramid.

هَزِيع part of the night.

هُزَال thinness.

قَطَلَ (i) to send rain.

هَلْ particle of interrogation.

هَلَّ X. to appear first (new moon), begin.

هَلَكَ IV. to destroy utterly — هَلَاكٌ destruction.

هَلُمَّ and هَلُمَّ جَرًّا come hither!

هُمَا they two.

هُمْ they (masc.).

هَمَّ (i) to be important, intend (with بِ), be anxious about (with إِلَى) — VIII. to take great pains — هَمٌّ plur. هُمُومٌ care — هِمَّةٌ care — مُهِمٌّ plur. مَهَامُّ important — مَهْمُومٌ anxious.

هَنِئَ (a) to be pleasant (of food etc.) — II. congratulate — هَنِيئًا good wish!

هُنَا here — هُنَاكَ and هُنَالِكَ there. — هُنَيْهَةً a little.

هِنْدٌ n. pr. of a woman.

مُهَنْدِسٌ engineer.

هُوَ he.

هَانَ (هون) III. to moderate (price).

هُوَذَا see!

هَانَ (هون) u) to be or become easy — IV. to offend, affront.

هَوًى passion — هَوَاءٌ air, weather.

هِيَ she.

هَاءَ (هيء) II. to prepare.

هَابَ (هيب a) to fear.

هَاجَ (هيج i) to stir up.

هَامَ (هيم i) to be passionately in love.

هَيَّا up! — هَيَّا بِنَا up, lev us go!

وَ and, by (with genit. in oath) — وَلٰكِنْ but.

وَا oh!

وَبَالٌ misfortune, evil consequences.

وَتَدٌ peg.

وَثِقَ (يَثِقُ) to trust — vn. وُثُوق — وَثِيقَة certificate.

وَجَبَ (يَجِبُ) to be necessary, incumbent on (with عَلَى) — IV. to cause — X. to deserve — إِيجَاب affirmation — وَاجِب incumbent on (with عَلَى) — بِمُوجِبِ in accordance with.

وَجَدَ (يَجِدُ) to find — وُجُود existence — إِيجَاد finding — مَوْجُود existent, on hand.

وَجِيز small.

وَجَع plur. أَوْجَاع pain.

وَجْنَة cheek.

وَجَّهَ II. to turn to — V. to make for — VIII. to turn — وَجْه plur. وُجُوه face, fashion — جِهَة side, district — وَجِيه respected.

وَحْدَ alone (with suffixes) — وَاحِد one — وَحِيد alone, single.

وَحْش plur. وُحُوش wild beast.

وَدَّ (a) to love — وِدَاد friendship.

وَدَعَ (يَدَعُ) to lay down, leave (only in imperf. and imper.) — II. to bid farewell to (with accus.) — IV. to store — وَدَاع departure.

وَادٍ valley.

وَرَاءَ behind.

وَرَدَ (يَرِدُ) (properly = to go down to water) to arrive — IV. to bring — إِيرَادَات revenues — وَرْدِيّ rosy.

وَرَق paper.

وَزِير plur. وُزَرَاء vezir, minister.

وَزَّعَ II. to share, allot.

مِيزَان (وزن) balance — مِيزَانِيَّة budget.

وزى III. to be parallel

وَسِخ dirty.

وَسْط middle — وَاسِطَة means — أَوْسَط fem. وُسْطَى middle.

وَاسِع wide, roomy — سَعَة width, comfort.

وَسَلَ V. to get the means for (with إِلَى) — وَسِيلَة means.

وَسْوَسَ to whisper, suggest — وَسْوَاس suggester (satan).

وَصَفَ (يَصِفُ) to describe — صِفَة attribute.

وَصَلَ (يَصِلُ) to arrive — وَصَلَنِي I have received — II. to bring — III. to enter into relation with — IV. to make to arrive, lead — V. to reach — VIII. to unite, reach (with إِلَى) — وُصُول arrival, reception, receipt — وَصْل receipt — مُوَاصَلَة union.

وَصَى II. to make a will, recommend — IV. to charge — وَصِيَّة charge (of parents to children etc.) will.

وَضُوء V. to wash oneself (in religious ablutions).

وَضَحَ IV. to explain — وَاضِح obvious, clear.

وَضَعَ (يَضَعُ) to set, place, lay, bring into the world, edit — vn. وَضْع — مَوْضِع place.

وَطِئَ (يَطَأُ) to tread on.

وَطَن plur. أَوْطَان home — وَطَنِيّ indigenous — مَوْطِن native land.

وَعَدَ (يَعِدُ) I. to promise (with accus. of person, بِ of thing) — IV. to threaten, promise — مِيعَاد appointed time.

وَعْر and وَعْرَة ruggedness.

وَعَظَ III. to be exhorted.

وَفَدَ (يَفِدُ) to reach.

وَافِر abundant.

وَفِقَ II. to help (of God) — III. to be suitable, correspond to, agree to (with عَلَى) — VIII. to agree, happen — تَوْفِيق success (from God).

وَفَى II. to fulfil (with بِ) — V. (pass.) to die — وَفَاء fulfilment (of a promise), payment (of a debt) — وَفَاة plur. وَفَيَات death — وَفِيّ perfect, complete.

وَقَبَ (يَقِبُ) to be eclipsed (of the moon).

وَقْت plur. أَوْقَات time — وَقْتَئِذٍ at that time.

وَقَعَ (يَقَعُ) to fall, happen — IV. to let fall — وَاقِعٌ situated — وَاقِعَةٌ plur. وَقَائِعُ event, battle — وَاقِعَةُ ٱلْحَالِ state of affairs — إِيقَاعٌ name of a dog.

وَقَفَ (يَقِفُ) to stand still, acquaint one with (with عَلَى) — IV. to refrain from (with عَنْ) — وُقُوفٌ experience of (with عَلَى) — وَقْفٌ plur. أَوْقَافٌ pious foundation or benefaction.

وَقَى VIII. to fear — تَقْوَى piety.

وَكَأَ (اِتَّكَأَ) to support oneself — مُتَّكَأٌ cushion.

وَكَلَ II. to represent — V. and VIII. to trust, rely on — وَكَالَةٌ representation — وَكِيلٌ representative.

وَلَدَ (يَلِدُ) to bear, beget — وَلَدٌ plur. أَوْلَادٌ boy, son — وَالِدٌ parent, father — وَالِدَةٌ mother — وِلَادَةٌ birth — مَوْلِدٌ birthday — مِيلَادٌ plur. مَوَالِيدُ time of birth, Christmas — ٱلْوَلِيدُ n. pr.

وَلْوَلَ to howl.

وَلِيَ (يَلِي) to be near — II. to make governor, flee — X. to master (with عَلَى of a thing) — وِلَايَةٌ province of a wāli (governor) — وَالٍ wali, governor — وَلِيٌّ master — مَوْلًى master — أَوْلَى better, more suitable.

مُومَأٌ إِلَيْهِ mentioned.

وَهَبَ (يَهِبُ) to present — وَهَّابِيٌّ wahhabite.

وَهْمٌ plur. أَوْهَامٌ imagination, prejudice.

وِيس قُنْصُل vice-consul.

وَيْلَاهْ alas!

يَا o! (particle of address).

يَئِسَ (يَيْأَسُ) to despair — يَأْسٌ despair.

يَافَا Jaffa.

يَبْس dry (land etc.).

يَد plur. أَيْدٍ hand, help — بَيْنَ يَدَيْهِ before him, in his presence.

يَسَّرَ II. to make easy — V. to be made easy, possible — يَسِير easy, small.

يَعْقُوب Jacob.

يَقِظَ IV. to waken — V. to be awakened — X. to wake up.

يَقِنَ (a) to be certain — V. to convince oneself.

يَمِين right hand.

يَنَايِرُ January.

يَانِع ripe.

يُوسُف Joseph.

يَوْم plur. أَيَّام day — يَوْمُ ٱلدِّينِ day of judgement — اَلْيَوْمَ to-day — يَوْمًا فَيَوْمًا from day to day — يَوْمًا once — ذَاتَ يَوْمٍ one day.

يُونِيه June.

English-Arabic Vocabulary for the Exercises in Part II.

Able — to be able to قَدَرَ with عَلَى

about فِي

accompany رفق III.

acquaint — to be acquainted with أنس (a)

after بَعْدَ

age دَهْر

Ali عَلِيّ

alight نَزَلَ

all جَمِيع, كُلّ

allow — to be allowed جَازَ

alms صَدَقَة

amazed مُنْدَهِش (with بِ)

ambassador سَفِير plur. سُفَرَاء

amen آمِين

angel مَلَك (مَلْأَك) plur. مَلَائِكَة

answer جَوَاب — to answer أَجَابَ

Arab عَرَب (coll.), Arabic عَرَبِيّ

arrive وَصَلَ (يَصِلُ) — وَرَدَ (يَرِدُ)

ask سَأَلَ (a)

astonish — to be astonished عجب V.

atmosphere جَوّ

attached — to be attached عَلَّقَ II. (pass.)

Back ظَهْر

balance مِيزَان

bath حَمَّام

be كَانَ (u)

befall أَصَابَ

before أَمَامَ

begin أَخَذَ (u)

beggar سَائِل

Beirut بَيْرُوت

beseech تَضَرَّعَ

best الأَحْسَن

better أَحْسَنُ
between بَيْنَ
bind قَيَّدَ
bitter مُرٌّ
black أَسْوَدُ
bold شُجَاعٌ
book كِتَابٌ plur. كُتُبٌ
book-shop مَكْتَبَةٌ
borrow إِسْتَعَارَ
boy غُلَامٌ plur. غِلْمَانٌ — صَبِيٌّ
plur. صِبْيَانٌ
bread خُبْزٌ
bring وَصَّلَ
bring back أَرْجَعَ
bringing إِهْدَاءٌ
broom مِكْنَسَةٌ
brother أَخٌ
buy إِشْتَرَى
Cairo مِصْرُ
calamity مُصِيبَةٌ plur. مَصَائِبُ
caliph خَلِيفَةٌ
call دَعَا
calm هَادٍ
canal تُرْعَةٌ
cannon مِدْفَعٌ
captain قَبْطَانٌ
captive أَسِيرٌ
carry حَمَلَ (i)
cause سَبَبٌ plur. أَسْبَابٌ
cease زَالَ (u, a)
certain — a certain بَعْضٌ
chain سِلْسِلَةٌ
chamber غُرْفَةٌ
chance صُدْفَةٌ
character أَخْلَاقٌ
cheerful بَهِجٌ
chief رَئِيسٌ
circumstance حَالٌ plur. أَحْوَالٌ
city مَدِينَةٌ
clear رَائِقٌ
clever شَاطِرٌ

clothe كَسَا (u)

come جَاءَ

comfort سَلَّى

command أَمَرَ

commander أَمِيرٌ

compelled مَلْزُومٌ

concerning عَنْ

condition حَالٌ

content أَقْنَعَ

continuance دَوَامٌ

continue مَا زَالَ

corsair (adj.) قُرْصَانِيٌّ

country بِلَادٌ. وَطَنٌ

court صَحْنٌ

crowd إِزْدِحَامٌ

custom عَادَةٌ plur. عَوَائِدُ

cut قَطَعَ (a)

Danger خَطَرٌ plur. أَخْطَارٌ

dawn لَاحَ

day يَوْمٌ

dear عَزِيزٌ

death مَوْتٌ

deceive خَادَعَ

deed فِعْلٌ

defend — to defend oneself دَافَعَ عَنْ نَفْسِهِ

deliver أَنْقَذَ

deliverance خَلَاصٌ

demand طَلَبَ (u)

describe وَصَفَ

desert صَحْرَا

despair يَئِسَ — despairing مَأْيُوسٌ

destruction هَلَاكٌ

determine عَزَمَ

die مَاتَ (u)

different مُخْتَلِفٌ

diligence إِجْتِهَادٌ

disappointed خَائِبٌ

disturb شَغَلَ - disturbing مُزْعِجٌ

do فَعَلَ (a)

dog كَلْبٌ

door بَابٌ

doubt شَكّ

dream حُلْم

drink شَرِبَ

drive out أَخْرَجَ

during فِي

dwell سَكَنَ (u), vn. سُكْنَى

dynasty دَوْلَة

Each كُلّ

earth أَرْض

east مَشْرِق

easy — to make easy سَهَّلَ

Egypt مِصْر — Egyptian مِصْرِيّ

encircle أَحَاطَ

encroachment تَعَدّ

enemy عَدُوّ plur. أَعْدَاء

energy جَهْد

enmity عُدْوَان

entangle — to be entangled اِشْتَبَكَ

escape ر vn. فِرَار — there is no escape لَا بُدّ

especially لَا سِيَّمَا

eternity بَقَاء

every كُلّ

evil شَرّ

exalted عَلِيّ

examine إِطَّلَعَ with عَلَى

excellency حَضْرَة

excellent عَظِيم

except سِوَى

excess مَزِيد

existing things مَوْجُودَات

expend بَذَلَ - expenses مَصْرُوفَات

experience شَاهَدَ

Ezbekiya الازبكية

Face وِجْه

fair جَمِيل

faith إِيمَان

faithful مُوْمِن

farewell — to say farewell to وَدَّعَ

father وَالِد

Fatima فَاطِمَة

festivity إِحْتِفَالٌ
fifteen see Less. 32
filled with مَمْلُوءٌ
fight مُحَارَبَةٌ
find وَجَدَ, رَأَى
finish إِنْتَهَى with مِن
fire أَطْلَقَ
first see Less. 33
five see Less. 32
follow دَاهَمَ — following آتٍ
food مَأْكُولَاتٌ
fortress مِتْرَاسٌ
free خَلَّصَ
Frenchman فَرَنْسَاوِيٌّ
friend صَدِيقٌ, حَبِيبٌ plur. أَصْدِقَاءُ friendship صَدَاقَةٌ
from مِنْ
fulfil قَضَى
Garden بُسْتَانٌ
garment ثَوْبٌ
give أَعْطَى

go ذَهَبَ (a), سَارَ (i) — go out خَرَجَ — go away ذَهَبَ
God اللهُ
good خَيْرٌ
governor حَاكِمٌ plur. حُكَّامٌ
grade دَرَجَةٌ
grain ذُرَةٌ
great عَظِيمٌ, شَدِيدٌ
greeting سَلَامٌ
grieve سَاءَ grievous مُحْزِنٌ
guard وَقَى
guest — to be a guest of زَامَلَ
gun بَارُودٌ
Half نِصْفٌ
hall قَاعَةٌ
hand يَدٌ plur. أَيْدٍ — hand over سَلَّمَ
happen جَرَى
happiness سَعَادَةٌ
harm ضَرَرٌ plur. أَضْرَارٌ
hatred كَرَاهِيَةٌ

health صِحَّة

hear سَمِعَ (a)

heart قَلْبٌ plur. قُلُوبٌ

high عَالٍ

hither إِلَى هُنَا

honour أَكْرَمَ — honourable فَخِيمٌ

hope أَمَلٌ plur. آمَالٌ

horse خَيْلٌ (coll.) — فَرَسٌ

hour سَاعَة

house بَيْتٌ — مَنْزِلٌ

Important — most important جُلٌّ

improve أَصْلَحَ

increase زَادَ (i)

incumbent وَاجِبٌ

indebted — I shall be indebted to thee كَانَ لَكَ عَلَيَّ

indisposition إِنْحِرَافٌ

inducement دَاعٍ

inform أَخْبَرَ

inhabitant plur. أَهَالٍ

ink حِبْرٌ

inner دَاخِلِيٌّ

intelligent عَاقِلٌ

intend قَصَدَ

intercessor شَفِيعٌ plur. شُفَعَاءُ

Jacob يَعْقُوبُ

Joseph يُوسُفُ

journey سَفَرٌ

joy سُرُورٌ

Key مِفْتَاحٌ

kill قَتَلَ

king مَلِكٌ

kiss قَبَّلَ

knock قَرَعَ

know عَرَفَ (i)

Land وَطَنٌ — بِلَادٌ — by land بَرًّا

language لُغَةٌ

large كَبِيرٌ

last آخِرٌ

lasting دَائِم

latter days أَوَاخِر

learn تَعَلَّمَ — learned عَالِم plur. عُلَمَاء

least أَقَلّ

leave إِنْصَرَفَ

legally شَرْعًا

lend أَعَارَ

letter مَكْتُوبَة

life عُمْر — manner of life سِيرَة

light ضَوْء

light upon عَثَرَ with عَلَى

little شُوَيَّة

lord رَبّ

love حُبّ — مَحَبَّة

Make جَعَلَ

make for قَصَدَ

Mamluke مَمْلُوك plur. مَمَالِيك

man رَجُل

many كَثِير

market سُوق

matter شَأْن

meet لَقِيَ

memory ذِكْرَى

mighty جَبَّار

mind فِكْر

minister وَزِير

misfortune مُصِيبَة plur. مَصَائِب

money أَلدَّرَاهِم (plur.)

morally ذِمَّةً

morning صَبَاح

Moslem مُسْلِم

mosque مَسَاجِد

mouth فُو plur. أَفْوَاه

must — you must لَا بُدَّ لَكَ مِن

Mu'tasim أَلْمُعْتَصِم

Name إِسْم

nay rather بَلْ

necessary — it is necessary لَا بُدَّ مِن

need حَاجَةٌ

needle إِبَر (coll.)

noble شَرِيف, كَرِيم

northwards شِمَالًا

November شَهْرُ تِشْرِينَ ٱلثَّانِي

Offer عَرَضَ (i)

official مَأْمُور

once — at once حَالًا

one وَاحِدٌ fem. إِحْدَى — one another بَعْض

open فَتَحَ

order نِيشَان

other آخَر fem. أُخْرَى

Pain أَلَم

paleness إِصْفِرَار

park حَدِيقَةٌ

part of مِنْ

party فَرِيق

pass by مَرَّ

pasturage مَزْرَعَةٌ

patience صَبْر — patient صَبُور

pay دَفَعَ (a)

people أَهْل

perfection كَمَالٌ

perhaps عَسَى أَنْ

permit سَمَحَ (a)

perpetuate خَلَّدَ

person شَخْص

philosopher فَيْلَسُوف pl. فَلَاسِفَةٌ

piece قِطْعَةٌ

pious تَقِيٌّ

pleasant — to be pleasant حَلَا (u)

please شَاءَ (a) — pleasure جَمِيل

pledge ضَامِن plur. ضُمَنَاء

pool بِرْكَةٌ

porter حَمَّالٌ

possessing حِيَازَةٌ

possessor صَاحِب

possible — to be possible أَمْكَنَ

pour down هَطَلَ (i)

power طَاقَةٌ — powerful قَدِيرٌ

praise مَدَحَ - praise (subst.) حَمْدٌ

prayer صَلَاةٌ

preacher وَاعِظٌ

precious عَزِيزٌ

prepare أَعَدَّ — (intr.) تَهَيَّأَ

preserve أَبْقَى

pride تَكَبُّرٌ

prince أَمِيرٌ — princess أَمِيرَةٌ

prisoner أَسِيرٌ plur. أُسَرَاءُ

prophet نَبِيٌّ plur. أَنْبِيَاءُ

protect حَفِظَ

punish عَاقَبَ

purpose مَقْصَدٌ plur. مَقَاصِدُ

Raging عَجَّاجٌ

rail أَلسِّكَّةُ ٱلْحَدِيدِيَّةُ

rain مَطَرٌ plur. أَمْطَارٌ

raise رَفَعَ, عَلَّى

rank مَقَامٌ

reason, for this reason لِهٰذَا — by reason of بِسَبَبِ

rebellion عِصْيَانٌ

receive إِسْتَقْبَلَ — أَخَذَ — we received وَصَلَنَا

recovery عَافِيَةٌ

refresh — to be refreshed إِنْتَعَشَ

refuge — to take refuge إِعْتَصَمَ

reject رَفَضَ

rejoice فَرِحَ, سُرَّ (u)

rely إِتَّكَلَ

remember ذَكَرَ (u)

request سُؤَالٌ

requite جَازَى with 2. accus.

residence مَقَرٌّ

resist قَاوَمَ

return عَادَ (u)

ride رَكِبَ

rise قَامَ (u)

robber لِصٌّ plur. لُصُوصٌ

room حُجْرَةٌ

root out إِسْتَأْصَلَ

ruler مَلِيكٌ

Saddle سَرْجٌ

safe سَالِمٌ — يَقِينٌ

sailor بَحْرِيٌّ

same نَفْسٌ with genit.

say قَالَ (u)

scholar تِلْمِيذٌ plur. تَلَامِذَةٌ

school مَدْرَسَةٌ plur. مَدَارِسُ

science عِلْمٌ plur. عُلُومٌ

sea بَحْرٌ

sea-sickness مَرَضُ ٱلْبَحْرِ

season فَصْلٌ

secretly سِرًّا

security سَلَامَةٌ

see رَأَى (a) — شَاهَدَ

seek طَلَبَ

seem ظَهَرَ (a)

send أَرْسَلَ — send back رَدَّ (u)

sentence جُمْلَةٌ

separate أَبْعَدَ

servant خَادِمٌ

sew خَاطَ (i)

sheikh شَيْخٌ

shepherd رَاعٍ plur. رُعَاةٌ

ship مَرْكَبٌ plur. مَرَاكِبُ

show أَظْهَرَ

side جَانِبٌ

sigh أَنَّ — sighing أَنِينٌ

since مُنْذُ

sit down جَلَسَ

skin سَلَخَ (a)

slay قَتَلَ

slave عَبْدٌ plur. عَبِيدٌ

smite ضَرَبَ

soldier عَسْكَرٌ plur. عَسَاكِرُ

son إِبْنٌ plur. بَنُونَ

soon عَنْ قَرِيبٍ

sorrow حُزْنٌ

soul نَفْسٌ

sound صَوْتٌ

southwards جَنُوبًا

speak تَكَلَّمَ

speech كَلَامٌ

spirit نَفْسٌ

standard عَلَمٌ plur. أَعْلَامٌ

steed جَوَادٌ

stick عَصًا

still سَاكِنٌ

stone حَجَرٌ plur. حِجَارَةٌ

strange غَرِيبٌ

strike ضَرَبَ

strong شَدِيدٌ

stubbornness قَسَاوَةٌ

success تَوْفِيقٌ

Sultan سُلْطَانٌ

sweep كَنَسَ

Syria اَلشَّامُ — Syrian شَامِيٌّ

Tailor خَيَّاطٌ

take تَنَاوَلَ

teacher مُعَلِّمٌ

tell قَالَ (u) with لِ

ten see Less. 32.

than مِنْ

that (conj.) أَنَّ

think ظَنَّ

this هٰذَا fem. هٰذِهِ

thought ظَنٌّ plur. ظُنُونٌ

threaten تَهَدَّدَ

throw رَمَى (i)

thrust طَرَحَ

thwart عَانَدَ

time وَقْتٌ

to-day اَلْيَوْمَ

together جَمِيعًا

tomb مَدْفِنٌ plur. مَدَافِنُ

to-morrow غَدًا

torn — to be torn قُدَّ

track أَثَرٌ

transitoriness اَلْفَنَاءُ

travel سَافَرَ — traveller مُسَافِرٌ

tree شَجَرٌ

trouble وَرْطَةٌ — كَدَرٌ plur أَكْدَارٌ

true وَفِيٌّ

truly إِنَّ

trust وَثِقَ

trusty أَمِينٌ

turn away صَرَفَ

two see Less. 32.

Unite جَمَعَ

Vain فَارِغ

vegetables خَضْرَوَات

verily إِنَّ

very كَثِيرًا

village قَرْيَة

visiting زِيَارَة

Walk — **to take a walk** إِنْتَزَهَ

war — **to make war on** حَارَبَ

warning عِبَر

watchful حَارِس

water-carrier سَقَّاء

way طَرِيق **plur.** طُرُق — **in the way of** . . مِن

weapon سِلَاح **plur.** أَسْلِحَة

weather هَوَاء

weep بَكَى **(i)**

weigh وَزَن

well خَيْر

well-being سَلَامَة

west مَغْرِب

what مَا

wheat حِنْطَة

when لَمَّا

whence مِن أَيْنَ

wherever حَيْثُمَا

white أَبْيَض **fem.** بَيْضَاء

whither إِلَى أَيْنَ — إِلَى حَيْثُ

wine نَبِيذ — **wine-skin** قِرْبَة **plur.** قِرَب

winter شِتَاء

wish أَرَادَ

with بِ — عِنْدَ

withstand قَاوَمَ

woman إِمْرَأَة

world دُنْيَا — عَالَم

writing كِتَابَة — تَحْرِير

Year سَنَة

yearning مُشْتَاق

yes نَعَم

yesterday أَمْسِ

yet فَأَنَّ

youth شَابّ — غِلْمَان **(plur.)**.

I. Arabic Index

(arranged alphabetically without regard to roots).

The numbers refer to the pages.

II. English Index.

Printed by C. F. Winter, Darmstadt.